WINGS
OF FAME™

Aerospace Publishing Ltd
AIRtime Publishing Inc.

Published quarterly by
Aerospace Publishing Ltd
179 Dalling Road
London W6 0ES
UK

Copyright © Aerospace Publishing Ltd
1998

ISSN 1361-2034
Aerospace ISBN 1 86184 017 9
                  (softback)
                1 86184 018 7
                  (hardback)
AIRtime ISBN   1-880588-23-4

Published under licence in USA and
Canada by AIRtime Publishing Inc.,
10 Bay Street, Westport,
CT 06880, USA

Editorial Offices:
WINGS OF FAME™
Aerospace Publishing Ltd
3A Brackenbury Road
London W6 0BE UK
E-mail: info@aerospacepbl.co.uk

Publisher: Stan Morse
Managing Editor: David Donald
Editor: John Heathcott
Deputy Editor: Jim Winchester
Contributing Editor:
   David Donald
Sub Editor: Karen Leverington
Editorial Assistant: Tim Senior
US Correspondent: Robert F. Dorr

Artists: Mike Badrocke
         Chris Davey
         Keith Fretwell
         Tim Maunder
         Mark Rolfe
         Kata Vida
         John Weal
         Iain Wyllie
Origination by
   Chroma Graphics, Singapore
Printed by
   Officine Grafiche DeAgostini,
   Novara, Italy

The editors of WINGS OF FAME™
welcome photographs for possible
publication, but cannot accept any
responsibility for loss or damage to
unsolicited material.

The publishers gratefully acknowledge the
assistance given by the following people:

The author of the P-80 article would like
to thank the following for their assistance:
Lee Attwood, Warren M. Bodie, John M.
Campbell, Bob Clark, Ruth Collins of the
NASA Ames Research Center, Bob
Esposito, John Henderson, Tom Kaminski,
Craig Kaston, Denny Lombard of the
Lockheed Martin Skunk Works, David R.
McLaren, David W. Menard and Norman
Taylor

Thanks to Clive Richards for his help with
the No. II (AC) Squadron article

The authors of the MiG-19 article would
like to thank Tranh Dinh Kiem, Nguyen
Van Dinh, Vietnamese Embassy
(Budapest), Ministry of Foreign Affairs
(Hanoi), VPAF Museum (Hanoi), Da
Nang Air Base, Phu Cat Air Base

Keith Fretwell
1944 – 1998

It is with great sadness that we report the
death of Keith Fretwell, the aviation artist
who created so much wonderful artwork
for our publications over the past 25 years.

It was Keith who pioneered our first
spectacular three-view drawings and
again, later, the giant fold-out artworks.
Each one of Keith's pieces was a work of
genius, recording not only the technical
detail but the speed, excitement, war
history and even, it sometimes seemed, the
roaring sound of his subjects.

His artworks have travelled the world and
have featured in many millions of copies of
magazines and books. There is no telling
how many young aviation enthusiasts have
been inspired by Keith's work to enhance
their interest, try their hand at aviation art,
or take up flying as a pleasure or career.

What we can be sure of is that Keith made
a remarkable contribution to aviation
publishing, and his work will live on as a
testament to his unique and very special
talent.

Stan Morse
Publisher

For subscription information and
details of other products, visit the
new *Wings of Fame* web site
http://www.wingsoffame.com

Wings of Fame™ **is a registered
trademark in the United States of
America of AIRtime Publishing Inc.**

Wings of Fame™ **is published
quarterly and is available by
subscription and from many fine book
and hobby stores.**

**SUBSCRIPTION AND BACK
NUMBERS:**

**UK and World (except USA and
Canada) write to:**
Aerospace Publishing Ltd
FREEPOST
PO Box 2822
London
W6 0BR
UK

**(No stamp required if posted in the
UK)**

USA and Canada, write to:
AIRtime Publishing Inc.
Subscription Dept
10 Bay Street
Westport
CT 06880, USA
(203) 838-7979
Toll-free order number in USA:
1 800 359-3003

**Prevailing subscription rates are as
follows:**
Softbound edition for 1 year:
   $59.95
Softbound edition for 2 years:
   $112.00
**Softbound back numbers (subject to
availability) are $16.00 each, plus
shipping and handling. All rates are
for delivery within mainland USA,
Alaska and Hawaii. Canadian and
overseas prices available upon request.
American Express, Discover Card,
MasterCard and Visa accepted. When
ordering please include card number,
expiration date and signature.**

U.S. Publisher:
   Mel Williams
Subscriptions Director:
   Linda DeAngelis
**Charter Member Services
Manager:**
   Janie Munroe
Retail Sales Director: Jill Brooks
Shipping Manager: E. Rex Anku

WINGS OF FAME ™

CONTENTS

Volume 11

F-86 Sabre in Korea

The deployment of the F-86 to the Korean War brought the USAF's most modern fighter face-to-face with its opposite number from the Soviet Union – the MiG-15. Here the exploits of the USAF in 'MiG Alley' are described and illustrated with contemporary colour photographs

4

Larry Davis, with additional material from Warren Thompson

Supporting the front line

A photo-essay of some of the airlift, liaison and rescue types in service with the US Air Force in the 1950s

28

From the collection of Robert F. Dorr

Fairey Deltas

Fairey Aviation designed two delta-winged jet aircraft in the 1940s and 1950s. Though the FD.1 faded into relative obscurity, and the FD.2's potential as a fighter went virtually unnoticed, the latter went on become a world speed record holder and the basis of the BAC 221 'ogee wing' testbed

32

Jon Lake

Messerschmitt Bf 109: the later variants

Despite the fact that the design was losing its supremacy, the Bf 109 continued in production and widespread service throughout World War II, and spawned a family of related designs, including those built post-war in Czechoslovakia and Spain. This article relates the story of the Bf 109F and all subsequent models

46

David Donald

MiG-19 in Vietnam

After the MiG-17 and MiG-21 had entered service, the Vietnamese People's Air Force took delivery of Chinese-built MiG-19s in the late 1960s. Here the type's combat history and victories against American Phantoms is described in unprecedented detail

110

Dr Zoltán Buza and Dr István Toperczer

P-80 Shooting Star Variants

America's first jet fighter just missed a combat debut in World War II, but went on to form the backbone of the USAF's ground-attack forces in the Korean conflict. This first instalment of a two-part briefing looks at the single-seat P-80 variants

114

Robert F. Dorr

MiG Ye-150/Ye-152

Though it was hampered by engine development snags and changing air force requirements, Mikoyan's Ye-150/152 programme produced the first Soviet aircraft able to exceed Mach 2.5 and attain an altitude of 22 km

134

Yefim Gordon, original translation by Dmitri Komissarov

No. II (AC) Squadron

'Shiny Two' has the distinction of being the longest-established of the RAF's front-line squadrons. This *Unit Heritage* feature tells the story of the squadron from its establishment in 1912, though its service during World War II and the Gulf in the 1990s, primarily in the tactical reconnaissance role

140

John Heathcott

Index

158

Air Combat
'MiG Maulers'
F-86 Sabre in Korea, 1950-53

The ultimate test of any aircraft design is how it performs the mission it is assigned, whether that is fighting an enemy aircraft or carrying passengers or ordnance. In the case of the F-86 Sabre, that test was against the Mikoyan-Gurevich MiG-15.

When the Korean War broke out in June 1950, neither the Sabre nor the MiG were committed to the fighting. During the early days of the conflict the North Korean Air Force was very aggressive against the South Korean defences, which was not difficult since the only 'modern' aircraft in the RoKAF arsenal were a couple of T-6 Texan trainers. As effortless as the North Korean defeat of the RoKAF was, the total defeat of the North Korean Air Force by the US 5th Air Force was even more so. North Korean Yaks were easy prey in the gunsights of 5th AF F-51Ds, and even easier in the gunsights of the F-80C Shooting Star jets. In the ensuing four months of combat, 5th AF aircraft literally owned the skies over Korea, North and South.

In the beginning of November the situation changed drastically, on the ground and in the air. The Chinese Communists were about to enter the war, and they brought with them a new and much better foe for the pilots of 5th AF. Early in the afternoon of 1 November 1950, a flight of F-51Ds was escorting an RAF Mosquito photo-reconnaissance aircraft. Nearing the Yalu River, the flight was suddenly attacked by swept-wing jet fighters. The Reds had introduced the best aircraft in their inventory to the fighting in Korea – the MiG-15.

Air superiority evaporates

Overnight, the air superiority the 5th AF had won over Korea evaporated. The MiG was almost 100 mph (160 km/h) faster than the best aircraft in the 5th AF, the F-80C. Had the Communists pushed this new-found advantage, combining it with the all-out Chinese ground offensive that was driving the UN forces back down the Korean peninsula, they might very well have forced the UN right out of Korea. But they did not press their advantage, preferring to remain behind the invisible wall erected at the Yalu River that prevented UN air forces from attacking them. This *faux pas* gave the 5th AF time to muster reinforcements to counter the new threat – the reinforcements included the F-86A Sabre.

On 9 November 1950 the 4th Fighter Interceptor Group was alerted for temporary duty with the Far East Air Force, in Korea. This

A North Korean pilot ejects as his MiG-15 falls to 0.5-in (12.7-mm) machine-gun fire from a 16th FIS Sabre flown by 2nd Lt Edwin E. Aldrin Jr on 14 May 1953, during a six-day period in which USAF Sabres shot down 36 MiGs. 'Buzz' Aldrin was perhaps better known as a 'Gemini' astronaut and the second man to set foot on the moon from Apollo 11 in July 1969.

F-86 Sabre in Korea

all the aircraft shipped from the United States had suffered some sort of salt water corrosion damage. Parts were scarce. Base and airfield conditions ranged from terrible to abominable. The taxiways at K-13 were non-existent. Indeed, inbound Sabres landing at Suwon (K-13) had to land on one side of the runway as other Sabres were taxiing back to their parking spots on the other side of the same runway. Less than 10 ft (3 m) separated the landing and taxiing Sabres.

Maintenance as a whole was outstanding, considering the conditions. North American Tech Reps, coupled with fine mechanics and crew chiefs, kept the F-86s flying and fighting. Even though they had to fly from a base (Suwon) that was an additional 30 miles (48 km) from 'MiG Alley', the toll of MiG victories continued to climb steadily in favour of the Sabre pilots. By May 1951, victories stood at 22 MiGs shot down for the loss of just a single Sabre.

First jet versus jet ace

In May 1951, the world's first jet vs jet ace was crowned. On 20 May 1951, the MiGs came up and the 4th FIG made a maximum effort. Captain James J. Jabara was flying that day, and had four MiGs to his credit. He was already over the 100-mission limit and was scheduled to be rotated home. As the fight developed, it seemed that somebody was bent on keeping him from getting his fifth MiG. With MiGs everywhere, Jabara ordered his flight to drop tanks, but his right wing tank would not come off. Standing orders were to take yourself and your wingman and head for

'temporary duty' would last until 1957. The Sabre was going to war. Prior to flying to the West Coast, since most of their aircraft were older '48 model Sabres, the 4th FIG was authorised to obtain the best 'low time' aircraft from the other Sabre units. The 334th and 335th Fighter Interceptor Squadrons (FIS) flew to San Diego, and were loaded aboard the Navy escort carrier USS *Cape Esperance*. The 336th FIS went to San Francisco and was loaded aboard a waiting tanker for the two-week trip to Japan. Arriving in Japan in early December, aircraft of the 336th FIS were in place at Kimpo AB (K-14) near Seoul the morning of 15 December. They flew an orientation flight that afternoon. Snow cancelled all air operations on the next day, but on 17 December the skies cleared and the runways were plowed clear of snow. Late that morning, the Sabres were taxiing to the runway for their first taste of combat against the vaunted MiG. But the MiGs would not come up.

First combat with MiGs

In the early afternoon of 17 December, Lieutenant Colonel Bruce Hinton led the 336th north toward the Yalu. Flying F-80 patterns and using fighter-bomber radio callsigns, Hinton lured the MiGs into a fight near the mouth of the Yalu River, an area later known as 'MiG Alley'. Minutes later, the Sabres were joined in combat with four very surprised MiGs. When it

was over, only three of the MiGs went home. Lieutenant Colonel Hinton had scored the first of 792 confirmed victories over the MiG-15 during the Korean War. This was against an official loss of 78 F-86s, a 10:1 kill ratio.

The 4th FIG F-86As kept the MiGs at bay throughout the spring and summer of 1951, despite some of the most miserable operating conditions in the history of air warfare. Almost

Kimpo Air Base (K-14) is seen here in 1954, only months after the cessation of hostilities between the Democratic People's Republic of Korea in the north and the Republic of Korea. Four bases (including Taegu/K-2 briefly in early-1951) played host to USAF F-86s during the 'police action'.

On 11 November 1950, the 4th Fighter Interceptor Group left its bases around Washington, DC, bound for 'temporary duty' (TDY) in Korea. The TDY would last for six years! The 4th FIG F-86A-5s were flown west and loaded aboard the escort carrier USS Cape Esperance (CVE-88) at NAS North Island, San Diego, arriving at Yokosuka, Japan on 1 December. (The 336th FIS went to San Francisco and loaded onto a tanker.) Note the different tail markings on the aircraft. The 4th traded all its high-time Sabres for newer models serving with other units.

Left: With no hangars or revetments to shelter the aircraft, the 4th FIG resorted to using World War II camouflage netting in an attempt to hide the Sabres from 'Bedcheck Charlie', the night raider that dropped small bombs on aircraft targets at K-14. The Bearded Clam was F-86A-5 49-1298, a 336th FIS Sabre transferred from the 1st FIG before the deployment to Korea. It was lost in combat on 19 June 1951.

home if the tanks would not drop. Captain Jabara opted to ignore the orders.

He and his wingman found the MiGs, 12 of them; and the MiGs found them. As Jabara lined up on one MiG, three more bounced him and his wingman. Desperately, Jabara and the wingman slowed their Sabres down and the MiGs overshot them. Jabara latched onto the last one in the flight and chased him down to about 10,000 ft (3048 m), where he put a long burst of 0.50-in fire into the MiG. The MiG snap-rolled to the right, started into a spin, and the pilot bailed out. That was Jabara's fifth kill. However, he was not done yet. With MiGs everywhere, Captain Jabara found a flight of six

Below: Normal maintenance, including engine changes, was performed on the open ramps at both Kimpo and Suwon in 1951. The B-29 in the background had been forced down at Suwon due to battle damage. Since it was the only cover available, the B-29 is being used as an open-air engine shop, with a tarp layed over its wing.

more, and moved into a good firing position. A long burst into a fuselage and a MiG flamed out. Smoke started pouring from the exhaust and the aircraft began to slow. Jabara put another heavy burst into the dying MiG and it started to burn. He followed the MiG down to below 6,500 ft (1980 m) and watched as it impacted the ground.

Close call

That was number six, but it almost cost him his life. While Jabara was watching his sixth victory crash into the Korean mountains, two more MiGs were pulling in behind him and getting into a very good firing position. His wingman had been driven off by several other MiGs and Jabara had no warning that he was under attack.

Breaking left and right as hard as the aircraft would manoeuvre, Jabara watched for several minutes as the large orange 23-mm 'ping-pong

balls' came toward him. Whoever was flying those MiGs was good – and they were mad. Jabara jinked, broke to his left, jinked again, dove for the ground; those two MiGs were still there. Finally someone said, "Hey, there's an F-86 in trouble down there!" Help was on the way as two F-86s rolled in on the attacking MiGs. One of the Sabres hit one of the MiGs and both MiGs suddenly broke off their attack on Jabara and ran for home.

Captain James J. Jabara landed at K-13 some 15 minutes later. The gun ports on his F-86A, serial 49-1319, were smoked and his right wing tank was still there. He had his fifth (and sixth) victories, making him the first ace in the Korean War, and the world's first jet ace. The Air

F-86 bases, Korea 1950-53

Yalu River

'MiG Alley'

● PYONGYANG

38th Parallel

K-14 (Kimpo)   ● SEOUL
                ● K-13 (Suwon)
                ● K-55 (Osan)

● PUSAN

F-86As of the 336th FIS are seen on the PSP ramp at Suwon (K-13) during the spring of 1951. When Chinese forces overran Kimpo in January 1951, the 4th FIG was forced to move out of Korea, returning to Suwon and operations over the Yalu in March 1951. K-13 had only a concrete runway, with PSP taxiways; this soon became untenable for the Sabres, forcing them to land on one side of the main runway, and taxi to their parking spots on the other side as other Sabres were still landing.

Force immediately grounded him and sent him home.

During the late summer of 1951, the MiG threat began to grow larger and larger. Out-numbered five to one on any given day, and sometimes as high as 10 to one, the 5th AF requested more Sabres to counter the growing number of MiGs across the Yalu. During the first six months of combat, the 5th AF only committed two Sabre squadrons to combat at any one time; the third was held in reserve at Johnson AB, Japan. During the summer of 1951, after committing the third Sabre squadron to combat, and moving the 4th FIG from Suwon back to Kimpo (K-14), the 5th AF got permission to convert one of the fighter-bomber groups to the fighter interceptor mission and equip it with F-86s.

The 51st converts

The 51st FIG based at Suwon was chosen to convert from F-80Cs to Sabres. And not just any Sabres: the 51st FIG would be equipped with new F-86Es with the new 'all-flying tail'. The F-86E had been introduced into the Kore-an combat with the 4th FIG beginning in July. Colonel Francis 'Gabby' Gabreski, the 56th FG World War II ace, transferred from the 4th FIG in October 1951. He would take command of the 51st. The two squadrons of the 51st FIG, the 16th and 25th FIS, were combat ready and flew their first mission on 1 December 1951.

Lieutenant Paul Roach in the 25th FIS scored the first kill for the 51st FIG on its second day of combat, 2 December.

The 5th AF could put up a maximum force of about 60 Sabres when everything was 'right', meaning that each squadron would put up three flights of four aircraft. The rest of the Sabre force remained at Kimpo or Suwon on alert, or was simply down for maintenance problems. Even at maximum levels, though, the Sabres were still greatly outnumbered as the MiGs came across the Yalu in 'trains', with each 'ban-dit train' numbering 25 MiGs or more, in addi-tion to the usual six 'trains' sent from Antung Station. By late 1951, the Red Air Force had so many MiGs available that they made an attempt to move two squadrons of MiGs back into the

Left: It was not always a one-sided affair in Korea. Sometimes the MiG pilots were very aggressive and quite often displayed great skill in the air. This F-86A, with the 335th FIS, was struck by accurate 37-mm cannon fire over the Yalu River, but the pilot brought the aircraft back to K-14 in September 1951.

base at Uiju, North Korea. B-29s and F-84 fighter-bombers soon made the base untenable, and the MiGs were forced back across the Yalu.

Five more aces

By late 1951, the 4th FIG had crowned five more aces. Dick Becker and 'Hoot' Gibson both got their fifth MiGs on 9 September; Dick Creighton got his fifth on 27 November. On 30 November, the Communists tried to knock out the UN radar site located on Cho-Do Island, which was about 75 miles (120 km) behind their lines, using Tu-2 propeller-driven bombers. It was a major effort on their part, including 12 Tu-2s with an escort of 16 La-9 fighters – plus a large formation of MiG-15s for good measure. Fifth AF intelligence knew about the impending movement and set a trap: the 4th FIG was waiting when the propeller-driven aircraft crossed the Yalu. It was a turkey shoot. Major Winton 'Bones' Marshall shot down one Tu-2 and an La-9. Major George Davis shot down three Tu-2s, and saw a fleeing MiG on the way home. Davis turned and dove on the unsuspecting MiG, shooting him out of the sky. The final tally for the day was eight Tu-2s, three La-9s and one MiG-15 destroyed. Major Davis was crowned the fifth ace in Korea, and Major Marshall the sixth.

Both the MiG inventories across the Yalu River, and the 5th AF victories, continued to climb throughout 1952. Even after a third squadron was added to the 51st FIG (the 39th FIS, in June 1952), the MiGs still outnumbered the Sabres almost 1,000 to 150 during late 1952.

Left: 4th FIG crew chiefs ready the F-86As of the 334th FIS for the afternoon MiG sweep in June 1951. The different-coloured noses – some dark red, some off-white, some silver – are the result of different colours of fibreglass used to make the nose cap, not a unit colour marking.

4th Fighter Interceptor Wg
(334th FIS, 335th FIS, 336th FIS)

The more MiGs there were, the better the Sabre pilots liked it. Seventeen more aces were crowned in 1952, including three that had been aces in World War II: Bill Whisner, 'Gabby' Gabreski and Harrison Thyng. The first double ace was crowned on 13 December 1951, when Major George Davis shot down two MiGs on the morning mission to bring his total to 10. He got two more on the afternoon mission, giving him 12. Sadly, Major Davis was himself shot down on 10 February after getting his 14th victory. Having already shot down two MiGs, Davis was pulling lead on a third MiG, when a bunch of MiGs jumped him. He received the Medal of Honor for the mission.

MiG bases on the Yalu

By the end of 1952, MiG inventories were growing at an alarming rate. MiG squadrons were based all along the Yalu River, with at least six bases handling two squadrons each. Antung was the hub of the MiG base complex, home for the Soviet 3rd Air Division. In addition, the Chinese had a formidable MiG force at the bases surrounding Antung. At Mukden, the Communists had some 500 MiGs in readiness. It was one of the primary MiG training bases, where both Chinese and North Korean fliers were taught how to fly and fight in the MiG-15. Had the Communists wanted to do

On 17 June 1951, 'Bedcheck Charlie' scored a hit on this F-86A-5, 49-1334, completely destroying it on the ramp at Suwon. During the raid, shrapnel struck GE Tech Rep Leo Fournier, for which he was awarded the Purple Heart. In the background are the pilots' tents of the 335th FIS.

so, they could have brought all these forces into the combat arena of northwest North Korea – the area known as 'MiG Alley'.

At this time the 5th AF sought and was granted approval to convert two more fighter-bomber groups to the F-86. Both the 18th FBG at Osan (K-55) and the 8th FBG at K-13 converted to F-86s in early 1953. Their primary mission would remain fighter-bomber, but they could and would be able to successfully mix it up with the MiGs if they encountered them. Thus, the 8th and 18th were the first groups equipped with the new F-86F-30 fighter-bomber variant of the Sabre; these early F-30s had the underwing stores pylons to carry a pair of 1,000-lb (454-kg) bombs, in addition to their standard 120-US gal (454-litre) drop tanks.

The end

The Korean War ended on 27 July 1953, much as it had begun. The Communists held North Korea and the Allies held South Korea, roughly along the line of the 38th Parallel, where it had begun. That was on the ground. In the air, it was all UN, from the Yalu River to the southern tip of Korea. The Communists had suffered enormous losses. Even the Russian archives refer to the slaughter, admitting to at least a 12:1 mauling for both the Russian- and Chinese-flown MiGs. Officially, 5th Air Force

Below: In mid-January 1951, the 4th FIG returned one squadron to Korea, this time flying from Taegu AB in southeastern Korea as both K-13 and K-14 were in Chinese hands. Since it could not reach the Yalu River from Taegu, the 4th began flying limited air-to-ground missions armed with 5-in HVARs. This F-86A was assigned to Lt Col Glen Eagleston, commanding the 334th FIS. Note the 5-in HVAR just inboard of the drop tank.

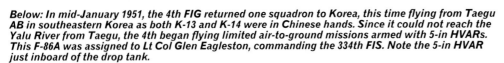

Above: Pilots of 335th FIS sit in the cockpits for the signal to 'start engines' prior to the afternoon sweep of 'MiG Alley' in June 1951. It was approximately 230 miles from K-13 to the Yalu River, and although the weather could be sunny on the K-13 ramp, it might have been completely 'socked in' for the MiGs based on the Yalu. Note the different-coloured noses on the aircraft.

Below: The date is 20 May 1951 and Captain James J. Jabara returns to a hero's welcome in his F-86A, 49-1319. Jabara had shot down his fifth MiG, becoming the first Sabre pilot to do so. Serving with the 334th FIS, 4th FIW, Jabara finished the war with some 15 kills, the second-highest tally of the war.

Above: GE gunsight Tech Rep Leo Fournier proudly stands beside the F-86A-5 flown by Captain James Jabara on the 20 May 1951 mission on which he became the first jet ace in history. Capt. Jabara could not drop his right wing tank, and, contrary to standing orders to return to base, engaged the MiGs anyway. He shot down two MiG-15s. The lack of identifying markings, such as crew names and victories, was normal for the 4th at this time. Aircraft were routinely flown by several pilots, even though many pilots had 'assigned' aircraft.

Sabre pilots were credited with 792 MiG-15s destroyed, although the number was probably higher. In return, the 5th Air Force lost somewhere between 58 and 78 F-86s; the number is unclear. On 29 July 1953, two days after the ceasefire, the 5th Air Force put out a communiqué stating it had lost 58 F-86s to the MiGs, but that figure was later changed to 78 F-86s shot down by MiGs.

The 5th Air Force had 39 Sabre aces, including six double aces and two triple aces. The top scorer of the war was Captain Joseph McConnell of the 39th FIS, who shot down 16 MiG-15s. Right behind him was Major James Jabara, with 15 MiGs. The 4th FIG shot down 502 enemy aircraft, with the 51st FIG getting credit for 303 aircraft destroyed. Of the 39 aces, the 4th FIG had 23, the 51st FIG had 15 aces, and the 18th FBG had one ace – Major James Hagerstrom. The final official ratio was 10:1, according to 5th Air Force statistics. However, that subject is open for debate.

Korean War credits and losses

In the 45 years since the end of the Korean War, aviation historians have been amazed at the kill ratio achieved by 5th Air Force pilots. Amazed – and often incredulous. Historians have tried many times, using every conceivable formula and information source, to reduce the kill ratio in Korea. USAF statistics themselves differed at times. One 'historian' tried to equate the number of Sabre sorties against MiGs sighted, resulting in a conclusion that the kill ratio

was only 4:1 since there were far fewer MiGs sighted, and the Sabres were in greater numbers than previously stated. Of course, he did not take into account the fact that in 1953 six of the 13 F-86 squadrons in Korea were fighter-bomber units rarely flying counter-air missions. And one squadron was a reconnaissance unit. In 1953, six squadrons – approximately 150 aircraft when at full strength – were available for counter-air missions.

Two squadrons

The key words here are "when at full strength". During the first full year of F-86 operations, from December 1950 to December 1951, only the 4th Fighter Interceptor Group's three squadrons – 334th, 335th and 336th FIS – were available to oppose the MiG threat. And

On 17 December 1950, Lt Col Bruce Hinton, commander of the 336th FIS, led a four-ship sweep to the Yalu. Using flight tactics and callsigns of the F-80 fighter-bombers, Hinton's Sabres lured the MiGs into battle. Lt Col Hinton shot down one of the MiGs for the first Sabre victory of the war.

until the summer of 1951, 5th AF would only allow two of the three squadrons to be based in Korea close enough to 'MiG Alley' to join in combat with the MiGs across the Yalu River. The third squadron remained at Johnson AB, Japan in both a defensive and training role. The 51st FIG was operational in F-86Es on 1 December 1951, but had only two squadrons assigned, the 16th and 25th FIS. The third squadron, the 39th FIS, did not become operational until 1 June 1952. Against this reasonably small number of Sabres were the MiGs based

MiG-killing F-86A

Named *Paul's Mig-Killer*, this F-86A was adorned with a huge sharkmouth marking. Although popular earlier in the war, these markings were, in some cases at least, removed in deference to the local community, who may have misinterpreted such 'demonic' features. Fields scored a MiG-15 kill outright on 21 September 1952, sharing another on 25 October with an RAF exchange officer, Sqn Ldr Graham Hulse.

F-86A-5-NA 49-1175
1st Lieutenant Joseph E. Fields
336th Fighter Interceptor Squadron,
4th Fighter Interceptor Wing

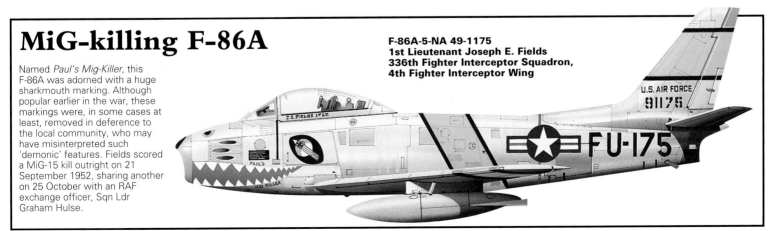

Air Combat

Right: The 335th FIS, 4th FIW operated a number of Canadair-built F-86E-6-CAN aircraft, including 52-2856 Betty Boots. '856 was the personal aircraft of Captain Karl Dittmer, a MiG-killer and a talented artist much in demand by other pilots keen to decorate their Sabres. Like their North American-built brethren, survivors of the 60 Canadair Sabres (CL-13 Sabre Mk 2s) shipped to Korea were distributed among Air National Guard units after the war.

Left: One of the 336th Fighter Interceptor Squadron's F-86E-10s is seen here at K-14, in the company of a C-47 and a couple of T-6s. All aircraft carry the yellow fuselage and tail bands introduced by the Far East Air Force in 1952 as a readily identifiable theatre marking, although, in the case of the Sabre, the yellow tail marking was restricted to the 4th FIS.

Major Richard Ayersman flew Baby Linda, one of the last F-86Es built, 51-2835, with the 334th FIS at K-14 in late summer 1952. Baby Linda shows one of the markings oddities of the 4th FIG – victories shown under the windscreen on the left side belong to the pilot, while those under the crew data block were 'awarded' to the crew chief of that aircraft when the score was confirmed. Solid red stars indicate a victory; those containing a 'P' indicate a 'probable' victory; a 'D' indicated a 'damaged' aircraft.

just across the mouth of the Yalu River in northwest Korea.

Recently released Russian archives material confirm what US sources had known along – that Soviet fighter squadrons were rotated through the MiG bases across the Yalu. Soviet air force MiGs opposed the F-86s from bases at Antung, Fengcheng, Tak Tung Kao, Takushan, Kuantien, and others near the Yalu. At Mukden, Manchuria, large numbers of MiGs – up to 500 based on intelligence information – lined the runways waiting to replace those lost in combat or rotating home to Mother Russia. Eastern Bloc squadrons supplanted the elite V-VS units throughout the war.

This takes no account of the Communist Chinese or North Korean squadrons being combat trained by Soviet pilots. 5th AF reconnaissance flights, flown by RB-45C Tornados and RF-80A and RF-86 fighters, routinely penetrated Manchurian airspace as far as Mukden to get photos of the MiGs. The photos

Above: Designed by Capt James Horowitz (a.k.a. James Salter, author of the 1956 novel about fighter pilots in Korea, The Hunters), this patch was worn by 'D for Dog' Flight, 335th FIS ('The Mach Riders of the Sky') and is believed to have been the rarest of Korean War patches. The caricature represents 'D' Flight's leader, Capt. Phil Colman, who led the flight to score 24 confirmed kills, the highest total by a single flight during the war.

clearly reveal row after row of MiG-15s, up to 1,000 in the spring of 1953. The Communists had enough MiGs north of the Yalu by November 1951 to feel sufficiently confident to attempt to put a MiG base at recently modernised Uiju, North Korea. A B-29 raid, with Sabre support, put a stop to MiGs based south of the Yalu.

CIA estimates

Conservative estimates, based on intelligence photos and clandestine CIA operations across the Yalu River, show that at any given time during 1951/52, up to 900 MiGs directly opposed the (up to) 125 Sabres available for patrolling the Yalu River. Maintenance problems caused by crude Korean base conditions (major maintenance facilities were in Japan),

JoAnn was the F-86E-1 assigned to Winton 'Bones' Marshall in November 1951, when he became the sixth ace in Korea. The aircraft carried the name Mr Bones V at the time. A note about 4th FIG kill markings: all MiG kills scored on the right side of the aircraft are credited to the aircraft itself. The yellow tail bands were a 4th FIG group marking applied in the summer of 1952, sometimes directly over the old black stripe tail markings.

Above: An example of the fine artwork by Capt. Karl Dittmer is Lt Hank Cresibene's Newark Fireball, F-86E-10 51-2794 with the 335th FIS in 1952. Lt Cresibene had one MiG victory on 4 August 1952.

Above: Certainly one of the most colourful of the Sabres in Korea was Captain Chuck Owens's Liza Gal/El Diablo, a 336th FIS F-86E-10. Captain Owens's Sabre shows eight MiG victories, 15 truck kills, and a tank kill. In 1952, Col Walker Mahurin cleared the pilots returning from 'MiG Alley' to fire on targets of opportunity, i.e., trucks, trains and the like.

Below: Little Butch, an F-86E-10 assigned to the 335th FIS at Kimpo in the summer of 1952, is seen being towed to the alert ramp for a possible scramble against either incoming MiGs (rare), or to join an ongoing fight at the Yalu where aircraft might need help to get home again. The peeled condition of the ID bands is the result of combat at near supersonic speeds.

and replacement parts being few and far between at times, kept the amount of combat-available F-86s at about 70 per cent, or less than 90 aircraft. There were even fewer in late 1951/early 1952.

Rules of Engagement

The Sabres were further hampered by something new to warfare – Rules of Engagement. The rules were simple – any Communist aircraft south of the Yalu River could be attacked. And, on orders issued by the United Nations in October 1950, no UN aircraft were permitted to violate the Manchurian border, which began on the north side of the Yalu River, for any reason.

The Communists knew this and took full advantage of the 'rules'. They would form up and get into attack position well north of the Yalu, most of the time being well above the service ceiling of the F-86. The Sabres could not get into a good defensive position even when they saw an attack forming. The MiGs dove on the UN aircraft, made their attack, then broke for safety back across the Yalu

Sabre operations in 'MiG Alley' were hampered throughout the war by a shortage of wing drop tanks, despite the fact that a tank production line had been set up in Japan. Here, F-86E-10 51-2791 of the 4th FIW sits in its revetment at Kimpo, having just received a new pair.

Above: The 335th FIS five-minute alert ramp at Kimpo shows a mixed batch of F-86E-1s, E-6s, and E-10s. Throughout the war, both the 4th and 51st FIG flew different aircraft types in the same squadrons and flights. Of course, the experienced pilots always got the newer types. Both Col Thyng and Major 'Bones' Marshall flew F-86E-1 50-680 to victories.

River. It worked well. In late 1951, 5th AF modified the rules slightly, introducing something called 'in hot pursuit'. UN pilots were allowed to cross the Yalu River when they were 'in hot pursuit' of a fleeing enemy aircraft and were in position for a possible victory. This was the only 'official' reason for crossing the Yalu. Of course, reconnaissance flights routinely crossed the river – and they always had Sabre escorts.

There were also many instances when 5th AF pilots simply went north of the river looking for trouble. 5th AF F-51Ds strafed Antung in August 1950. Two F-80 pilots went all the way to Vladivostok, Russia in October 1950, strafing the MiG base there. F-86 pilots, too, often went north of the Yalu looking for MiGs.

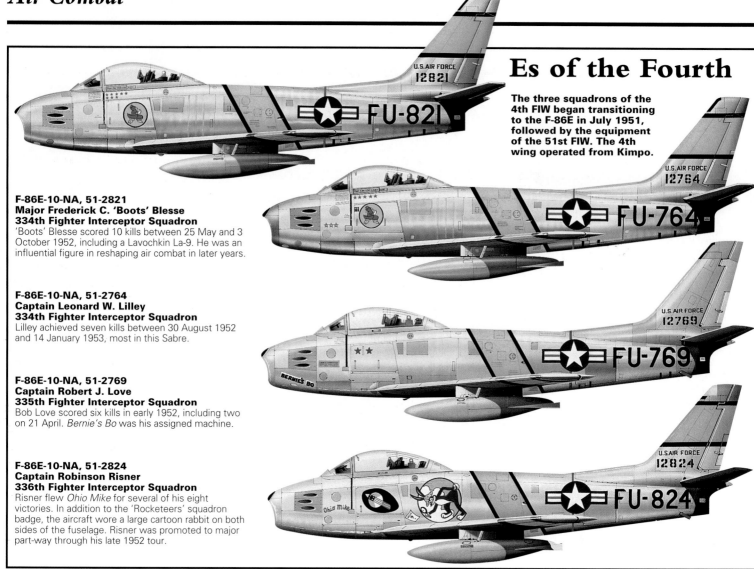

Es of the Fourth

The three squadrons of the 4th FIW began transitioning to the F-86E in July 1951, followed by the equipment of the 51st FIW. The 4th wing operated from Kimpo.

F-86E-10-NA, 51-2821
Major Frederick C. 'Boots' Blesse
334th Fighter Interceptor Squadron
'Boots' Blesse scored 10 kills between 25 May and 3 October 1952, including a Lavochkin La-9. He was an influential figure in reshaping air combat in later years.

F-86E-10-NA, 51-2764
Captain Leonard W. Lilley
334th Fighter Interceptor Squadron
Lilley achieved seven kills between 30 August 1952 and 14 January 1953, most in this Sabre.

F-86E-10-NA, 51-2769
Captain Robert J. Love
335th Fighter Interceptor Squadron
Bob Love scored six kills in early 1952, including two on 21 April. *Bernie's Bo* was his assigned machine.

F-86E-10-NA, 51-2824
Captain Robinson Risner
336th Fighter Interceptor Squadron
Risner flew *Ohio Mike* for several of his eight victories. In addition to the 'Rocketeers' squadron badge, the aircraft wore a large cartoon rabbit on both sides of the fuselage. Risner was promoted to major part-way through his late 1952 tour.

Colonel Walker Mahurin, CO of the 4th FIW, told of a pilot who went to Mukden, about 100 miles (160 km) north of the Yalu, before turning back – and accidentally left his IFF beacon on for everyone in 5th AF to monitor.

Victories on the 'wrong' side

Several F-86 pilots got victories on the wrong side of the Yalu. When caught, the results could be hazardous to a pilot's career. Well north of the boundary, one 51st FIG ace shot down a pair of MiGs that themselves had shot down his leader. Unfortunately, both the Sabre and one of the MiGs crashed near a train that contained the UN peace delegation. The ace was sent home and stripped of his victories.

Often, these victories were not credited – except on the Soviet ledgers. The reason was 5th AF verification rules, which were even stricter than the rules of engagement. In interviews with a large number of combat pilots from the Korean War, including Captain (now Brigadier General) Erwin 'Sandy' Hesse, Operations Officer for the 4th FIG in Korea and in charge of filing MiG claims, the rules as to how a claim for a MiG was verified were clearly spelled out. 'Bones' Marshall, Ralph Parr, and Jim Low confirmed those rules almost verbatim.

During the debriefing following a mission on which MiGs were encountered, any pilot putting in a claim had to have his gun camera film show one of the following to have the claim verified as 'confirmed destroyed': 1) Sus-

Above: 1st Lieutenant Joe Fields flew this gaudily decorated 336th FIS F-86A (49-1175) named Peg 'O' My Heart/Tiger.

Left: This F-86E of the 336th FIS carries eight kill markings under its cockpit. It was assigned to Captain Clifford Jolley, the 18th ace of the Korean conflict, and the first National Guard pilot to become a jet ace. During World War II, Jolley flew P-40s and P-38s from the Aleutians.

Lt Martin Bambrick
335th FIS

Martin Bambrick (left) and Hank Cresibene beside F-86A 49-1272 Wham Bam, *in which Bambrick shot down a MiG in September 1952.*

"On 4 September 1952, I was to lead a flight of four Sabres up to the Yalu. I was flying the only A-model in the flight. We were assigned to cover a squadron of F-84s that were going to be working over some ground targets. We would be over them at 29,000 ft (8839 m). As we began to orbit, I attempted to contact the bomber lead, but didn't have any luck. I switched over to the 'E' channel on the VHF and still no luck. At that moment, I noticed two silver, swept-wing aircraft flying toward the '84s. I yelled out to the leader of the bombers that there were MiGs coming in on him. I didn't have a chance to see if he reacted, because my flight was in the process of dropping tanks and getting down into the middle of the MiGs.

"These guys were moving at a very high rate of speed. Before we could get down on their level, they had flown right through the middle of the F-84 formation, without firing a shot! Down around 10,000 ft (3048 m), one of the MiGs started a gradual turn to the left, heading south along the MSR. I pulled in at his level, too far behind him, and he was just too fast for my 'A'. So I'm sitting there at 1,200 ft (366 m), firing short bursts at him.

"I know I hit him a few times, in the engine section and left wingroot. After the MiG had taken four or five bursts, some pieces came off his vertical stabiliser and he began a shallow left turn. I was able to cut him off and put a few more bursts into the MiG's wing. At that time, he slowly did a nose up and, by this time, he was widening the gap between us. His speed never seemed to falter and he probably had it at full throttle for the entire time we were engaged. He was almost into the protective overcast. As he got into the soup, he punched out! I don't know what shape his aircraft was in or why he punched out, but I knew I had made a 'kill'.

"I flew on the wing of ace Captain Cliff Jolley many times. I can recall one mission that Jolley was leading. I was lead on the second element in the flight. Jolley was extremely aggressive against the MiGs. On one mission we were at altitude over 'MiG Alley' when someone called out a lone MiG below us. It was making a high-speed run toward the safety of the Yalu. Jolley immediately pitched over and went after him. At this time, he didn't drop his speed brakes and also didn't drop his tanks! He started a very tight spiral-like, continuous barrel roll almost straight down to get behind this guy. The MiG was probably 10,000 to 12,000 ft below us. When all of this began, we were probably at 35,000 or higher.

"Jolley's wingman called out that he couldn't stay up with him in such a tight manoeuvre! I hooked up with him, keeping my hand on my *g* suit valve button to keep it down all the way, so I would not black out from the *g* forces. The MiG led us into a traffic pattern at one of the air bases in the area. I don't remember which one it was, but I'm sure it wasn't Antung. Even then, Jolley still did not let up! To avoid the flak, he put us down on the deck and we could not see very much. We lost sight of the MiG, so we popped up a little bit and here we were, on the end of the runway of this MiG base! We screamed down the runway, pulling streamers off of our canopies.

"By this time, of course, our external tanks were gone. Out of the corner of my eye, I could see the blinking of small-calibre fire coming from both sides of the runway. We were running the gauntlet! Neither one of us was hit, and by this time our wingmen had gone out off the coast to wait for us to join up. Jolley took us out over the ocean at about 25 ft (7.6 m) altitude. We joined up with the other two Sabres and the flight back to Kimpo was mild compared to what we had been through. That was probably one of the most frightening experiences I have ever had in my life! Jolley went on to become the 18th jet ace of the war, with a total of seven confirmed kills.

"I can remember another mission where we were patrolling at an extremely high altitude. Every member of the flight had a pair of binoculars. We were floating along at 45,000+ ft (13716+ m). And, I do mean 'floating'. When we were sitting this high up, we had a tremendous view and the binoculars helped us spot MiGs long before they could see us. All of a sudden, about 50 yd (46 m) in front of us, were two huge bursts of flak … big orange balls of flame. At that altitude, it was unheard of to run into flak! We immediately varied our course to the left … the radar-directed AAA never corrected. They kept firing the direction we had been headed, but we were clear of them by that time. This was the first high-altitude flak that I had ever seen. This proved to all of us that we weren't safe, at any altitude!"

1st Lieutenant Martin Bambrick, 335th FIS

Col Harrison Thyng, 4th FIW commander in 1952, was the 16th ace of the Korean War. His assigned aircraft was Pretty Mary and The Js, *F-86E-1 50-623. Col Thyng's Sabre was one of the first assigned to the 335th FIS, arriving in late July 1951.*

tained flame emanating from a vital area of the aircraft. 2) Aircraft abandonment, i.e., pilot bailout. 3) Aircraft crash. 4) Aircraft disintegration, i.e., major portions leaving the aircraft, such as a wing or tail assembly. The last item would obviously cover any aircraft exploding in mid-air.

A 'probable' victory would have the film show damage that did not fit the 'destroyed' category, but appeared to show that the aircraft probably did not make it back to its base: 1) No visible flame but smoking heavily from vital areas. 2) Aircraft in an obviously uncontrolled spin into a low undercast that hid the aircraft crash site. 3) A large number of hits, and debris departing the enemy aircraft, but, again, no crash is seen either due to cloud cover or the aircraft being able to successfully cross the Yalu River boundary. A 'damaged' was credited for any pilot with film showing at least 15 hits on an enemy aircraft. However, during the first year of the war, the 4th FIG had no 'probable' category, only 'destroyed' or 'damaged'.

Rules modified

Late in the war, the rules were modified, at least in the 51st Fighter Interceptor Group. Major John Bolt, USMC, a World War II ace with six Japanese victories, was an exchange pilot flying with the 39th Fighter Interceptor Squadron at K-13. Major Bolt recounted, "The 'kill rules' were, if you got seven hits on a MiG in a vital area, the Claims Board would award you a kill. The reason being that the MiG did not torch off at high altitudes (above 40,000 ft/12192 m). They simply would not burn because of the air density. So the Claims Board would count the incendiary hits on the film. (We had good gun cameras.) They figured that if you got seven vital hits in the fuselage, the odds were that it was dead. Counting the incendiary hits, which they knew was every third round being fired, if you got three incendiary hits showing on the gun camera film, it meant you hit the MiG at least nine times, and they would say that was a dead MiG."

It is interesting to note here the remarks of Lieutenant No Kum-Suk, a pilot with the North Korean Air Force who defected with a North Korean MiG-15 to Kimpo AB on 21 September 1953, concerning the flyability of a

Nose art was very prevalent in the 4th FIG during 1952. Gopher Patrol/Virginia Belle *was flown by Major William Thomas, who scored one MiG victory in May 1952. Many times, nose art or personal names were not removed when the aircraft changed pilots or crew chiefs; the new person simply added his own personal marking. Major Thomas also had two train kills, as seen just above the 335th 'Indian Head'.*

51st Fighter Interceptor Wg
(16th FIS, 25th FIS, 39th FIS)

MiG after being hit. When asked about the high kill ratio in a recent interview, Lieutenant No responded, "It had to be estimated (the US claims). The MiG-15 was a simple design with primitive and minimal hydraulic control systems, which gives the pilot an advantage of not suffering a hydraulic system loss, thus a loss of flight controls. The MiG-15 was flyable even when the hydraulic system was severely damaged. And many MiGs were able to return home with much damage – unless the aircraft exploded.

Exaggerated claims

"However, Communist claims of downing so many American aircraft were highly exaggerated. Quite simply, as often as they (the Communists) recovered a damaged MiG either in North Korea or across the border in Manchuria, they could not find many downed American aircraft.

"Based on my personal observations, the two elite Soviet V-VS fighter divisions out of the Moscow Defence District, that deployed to Manchurian bases for Korean combat between March 1951 and February 1952, had about an even ratio against all types of American aircraft. The Soviet pilots claimed a 2:1 kill ratio in their favour, but I don't believe it! Their success of achieving an equal ratio against the world's best-trained pilots was remarkable in itself.

"They were lucky that everything was in their favour. They were the best pilots in the Soviet air force, they flew an advanced model of the MiG-15 (the MiG-15bis), the Manchurian sanctuary was strictly observed by the Amer-

The men and aircraft of the 25th FIS line the ramp at Suwon prior to the afternoon mission in the spring of 1953. The near aircraft was flown by Major Herman Visscher, operations officer for the 25th FIS and a flight commander, as denoted by the two red bands around the nose. The obviously busy ramp indicates a maximum effort for the upcoming mission.

icans, the F-86s were never at full strength at K-13 and K-14, and the F-86F had not yet been introduced. These elite Russian pilots were replaced by younger pilots beginning in February 1952.

"As soon as the Manchurian sanctuary was lifted during the second week of April 1952, the ratio ballooned to at least 10:1 in favour of the Americans for the rest of the war, no matter who was flying the MiGs. Sabres shot down many MiG-15s during take-off and landing in Manchuria. Although the MiGs kept flying, the Communist air effort was hopelessly defeated by the summer of 1952. The Russians kept rotating in fresh, young pilots to replenish their losses through to the end of the war in July 1953. The Chinese had no replacement pilots by the late spring of 1953. The North Korean air force also lost heavily. But our mission was against American fighter-bombers, and we could usually avoid contact with the Sabres."

Less than reliable gun camera

All of the above criteria were essential for confirmation of any claim using the gun camera film. However, the type N6 gun camera was not always the most reliable unit, suffering from a variety of malfunctions as well as poor film. Thus, all filmed claims had to be substantiated

Above: The badge below the cockpit and red tail stripe identify this aircraft as a 25th FIS machine, specifically an F-86E-10 flown by 'Tiger Flight', hence the 'tiger teeth'. '793 is believed to have been flown by North American's chief test pilot, Bob Hoover, while in Korea to help alleviate concerns regarding the Sabre's gunsight.

Left: As the crew chief buttons up the gun bay after charging the M3 0.5-in (12.7-mm) guns, the pilot of Miss B, a 16th FIS F-86E-1, begins the starting sequence as he prepares for a mission to 'MiG Alley' in April 1952. The black-and-yellow bands on the fuselage and wings were a 51st FIG unit marking, which was later adopted by FEAF as an operational marking for all F-86s operating in the Far East.

Right: The lead F-86E-10 in this famous photograph is 51-2721, the aircraft in which Major Fred Ascani broke the world closed-circuit speed record on 17 August 1951, with a top speed of 635.31 mph (1022.4 km/h). Shipped to Korea and issued to the 51st FIW, FU-721 was named Lady Margaret *and, later,* This'll Kill Ya.

Above: Nina II, *showing two of Colonel Bob Baldwin's five MiG victories, sits on the ramp at K-13 in June 1953. Col Baldwin was the group commander of the 51st FIG, the combat operations portion of the 51st Wing. The three colour bands around the nose indicate either the group or wing commander's aircraft.*

by sworn affidavit by an eye witness to the claim. Lacking any film results, the claim had to be verified by two witnesses – one witness could be the claimant himself; the other witness could be his wingman, and/or another eye witness to the event. The 'other eye witness' could be another pilot in the area, or a witness on the ground.

It has recently come to light that 5th AF had intelligence people on the ground near the MiG bases inside Manchuria, or near to it. Both the CIA and the Australians had intelligence operations on some of the islands in the mouth of the Yalu River, as well as on both banks of the river. These intel teams that would call out interesting things, like – "Bandit train number 6 leaving the station! Casey Jones at the throttle!" Yes, the legendary 'Casey Jones' did exist, although he was also known as 'Honcho', 'The Professor', etc.

Personalised MiGs

How did the intel teams know who was flying the MiG aircraft? Because, as with most aggressive pilots, the MiG pilots personalised their aircraft, sometimes with stripes on the fuselage, or a tail marking. One even had a large dragon painted on the side. The intel people were trained to watch for these special markings and call them out to the incoming 5th AF formations. The intel operations on the ground could also verify aircraft claims, either by seeing

F-86Es of the 51st FIW are seen here in their sandbagged revetments at Suwon. To the left of the picture is an aircraft of the 25th FIS, known as the 'Tiger Flight', which applied 'tiger teeth' to a number of its F-86Es.

Checkertail Es of the 51st FIW

The 51st began its transition from the F-80C to the Sabre in late 1951, initially with two squadrons (16th and 25th). The 51st Sabres flew their first combat mission on 1 December.

F-86E-10-NA, 51-2738
1st Lieutenant Cecil Foster
16th Fighter Interceptor Squadron
This, Foster's second Sabre, was known as *Four Kings and a Queen*. He had earlier flown another F-86E, 51-2737 *Three Kings*. Foster himself was the top-scoring 16th FIS pilot, with nine victories. He twice achieved double kills, on 26 September 1952 and 24 January 1953, and was promoted to captain during the tour.

F-86E-1-NA, 50-649
Lieutenant Walter Copeland
25th Fighter Interceptor Squadron
Copeland scored his single kill in *Aunt Myrna* on 9 September 1952, one of six MiG-15s officially credited that day. The 25th's leading scorer was Iven Kinchloe, with nine.

Only when the previously mentioned criteria was met was that claim confirmed as either 'destroyed', 'probably destroyed', or 'damaged'. Often, other pilots and/or the intel people that were interviewed got a claim changed from Destroyed to something else. It was not easy to get a confirmed victory in Korea.

Loss classifications

Although the rules for claims were clear, the rules for losses were not. 5th AF and Far East Air Force (FEAF) seemed to take different approaches as to what constituted a combat loss. There were five classifications for losses: 'M' – combat loss due to enemy action; 'P' – cause unknown on a combat mission; 'N' – flying accident on a combat mission; 'Q' – enemy action not on a combat mission, i.e., destroyed on base of operations; 'A' – flying accident.

There were times when an aircraft would be shot to pieces, either by MiGs or anti-aircraft fire, crash and not be counted as a combat loss. This was especially true with B-29 losses. Officially, the USAF confirms the loss of 17 B-29 aircraft, but they were just B-29s actually shot down over enemy territory. A great many B-29s made it out of North Korea, only to crash at sea, make an emergency landing in South Korea, or make it back to home base but never fly again. Over 100 B-29s fall into this category and were not carried as a combat loss.

Was this done with F-86 losses? Again, research results are inconclusive. Some F-86s are known to have made it back to bases in South Korea after suffering heavy damage from

Above: Colonel Francis 'Gabby' Gabreski, commander of the 51st FIW at K-13 beginning in November 1951, stands in the cockpit of Major William Wescott's Lady Frances, F-86E-10 51-2746. Although 'Gabby' got a victory in Wescott's Sabre, the victories shown above the gun bay are Wescott's. Col Gabreski's regular Sabre was named Gabby.

Above: The 10th ace of the Korean War was Captain Iven C. Kinchloe Jr, who shot down five MiG-15s and four Yak-9s between January and May 1952. Captain Kinchloe and Ivan (F-86E-10 51-2731) were assigned to the 25th Fighter Interceptor Squadron at K-13.

the MiG crash or explode, or the pilot bail out below the cloud deck.

The facts are clear. All claims went from the fighter wing headquarters to the 5th AF Claims Board. The Claims Board first checked the gun camera film for verification. If the film was inconclusive, the Board would interview the wingman or any other pilot in the area. If the claim could be verified by the ground intelligence people, that operator was interviewed.

1st Lt Philip C. Davis
Flight Leader, 16th FIS

Lt Philip Davis is seen here in the cockpit of a 16th FIS Sabre. Next to the 'bullseye' marking is the inscription 3 shots for 25.

"My first kill was in April 1953. At this time, I was 'C' flight commander in the 16th FIS. Since you had to have a tremendous amount of combat experience to lead, I had already flown at least 80 missions. I had had several opportunities to score while flying wing, but due to the fact that I considered myself an excellent fighter pilot and a lousy shot, I had fumbled all of my chances! I was determined to get the next one, even if I had to ram him!

"We always started out in flights of four, but, on numerous occasions, we would end up as an element of two – usually because someone in the flight had a 'hung' tank. This meant that his wingman had to escort him out of the area. This left two Sabres from the original flight. On the day in question, this was what happened. After sending the element back to Suwon, my wingman and I continued the patrol. We turned down the Yalu at the 'Mizou' at 40,000 ft (12192 m). Shortly after we rolled out of our turn, I spotted a single

MiG-15 ahead and slightly below. He was on a parallel course with us.

"I called the 'bounce' and told my wing to cover me. I let down and closed on the MiG. The range finder dropped from 1,200 ft (366 m) to 1,000 ft (305 m) to 800 ft (244 m). At this point I gave him a quick burst from the '50s'. I do not believe he saw me until I started firing. In any event, I observed hits with my first burst and he must have flamed out. He immediately started emitting heavy white vapour from his tailpipe. We were not in the cons [contrail zone], so I knew he was in trouble.

"Without wasting any time, the MiG pilot rolled over into a vertical dive. I followed, firing short bursts while headed downhill. When my altimeter rapidly approached the 10,000-ft (3048-m) mark, I began to get worried about being able to pull out! At that instant, he initiated what must have been about a 7g or 8g pullout. I know this is accurate because I was pulling almost 7g and I watched him disappear out the top of my windscreen (with my chin on my chest)! Although the g forces didn't black me out, I could not hold my head up. We ended up in an almost vertical zoom, then he abruptly rolled off and dove into the ground!

"In retrospect, I believe one of my early bursts may have killed or disabled the pilot and the subsequent dive, pullout and final dive may have been the airframe response to him slumping against the controls. About midway through the encounter, my wingman began yelling that another MiG was jumping him. (As we subsequently realised, this was a standard MiG tactic: a second MiG would be about 3 miles/0.9 km in trail to jump you while you were engaging the leader...I have always wondered how they talked their pilots into leading!) I started looking around for my wingman about the time my MiG was in his final dive. I couldn't find him, but I sure could hear him. He finally shook the second MiG and we both got the hell out of there – independently! As a consideration for his harrowing

experience and a reward for keeping MiG No. 2 out of my six o'clock, I split the kill with him.

"As an additional comment to all of this, about midway through my tour, there was a rumour that the MiG-15 could only pull 5g. Since I could pull at least 6g without a suit on, as long as the F-86 could, I quit wearing a g suit. I almost changed my mind after that experience!

"My second kill was more routine than spectacular. It was during the early months of the summer of 1953. The war was winding down rapidly. We were involved in a routine patrol over the mouth of the Yalu River. We were up around the 42,000 ft (12802 m) marker. We had just started an easy turn to the south (at that altitude, you had to be smooth and easy to keep your Mach up). Midway through the turn, I spotted a single MiG heading south out of Antung. It was travelling at a high Mach down about 5,000 ft (1524 m) altitude. We didn't hesitate. I called the bounce, opened the 'trombone' (canopy defroster), chopped the power and headed downhill!

"I closed at his 6 o'clock to about 800 ft (244 m) Unless this was a trap, we had the element of surprise, because the pilot had not taken any evasive action. He was lined up perfectly and I squeezed off a quick burst. There were numerous hits. The MiG pilot instantly broke to the left and up … I followed. We were both pulling 4g or 5g … I managed to pull harder and gradually got a good lead on him. Firing another few rounds, I got more hits. I found myself yelling for him to go ahead and 'blow up'. At that instant, the pilot ejected. I was still firing, completely oblivious to his ejection until my wingman (Alvin 'The Wiley Coyote' Bouchard) yelled to stop firing. I finally realised that the MiG was pilotless and broke it off. We headed back for base without seeing any other activity in our vicinity. I finished my tour with 1.5 kills."

1st Lieutenant Philip C. Davis

1st Lt Walt R. Copeland
25th FIS

1st Lieutenant Walt Copeland is seen here with a 25th FIS Sabre at Suwon.

"It was 9 September 1952. There was heavy air traffic in and out of Suwon because of the numerous air strikes being carried out by the fighter-bombers over North Korea. The 25th's mission (#51-01) for today was to fly top cover over 24 F-84s. The possibility of mixing it up with the MiGs was excellent. The assigned target for the bombers was the Officers Candidate School at X-Ray/Easy 8150. The time over the target was to be precisely 12.00. I was part of 'Hawk' flight and we were being led by Captain Carr.

"We all knew this would be a good mission because there was a good possibility that the MiGs would be forced to defend some of the many targets being attacked today. Ours was only a few minutes flying time from the big base at Antung. We all checked and rechecked the footage indicators on the film packs because we knew that we would be firing our guns. We strapped in and hit the master switch at 11.28. We

were airborne and heading north at 11.35. Our ingress altitude was pegged at 35,000 ft (10668 m), which gave us a great view over any possible danger to our F-84s...

"Up ahead, another group of F-84s were hitting targets and meeting a lot of resistance, in the form of MiG-15s. 'Cobra' flight, a few minutes ahead of us, radioed that several bombers were getting bounced as they came off their bomb runs. At that point, we were close enough to punch off our drop tanks. Our '84s were already initiating their bomb runs, so we dove into the fracas. Right below us, at a very low altitude, were some bombers being chased by two MiG-15s. They were at treetop level.

"The enemy fighters were at 7 o'clock low. 'Hawk' flight made a hard right descending turn. I was leading the second element, trying to close. I found myself dropping back, so I notified lead of this fact. We proceeded, trailing behind. Seconds later, I spotted a single MiG climbing through 10,000 ft (3048 m). He was at a range of about 4,000 ft (1219 m), doing what the MiGs do best – climbing straight up at a terrific rate of speed! I pushed the throttle all the way and, for a second, I thought I would be able to get off a long shot, but he disappeared into a dense cloud layer and I turned my attention back to the bombers that were scattered all over the place. It did not take long to observe that there were still MiGs all over the place! It was two flights of four MiGs that caught my attention. They were flying in tight formation. As I closed, I noticed they were all painted in a dull green scheme and their easterly course would put them in the middle of our F-84s in minutes. I popped my speed brakes and retarded the throttle, heading into a steep dive with a descending right turn. Adding power put us in a very high Mach number and we dropped in about 500 ft (152 m) behind the No. 3 MiG. As I approached from his 6 o'clock position, the entire flight of eight MiGs dropped their tanks. I believe they were focused on the F-84s.

"At that instant, I opened fire with a few short bursts, and in seconds one of the green MiGs burst into

a bright orange fireball. He plummeted straight down. I flew through the debris, smoke and flames and commenced firing at the No. 4 man, which had been on the No. 3's left side. I fired several long bursts, but due to the turbulence from the low altitude (we had dropped down to just a few hundred feet above the terrain), I had difficulty hitting him. I do remember scoring a few hits on one of his wingroots and the fuselage. Suddenly, there was silence...I had completely fired out my ammunition.

"I called for my wingman to take over the attack. All this time, the MiG was steadily pulling away. As he moved into position, he called out that my speed brakes were still partially extended. As I pulled them in, I told him to keep an eye on his fuel gauge, because we had been working at low altitudes at full throttle. At this point, we found out that the remaining MiGs had come in behind us and their leader began firing. As I broke hard right, I looked back and noticed the MiG's nose light up again. He was firing from about 5,000 ft (1524 m) out. We reversed our turn, continuing violent evasive action for several minutes. Luckily for us, the MiGs broke off the attack and headed back across the Yalu River. They were probably having the same problem we were having; low fuel.

"We immediately withdrew from the area and nursed our Sabres back up to 40,000 ft (12192 m); just in case we flamed out, we would have sufficient altitude to glide back safely to Suwon. We touched down at 12.55. The fight had ... lasted a few minutes, but it sure seemed that we had been airborne for longer than we had!"

1st Lieutenant Walt R. Copeland

Note: Over the mountainous terrain of North Korea, flying at high speed below 2,000 ft (610 m) was treacherous. It was tough enough to control the aircraft, much less hold a MiG in the gunsights. That said, many kills were scored below 1,000 ft (305 m).

Right: This pair of 25th FIS F-86Es is on five-minute alert at K-13 during early June 1952. Pilots on five-minute alert could often relax in the alert shack, or play games like horseshoes at nearby facilities. The aircraft were plugged in and ready to go. Aircraft on one-minute alert had the pilots strapped in and ready to start engines. The metal nose cap with the small radome was installed on aircraft from F-86E-10 onwards.

Above: Benjo Nazume (Outhouse Mouse)/The Tokay Flame was one of the new F-86E-10s assigned to the 25th FIS at Suwon in October 1951. The F-86E-10 Sabres were drawn from aircraft assigned to the 1st FIG at George Air Force Base, California, which were then rushed to Korea and distributed to both 4th and 51st FIG squadrons. The green wingtips are a flight colour marking.

Right: An F-86E-1 shares the ramp at Suwon with some of the brand new F-86E-10s recently arrived from the States. F-86Es began arriving in Korea as early as late July 1951, being assigned to the 4th FIG. Note the absence of tail markings at this point.

Lt Jim Thompson flew an aircraft called **The Huff**, *F-86F-1 51-2897, with the 39th FIS. On 18 May 1953, the same day Joe McConnell got his 15th and 16th victories, Lt Thompson met a MiG-15 with a large green dragon painted on the side, successfully shooting it down for his first victory. The next day the crew chief had a large dragon painted on the side of Thompson's F-86F. Thompson got another MiG-15 on 16 June 1953.*

Lieutenant Colonel George Ruddell, posing here for press photographs, was the commander of the 39th FIS at K-13 in 1953, when he became the 30th ace in the Korean War. His aircraft, **MiG Mad Mavis**, *was F-86F-1 serialled 51-2940. Colonel Ruddell finished the war with eight victories. His aircraft was another of the early Fs retrofitted with one of North American Aviation's '6-3 hard wing' kits.*

The 'ace of aces', Capt. Joseph McConnell, scored 16 victories flying with the 39th FIS. His F-86F-1 **Beautious Butch II** *had the '6-3 hard wing' retrofitted. This photograph was taken at K-13 on 19 May 1953, the day after he scored kills 15 and 16. The aircraft originally had MiG silhouette victory markings; they were replaced with small red stars for PR purposes. The name was misspelled when reapplied for the photos.*

2nd Lt Ronald Wilson 39th FIS

Ronald Wilson poses with a DHC L-20 Beaver, the 'General's Jeep', in this case belonging to Lt Gen Glenn O. Barcus.

"It was 15 February 1953, still bitter cold and the type of day that all of us Sabre pilots both loved and hated! It was crystal clear with unlimited visibility. On the other hand, we would be throwing heavy, persistent contrails that made you feel like you were under easy viewing by everyone, especially MiG pilots.

"This was my 32nd combat mission with the 39th and all of them had been in the F-86F models. Due to my junior level, I was still relegated to the worst wing position: number four in a flight of four. This was known as 'tailend Charlie'. If attacked, the number four position was usually the first to get fired upon! Our formation was the standard four aircraft flying in a fingertip configuration. Number one in the formation was the flight leader, number two was his wingman, number three was element leader, and my position was wingman for him. If separated, each leader and his wingman stayed together to form the basic minimum of the two-fighter unit. If, for some reason, you got separated from your element and could not join up, the rule was to withdraw from the hostile environment and go home. This was never a one-man show.

"Since we all flew in the 39th squadron, all of our callsigns were names of snakes. In this case, we were 'Cobra' flight. This meant that all radio chatter pertaining to me would be COBRA 4. We departed our base at Suwon (K-13) early in the morning, proceeding to climb on a northerly heading. Our objective was to arrive over the Yalu River with as much fuel as possible and a very high altitude. On this day, we would hit our patrol area at 45,000 ft (13716 m).

"As we approached our sector, just south of the Suiho Reservoir, we could tell that the air activity would be much heavier than normal! There were contrails all over the place. There was no way to tell how long they had been there or if they had been made by friendlies or the enemy. Then the radios started up, with other flights calling in bandits and taking bounces on the enemy. You could hear the strain in the voices, but you couldn't see where all of it was coming from. Nevertheless, our heads were on swivels!

"The next thing I heard was 'Cobra Flight, this is Cobra lead … drop tanks!' We all punched off our external fuel tanks (they were already empty). This transmission was immediately followed by 'Cobra Flight … break left!' We were being jumped by MiGs. It was a hard, violent turn and we were pulling a lot of gs. As I was No. 4 on the left of the flight, the turn was into me and, therefore, very difficult. I managed to maintain contact with my leader, COBRA 3, but when we rolled out, there were no other aircraft to be seen! There was only the two of us. We had lost some altitude, so we proceeded to climb as fast as we could. Well into our climb, I looked up and saw four MiGs above us and called them out to element lead.

"He turned and took a bounce on the last aircraft and fired. The long burst scored numerous hits all over the MiG, but he continued on course. The element of surprise was gone, because the bandits scattered in all directions. The temptation to go after one of them didn't win out over the air discipline that had been engrained in me. I stayed on my wing position to keep my leader clear from behind. The damaged MiG continued to head north for the safety of Manchuria. COBRA 3 radioed that he was out of ammunition and that I should slide in and take over pursuit of the enemy fighter.

"We were about 2,000 ft (610 m) behind and slowly closing the gap. Our problem with this was that the MiG was climbing slightly, making it more difficult to close fast. I squeezed off a couple of bursts. My aim was accurate and, once again, the enemy fighter took 50-calibre hits in both wingroots and the aft part of its fuselage. As I let up on the trigger, the MiG began trailing a plume of smoke and its nose dipped, causing a loss of altitude. By this time, he was over the Yalu and, most probably, we were too. We eased up and watched the MiG continue to dive and smoke. I saw him crash, but my leader did not, so it was officially declared a 'probable'. It was very unfortunate for me that there were no witnesses. Low on fuel, we headed back to the safety of our base at Suwon."

2nd Lieutenant Ronald Wilson

Aircraft of the commanders

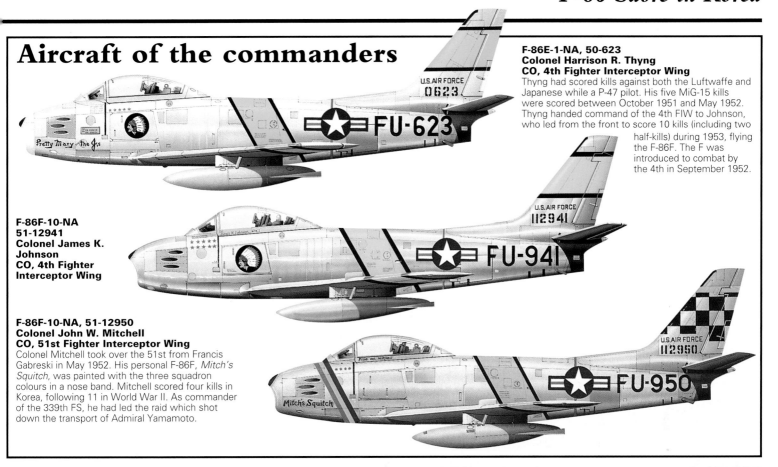

F-86E-1-NA, 50-623
Colonel Harrison R. Thyng
CO, 4th Fighter Interceptor Wing
Thyng had scored kills against both the Luftwaffe and Japanese while a P-47 pilot. His five MiG-15 kills were scored between October 1951 and May 1952. Thyng handed command of the 4th FIW to Johnson, who led from the front to score 10 kills (including two half-kills) during 1953, flying the F-86F. The F was introduced to combat by the 4th in September 1952.

F-86F-10-NA
51-12941
Colonel James K. Johnson
CO, 4th Fighter Interceptor Wing

F-86F-10-NA, 51-12950
Colonel John W. Mitchell
CO, 51st Fighter Interceptor Wing
Colonel Mitchell took over the 51st from Francis Gabreski in May 1952. His personal F-86F, *Mitch's Squitch*, was painted with the three squadron colours in a nose band. Mitchell scored four kills in Korea, following 11 in World War II. As commander of the 339th FS, he had led the raid which shot down the transport of Admiral Yamamoto.

F-86 Maintenance and Test Flight, Rear Echelon Maintenance Combined Operations (REMCO), Tsuiki Air Base, Japan

Above: The base at Tsuiki, Japan was designated the Rear Echelon Maintenance Combined Operations facility, commonly called the Tsuiki REMCO. All F-86s, no matter what unit they were from, had major maintenance performed at Tsuiki. The Tsuiki ramp was full of F-86s of various types and from every unit, when this photo was snapped in the summer of 1953.

Right: F-86Fs began arriving in Korea in late summer 1952, equipping both the 4th and 51st FIGs equally. This flight of 25th FIS F-86Fs is en route to 'MiG Alley' in the spring of 1953, in a 'finger-four' formation, the typical combat formation. All aircraft carry standard 120-US gal (454-litre) combat drop tanks.

Left: Pilots on five-minute alert with the 39th FIS play a game of horseshoes directly behind the alert aircraft at K-13 in the late spring of 1953. There was also an 'alert shack' nearby where pilots could relax, read, write letters, or talk tactics while waiting for the alert horn to sound.

Above: The 12-in (30-cm) black-and-silver checks on the fin of the 51st FIW Sabres represented a revival of the markings worn by the 25th FS while based in China during World War II. At least one Sabre carried a variation using 4-in (10-cm) checks. The nearest aircraft is an early production F-86F of the 39th FIS and is seen at Suwon in early 1953.

Above: Lt Gen. Glenn O. Barcus, commander of Fifth Air Force, flew this F-86F, Barcus' Carcus, on several missions into 'MiG Alley' during 1953. The aircraft was assigned to the 39th FIS at Suwon, and carried Barcus's three general's stars on the gun bay door. When Gen. Barcus flew, his flight was always made up of the best pilots available. Even Capt. Joseph McConnell flew 'wing' in this flight.

Fs of the 39th FIS

The 39th FIS was reassigned to the 51st FIW on 12 June 1952 and transitioned to the Sabre. F-86Fs were received later in the year.

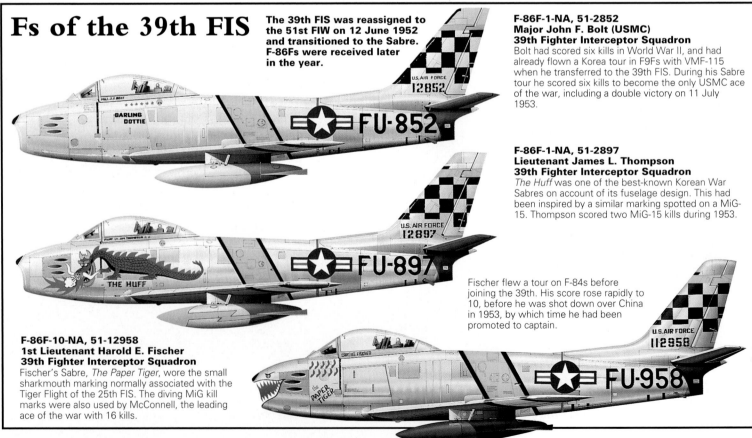

F-86F-1-NA, 51-2852
Major John F. Bolt (USMC)
39th Fighter Interceptor Squadron
Bolt had scored six kills in World War II, and had already flown a Korea tour in F9Fs with VMF-115 when he transferred to the 39th FIS. During his Sabre tour he scored six kills to become the only USMC ace of the war, including a double victory on 11 July 1953.

F-86F-1-NA, 51-2897
Lieutenant James L. Thompson
39th Fighter Interceptor Squadron
The Huff was one of the best-known Korean War Sabres on account of its fuselage design. This had been inspired by a similar marking spotted on a MiG-15. Thompson scored two MiG-15 kills during 1953.

Fischer flew a tour on F-84s before joining the 39th. His score rose rapidly to 10, before he was shot down over China in 1953, by which time he had been promoted to captain.

F-86F-10-NA, 51-12958
1st Lieutenant Harold E. Fischer
39th Fighter Interceptor Squadron
Fischer's Sabre, *The Paper Tiger*, wore the small sharkmouth marking normally associated with the Tiger Flight of the 25th FIS. The diving MiG kill marks were also used by McConnell, the leading ace of the war with 16 kills.

Right: The nearest of these two 336th FIS F-86Fs is 52-4539 Slo-Mo-Shun II. While its pilot at this time was unknown, the aircraft was initially assigned to Colonel D. P. Hall, commander of the 4th FIW in summer 1953.

Below: Boomer was the F-86F-30 flown by Captain Clyde Curtin. Assigned to the 335th FIS, Capt. Curtin was the 38th ace crowned during the Korean War, with a total of five victories.

the MiGs. Case in point is that of Lieutenant Colonel Glenn Eagleston. 'Eagle' ran into 'Casey Jones', who calmly shot to hell Eagleston's F-86A. After Lieutenant Colonel Bruce Hinton chased off the MiG, they limped the Sabre back to Suwon. It was crash-landed at K-13 and written off. This aircraft was carried as 'M' – combat loss due to enemy action.

Others were not, being carried as 'P' – unknown cause, or 'N' – flying accident on a mission. The number of 'P' and 'N' losses caused by the MiGs is unknown, and probably will remain that way. We are left with the numbers readily available, but even those vary at different times. The first 'ratio' of MiGs shot down to Sabre losses is the legendary 14:1 ratio. This is a result of an 'official' Air Force score of 808 MiGs shot down for the loss of 58 Sabres. These numbers are used frequently in Air Force publications such as *Encyclopedia of US Air Force Aircraft and Missile Systems*, Vol. 1, put out by the Office of Air Force History in 1978. They were first brought to light two days after the ceasefire went into effect. In a 5th Air Force communiqué dated 29 July 1953, Sabre losses were stated to be 58, and MiG victories stood at

808 – a ratio of 13.79:1.

But these numbers "818-58" do not concur with official lists such as *USAF Historical Study #81, USAF Credits for the Destruction of Enemy Aircraft, Korean War*, and the *USAF Statistical Digest*, Fiscal 1953. In Study #81, F-86 pilots flying with 5th Air Force units are officially credited with the destruction of 792 MiG-15 aircraft. The 1953 *USAF Statistical Digest* lists a loss of 78 F-86 aircraft during the Korean War – a 10:1 kill ratio. How the number of Sabre losses rose from 58 to 78 is not explained. Nor is the reduction of MiG victories. Some Sabres that had been carried as "Lost to Unknown Causes (P)", were probably re-evaluated and changed to "Lost To Enemy Action (M)". Some MiG victories, especially in the last three months of the war, were also probably re-evaluated and changed to 'probable'.

Interesting figures

The same Statistical Digest contains some other interesting figures, including Total Enemy Aircraft Destroyed (MiGs, all other types, air and ground kills) by F-86s – 810, with 814 Damaged. Total F-86 Aircraft Lost To Enemy

Below: Capt. Jim Jabara, first ace in the Korean War, returned to the 4th FIG in 1953 as a major, and scored nine more victories before the war ended. Major Jabara was assigned to HQ Squadron, 4th FIG in 1953, and flew any aircraft that was available. This aircraft, F-86F-30 52-4519, shows 12 of his 15 total victories.

Right: Two of the 4th FIW's F-86Fs, 51-12954 and 51-12963, are seen here en route to the Yalu River in October 1952. As both aircraft are bereft of nose art of any description, this photograph was evidently taken soon after delivery.

In the autumn of 1952, three F-86Fs from the 335th FIS were flown to Tsuiki REMCO facility, where they had three JATO bottles installed under the J47 engine. The JATO could be fired in flight, and was especially useful when trying to catch a fleeing MiG-15. However, Capt. Cliff Jolley reported that the JATO aircraft were quite uncontrollable, and the aircraft centre of gravity had to be readjusted after firing the JATO bottles. The idea was scrapped in November 1953. This aircraft is one of the JATO-equipped F-86Fs.

The 'Grey Fox'
F-86F-10-NA, 51-12953
Lieutenant Colonel Vermont Garrison
CO, 335th Fighter Interceptor Squadron

With 10 kills, Vermont Garrison, the 'Grey Fox', shared with Lonnie Moore the distinction of being the 335th's top scorer. As a major, Garrison opened his account on 21 February 1953, scoring regularly for the remainder of the war. His promotion occurred in June. His squadron was responsible for fielding the Gunval aircraft, armed with 20-mm cannon.

A pair of F-86F-10s assigned to the 335th FIS is seen in the revetments at K-14 in 1953. The second aircraft is Col James K. Johnson's F-86F. Col Johnson was the 4th FIW commander in 1953, and shot down 10 MiG-15s to become the 29th ace of the Korean War.

Action – 110: 78 in air-to-air action, 13 to unknown causes, and 19 lost to ground fire. Total sorties flown by F-86s was 87,177 between 14 December 1950 and 27 July 1953. But, of that number, 25,604 were flown between 1 April 1953 and 27 July 1953, when both the 8th and 18th FBW were operational, flying fighter-bomber missions at a rate of up to four per day.

Russian archives data revealed a loss officially of 345 MiG-15s to UN aircraft of all types. This is strictly Soviet-piloted MiG-15 losses; there are no numbers available for losses of Chinese and North Korean MiGs. However, both Russian and US authorities agree that by the early spring of 1953, most of the MiG force was being flown by Chinese and North Korean pilots. In the months of April, May, June and July 1953, F-86 pilots claimed 191 MiGs destroyed. Most were probably not Soviet-piloted MiGs. Soviet sources confirm that Chinese and North Korean pilots had been flying MiG combat air patrols as early as spring 1951.

Conflicting claims

Interestingly, the same Soviet sources that claim only four Soviet MiGs were destroyed against the destruction of one Sabre also state that the Chinese MiG losses alone were at least

Above: Colonel Royal Baker, 21st ace of the Korean War, discusses with the press how he achieved his 11th kill on 19 February 1953. The aircraft, F-86F-10 51-12955, is not Col Baker's regular F-86F; that was F-86E 51-2822. Baker was the wing commander of the 4th FIW at the time, and finished with 13 victories.

Below: Gunval was the result of attempts to find heavier-calibre guns for the Sabre. Eight F-86F-1s, fitted with four T-160 20-mm cannon as F-86F-2s, were assigned to the 4th FIW in January 1953 for 16 weeks of combat testing. Although firing all four guns caused engine compressor stalls, the trials were judged a success. The T-160 later entered production as the M39 and was installed in the F-86H and F-100.

Below: Bearing the badge of the 334th FIS, this F-86F-30 (52-4794/The Mauler) was the mount of Lieutenant Marvin Lamb who flew with the unit in 1953 but did not record any kills. The name under the cockpit on the starboard side of the aircraft was that of Airman 2nd Class Bill Mack, the machine's crew chief.

15th Tactical Reconnaissance Squadron, 67th Tactical Reconnaissance Wing

Above: Mig Killer *(48-196) was one of the F-86A-5s converted to RF-86A standard under Project Ashtray for service with the the 15th TRS at K-14, where it is seen in late 1952. At least five A models were converted in Japan to Ashtray standard, with two K-9 cameras installed, one in each gun bay. These followed the two F-86As modified to Honeybucket standard with a single K-25 in the right-hand gun bay. This particular aircraft was destined to serve with the California ANG after the war.*

Right: Before the RF-86 entered service, reconnaissance near the Yalu River and 'MiG Alley' was carried out by RF-80s and RB-45s. Both types suffered at the hands of the MiGs and an alternative platform was needed, preferably based on the F-86. Despite a lack of official backing at first, 67th TRW personnel eventually devised a camera mounting for installation in two war-weary 4th FIW F-86As (Project Honeybucket). These entered service with the 15th TRS, alongside its RF-80s, in late 1951. Here we see one of the later Ashtray aircraft, named Ave Maria, *in a revetment at Kimpo.*

8:1. Using the Soviet sources, adding the Chinese and Soviet loss ratios together, results in a 12:1 ratio in favour of the F-86s, without factoring in any North Korean losses. It now seems that the often reported 1953 ratio of 14:1 is actually closer to correct than the 'official ratio' of 10:1 based on later statistics. In the past several years, a document titled 'Sabre Charlie Measures Report' has been circulating through the aviation historian community. Reputedly a US Air Force document, many officials at

The Ashtray RF-86A conversions, including that performed on 48-195 Nancy, *were far from consistent in their execution. Most had their guns completely removed; some retained the upper pair only, though they could not be fired without the vibration upsetting the delicate camera gear. A few of these aircraft also carried a K-14 'dicing' camera in the upper 'lip' of the engine air intake, in place of the APG-30 ranging radar set.*

Right: The 15th TRS 'Cotton Pickers', a component of the 67th TRW, operated RF-86s alongside its RF-80s in Korea. Both types are seen here in a revetment at Kimpo in late 1952. The 67th also flew RB-26s and RF-51s in the Tac/R role during the 'police action'.

18th Fighter-Bomber Wing
(12th FBS, 67th FBS, No. 2 Sqn SAAF)

Above: An F-86F assigned to No. 2 Squadron, SAAF taxies past other F-86Fs of the 18th FBG at K-55 in the late spring, 1953. No. 2 Sqn flew over 2,000 sorties in the Korean War, the biggest percentage being fighter-bomber strikes. Its F-86Fs were returned to USAF control in October 1953, when No. 2 Sqn rotated home. The 18th FBG F-86Fs carry the early tail markings of the 67th FBS. The squadron was assigned to the 18th FBW when that unit was still flying F-51Ds.

Left: No. 2 Sqn F-86F 617/I displays the SAAF springbok roundel, orange/white/blue fin flash and an individual aircraft code letter.

USAF history offices knew nothing about it. According to many writers who had copies of the 'Sabre Charlie Measures Report', the report concluded that the kill ratio in Korea was actually 7:1 rather than the 10:1 official ratio that had generally been conceded as correct.

'Saber Measures (Charlie)'

This author finally located a copy of the report through the efforts of Air Force Historical Research Archives at Maxwell AFB. The report, actually titled 'Saber Measures (Charlie)', was written in 1970 as part of Project Coronet Harvest. It deals with "The Relationship Between Sortie Ratios And Loss Rates For Air-To-Air Battle Engagements During World War Two And Korea", and is an analysis of "the outcome of conflicts and the relative numerical strengths of the contending forces".

It is full of interesting notes, not the least of which is the following, which is taken from the Forward: "History is made by people, and people do not like to record their own failures".

'Saber Measures (Charlie)' relates the sortie ratio to the loss rates (air-to-air only) per 1,000 sorties of both contending air forces. It was noted that "in Korea, the air war was quite different from World War II. The Blue Forces (UN) was constrained by limited war aims, in that the Communist Forces were granted sanctuary north of the Yalu River. Thus, Communist Force aircraft could refuse to engage the Blue Forces by simply staying within their refuge, emerging only when they chose to fight."

Careful scrutiny of the report reveals various monthly loss ratios between the MiGs and the F-86s, with a low ratio of 4.73 MiGs to 1 Sabre

Below: Lt Robert Hard of the 67th FBS flew Hard's Hornet from K-55 (Osan) in June 1953. Though initially a marking applied to No. 2 Sqn, SAAF aircraft, the fin flash was eventually adopted by the rest of the 18th FBW.

Above: An F-86F-30 from the 67th FBS has its APG-30 radar bay open for maintenance on the hard stand at K-55 in the summer of 1953. A jeep with a fitted toolbox was standard equipment at any Sabre installation from the early 1950s. The M44 1,000-lb (454-kg) general-purpose bombs have all been fitted with the new-style conical-design tail fins.

Left: This 12th FBS F-86F was struck by anti-aircraft fire, the pilot attempting to put the aircraft down at the first airfield on his map. Unfortunately, this was K-47 (Chunchon), the home of the North American LT-6 Mosquito squadrons, with a runway measuring just 4,200 ft (1280 m). The aircraft's tail markings are in the early style used by the 18th FBG; yellow bands were used by the 12th FBS.

'Flying Cheetah'

No. 2 Sqn, SAAF, the 'Flying Cheetahs', received 22 F-86F-30s on loan, which it flew mainly in the ground attack mission from March 1953 to the end of the war. Operating as part of the 18th FBW, the aircraft wore large South African tricolour fin flashes, which were subsequently adopted by the 18th's two USAF squadrons. The original wing markings of a dark blue band with white stars had caused the F-86 to resemble a MiG-15 from certain angles.

F-86F-30-NA, SAAF 607/52-4320
No. 2 Squadron, SAAF
18th Fighter-Bomber Wing

Above: 12th FBS mechanics install a J47-GE-27 engine in Puddy Tat, *one of the new F-86F-30s, on the open ramp at K-55 in April 1953.*

Above right: 18th FBG armourers unload M44 bomb casings behind The Stinker, *an F-86F assigned to the 12th FBS. During the summer of 1953, most of the F-86F-30s had the '6-3 hard wing' fitted, adding another 30 US gal (114 litres) of fuel as well as increased manoeuvrability.*

in February 1952, and a high of 65.63 MiGs to 1 Sabre in June 1952. These numbers are theoretically based on 1,000 sorties. Studying the figures further, it was apparent that during every month of combat in Korea, the Blue Force sorties were higher than the Communist Force sorties!

Did this mean that there were more F-86s than MiGs? Absolutely not! It only meant that the number of F-86 flights recorded was greater than that of MiGs engaged. Often the Sabres would patrol south of the Yalu River, as the MiGs patrolled north of the Yalu River. If the MiGs did not initiate an engagement, both sides went home with nothing to show for their efforts except another marker in the F-86 sortie

Above: The F-86F-30 was the first of the multi-role Sabres to serve in Korea. It had a strengthened wing capable of holding four drop tanks, or two 1000-lb (454-kg) bombs and two drop tanks. This F-86F assigned to the 67th FBS carries two Misawa-built drop tanks on the inner pylons, with a pair of standard combat tanks outboard.

Right: 52-4536 was an F-86F of the 67th FBS, indicated by the red nose marking, seen here in the summer of 1953. Yellow-nosed aircraft belonged to the 12th FBS, while No. 2 Sqn, SAAF identified its aircraft with their distinctive springbok roundel. Note also the 'U. S. AIR FORCE' titling. The F-86F allowed Sabre pilots to outperform the MiG-15 in every regime for the first time. The F model could operate at 52,000 ft (15850 m), had an improved climb rate and a tighter turning circle, and was marginally faster than the F-86E.

8th Fighter-Bomber Wing
(35th FBS, 36th FBS, 80th FBS)

Each aircraft in this flight of 36th FBS F models, including 52-4796 bringing up the rear, has 1,000-lb (454-kg) bombs on its inboard pylons. 'U.S. AIR FORCE' titling is just visible on their fuselages, indicating that the photograph was taken towards the end of the war.

column. MiG sorties were not counted unless the MiGs engaged the Sabres. Thus, if a maximum effort put 50 F-86s on the Yalu, and 100 MiGs stayed on their side of the river, 50 sorties went into the Sabre statistics, while no MiG sorties were recorded. From April 1953, the F-86 sortie rate was greatly inflated by fighter-bomber sorties as the 8th and 18th FBGs became operational in the F-86F.

10.32:1 loss ratio

Using the 'Saber Measures (Charlie)' loss rates per 1,000 sorties, and averaging that by the number of recording months (25), gives an average of 24.49 MiG losses per 1,000 sorties. Of course, this is all theoretical, and the report

also flatly states that the official ratio was 10.32 MiGs shot down for the loss of one Sabre. This number is based on the actual number of aircraft recorded in 5th Air Force records, 792 MiGs shot down to 78 F-86s.

Other figures of note found in the report: during the first year of F-86 operations from December 1950 through December 1951 – i.e., only 4th Fighter Interceptor Group operations against Soviet pilots – the F-86 losses totalled 16, while MiG victories totalled 102 – a ratio of 6.37 over 'the best in the Soviet air force' according to their admissions as who was committed and when. In 1953, when the Communist forces were mostly young Russian, Chinese and North Korean pilots, F-86 losses totalled 12

Below: Last unit to convert to the F-86 during the Korean War was the 8th FBG at Suwon. The 8th transitioned from Lockheed F-80Cs to new F-86F-30 fighter-bombers beginning in May 1953. This 35th FBS F-86F carries a pair of M43 500-lb general-purpose bombs, plus a pair of the 120-US gal 'Misawa' drop tanks.

Above: Colonel Woodrow Wilmot flew Miss Tena when he commanded the 8th FBW in the summer of 1953. His aircraft carries the three coloured command stripes on the nose, indicating either a wing or group commander's aircraft. The three colours (blue, red and yellow) represented the fin stripes applied to the tails of aircraft of the three squadrons that made up the wing (the 35th, 36th and 80th, respectively). The machines in the background appear to belong to the 35th FBS. Miss Tena is armed with a pair of M57A-1 250-lb (113-kg) GP bombs that have yet to be fitted with tail fins.

Right: The 36th FBS is seen on the ramp at K-13 (Suwon) in the summer of 1953, following an inspection by 5th Air Force officers who are visible in the distance, departing in blue cars. The nearest aircraft is the squadron commander's, as denoted by the three red stripes around the nose. The parking area at K-13 was PSP matting.

aircraft, while MiG kills were an astounding 287 – resulting in an even more spectacular 24:1 kill ratio based on 'actual' numbers!

Does it really matter? 14:1, 10:1 or 7:1, the point is that F-86 pilots in Korea mauled the MiG forces that were trying to win air superiority. Even the 4:1 ratio conceded by the Russians over their best pilots is considered outstanding in any military handbook, especially in light of the many handicaps with which the F-86 pilots were operating – operating over enemy territory 100 per cent of the time, at the extreme end of their range, which limited patrol time to less than 15 minutes along the Yalu River. The MiGs entered combat when they wanted, were always over friendly territory, and broke off combat when they wanted. The Sabre missions were flown under strict rules of engagement, while the MiGs operated under no such rules. Sabre victories were scrutinised by authorities at a level more intense than that during World War II, and are being scrutinised today, 45 years after the fact. The margin of victory of the F-86 over the MiG-15 remains at least 10.32:1, depending on whose sources you choose to accept. A 10:1 victory margin is, in anyone's mind, a thorough beating!

Larry Davis; pilot accounts compiled by Warren Thompson

*Above: These two Sabres of the 35th **FBS**, 8th **FBW** are F-86F-30s, the first of which were delivered in January 1953. These were the first 'dual store' fighter-bomber Sabres, able to carry two underwing drop tanks per wing, or one set of tanks outboard and a 1000-lb (454-kg) on each inboard station. The latter are clearly visible in this photograph.*

*Above: The 36th **FBS** commander flew this F-86F-30 in 1954. Command stripes indicate the 'flight rank' – three was the squadron commander's marking, two was a flight leader, one was an element leader. The '**U.S. AIR FORCE**' legend began to appear on combat aircraft in July 1953.*

*Above: 35th **FBS** armourers deliver M44 1,000-lb (454-kg) **GP** bombs, with the new conical-design tail fins, to aircraft waiting on the ramp at K-13 in late spring, 1953. 8th **FBG** F-86Fs flew fighter-bomber missions exclusively until the war ended, when their mission became multi-purpose, adding 'MiG sweep' to the fighter-bomber task.*

*Right: Typical of the revetments at Suwon is this 80th **FBS** structure in 1953. The revetment could hold two aircraft, had a **PSP** floor, and was surrounded by sandbags to a height at least 12 in (30 cm) higher than that of the fuselage of an F-86. Some revetments at K-13 and K-14 were constructed to hold just a single aircraft.*

Supporting the front line
USAF Airlift and Rescue in the 1950s

In the 1950s the USAF's fighter and bomber forces grew at a dramatic rate as the Cold War deepened. To provide support for its far-flung forces, the USAF operated a massive network of transports while establishing a comprehensive rescue service for its front-line aviators.

Right: The Boeing KC-97G was a dual-role tanker/transport. It featured underwing fuel tanks.

Above: First delivered in 1950, the Douglas C-124A was vital for ferrying large items of equipment.

Above right: Workhorse of the airlift fleet was the Fairchild C-119. This C-119C is seen in Korea in 1952.

Right: The Douglas C-54 was used to move men and materiel on long-range flights. This pair is seen in Korea in 1954.

Left: The graceful Constellation was used for long-range transport. The C-121C, of which 33 were procured, was the military version of the L-1049. It wears the markings of the MATS Atlantic Division.

Above: With its giant hold and clamshell doors, the Globemaster could swallow large loads with ease. The C-124C introduced a weather radar in a nose radome, subsequently retrofitted to C-124As.

Below: Queen Bee of the 'Blue Tail Flies' taxis out at Kimpo in 1953. The C-119 was vital to the Korean War effort, trucking spare parts, equipment and men between bases in the Pacific theatre.

Above: The high-wing, twin-boom layout of the Fairchild C-119 was adopted to provide an unobstructed hold with its floor at truck-bed height. Loading and unloading was accomplished easily, as demonstrated here by a C-119B in Korea.

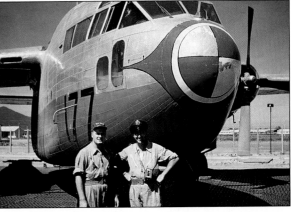

Left: We Go? was a C-47A flying from K-46 Hoengsong in Korea in December 1950. It was employed on nocturnal flare-dropping missions in addition to general transport duties.

Below: The long-suffering Douglas C-47 continued to provide excellent service in general transport roles long after the end of World War II. This camouflaged example is seen flying over the Far East in 1950.

This C-119 and its crew were from the 50th Troop Carrier Squadron, based at Clark AB in the Philippines, one of the USAF's main transport hubs in the region. The photograph was taken at Kimpo in 1954. Korea remained an important destination for the transport fleet long after the war ended.

Left: The de Havilland Canada Beaver won a 1951 competition for a liaison type and was employed in large numbers by both the Army and Air Force under the designation L-20. This Beaver is seen in Korea, where the type performed sterling work on casualty evacuation, command transport and liaison duties.

Below: During the 1950s the standard USAF air-sea rescue vehicle was the Grumman SA-16A Albatross. This example served with the 31st ARS, based at Clark AB in the Philippines.

Above: The Convair L-13 general-purpose light aircraft is little known today. This is one of the 28 L-13Bs built, winterised for use in the Arctic for which it could be fitted with wheels, skis or floats.

Above: This 50th TCS C-119C was one of the aircraft painted up in French markings and flown by US aircrew on supply drops to the beleagured French outpost at Dien Bien Phu, Indo-China, in 1954.

Below: A wartime survivor was the Consolidated Catalina which, designated OA-10, operated for many years in the air-sea rescue role. This example is seen in Alaska.

By the time of the Korean War, the helicopter had matured into a versatile and useful military vehicle. The US Air Force used its Sikorsky H-5 Dragonflies principally on casualty evacuation and combat rescue missions with the Air Rescue Service. For this work two litters could be mounted externally, fitted on to a pole mounting which projected from the cabin. A winch was also provided. Shown here are two H-5Gs of the 3rd ARS in Korea (above and left), and a YR-5A (below) seen in an early (1946) trial at Eglin Field in Florida.

Superseding the H-5 in the Air Rescue Service from 1951 was the larger and more capable Sikorsky H-19A, two examples of which are seen here practising winching. The H-19A had a narrow-chord vertical fin and a straight tailboom.

Fairey Deltas
FD.1, FD.2 & BAC 221

Two very different designs linked by a common design feature – the delta wing – the Fairey Deltas were both conceived with service use in mind. In the event, neither entered service, the FD.1 fading into relative obscurity. The FD.2, however, achieved fame as a 1,000+ mph world speed record breaker, raising the profile of Fairey Aviation and the British aircraft industry as a whole. Rebuilt as the BAC 221, the Delta 2 went on assist the British SST programme.

At the end of World War II, Britain probably led the world in aeronautics. The Royal Air Force operated the world's only truly practical jet fighter, in the shape of the Gloster Meteor. The hopeful Messerschmitt Me 262 was fatally compromised by its unreliable, 25-hour-lived engines, while the American P-59 was little more than a testbed for British engines. Britain's lead was perhaps most dramatically demonstrated by the de Havilland Vampire, whose unique twin-boom design bestowed a compact layout, superb agility, and a very short and thus very efficient jetpipe.

Britain's aircraft industry has often been portrayed as having been almost fatally conservative, ignoring the problems of transonic flight, and either ignoring or misunderstanding the importance of things like swept wings. In fact, while mainstream companies produced a first generation of cautiously conventional jet fighters which marked an evolutionary improvement over the last of the piston-engined fighters, the Ministry of Aircraft Production was remarkably far-sighted in laying the foundations for later generations of jet fighters. In the autumn of 1943, Specification E.24/43 was issued for a research aircraft which would not only exceed Mach 1.0, but which might also fly at up to and beyond 1,000 mph (1610 km/h). This specification resulted in the Miles M.52, now widely acknowledged as having been considerably more advanced than the Bell X-1, with an all-flying tail and other highly original features.

Unfortunately, the M.52 was cancelled before it could be flown, perhaps because it had a straight wing, perhaps because of concerns for the safety of test pilots who might have to fly the aircraft. The test results from the M.52 project were given to the USA, and the Bell X-1 gained the honour of becoming the first aircraft to officially break the sound barrier.

As if to prove how capable the M.52 would have been, a model based on the same configuration exceeded Mach 1.38 in level flight on 10 October 1948. The X-1 had struggled to get to Mach 1.03. The abandonment of the aircraft was a near-fatal blow to the British aircraft industry, which stagnated while the US industry cleverly assembled a combination of German aerodynamics and British engine and control technologies to produce aircraft like the F-86.

Britain was not as far behind the USA as has

Above: The FD.2 probably had the smallest possible airframe that could be built around its Rolls-Royce Avon engine.

Left: The impracticalities of the FD.1 concept, inspired by the Bachem Natter, were soon made obvious. Thus, VX350 was to be the sole flying example and finished up on a gunnery range. In this photograph, leading-edge slats, deleted during repairs to the aircraft after a crash in 1951, are clearly visible.

The worldwide fascination with the delta wing manifested itself in Great Britain in the Fairey Delta 2. It was to be the last fixed-wing aircraft designed and built by Fairey Aviation Limited.

sometimes been assumed, as was proved when Britain's first swept-wing jets (the Hunter and Swift) set new world speed records. Unfortunately, these aircraft were drastically delayed in entering service. Even before these types did enter service, the next generation of fighters was already in preparation, at least in the form of advanced research aircraft.

Delta One

Specification E.10/47 of 1947 was issued to cover the development of a piloted Delta-winged research aircraft which was primarily intended as a proof-of-concept vehicle for an advanced ramp-launched fighter. Ramp-launching was briefly all the rage, from semi-prepared forward airstrips and also for shipborne applications. Fairey received an order for three aircraft, to be serialled VX350, VX357 and VX364. At the end of the day, the very concept of a ramp-launched fighter seems in retrospect to have been fundamentally flawed, since the need to obtain a low launch weight imposed severe constraints, while recovery to anything but a conventional runway meant turnaround times became unacceptably long. Nevertheless, ramp-launch was glamorous, and was so impractical that it seemed undeniably futuristic. Typically, perhaps, Britain had allowed itself to be influenced by the more esoteric work conducted in Germany during the war, rather than by the more useful and more practical mainstream. Thus, Fairey took as its inspiration for the FD.1 not the marginally practical

Me 262, but instead the hare-brained Bachem Ba 349 Natter, whose first flight had ended in predictable tragedy and the death of its test pilot.

Fairey had already built and test-flown a series of small-scale, radio-controlled, delta-winged, ramp-launched models, progressing to vertical launches by 1949. Built and tested under an Air Ministry contract, the models were tailless deltas, using what was known as

the Fairey-Heston delta wing, which had 48° 12' sweep on its leading edge and a thickness/chord ratio of 10 per cent. The models were successful enough, but two accidents led to trials being moved from their original land site to an anchored landing craft (HMS *Suvla*) in Cardigan Bay, and eventually to the wilds of Woomera, Australia.

The full-scale, manned FD.1 emerged as a very similar configuration, with a 19-ft 6.5-in

The ultimate incarnation of the Fairey Delta family, the BAC 221, was an extensive rebuild of the first FD.2, WG774. The aircraft is seen here, watched by spectators atop Farnborough's control tower.

Left: The rocket-powered VTO models were each propelled into the air by a pair of bi-fuel Beta 1 engines designed by the Royal Aircraft Establishment and built by Fairey. Each developed 4 kN (900 lb) thrust, to which was added the 2.67 kN (600 lb) thrust of each cordite booster rocket for take-off and initial acceleration. Signals from an autopilot (adapted from that fitted to the German A4 rocket) maintained attitude in pitch and yaw by swivelling the Beta engine's nozzles through small angles.

Fairey's Heaton Chapel works (above) was assigned the task of building the E.10/47, or FD.1 as it was later known. In this underside view (below) of the FD.1, the rocket booster housings either side of the jetpipe can be seen. As the boosters were never installed, streamlined 'cones' were fitted over the end of the rocket housings, which were eventually replaced altogether with fillets.

(5.9-m) span cropped delta wing and a small slab T-tail atop the fin. In order to generate sufficient thrust for a ramp launch, reliance was placed on four jettisonable solid-fuel rocket packs at the wingroots. They would have produced some 5,000 lb st (22.24 kN) for about six seconds. The main powerplant was a Rolls-Royce Derwent turbojet (a Derwent 5 RD7 rated at 3,500 lb st/15.57 kN for the first aircraft, with a 3,600-lb st/16.01-kN Derwent 8 in the subsequent prototypes). For control at the very low speeds encountered during a ramp (or vertical) launch, the aircraft was intended to feature four gyroscopically-controlled servo units, each driving a swivelling jetpipe arranged around the main jet nozzle. Virtually full-span powered elevons were fitted on the trailing edge, with a small split airbrake inboard. The aircraft also had fixed leading-edge slats outboard.

First prototype

The first FD.1 prototype came to be intended as an aerodynamic testbed for the planned configuration (apparently at the insistence of the Ministry of Supply), rather than as a prototype to test launch procedures, so it was accepted that the first aircraft would take off and land conventionally. The tiny aircraft was thus completed with a retractable tricycle undercarriage and a conventional jetpipe, with empty fairings where the swivelling jetpipes would have been. The second and third aircraft

Above: Fairey's delta model was initially tested at Aberporth, Wales, but after safety concerns were raised following two incidents involving the aircraft's highly volatile fuel, they were moved offshore, to a naval landing craft, HMS Suvla. This brought its own problems, with the result that the remainder of the test programme was conducted at the Long-range Weapons Establishment at Woomera, Australia.

were to have been ramp-launched, however.

Plans for ramp launching reached an advanced stage, with a site for the ramp being selected beside runway 24's threshold at Boscombe Down. A special mobile crane was also designed, to allow a fully laden aircraft to be lifted onto the ramp, which would begin at a modest 45° elevation, increasing to 80° by the end of the trials. The idea of ramp-launching fighters was soon abandoned, although the development of mixed-powerplant (turbojet and rocket) interceptors continued at Saunders Roe and Avro. Fairey, meanwhile, had already been contracted to produce a pair of experimental transonic research aircraft under Specification ER.103, and was working flat-out on the new Gannet anti-submarine aircraft. The first FD.1 was completed as a basic aerodynamic research aircraft, intended to gain experience of the Delta wing. The second FD.1 (already almost complete, with its engine installed) and the third aircraft were cancelled and scrapped.

Smallest delta

The first FD.1 was completed at Fairey's Heaton Chapel, Stockport factory in early 1950, and began taxi trials at Fairey's flight test facility at Manchester's Ringway airport on 12 May 1950. Remarkably, the aircraft was then dismantled and was taken to Boscombe Down by road, where it made its 17-minute maiden flight on 12 March 1951, in the hands of Group Captain R. Gordon Slade. At the time, the aircraft was the smallest delta-winged aircraft flown, but proved to have reasonable handling characteristics with adequate stability and an impressive roll rate. It was judged difficult to fly

Carrying the name Fairey Delta, VX350 is seen getting airborne, possibly during the 1954 SBAC show, at which it participated in the flying display. It possessed one of the fastest landing speeds of any aircraft at the show that year.

accurately, however, due to its large control surfaces, which were necessary in very-slow-speed flight during a vertical or ramp launch. Damaged in a landing accident in September 1951, the aircraft did not fly again until May 1953, by which time it had lost its (empty) swivelling nozzle fairings. The FD.1 was soon grounded again as a 'dangerous aircraft'. The FD.1 returned to flying status after removal of the leading-edge slats, and the wingtip-mounted anti-spin parachutes.

Following a minor landing accident (which effectively removed the undercarriage) on 6 February 1956, the aircraft was deemed to be uneconomical to repair, and was donated to Farnborough's Mechanical Engineering Department. It was not a very useful instructional airframe, however, and on 9 October 1956 was transported to Shoeburyness where it was used as a gunnery target, assessing the effect of gunfire on 'modern' airframes. It may be imagined that the small and flimsy FD.1 did not last long.

Delta Two

Whereas few remember the FD.1, the FD.2 became something of an icon during the late 1950s, its startling lines making it every boy's idea of what a jet fighter should look like. In

Above: Fairey's chief test pilot Gordon Slade took VX350 into the air for the first time on 12 March 1951, the flight lasting 17 minutes. Slade, an ex-RAF group captain, went on to fly the FD.2.

Left and above: Structural limitations of the FD.1's tail design restricted its top speed to a figure far below the projected 628 mph (1011 km/h). Though it had an impressive roll rate, the FD.1 was notoriously difficult to fly accurately, thanks to its large control surfaces. The wingtip-mounted fairings contain anti-spin parachutes, later deleted.

Specification

FD.1 (VX350)

Powerplant: one Rolls-Royce Derwent 5 RD7 turbojet rated at 3,500 lb (15.57 kN) thrust, plus four booster rocket engines together rated at 5,000 lb (22.24 kN), later deleted

Performance (estimated, without horizontal tail): maximum speed 628 mph (1011 km/h) at 10,000 ft (3048 m); initial climb rate 9,300 ft/min (47.2 m/sec); time-to-height 1.9 min to 15,000 ft (4572 m); 4.5 min to 30,000 ft (9144 m); maximum range 830 miles (1335 km)

Weights: loaded 6,800 lb (3084 kg)

Dimensions: span 19 ft 6.5 in (5.95 m); length 26 ft 3 in (7.99 m)

Fairey Delta One

1 Bifurcated air intake
2 Aft-retracting nosewheel with anti-shimmy tyre
3 Instrumentation bay
4 Rudder pedals
5 Control column
6 Instrument panel
7 Engine throttle lever
8 Frameless windscreen panel
9 Aft-sliding cockpit canopy
10 Martin-Baker ejection seat
11 Oxygen bottle
12 Fuel collector tank

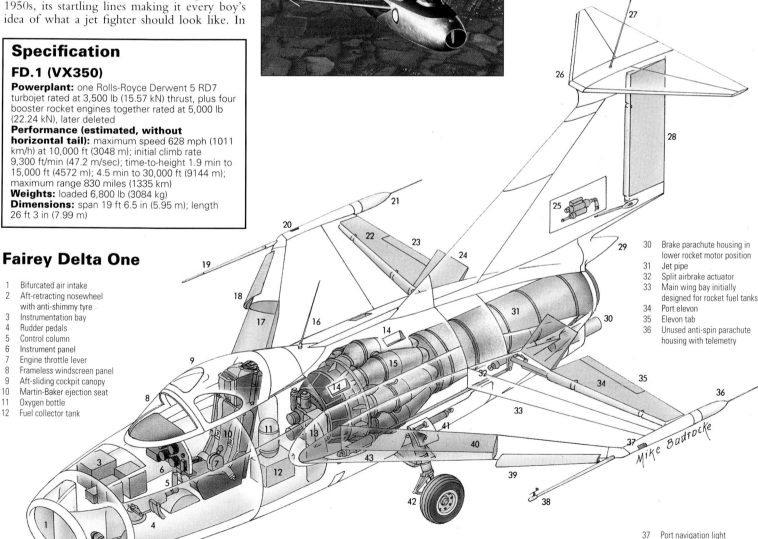

13 Engine oil tank
14 Engine bay suction relief doors
15 Rolls-Royce Derwent 5 engine
16 VHF antenna
17 Starboard fuel tank
18 Fixed leading-edge slat, deleted after early flight trials
19 Pitot head
20 Starboard navigation light
21 Anti-spin parachute housing
22 Starboard elevon
23 Elevon trim line

24 Split trailing edge airbrake
25 Rudder equator
26 Fixed horizontal tailplane
27 Standby VHF antenna
28 Rudder
29 Fairing over initially proposed rocket motor housing (4)

30 Brake parachute housing in lower rocket motor position
31 Jet pipe
32 Split airbrake actuator
33 Main wing bay initially designed for rocket fuel tanks
34 Port elevon
35 Elevon tab
36 Unused anti-spin parachute housing with telemetry

37 Port navigation light
38 Yaw vane
39 Port leading-edge slat
40 Port fuel tank
41 Main undercarriage hydraulic retraction jack
42 Aft-retracting mainwheel
43 Elevon hydraulic actuator in wingroot fairing

Below: The second FD.2, WG777, shows the adjustable 'eyelid' tailpipe of the aircraft's Rolls-Royce Avon turbojet, essentially an afterburning version of the Avon fitted to the Vickers Valiant bomber. The FD.2's first flights were made without afterburner as the engine had sufficient dry thrust to reach Mach 1.1. Though crude and untried, this 'all or nothing' afterburner was an improvement over earlier concepts that employed fixed nozzles fitted on the ground.

Above: Nose markings on this aircraft help to identify it as WG774, seen here over English countryside in about 1956.

Below: Peter Twiss received a Queen's Commendation for Valuable Service in the Air following WG774's successful forced landing after its 14th flight. The flight, on 17 November 1954, developed problems as Twiss levelled off at 30,000 ft (9144 m) after taking off from Boscombe Down. Engine failure led to a loss of hydraulic pressure which threatened to render the aircraft uncontrollable, but Twiss was able to bring it down with comparatively little damage. A ram air-driven hydraulic pump was subsequently fitted to the FD.2s.

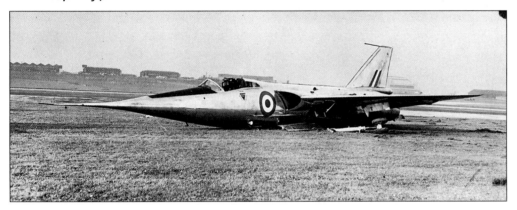

many respects, the FD.2 was an incarnation of the classic 'paper dart' shape. It is widely suspected that the design had as great an influence on Dassault as it did on Britain's schoolboys, and, while the basic Mirage I/II may have been a genuinely original design, there seems little doubt that the stretched and area-ruled Mirage III was heavily influenced by the British machine. The aircraft was used to set a new world speed record, beating the F-100's previous record by some 310 mph (500 km/h) – an astonishing 37 per cent – and giving both company and aircraft massive publicity. The second FD.2 continued flying in its original form until July 1966, while the first aircraft flew until 1973, albeit in modified form as the BAC Type 221. Both prototypes then retired to high-profile museum display.

The FD.2 was originally designed to meet

A newly repaired WG774 poses among other new aircraft exhibited at the 1955 SBAC show at Farnborough. Next to the FD.2 is Armstrong-Whitworth's AW.55 Apollo turboprop transport and two of Short's Seamew anti-submarine aircraft. The way in which the pilot's forward vision benefited from the Delta 2's 'droop snoot' is clearly evident. Ten degrees of 'droop' was available from the hydraulically-powered nose.

the same requirement which resulted in the English Electric P.1 (and which in turn formed the basis of the Lightning interceptor). Before designing the FD.2, Fairey sketched a number of alternative configurations, with the early front-runner being very similar to the P.1, albeit with a single engine. By December 1949,

however, the design had become a delta, with a minimum-diameter fuselage housing an afterburning Avon engine fed by wingroot intakes. (An afterburning Sapphire engine was briefly considered as an alternative to the Avon, but was rejected.) The intakes themselves were fixed, but were carefully tailored to allow flight at very high Mach numbers. The intakes had highly swept sharp lips and were staggered, with the lower lip well behind the upper, keeping it within the shockcone generated by the top lip.

Fuel shortage

The clearance between engine and fuselage was negligible. Sufficient fuel was provided to meet the specification (and no more), which would later handicap the aircraft when it came to make attempts on the world speed record, where two runs had to be made within 30 minutes. The specified fuel load had to be sufficient for start-up, take-off without afterburner, a climb to 45,000 ft (13715 m), 15 minutes' cruise (both without recourse to afterburner) and 10 minutes at full power with afterburner, with 80 Imp gal (365 litres) remaining for the descent and landing. There was provision for a ventral fuel tank to be fitted, but the tank was probably never built, and was never used. Still, the aircraft's inadequate fuel capacity was recognised as a severe limitation, and when the first

10 March 1956: FD.2 captures world speed record

FD.2 WG774 became the first aircraft to officially reach a speed of 1,000 mph (1609 km/h) when, with Peter Twiss in the cockpit, it took the World Absolute Speed Record in 1956. The previous mark set by an F-100 was bettered by a margin that has not been repeated since. The new record lasted one year, nine months and two days.

Right: It was only badgering by Peter Twiss that persuaded Fairey management to permit an attempt at the world air speed record. The Ministry of Supply did not believe that the aircraft was capable of 1,000 mph (1610 km/h), let alone a world record speed!

Below: The speed mark bettered by WG774 was that set by USAF Colonel Howard A. Hanes in the first North American F-100C Super Sabre, 53-1709, on 20 August 1955. At 822.135 mph (1323.062 km/h), this was the first supersonic world speed record. Unlike the FD.2, the F-100C was a service aircraft, a feature it shared with the type which was to take the FD.2's record back to the US – the McDonnell F-101A (designated JF-101A for the duration of concurrent J57 testing by Pratt & Whitney), which pushed the speed up to 1207.6 mph (1943.39 km/h) on 12 December 1957.

Above: Representatives from Fairey (including Fairey's chief test pilot, Gordon Slade, left), the RAeC (representing the FAI) and the RAE (including Mr W. J. G. Cox, with microphone) monitor the progress of Twiss and WG774 during the record attempt. The object to the left is the theodolite camera used to track the aircraft.

Below: Peter Twiss and Gordon Slade with their respective wives admire the record-breaking WG774 for the press, some weeks afterwards. By this time the aircraft carried the legend "World Speed Record, 1132 mph, March 10th 1956".

FD.2 was modified to become the BAC 221, fuel capacity was almost doubled.

The main load-bearing frames were very small, and to gain sufficient strength were machined from solid forgings. From the aft cockpit bulkhead back to the tail, the fuselage was of constant section, tapering to the afterburner nozzle and to the nose-mounted test instrumentation boom. It was an interchangeable fitting, and booms of different lengths were carried depending on the task in hand, accounting for the variation in length figures

given in specifications over the years. The nozzle and rear part of the jet pipe was surrounded by four petal-type airbrakes, each actuated by an independent hydraulic jack, hinged at the leading edge. Every effort was made to reduce weight to an absolute minimum, and to give the lowest possible frontal cross-sectional area, to reduce drag. Thus, the three-spar wing, with a thickness/chord ratio of only 4 per cent, was the thinnest then attempted, and used skins of exceptional thickness and strength in order to 'beef up' the

flimsy structure. The design team was led (from October 1951) by R. L. Lickley, brought in from Cranfield, under the overall command of chief designer H. E. 'Charlie' Chaplin.

Contracts placed

Contracts were placed with English Electric and Fairey (each for the construction of two prototypes) in October 1950. The original FD.2 design included a small horizontal slab tailplane atop the fin, but by May 1951 this was regarded as being entirely superfluous and was removed,

WG774

Completed with an unpainted 'natural metal' finish, WG774 was sprayed a 'royal purple' shade with a cream cheatline in 1957. Stripped when converted to BAC 221 standard, '774 was later finished in a dark blue shade, again with a white cheatline.

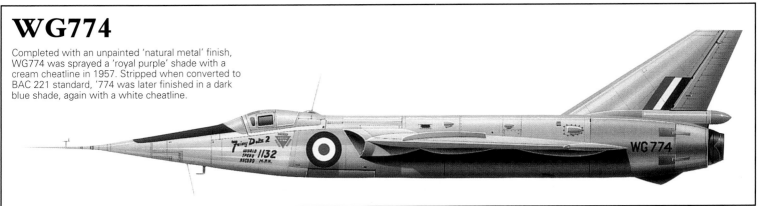

Above: The glorious sight of both Delta 2s at Farnborough, September 1956. Supersonic opposition passes at 38,000 ft (11582 m) were made by pilots Twiss (in WG774) and Slade (in WG777) during each day's flying display, but overcast weather conditions meant that their execution went unseen. The combined sonic booms, however, were plainly audible and resulted in a Mach 1.25 limitation being placed on the aircraft.

reducing drag and the structural weight of the tailfin. Before the aircraft flew, the rear fuselage was redesigned to allow access to the engine by removing the rear fuselage, rather than by dropping it through doors in the lower fuselage. The decision was also taken to remove the trailing-edge flaps from the design, although, when the prototype made its maiden flight, the prototype still had flaps fitted, albeit locked closed.

The Fairey Delta Two was packed with advanced features, many of which subsequently became standard. The aircraft was the first in Britain to fly with irreversible power controls, which had no means of manual reversion, for example. Although designed as an experimental research aircraft (and thus as a platform which would do very little flying), the aircraft was made remarkably easy to service and turn around, with an exceptional degree of easy access to its systems.

'Droop snoot'

The aircraft was eventually designed with a nearly-flush, highly-streamlined cockpit canopy and fairing, which gave a very poor view forward over the nose. The windscreen was raked at 62°. In order to improve visibility on approach, Fairey designed and patented a drooping nose ('droop snoot') in which the entire nose (from the cockpit's aft bulkhead) dropped down through 10° on approach. Interestingly, when Fairey was taken over by Westland, the patent passed to the latter company, and was purchased by BAC for use on Concorde. When the nose was drooped, the nose-gear doors were sequenced to open, whether or not the undercarriage was lowered; this explains why so many photos of FD.2 show

the aircraft with its landing gear retracted, but with the nose bay doors hanging. The cockpit itself was extremely cramped, and made use of especially miniaturised instruments to save weight and space. The view from the modified Martin-Baker Mk 3FDV seat was poor, with the pair of single-curvature windscreen panels separated by a metal pillar, and with tiny windows set into the cast magnesium alloy canopy frame. They gave only the most limited view out to the sides and directly above, and made the cockpit unpleasantly dark and claustrophobic. The pilot had no rearward vision at all.

Work on the FD.2 was delayed by the priority placed on the Gannet ASW aircraft, and drawings were not issued until September 1952, finally allowing construction and component manufacture to begin. Built at Hayes, the Fairey Delta Two was trucked to Boscombe Down for its 6 October 1954 maiden flight. This was made by Lieutenant Commander Peter Twiss, DSC, RN (Retd), who prepared himself by

WG774 makes a damp landing at Farnborough. The three braking parachutes were stowed in the 'bullet' fairing above the jet pipe.

flying the FD.1 and by amassing a large number of supersonic dives in Hunters, Swifts and Sabres. The flight test programme proceeded rapidly and smoothly until Flight 14, on 17 November 1954. A fuel problem caused the engine to flame-out, and the pilot executed a successful dead-stick landing at Boscombe Down. Mindful of the drag, he lowered the undercarriage at the last moment, so that only the nose gear was fully extended by the time the FD.2 touched down, and the nose would not lower to the landing position. It later transpired that there was insufficient hydraulic power to lower the nose and all three undercarriage units with the engine out. This led to the provision of a ram-air turbine driving an emergency hydraulic pump. The aircraft's wing was badly damaged, and had to be replaced by the wing from the structural test airframe, though Twiss had undeniably acted with coolness and great skill, and received a thoroughly deserved Queen's Commendation for Valuable Services in the Air. The aircraft was effectively grounded for eight months, but was back in the air in time to make its public debut at the 1955 SBAC show at Farnborough.

Supersonic without 'burner

The FD.2 quickly exceeded Mach 1 (without recourse to the still untried simple 'bang-bang, on-off two position eyelid-type afterburner) on 28 October 1955, after supersonic wind tunnel testing had been conducted, but before the results could be analysed. It soon became apparent that once the afterburner was working, the aircraft would be very fast. The crudity of the afterburner was something of a worry.

Such was its power-to-weight ratio that even on dry thrust alone the FD.2 had an impressive rate of climb. In just 2.5 minutes a Delta Two could reach 45,000 ft (13716 m) at a speed of Mach 0.93.

When engaged at 36,000 ft (10970 m), the pilot gained an almost instantaneous doubling of thrust virtually 'at the flick of a switch', and the resulting acceleration felt almost like a loss of control. Still, it was undoubtedly better than the original afterburner concept which used optional fixed nozzles that had to be selected and fitted on the ground, for afterburning or non-afterburning flights.

Despite official indifference which bordered on apathy, the decision was taken to make an attempt on the world speed record, at the urging of Gordon Slade, the company's chief test pilot, and his newly-recruited deputy, Peter Twiss, DSC, the Fairey Delta Two project pilot. Rolls-Royce did not support the attempt, suggesting that the aircraft's intakes were unsuitable for flight above Mach 1.5, and that the engine might break up as a result, although this statement was not made with the benefit of any experience or detailed research or modelling. The Air Ministry reluctantly loaned the aircraft to Fairey for the record attempt, but the company had to pay its own insurance and even had to pay for the recording team from the RAE. Fortunately, others involved in the

Above and right: In recognition of its world speed record achievements, '774 lost its 'natural metal' finish in favour of a coat of colourful paint, in a similar way to other British record breakers. Mauve with a cream cheatline was the chosen scheme, complete with an RAF roundel and fin flash.

Left: Photographs of the second FD.2, WG777, appear to have been comparatively few, the aircraft spending almost its entire life at RAE Bedford. By the time this shot was taken, the aircraft had been resprayed blue and a white cheatline applied.

Specification

FD.2

Powerplant: one Rolls-Royce RA.14R Avon turbojet developing 12,000 lb (53.38 kN) thrust with afterburner (WG777 later fitted with RA.28R rated at 9,300 lb/41.37 kN dry thrust or 13,100 lb/58.27 kN with afterburner)
Performance: maximum speed 748 mph (1204 km/h) at low level; 1,122 mph (1805 km/h) above 36,090 ft (11000 m); initial climb rate 4,750 ft/min (24.1 m/sec); 15,000 ft/min (76.2 m/sec) with afterburner; time-to-height 2.5 min to 40,000 ft (12192 m) at Mach 0.93
Weights: loaded 13,884 lb (6298 kg) with RA.28R engine
Dimensions: span 26 ft 10 in (8.18 m); length 51 ft 7.5 in (15.74 m) including nose probe; height 11 ft (3.35 m)

Fairey Delta Two

1 Pitot head
2 Yaw vane
3 Nose, drooped position
4 Remote compass transmitter
5 Flush HF antenna
6 Oxygen bottle
7 Lower VHF antenna
8 Temperature probe
9 VHF transceiver
10 Rudder pedals
11 Instrument panel
12 Engine throttle lever
13 Control column
14 Centrally divided windscreen panel
15 Cockpit canopy, hinged to starboard
16 Martin-Baker Mk 3 ejection seat
17 Mechanical flight control linkages
18 Nosewheel leg strut
19 Twin nosewheels, aft retracting

20 Nosewheel drag/breaker strut
21 Nose section hinge mounting
22 Nosewheel hydraulic retraction jack
23 Drooping nose section hydraulic actuator
24 Upper VHF antenna
25 Hydraulic reservoirs
26 Hydraulic accumulators
27 Cockpit air conditioning system equipment
28 Instrumentation bay
29 Boundary layer splitter plate
30 Port air intake

31 Engine bleed air heat exchanger for conditioning system
32 Fuel collector tank and recuperator
33 Fuel filler
34 Engine starter
35 Rolls-Royce Avon RA14 engine

36 Starboard wing integral fuel tanks
37 Wing fence
38 Starboard wing integral fuel tanks
39 Aileron hydraulic actuator
40 Starboard aileron
41 Starboard elevator
42 Flight control system variable ratio gear boxes
43 Jet pipe/afterburner duct
44 Rudder hydraulic actuator
45 Rudder

46 Triple brake parachute housing
47 Two-position afterburner nozzle
48 Nozzle pneumatic actuators
49 Four-segment airbrake panels
50 Airbrake hydraulic jacks
51 Elevator hydraulic actuator
52 Port elevator
53 Port aileron

54 Aileron hydraulic actuator in ventral hung fairing
55 Port wing integral fuel tanks
56 Port mainwheel
57 Levered suspension axle
58 Shock absorber strut
59 Skew axis mainwheel leg mounting and side strut
60 Hydraulic retraction jack
61 Telescopic drag strut

Photographs capturing the BAC 221 and the surviving FD.2 together, let alone in formation, appear to be rare. In this example, the main differences between the two aircraft are visible.

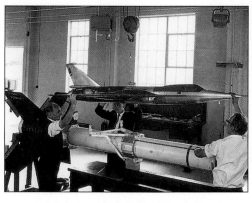

Above and below: Strapped to a rocket named Titania I, a scale model of the BAC Type 221 is prepared by engineering staff for a test flight prior to the conversion of the first FD.2 as a full-size test airframe.

record bid were more helpful than the Air Ministry. An RAF radar station at Sopley, and the RNAS at Ford, tracked and controlled the attempt, while Meteors from No. 29 Squadron at Tangmere and a specially calibrated Venom performed calibration work of the recording instruments and of the FD.2's altimeter and ASI under Exercise Metrical. The GPO provided communications lines, and the appropriate authorities erected markers at the sick quarters at RNAS Ford and on a sewage farm at Chichester. The record run was between Thorney Island and a point just west of

Worthing, with the aircraft operating from Boscombe Down. The aircraft climbed subsonically, over the New Forest, accelerating at Fawley, and then engaging 'burner just before Thorney Island. A similar 40-mile (64-km) acceleration was made on the westward run, passing over Rottingdean and Angmering.

Record run

After practices on 8 March 1956, the record-breaking flights were made by the first prototype (WG774) on 10 March. The aircraft had to make one run in each direction (within 30 minutes of each other) but lack of fuel meant that the pilot had to land, refuel and climb back to height between runs. The runs were flown at 38,000 ft (11582 m), providing observers on the

ground with a vapour trail to watch, and taking advantage of the optimum performance available at the tropopause. The aircraft clocked 1,117.6 mph (1798.6 km/h) on the first run and 1,146.9 mph (1845.7 km/h) on the second, averaging 1,132.136 mph (1821.95 km/h; Mach 1.731). With greater fuel capacity, the speed could have been much higher, since the aircraft was still accelerating as the fuel warning lights flickered on to signal the pilot to stop the run. Reports suggest that the aircraft was regularly reaching Mach 1.9 as it finished its runs, but did not have sufficient fuel to accelerate to Mach 1.9, do the run, decelerate and land. Despite an outside air temperature of -76°F (-60°C), skin temperature reached more than 122°F (+50°C). Colonel Horace Haynes, in his F-100, had managed only a 'cool' 822.26 mph (1323.26 km/h) to set the record so comprehensively shattered by the FD.2. The margin between old and new records (37 per cent, or 310 mph; 499 km/h) had never been so wide.

FD.2 number two

A second FD.2 (WG777) made its maiden flight on 15 February 1956, differing from the first prototype in minor detail, and in having no trailing-edge flaps. Interestingly, this aircraft (with its serial doctored for the occasion) served as the backdrop for photos of the record-breaking team taken after the event, while '774 was undergoing servicing and rectification. After brief manufacturer's trials, the new aircraft went

In these plan view drawings, the lines of the BAC 221's ogival wing can be compared directly with the FD.2's delta wing. The lengthened fuselage and absence of the leading-edge engine air intakes in the 221 are also evident.

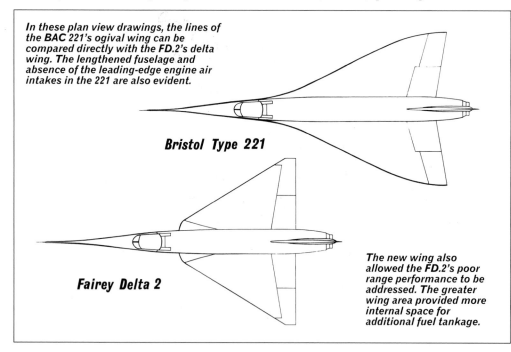

Bristol Type 221

Fairey Delta 2

The new wing also allowed the FD.2's poor range performance to be addressed. The greater wing area provided more internal space for additional fuel tankage.

*Below: As well as the ogival wing, the **BAC Type 221** featured a fuselage lengthened by 2 m (6.6 ft), and taller undercarriage. The design's type number was allocated by Bristol Aircraft (a subsidiary of **BAC**), which was given the task of completing the **FD.2** conversion project upon the reorganisation of the British aviation industry in 1960. While Fairey's rotary-wing projects were hived off to Westland Aircraft, Hunting Aircraft took responsibility for Fairey's fixed-wing machines, including the **FD.2**. Finally, in July 1960, the job was given to the Bristol factory at Filton, which would later build Concorde. In this photograph the original side-hinged cockpit canopy can be seen. This was later replaced with a clear, blown canopy, much improving visibility for the pilot.*

*Above: WG774 is rolled out from **BAC**'s Filton works in late 1963 and is seen here prior to engine installation. The Type 221 was fitted with a Rolls-Royce Avon RA.28R as retrofitted to the second FD.2. The four-petal airbrake forward of the jetpipe is readily discernible.*

sequently conducted in Norway (from Sola) during June 1958, by Twiss and Squadron Leader 'Jimmy' Matthews. The aircraft flew out to Sola via a refuelling stop at Newcastle. The Newcastle-Sola leg of the journey (363 miles/584 km) took 45 minutes.

Useful contribution

The first prototype was sent to BAC at Filton on 5 September 1960, for conversion to a new standard, as will be described, but WG777 continued flying until 1 July 1966, when its lack of UHF radio forced its premature retirement, with only 198 hours and 15 minutes logged. Despite this relatively low total, the aircraft (and its brother) had made an enormous contribution to high-speed aerodynamic research, and to the understanding of supersonic engine and intake performance in a very wide range of conditions. The aircraft was cannibalised to provide spares for the BAC 221, but the airframe was kept

to RAE Bedford for use by Aero Flight on high-speed research and trials. Teddy Donaldson's speed record-breaking Meteor had been painted bright yellow after its success; Neville Duke's record-breaking Hawker Hunter had been painted bright red prior to its record run; and Mike Lithgow's Swift had broken the record in an attractive pale blue colour scheme. Inevitably, the record-breaking Fairey Delta Two was repainted (in 1957), in a rather fetching mauve (officially, 'royal purple') with a cream cheatline and 'Holder of the World Speed Record' logo.

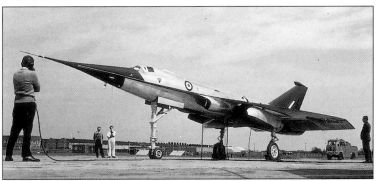

Below and right: WG774 is seen after engine installation and during ground running at Filton soon after completion. Initially, the aircraft was unpainted apart from its deep blue nose and tail. Later it was finished all over in blue to improve its looks and provide a good photographic background for the tufted starboard wing.

Farnborough '56

Both aircraft appeared at the 1956 Farnborough air show, staging high-altitude (38,000 ft/11582 m) Mach 1.25 opposition fly-pasts, but these were unfortunately obscured by cloud. Despite the world speed record, the FD.2's research programme was severely constrained by new regulations which effectively prohibited supersonic flying overland at altitudes below 30,000 ft (9145 m). Accordingly, the first prototype undertook low-level supersonic trials from Cazaux in the south of France from 11 October until 15 November 1956, flying 52 sorties and exceeding Mach 1 at altitudes from 3,500 ft (1067 m). On its return to the UK, WG774 joined Aero Flight at Bedford. Further low-altitude supersonic trials were sub-

improve high-altitude turn performance. This ambitious interceptor had a projected performance of Mach 2.26 at 55,000 ft (16765 m), and Mach 1.8 at 60,000 ft (18288 m), with a time to height of 45,000 ft (13716 m) in 1.9 minutes.

The most advanced fighter project stemming from the FD.2 programme was developed to meet the RAF's OR.329 (F.155T) requirement. This specification called for a mixed-powerplant, two-seat, radar-equipped interceptor, capable of climbing to 60,000 ft (18288 m) within 70 miles (113 km) of base, and of accelerating to Mach 2 within six minutes. In its 45-minute sortie time (76 minutes with external fuel), the aircraft would have to be able to intercept a target cruising at Mach 1.3 at 60,000 ft. The Fairey two-seat fighter was designed around a single Gyron turbojet, with two de Havilland Spectre rocket engines in fairings on each side of the rear fuselage. The rockets allowed a theoretical speed of Mach 2.5 at over 91,000 ft (27737 m), a speed which could be attained with reheat alone at 59,000 ft (17983 m). The proposed aircraft was to be armed with wingtip-mounted Firestreak Mk 4 (Red Top) missiles and fitted with a Ferranti AI.23 radar.

A revised submission to the RAF made in November 1956 detailed an even more ambitious aircraft, capable of collision course attacks and armed with Red Dean AAMs. The new version had twin RB.128 turbojet engines and no rockets, and promised to have potential in other roles. On 1 April 1957, the Ministry of Supply reportedly indicated to Fairey that its submission was likely to win the F.155T requirement, but, three days later, Duncan Sandys published his infamous White Paper, which effectively ended all manned fighter development ("from the Mk 1 Lightning") and which led to the immediate cancellation of a host of programmes, including the Fairey aircraft and its competitor, the Hawker P.1103.

SST support

As pure research aircraft, the FD.2 prototypes were virtually unaffected by the 1957 White Paper. The first prototype was converted to a new configuration under Specification ER.193D, following discussions between Fairey

Above: From the underside, the undercarriage bulges and repositioned engine intakes are visible.

Left: At Filton, Godfrey Auty is seen taking the 221 into the air for the first time on a potentially stormy 1 May 1964. The flight was of 23 minutes duration. Note that the 'droop snoot' (later to be adopted for Concorde) does not appear to have been 'drooped' for the first flight.

Below: WG774 is seen at rest in a hangar at Filton. The 221's UHF radio aerial may be seen under the nose.

intact, and was retired to display at the RAF Museum at Cosford, where it remains to this day, forming a vital part of the museum's display of significant experimental and research aircraft.

The FD.2 is remembered as a research aircraft and as a record-breaker, but the aircraft was almost developed into a front-line fighter, too. The seizure of the world speed record convinced Fairey that it had the right formula on which to base a supersonic fighter, and proposed an ER.103/B with a revised fuselage, provision for underwing drop tanks, a slight increase in span, and powered either by a de Havilland Gyron, or a Rolls-Royce RB.122. The proposed ER.103/C was more ambitious, with a Ferranti ARI 1495 monopulse radar, wingtip-mounted de Havilland Firestreak missiles and wings scaled up by 50 per cent to

and the RAE, which investigated the use of the basic FD.2 airframe with a new 'ogee' (ogival) 'slender delta' wing to provide aerodynamic data to support Britain's infant SST programme, then represented by a Hawker Siddeley project. Initially given to Hunting Aircraft (Fairey having by then been swallowed by Westland), the project was reallocated to Bristol at Filton as the new British Aircraft Corporation took shape.

Fairey had originally envisaged the new 'ogee-winged' FD.2 as having a 3-ft (0.9-m) fuselage stretch and new rectangular-section dorsal intakes at about 30 per cent chord, but this configuration promised to be troublesome, and BAC proposed two different configurations. One was very much a minimum-change conversion, using the same fuselage and undercarriage, while the other envisaged a 6-ft (1.8-m) fuselage stretch and a new, much taller undercarriage. The latter option was chosen, since it allowed a better simulation of the proposed airliner's slender shape, and offered a useful increase in fuel capacity.

Conversion begins

The first FD.2 was delivered to Filton on 5 September 1960, but conversion did not begin until April 1961, and was not completed until 7 July 1963. The original FD.2 fuselage was cut at Frame 194 (measured from an original datum at the wing trailing edge), which was located at the forward end of the centre-section. A basic 6-ft plug was added, carrying the nose forward and allowing the break for the nose-drooping mechanism to be clear of the widest part of the chines. To maintain the integrity of the chine even when the nose was lowered, the chine incorporated a series of sliding plates which moved to keep the gap closed. The upper fuselage and centre-section skinning was beefed up to cope with higher flight loads from the various new vortex flows, and the forward fuselage was modified to accommodate new instrumentation, extra fuel tankage and the very much longer nose oleo, which was adapted from a Gannet unit, with the original FD.2 live axle and a Lightning-type shimmy damper. The new main gear oleos were adapted from Lightning units, with universal joints to allow the oleos to rotate through 90° on retraction, so that the

The BAC 221 lacked the 'clean' aerodynamics of the FD.2, the fairings on the underside of the wing housing the redesigned undercarriage.

wheels could lie flat in the wing. Although the wheels were very slim, with lightened brake drums and reduced tyre pressures, the landing gear bays were covered by noticeable bulged fairings, which themselves faired into the underwing air intakes. The intakes were fixed, and were optimised for speeds of about Mach 1.6. Variable intakes were briefly considered, but the extra cost and complexity was not felt to be worthwhile. Fuel capacity rose from the original FD.2's 322 Imp gal (1464 litres) to 505 Imp gal (2295 litres) (15.75 Imp gal/72 litres of which were unusable) and the aircraft incorporated an afterburner cut-out when fuel levels reached a predetermined point. The aircraft received a new UHF radio, with a give-away blade antenna below the nose, and the windscreen was replaced. The new unit used gold film for de-icing, rather than a hot-air sandwich. Finally, the aircraft had a continuous

voice transmission VHF radio, allowing all of the pilot's comments to be heard on the ground and in the chase Hunter in real time, without the pilot having to press a transmit button.

The new wing was built around three mainspars and a number of chord-wise and span-wise formers. It was attached to the fuselage at the same points as the original wing. The sharp leading edge (the FD.2's had been blunt) was markedly swept, but curved gracefully forward to blend into nose chines forward, and had curving tips. 'Bonkers' were incorporated above and below the wings for flutter investigation; they were short-duration rocket motors,

In its revised form, WG774 made two appearances at the Farnborough SBAC show, in 1964 and 1966, during which it participated in the flying display. Here contrails spill from the wings of '774 as it lifts off during the 1964 event, Godfrey Auty at the controls.

Just visible in this photograph is tufting applied to the starboard wing of WG774 for airflow testing.

ogee wings were very different in detail to that eventually adopted for the Concorde. The BAC 221 was really too late to be of much relevance, and its wing, although of similar planform to that of the Concorde, lacked the larger aircraft's complex camber, droop and twist, and had a different thickness/chord ratio. As such, it behaved entirely differently, especially at high speeds. As a Concorde analogue, the BAC 221 was of limited usefulness.

'Slender delta' research

Nevertheless, after manufacturer's trials by Auty, 'Willie' Williamson and a Bedford pilot, the aircraft was delivered to the RAE at Thurleigh near Bedford for use by the Aero Flight on 20 May 1966. Here it joined the HP.115, which had been used for low-speed 'slender delta' research. By the time the aircraft arrived at Bedford it had gained an 8-in (20-cm) fin extension and an anti-spin chute, and the drooping nose mechanism had been modified to allow greater droop angles. The aircraft was accordingly used mainly for research into the Concorde's approach and landing, and was especially useful in developing the Concorde's auto-throttle system. This was somewhat ironic, in view of the type's Mach 1.6 intake, FD.2 airframe and powerful afterburning Avon RA.28R engine. The RA.28R (effectively an afterburning Valiant-type engine) was rated at 10,150 lb st or 14,000 lb st in reheat (45.14 or 62.26 kN), compared to the 9,500 lb st and 14,500 lb st (42.25 and 64.49 kN) ratings of the original FD.2's Avon RA.14R. During its life, the aircraft gained a clear, blown canopy, but was otherwise largely unmodified from its first flight configuration when it was retired to the Museum of Flight at East Fortune in June 1973. Subsequently, the aircraft was transferred to the Fleet Air Arm Museum at RNAS Yeovilton, forming part of a display dedicated to the Concorde, sitting (sometimes quite literally) in the shadow of G-BSST, the British Concorde prototype. **Jon Lake**

Fairings at the junction between the wing and fuselage covered the engine air intakes ducts. During conversion these were left in situ, but were fed via repositioned intakes below the wing's leading edge.

Left: Like the FD.2, the BAC 221 utilised a 'droop snoot', allowing the pilot to see over the aircraft's long nose. In the latter, this incorporated moving plates on either side in order to maintain the aerodynamic integrity of the chine. The need to open the undercarriage doors when the nose was lowered remained in the BAC 221.

formally known as lateral thrust units. The port wing incorporated chord-wise rows of pressure, boundary layer and temperature sensors in two rows across the upper surface. Three span-wise rows of pressure-only sensors were also incorporated, together with three chord-wise rows across the elevator and aileron. The wing was built to much tighter tolerances than that of the original FD.2, and the upper surface was exceptionally clean.

Shoestring budget

The BAC 221 was produced on a shoestring budget, with cost-cutting and frugality the order of the day from the start. Sometimes this was counter-productive. None of the aircraft's new systems was tested using ground rigs, so there was a further 10 months of ground runs and systems checks before the new aircraft, by now

designated BAC 221, was ready to fly. The maiden flight finally took place on 1 May 1964, with Godfrey Auty at the controls of the half-painted aircraft, and chased by a single-seat Hunter. The aircraft was fitted with a bullet fairing on the fin-cap, designed to house a ciné camera, in anticipation of the right wing being 'tufted' to allow airflow patterns to be recorded. The fin-tip also had a 'bonker', designed to generate flutter. By the time the BAC 221 flew, the Hawker Siddeley SST which the aircraft had been designed to support had been abandoned, and the various slightly later Bristol SST studies had been subsumed into the Anglo-French Concorde project. Some of the Bristol/BAC projects had featured ogival delta wings (including the six-engined long-range Bristol 198 and the smaller Bristol 223), but Britain had preferred a more straightforward planform, and its

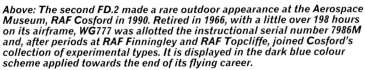

Above: The second FD.2 made a rare outdoor appearance at the Aerospace Museum, RAF Cosford in 1990. Retired in 1966, with a little over 198 hours on its airframe, WG777 was allotted the instructional serial number 7986M and, after periods at RAF Finningley and RAF Topcliffe, joined Cosford's collection of experimental types. It is displayed in the dark blue colour scheme applied towards the end of its flying career.

Retired in 1973, the BAC 221 (right) could be found, in 1998, at the Fleet Air Arm Museum, RNAS Yeovilton, Somerset. There it is displayed with Aérospatiale/BAC Concorde 002 G-BSST (top right), the first British-built prototype of the Anglo-French SST. When the Hawker Siddeley SST project, in support of which the BAC 221 had been originally conceived, was abandoned, WG774 had yet to fly. By the time that it did, in May 1964, the Type 221 could be of little real assistance to what had become, by then, the Anglo-French SST programme.

Specification
BAC Type 221
Powerplant: one Rolls-Royce RA.28R Avon turbojet developing 9,300 lb (41.37 kN) dry thrust or 13,100 lb (58.27 kN) thrust with afterburner
Performance: maximum speed 1060 mph (1706 km/h)
Dimensions: span 25 ft (7.62 m); length 57 ft 7.1 in (17.55 m); height 11 ft 4 in (3.45 m)

BAC Type 221

1 Pitot head
2 Yaw and pitch vanes
3 Nose drooped position
4 Remote compass transmitter
5 Oxygen bottle
6 UHF transmitter and receiver
7 UHF antenna
8 Standby VHF transceiver
9 Temperature probe
10 Nose ballast weight
11 Rudder pedals
12 Instrument panels
13 Engine throttle lever
14 Control column
15 Centrally divided windscreen panel
16 Cockpit canopy, hinged to starboard
17 Martin-Baker Mk 3 ejection seat
18 Mechanical flight control linkages
19 Nose undercarriage leg strut
20 Twin nosewheels, aft-retracting
21 Drag/breaker struts
22 Drooping nose section hinge mounting
23 Nose undercarriage hydraulic retraction jack
24 Drooping nose hydraulic actuators
25 Hydraulic reservoirs
26 Hydraulic accumulators
27 Cockpit air conditioning system equipment
28 Instrumentation and recording equipment bay
29 Fuselage fuel tank
30 Port air intake
31 Engine bleed air heat exchangers for conditioning system, port and starboard
32 Boundary layer spill duct
33 Stability augmentation system equipment bay
34 Fuel collector tank and recuperator
35 Fuel filler
36 Engine starter
37 Rolls-Royce Avon RA.28R engine
38 Starboard main undercarriage leg mounting
39 Starboard wing integral fuel tanks
40 Aileron hydraulic actuator
41 Ballast weight
42 Control surface flutter transducers
43 Starboard aileron
44 Starboard elevator
45 Flight control system variable rate gearboxes
46 Jet pipe/afterburner duct
47 Rudder hydraulic actuator
48 Fin-tip camera housing
49 Rudder flutter transducer
50 Rudder
51 Triple brake parachute housing
52 Two-position afterburner nozzle
53 Nozzle pneumatic actuators
54 Four-segment airbrake panels
55 Airbrake hydraulic jacks
56 Aft ballast weight
57 Elevator hydraulic actuator
58 Port elevator
59 Port aileron
60 Control surface flutter transducers
61 Port aileron hydraulic actuator
62 Port ballast weight
63 Port wing integral fuel tanks
64 Pressure plotting recorder
65 Port mainwheel
66 Shock absorber leg strut
67 Telescopic drag strut
68 Hydraulic retraction jack
69 Crash recorder

Messerschmitt Bf 109
Part 2: The later variants

The 1940 exploits of the Bf 109E 'Emil' firmly established the Messerschmitt fighter as the world's best. Building on those successes, the Augsburg company developed the Bf 109F, which was arguably the best variant of them all, and the spearhead of the devastating opening attack on the Soviet Union. However, it was not until the Bf 109G that the aircraft came to be built in huge numbers and in a wide variety of versions. By mid-war, the Bf 109 was beginning to lose its supremacy, yet it remained the backbone of the Luftwaffe fighter forces for the remainder of the conflict, and in the final days of the Reich late-model Bf 109Gs and Bf 109Ks were putting up fierce resistance to the overwhelming Allied forces. Even the close of the war did not spell the end for the Bf 109: the airframe continued to be developed in Czechoslovakia and Spain, seeing action in two post-war conflicts and surviving as a front-line type until the mid-1960s.

From 1991 to 1997 the only genuine flying Messerschmitt Bf 109 was the Bf 109G-2/Trop WkNr 10639 'Black 6', operated by the Imperial War Museum at Duxford, England. Originally laid down as an F-3 by Erla at Leipzig, the aircraft was completed as a G-2 Trop and issued to 8./JG 77 at Gambut in Libya. Here it was found by No. 3 Sqn, RAAF after the Germans had retreated. After spending some time with the Australians, it was allocated to the RAF's No. 1426 Enemy Aircraft Flight at Collyweston and was used for demonstration and evaluation flights. Soon after the war an unsuccessful attempt was made to put it back in the air. The final restoration began at RAF Lyneham in 1972, subsequently moving to Northolt and then to Benson, from where the aircraft made its 'first' flight in the hands of Group Captain Reg Hallam on 17 March 1991. The RAF restoration team was aided by Rolls-Royce, which overhauled the DB 605 engine, and many individuals. The result is a 100 per cent genuine Bf 109. Unfortunately, at the end of the show season in 1997, the aircraft was badly damaged in a landing accident and its future is uncertain.

Above: Bf 109Gs of 7./JG 27 escort a bomber at low level over the Adriatic from their base at Kalamaki, in Greece. The two aircraft in the background are G-6/Trops, fitted with underwing gondolas for MG 151/20 cannon (Rüstsatz-6). The nearest aircraft is a G-6 without tropical filter or additional cannon. All three carry the 300-litre centreline tank (Rüstsatz-3) which was regularly fitted to the late-model Bf 109s.

Right: Huge numbers of Bf 109Gs were produced by three factories. These G-6 aircraft are seen on Messerschmitt's own Regensburg line.

Far right: A Luftwaffe experte adds another victory to the tail of his Bf 109. Despite some reports to the contrary, the Luftwaffe was rigorous in its examination and award of victory claims. The term experte referred to a pilot with 10 or more kills, this figure having been used by the Germans, British and French to designate an ace since World War I. It was the US which introduced the five-kill figure.

When the Battle of Britain ground to an indecisive halt in late 1940, the German military machine had faced its first reversal in fortune. Unable to wrest control of the skies over Britain from the Royal Air Force, the Luftwaffe had not been able to provide the security blanket which the Wehrmacht had enjoyed during its previous successful campaigns, and it had been impossible for the invasion of Britain to proceed. The failure to capture Britain was of crucial importance to the outcome of the war for many reasons: it provided a bastion from which Britain and its allies could continue to attack, and eventually destroy, German military production; it provided a ready-made jumping-off point for the Allied invasion of Europe; it allowed Britain to retain control of the Atlantic and Mediterranean approaches; and it hammered the first dent into the morale of a buoyant German populace. Initially, while fighting alone, Britain could do little more than harass the Germans in mainland Europe, although the cross-Channel war diverted valuable forces away from other theatres.

Without doubt, the key weapon in the British inventory during the Battle of Britain and subsequent cross-Channel operations was the Supermarine Spitfire; this fighter had been the first to challenge the Messerschmitt Bf 109 for supremacy of the air. The Spitfire was aggressively developed throughout the remainder of the war, its airframe proving remarkably able to absorb ever greater power, loads and speeds. Furthermore, the Allies continued to develop new aircraft and bring them into service just as another type began to fade. It was forward planning and the full backing for rapid development that brought the P-47, P-51, Typhoon and Griffon Spitfire into the fray at a time when they could make a difference, and in more than sufficient numbers.

Left: It was on the Russian front where the late-model Bf 109s enjoyed their greatest successes, huge numbers of Soviet aircraft falling to the guns of the Luftwaffe experten. Always grossly outnumbered, the Jagdflieger continued their fight against growing odds, and against ever more capable opponents. Seen on a snowy airfield here are the Bf 109G-6s of I./JG 51, displaying a variety of winter finishes.

In Germany, things were different. The Focke-Wulf Fw 190 was essentially the only new fighter brought into widespread Luftwaffe service during the course of the war, and there were never enough to go around. Its own development problems also caused delays to its service introduction, giving the Luftwaffe something of a gap in capability during 1941/42. The otherwise excellent Jumo-powered Fw 190D arrived too late to make a difference, while the potentially war-winning jets were far too late and too few to make any impact. This failure to provide a seamless stream of new fighter types for the Luftwaffe occurred for a number of reasons, including the internecine way Germany itself was governed, internal friction in the RLM and a considerable amount of 'laurel-resting' in the first years of the war. Such was the scale and rapidity of the early military successes that few in Germany expected the war to last long enough to warrant the rapid development of follow-on weapons. Campaigns were expected to last weeks, not years.

When faced with the reality of the situation, the Luftwaffe and RLM had no choice other than to turn to its serving fighter, the Bf 109, to provide answers to many procurement questions. Only this aircraft could be made available in short order and in large numbers. Consequently, the Bf 109 was developed beyond its natural limit and at a pace forced by the exigencies of war. From the early G models onwards, the Bf 109 endured a slow and steady decline when compared with its enemies, gaining weight and speed but losing much of the fighting prowess with which the 'Emil' had been blessed. Yet huge numbers were built. In the right hands, of course, and in the right theatre, the late-model Bf 109s were still potent warplanes, but they never enjoyed the mastery of the skies achieved by their illustrious forebears. It would not be until the summer of 1941 that this fundamental planning weakness would begin to manifest itself.

Development of the 'Friedrich'

Eighteen months earlier, in early 1940, such a problem seemed to be impossible, and subsequent events would reinforce the delusion. Although numerically inferior and with woefully thin reserves, German forces swept through much of Europe with technologically superior weapons and superb tactics. Britain, the Soviet Union and the Balkans would surely follow.

In its Bf 109E, Messerschmitt had undoubtedly the finest fighter in the world, yet the company realised that a structured development would have to be implemented to protect that position. Daimler-Benz was promising developed versions of the DB 601, and Messerschmitt set about designing a new variant to harness the extra power in a way which would improve performance without losing the manoeuvrability and handling of the 'Emil'. The result would be the Bf 109F, arguably the finest version of all.

Compared to the Bf 109E, the F introduced a host of aerodynamic modifications, the structure remaining essen-

Above: This typical scene shows the pilots of II./JG 53 on Sicily in 1942, preparing to take their Bf 109G-2s to war in Tunisia. It would not be long before they would be back in Sicily, in full retreat from the Allied forces. In the Mediterranean theatre the Bf 109s were heavily employed in escorting the vulnerable Ju 52 transports.

Left: An increasingly common sight as the war progressed: a Bf 109G is caught by an RAF Spitfire. Although the Bf 109G was largely outperformed by Allied types in the last months of the war, it could still put up a more than credible fight in the right hands. Fortunately for the Allies, the once large number of experienced pilots had dwindled to just a handful, and the majority of Luftwaffe pilots were inexperienced and poorly trained.

Messerschmitt Bf 109

Bf 109F prototypes

Messerschmitt produced four Bf 109F prototypes (V21, V22, V23 and V24) in mid-1940. The first was powered by the DB 601A of the Bf 109E, albeit housed in the new, sleeker cowling. Subsequent aircraft all had the intended DB 601E.

Above: The most obvious new feature of the Bf 109F (fourth prototype V24 shown) was its streamlined cowling and enlarged spinner. The engine-mounted cannon, virtually never fitted to the Bf 109E, became a standard feature of all subsequent Bf 109s.

Below: The four prototype Bf 109Fs were fitted with short circular intakes for the supercharger. This aircraft is the V23 third prototype, which was the first to be fitted with the rounded wingtips which became standard.

Above: As originally designed, the Bf 109F had much shorter wings than the Bf 109E, as emphasised in this view of the V24. Although roll rate was significantly enhanced, the effect on handling was extremely detrimental, leading to the restoration of some wing area and span in the form of rounded wingtips.

The head-on view of the Bf 109F-0 highlights the shallow radiator configuration and the port-side supercharger intake. For the pre-production variant this had a square capture area, reverting to circular for production aircraft.

tially unchanged. Most noticeable at first glance was the redesigned engine cowling, which was deeper and more streamlined, and accompanied by a much larger, rounded spinner. The reduction in propeller diameter by a few inches further enhanced the visual effect of the new spinner.

Of more importance was the new wing design. Based on the E structure, the span was reduced by 2 ft (61 cm) and new ailerons were provided, of reduced span but greater chord. They were no longer interlinked to the flaps, and were changed from the slot to Frise type, with inset hinges and a bevelled upper leading edge. A new low-drag radiator was designed, which employed a boundary-layer removal system ahead of the intake, thereby allowing the radiator to project less far into the airstream, reducing drag. The boundary layer air was ejected through a duct above the flaps. The flaps themselves were split into two, the inboard sections being split horizontally. The upper and lower portions moved simultaneously to form a normal flap section for landing and take-off, but the upper and lower sections could move up and down independently, under control of a thermostat, to form a variable radiator ejector flap.

In the tail area, the Bf 109F introduced a semi-retractable tailwheel, while the tailplane was moved slightly forward of its position on the E. The bracing struts were removed. The rudder was reduced in size slightly, while the whole fin was given a cambered aerofoil section, as opposed to symmetrical, to reduce rudder inputs during take-off and climb. Following input from leading fighter pilots, the armament was changed to feature a single cannon firing through the engine hub, together with two MG 17 machine-guns in the upper fuselage decking. This concentration of firepower was thought to be entirely adequate, and the removal of the heavy cannon from the wings would have a beneficial effect on manoeuvrability and rate of roll.

Prototype construction

At about the time Bf 109Es were clearing the skies over France and the Low Countries, work began on Bf 109F construction, which consisted of four prototypes and a pre-production batch of 10 Bf 109F-0s. The first aircraft, Bf 109 V21, was fitted with the DB 601Aa engine which powered the Bf 109E-3 and E-4, offering 1,175 hp (876 kW) for take-off and 1,000 hp (746 kW) at 3700 m (12,140 ft). However, the second aircraft (V22) was powered by an early version of the Bf 109F's intended engine, the Daimler-Benz DB 601E. Both the third (V23) and fourth (V24) aircraft also had trials DB 601Es. The V22 was subsequently heavily employed in powerplant testing.

First flight (date not recorded) occurred in the summer of 1940, and immediately the F showed enormous promise, although the cut in wingspan severely hampered handling. Accordingly, the third aircraft was fitted with detachable rounded wingtips, which immediately restored the aircraft's

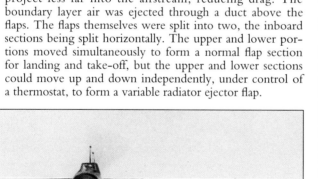

Bf 109F-0

Following on from the prototypes was a batch of 10 Bf 109F-0s, powered by the DB 601N pending delivery of the DB 601E. Similarly, the MG 151/15 cannon was not ready, so F-0s had the 20-mm MG FF/M installed in its place.

The rectangular supercharger air intake identifies this machine as one of the Bf 109F-0 pre-production aircraft. The armament consisted of only three weapons, as opposed to the four of the Bf 109E.

fine handling and were adopted as standard. The fourth aircraft had some minor changes applied, including a deeper oil cooler fairing under the nose, but it retained the short wings.

Bf 109F-0 pre-production aircraft left the factory in the late autumn, fitted with the rounded wingtips and deep oil cooler. The DB 601E engine was experiencing development problems, so the DB 601N (1,200 hp/895 kW for take-off and 1,270 hp/947 kW at 5000 m/16,400 ft) was employed instead, this engine having been used in the E-4/N and E-7 variants. Neither was the Mauser MG 151 engine-mounted cannon ready, so the trusty MG FF/M was substituted. Even with the E's engine, the Bf 109F showed a considerable advance over the 'Emil'. Performance and manoeuvrability were better in all respects, notably in terms of sustained turning and climb. The only retrograde step was the reduction of heavy-calibre firepower from two MG FFs to one, but the impending introduction of the MG 151 was expected to offset this.

In October 1940 the first Bf 109F-1 production aircraft left the assembly lines. It was similar to the F-0 except that it had a circular, as opposed to rectangular, supercharger air intake, as had been tested on the V24. DB 601Ns were fitted, burning high-octane (96) C3 fuel. Initially, they were for delivery to service evaluation units. A spate of crashes ensued, during which severe engine vibration was encountered. Naturally, attention was drawn to the powerplant, although, since it was the same engine which powered many Bf 109Es in service, it was not considered to be the cause. The Fs were grounded, but no cause could be found for the accidents. Flying resumed, whereupon another F-1 crashed. During the crash the engine sustained only minor damage, allowing it to be completely ruled out as the source of the problem. Instead, it was found that many of the rivets in the tail area were missing or loose. Further investigation revealed the true cause: the removal of the tailplane bracing struts had altered the rigidity of the tailplane, and at certain throttle settings an oscillation was set up in the spar. This overlapped that of the engine, causing resonance that eventually resulted in structural failure and a loss of control. The fix consisted of strengthening plates being attached externally.

'Friedrich' enters service

A handful of F-1s reached France as early as October 1940, to be flown by the most experienced pilots. The first production aircraft was used by Werner Mölders of Stab/JG 51, his first sortie being variously recorded as 6 or 25

Left: Werner Mölders is seen in the cockpit of an early Bf 109F-1. He was the first pilot to take the new variant into combat, flying it on the Channel front in October 1940. The following June, he led JG 51 into battle in the East, scoring rapidly in the first weeks of the campaign.

Far left: An early Bf 109F displays the rounded wingtips and angular mainwheel cutouts of the type. The F was widely regarded as the best of the Bf 109s from a pilot's standpoint, retaining much of the fine handling of the 'Emil' while enjoying better performance. It was well-matched with the Spitfire Mk V, enjoying some notable advantages such as diving speed.

October. Delay to the main issue of 'Friedrichs' was inevitable while the accidents were investigated and a cure devised. Therefore it was not until March 1941 that Bf 109F-1s entered service in any great numbers. Naturally, the first units to receive the type were the two Geschwaders of Luftflotte 3 remaining in France which, at the time, were the only Luftwaffe fighter units facing a real enemy. JG 2 'Richthofen' was the first to get the new fighter, closely followed by JG 26 'Schlageter', although II./JG 26 remained on the Bf 109E-7 pending the arrival of the first Focke-Wulf Fw 190A-1s in July. Several other units subsequently received F-1s, although none was ever fully equipped due to the small number produced.

Above: The 'Friedrich' was welcomed at the front line, especially in France where the Luftwaffe was facing the well-equipped RAF. This early aircraft served with II./JG 2 'Richthofen'. In the early days on the Channel, the Bf 109Fs usually sported all-yellow cowlings.

The first production series of Bf 109Fs (F-1 to F-3) retained the DB 601N engine, requiring the use of high-octane fuel. The deeper oil cooler bath under the nose was introduced on the fourth prototype and applied to all subsequent machines.

Messerschmitt Bf 109

Stars and roundels

A number of Bf 109s were captured intact by the Allies and subsequently flown in evaluation trials. The first was the Bf 109F-2 of Major Rolf Pingel (right), of I./JG 26, who was forced to make a wheels-up landing at St Margaret's Bay, Kent, on 10 July 1941. The aircraft was damaged only slightly, and was flown by the RAF until it crashed on 20 October.

Many Bf 109s were abandoned during the reversals in the desert, and some were flown as squadron 'hacks'. This F-4/Trop previously flew with III./JG 53.

The USAAF acquired this Bf 109F-4 from the USSR as a goodwill gesture. It arrived at Wright Field in March 1943, subsequently moving to Eglin in Florida.

In the East the Russians acquired at least one flyable Bf 109F (W Nr 7640), which was then put through its paces by the NII VVS, the Red air force's principal test establishment.

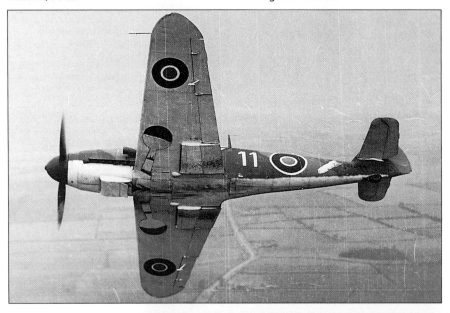

Deliveries of F-1s were undertaken alongside those of F-2s, which entered production in January 1941. They differed only by having the interim 15-mm MG 151/15 cannon (with 200 rounds) in place of the MG FF/M. The first few were built without the external stiffeners to the rear fuselage, but these were probably retrofitted.

At the same time, the RAF was introducing its first Spitfire Mk Vs on the Channel front, and, like the Spitfire Mk I/II and Bf 109E before them, the two proved to be remarkably well-matched. Just as its immediate predecessor had shown, the Spitfire Mk V could easily out-turn the Bf 109F, yet the 'Friedrich' still had the edge in diving and climbing. An early chance to fully evaluate the Bf 109F was handed to the RAF on 10 July 1941, when the aircraft flown by I./JG 26's Gruppenkommandeur, Hauptmann Rolf Pingel, was shot down near Dover and landed virtually intact. The damage to radiators and propeller was repaired, and the aircraft flew again (with RAF serial ES906) on 19 September at Farnborough. It was soon dispatched to Duxford for exhaustive testing against British fighters, but it crashed on 20 October, denying the chance for a quantitative test against the Spitfire Mk V.

Above: As 'White 11' of 10.(Jabo)/JG 26, this Bf 109F-4/B crash-landed at Beachy Head in Sussex on 20 May 1942. After repair, the aircraft flew again in October, assigned the RAF serial NN644 but retaining its Jabo markings. It was allocated to No. 1426 (Enemy Aircraft) Flight.

Although primarily day-fighters, Bf 109s were used in the nocturnal war, especially on the Eastern front during the early months of the campaign. Here they were employed against Soviet nuisance raiders. This Bf 109F of II./JG 54 displays 19 victory bars on the tail.

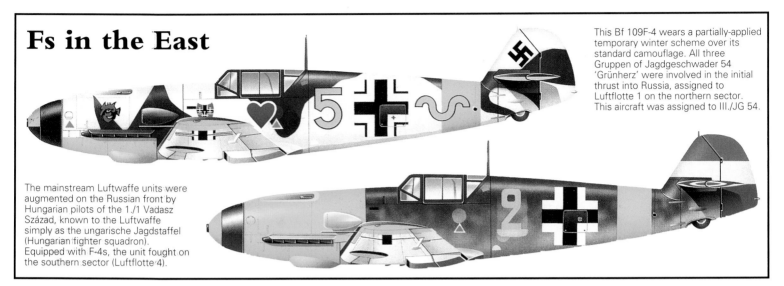

Fs in the East

This Bf 109F-4 wears a partially-applied temporary winter scheme over its standard camouflage. All three Gruppen of Jagdgeschwader 54 'Grünherz' were involved in the initial thrust into Russia, assigned to Luftflotte 1 on the northern sector. This aircraft was assigned to III./JG 54.

The mainstream Luftwaffe units were augmented on the Russian front by Hungarian pilots of the 1./1 Vadasz Század, known to the Luftwaffe simply as the ungarische Jagdstaffel (Hungarian fighter squadron). Equipped with F-4s, the unit fought on the southern sector (Luftflotte 4).

After having equipped the Channel front units, the next priority was to re-equip the Jagdgruppen which had been pulled back to Germany to await the assault on the Soviet Union. Bf 109Fs took no part in Operations Bestrafung, Marita and Merkur, the invasions of Yugoslavia, Greece and Crete, which were covered by units still flying the Bf 109E. However, by 22 June 1941 the majority of the Jagdgruppen involved in the opening attack on the Soviet Union were flying the 'Friedrich'. On the northern sector, Luftflotte 1 had I., II. and III./JG 54 'Grünherz' flying the F and no E units; covering the central sector, Luftflotte 2 had I., II., III. and IV./JG 51 (later named 'Mölders') and I., II. and III./JG 53 'Pik As' flying Bf 109Fs and a further two Gruppen (II. and III./JG 27) on Bf 109Es; on the southern sector, Luftflotte 4 had five Gruppen with Bf 109Es and three with Fs (I., II. and III./JG 3 – later named 'Udet').

Blitzkrieg in the East

Barbarossa was savage. By midday on the first day, the VVS had lost 1,200 aircraft, of which around 320 had been shot down, almost all by Bf 109s and the majority of these by Fs. The Russian Polikarpovs had a few tricks up their sleeves, relying almost entirely on the astonishing agility of the nimble fighters, but they were so hopelessly outperformed, especially by the Bf 109F, that the defence was futile, if brave. Once the Luftwaffe pilots had relearned the lessons of the Spanish Civil War and avoided tangling with the I-153s and I-16s in a slow, close-in fight, there was little the Polikarpovs could do. The Bf 109 pilots scythed into the Soviet defences using the dive and climb tactics which had been so successful in Spain and every campaign since; and, if a pilot should find himself in trouble, opening

'Black 3' was a Bf 109F of 8./JG 54, seen during the long winter of 1941/42 in the Leningrad area. The aircraft has a temporary white finish applied, and carries the Geschwader's large 'Grünherz' marking. Note the damaged radio aerial mast and sagging aerial.

the taps and diving away would almost certainly guarantee safety. The early Fs swept away the Red air force during the early weeks of Barbarossa, paving the way for the lightning ground advance that took the Wehrmacht almost to the gates of Moscow.

On the Russian front, Bf 109F *experten* began compiling scores that even bettered those of their compatriots in

One of the least popular roles was escort for the Ju 87s, Bf 109s being tied to the slow bombers instead of ranging free over the front. This Bf 109 wears the buzzard badge of JG 51 'Mölders'.

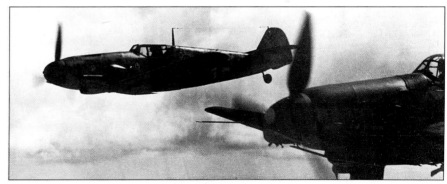

Operation Barbarossa

Barbarossa, the invasion of the Soviet Union, was delayed by the campaign in the Balkans, which was necessary to underpin the southern flank. This delay proved costly to the Germans, for the winter snows came early, stagnating the advance of the Wehrmacht tantalisingly close to Moscow. The 'Friedrich' spearheaded the German lunge into Russia, proving more than adequate for dealing with any Soviet fighters. A large proportion of the VVS had been destroyed in the opening blitz, either in the air or by strafing attacks. Those that survived the initial onslaught continued to fall in large numbers to the guns of the combat-hardened Jagdflieger.

A pilot brushes snow off his Bf 109F-2 during the winter of 1941/42. The harsh weather became a major factor in Luftwaffe operations. For all their lack of fighting capability, the Soviet aircraft of the time were able to operate in the coldest of weather, while the sophisticated Luftwaffe aircraft were often grounded. Note the fuel filler triangle, marked with 'C-3' to remind ground crew to only use 96-octane fuel.

Above: Providing a good illustration of how the Luftwaffe achieved such successes in the opening months of Barbarossa, a sleek II./JG 54 Bf 109F sits next to a portly and obsolescent Polikarpov I-16, the Luftwaffe's principal opponent in 1941.

Right: Ground crew refuel a III./JG 53 Bf 109F from fuel drums in the winter of 1941. In such extreme cold it was common practice to light a fire underneath the Bf 109's engine to get it started.

II./JG 27 flew in the assault on the Soviet Union, but in October 1941 was dispatched to North Africa. These are the Bf 109Fs of 5. Staffel.

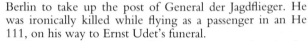

Berlin to take up the post of General der Jagdflieger. He was ironically killed while flying as a passenger in an He 111, on his way to Ernst Udet's funeral.

There were many candidates eager to take up the challenge, not that the Soviet air force represented much of an opposition in the last half of 1941. Several aces used the Bf 109F as the springboard to the 100-, 200- and even 300-kill marks, including Heinz Bär, Gerd Barkhorn, Gordon Gollob, Hermann Graf, Erich Hartmann and Joachim Müncheberg. Several élite units were subsequently transferred to the Mediterranean, and the Jagdgruppen operated at an alarmingly low level. In 1942 the VVS also began to represent a greater challenge: more competitive types entered service, and the Il-2 began to make its presence felt over the battlefield. Nevertheless, the Bf 109 held sway in the air war, although it was grossly outnumbered.

'Friedrich' heads south

As the Bf 109F was proving itself to be a worthy successor to the illustrious 'Emil' in the Russian summer, the variant began to reach another theatre where it would also make a considerable impact: the deserts of North Africa. Bf 109Es (of I./JG 27) had reached Libya in late April 1941, and had made an immediate impression on the air war in the theatre. In July the SAAF and RAF began to introduce the Kittyhawk Mk I into the theatre, and the Luftwaffe felt that it posed a threat to the Bf 109Es (erroneously, as it turned out). The consequence was an immediate request to convert JG 27 to the Bf 109F, a process initiated swiftly. In September, 'Friedrichs' arrived in Libya with II./JG 27, while the E-equipped Gruppe returned briefly to Germany to convert to the new variant. Their aircraft were designated Bf 109F-2/Trop and F-4/Z Trop, and they featured a dust/sand filter over the supercharger air intake (with a clamshell cover over the intake operated from the cockpit),

Libya. Heading the list was Werner Mölders, the Geschwaderkommodore of JG 51, and the leading German pilot in both the Spanish Civil War and Battle of Britain. By the end of June he had passed von Richthofen's score of 80, and shot down his 101st aircraft on 16 July. Deemed to be too valuable to be risked further, he was recalled to

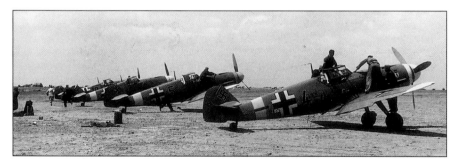

Tropical Fs

For service in the desert, F-2s and F-4s were given sand filters for the supercharger intake. The filter had a clamshell covering over the end, which was kept shut until the aircraft was airborne. It was then opened by the pilot, allowing the engine to develop its full power.

III./JG 53 was another unit which had fought in Russia, but which became heavily involved in the air war over Malta and Libya. Here one of the Gruppe's Bf 109F-4/Trops churns up the desert sand.

Desert wings

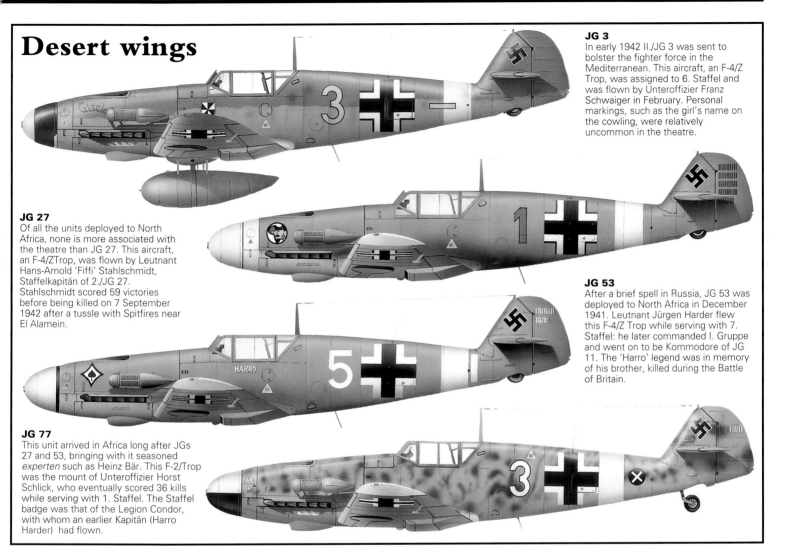

JG 3

In early 1942 II./JG 3 was sent to bolster the fighter force in the Mediterranean. This aircraft, an F-4/Z Trop, was assigned to 6. Staffel and was flown by Unteroffizier Franz Schwaiger in February. Personal markings, such as the girl's name on the cowling, were relatively uncommon in the theatre.

JG 27

Of all the units deployed to North Africa, none is more associated with the theatre than JG 27. This aircraft, an F-4/ZTrop, was flown by Leutnant Hans-Arnold 'Fiffi' Stahlschmidt, Staffelkapitän of 2./JG 27. Stahlschmidt scored 59 victories before being killed on 7 September 1942 after a tussle with Spitfires near El Alamein.

JG 53

After a brief spell in Russia, JG 53 was deployed to North Africa in December 1941. Leutnant Jürgen Harder flew this F-4/Z Trop while serving with 7. Staffel: he later commanded I. Gruppe and went on to be Kommodore of JG 11. The 'Harro' legend was in memory of his brother, killed during the Battle of Britain.

JG 77

This unit arrived in Africa long after JGs 27 and 53, bringing with it seasoned *experten* such as Heinz Bär. This F-2/Trop was the mount of Unteroffizier Horst Schlick, who eventually scored 36 kills while serving with 1. Staffel. The Staffel badge was that of the Legion Condor, with whom an earlier Kapitän (Harro Harder) had flown.

in addition to other desert modifications. It is not thought that any Trops were produced at the factory, aircraft being so altered in the field. Pitted against P-40s and Hurricanes, the Fs enjoyed a period of considerable ascendancy.

Despite the successes achieved in the opening months on the Russian front, there was still considerable attrition. Overall fighter production had been stepped up, but that of the Bf 109 was little increased. This was mainly due to the transition of three of the six factories which had hitherto built Bf 109s to the Fw 190 production effort. Fieseler was the first to go, in July 1941, followed by Arado and AGO before the end of the year. This left only Erla, WNF and the parent factory producing the Bf 109, although the latter contributed little in 1941.

Bf 109F developments

Nevertheless, new variants had been produced. A few F-2s had a centreline pylon for bomb carriage, being designated Bf 109F-2/B. At least one F-2/U1 is recorded as having seen combat (flown by none other than Oberstleutnant Adolf Galland of JG 26), this sub-variant featuring 13-mm MG 131 machine-guns in place of the MG 17s. The Bf 109F-2/Z was intended to introduce GM 1 nitrous oxide boosting, but probably never progressed further than test aircraft.

However, at the end of 1941 the intended engine, the DB 601E, finally became available. It had the advantage of running on low-octane (87) B4 fuel, which was easier to produce and more plentiful. The first DB 601E-powered variant was the Bf 109F-3, of which only a handful were built, closely followed bwy what was the definitive 'Friedrich': the Bf 109F-4. The latter differed in several respects from its forerunners, the most important change

being the installation of the 20-mm calibre MG 151/20 (with ammunition dropping to 150 rounds). At last, the originally intended Bf 109F armament and powerplant had been brought together. Other changes included revised self-sealing tanks and additional armouring, notably an angled plate above the pilot's head. Early F-4s retained the external stiffeners to the rear fuselage, but a more elegant solution of internal strengthening was applied to most of the batch.

This line-up is believed to be of the Bf 109F-3 variant, which was powered by the DB 601E. Only a few F-3s were built, differing in only minor detail (principally by retaining the MG 151/15 cannon) from the F-4 which followed.

Left: The Bf 109F-4 was the major production version of the 'Friedrich', and also represented the definitive standard with DB 601E engine and MG 151/20 cannon firing through the spinner. All F series aircraft retained the small quarterlight glazed panel, a useful recognition feature.

Bf 109F Jagdbomber

One of the success stories of the early cross-Channel operations were the 'hit-and-run' Bf 109E fighter-bombers, which caused considerable damage along the English coast. Some time after the fighter units had been re-equipped, the two Jabostaffeln transitioned to a dedicated version of the Bf 109F-4, fitted with an ETC 250 bomb rack under the centreline.

Above: 10.(Jabo)/JG 26 left the observer in no doubt as to the role of the Staffel. Clutching an SC 250 bomb to its belly, one of the unit's Bf 109F-4/Bs sets out for a mission across the Channel.

Above right: Partnering 10./JG 26 in the Jabo mission was 10./JG 2. The two Jabostaffeln specialised in anti-shipping attacks against coastal targets, and achieved a fair measure of success. Early warning of such attacks was often impossible, as the F-4/Bs operated in small formations (often just a pair) and crossed the Channel at very low level.

These Bf 109F-4/Trops are of I./JG 53, seen on Sicily. All carry the Rüstsatz-3 centreline drop tank.

On the Channel front, the F was used only briefly in the pure fighter role, as the Fw 190A-2/A-3 began arriving in numbers during the latter half of 1941. Only II./JG 26 operated the F-4, and that only briefly in the winter of 1941/42 while it gave up Fw 190As and waited for Bf 109Gs. However, at about this time, the Bf 109F-4/B was being introduced to Luftflotte 3's two fighter-bomber units. Both of the Channel front Geschwaders had a single Staffel assigned to hit-and-run duties, with shipping and coastal installations the main targets. Bf 109E-4/Bs had been used in this role throughout 1941, despite the re-equipment of the rest of JG 2 and JG 26 with Fw 190s. They were replaced in early 1942 with Jabo-roled Fs, which could carry a single 250-kg (551-lb) SC 250 bomb on a centreline ETC 250 rack. Bf 109F-4/Bs served with 10.(Jabo)/JG 2 at Beaumont-le-Roger and 10.(Jabo)/JG 26 at Poix, and achieved considerable success along the English coastline.

North African success

Events in the desert turned very much in the Bf 109F's favour. Facing opposition from Hurricanes, Tomahawks and Kittyhawks, the 'Friedrich' reigned supreme in the fighter v. fighter combat which dominated the air war. Several pilots began to amass large tallies, but no star shone more brightly than the 'Star of Afrika' himself – Leutnant Hans-Joachim Marseille of 3./JG 27. Marseille had already

scored five kills in the Battle of Britain (albeit with the loss of four Bf 109Es!), but it was when he arrived in the desert and began flying the Bf 109F-4Z Trop (at least four individual aircraft wore his famous 'Yellow 14') that his abundant skills began to show. An acknowledged master of deflection shooting, he astonished fellow pilots and ground crew by how few rounds he required to down his victims.

Marseille passed 50 kills on 22 February 1942, 75 on 6 June and reached 101 on 18 June, having been promoted

Above: A 'black man' catches up with his rest while the Bf 109F-4/Trops of 5./JG 27 sit at alert. The tropical filter was an Italian-designed unit.

Below: A group of 'Tommies' poses with a downed JG 27 Bf 109F. The desert was littered with aircraft from both sides – the recovery of downed pilots was a major problem.

Star of Afrika

This F-4/Z Trop is the aircraft used by Hauptmann Hans-Joachim Marseille after his return to Africa, and is seen as it appeared in September 1942, days before his death in a G-2/Trop. Marseille used at least four F-4/Z Trops during his reign in the desert, all coded 'Yellow 14'. The fin bears testament to 151 kills: he scored a total of 158 (all but seven in the desert). Marseille was a superb fighter pilot, but his high spirits ruined his chances for a meteoric rise to a plum command job. In June 1942 he was made Staffelkapitän of 3./JG 27.

'Pik As' in Sicily

Based at Comiso in May 1942, this Bf 109F-4 was one of the aircraft used by Oberstleutnant Günther Freiherr von Maltzahn, the Kommodore of JG 53. In addition to the Kommodore markings, the aircraft has its spinner tip painted blue, denoting the Geschwaderstab. Von Maltzahn scored 68 kills while with JG 53.

This F-4/Z wears typical Russian front summer camouflage, hastily applied with Mediterranean theatre bands for service with 5./JG 53 at Comiso in February 1942. The machine was the mount of Hauptmann Kurt Brändle, the Staffelkapitän, who went on to command II./JG 3, scoring 180 kills before being killed in November 1943.

to Oberleutnant and put in command of 3./JG 27. Days after, he was ordered back to Berlin to receive the Swords to his Ritterkreuz from Hitler himself. A two-month leave followed, after which Marseille returned to Libya, now promoted to Hauptmann. On 1 September, 'Jochen' achieved the near-impossible by downing 17 fighters in one day. More action in the month brought his total to 158. Having scored virtually all of his victories in a Bf 109F, Marseille was flying a G-2/Trop when he departed on a routine sortie on 30 September. Returning from a fruitless patrol, the DB 605 engine caught fire, leaving Marseille with no choice but to bail out. As he did so, his body struck the tailplane, and he fell to his death. He was just 22 years old.

Despite the arrival of the 'Gustav', the 'Friedrich' still reigned supreme in the Mediterranean theatre for some months, having been operated in North Africa by all of JG 27 (bar a Jagdkommando in Crete), III./JG 53 and the Jabo Staffel Afrika. The Stab. and II./JG 53 were in Sicily alongside I./JG 77. Reshuffling of units between Africa and Sicily, and between the theatre and the Russian front, was commonplace. By the time of Marseille's death, the Spitfire Mk V was being encountered in some numbers, considerably reducing the discrepancy between the two fighter forces, although the Spitfires were hampered by their cumbersome Vokes filters. Furthermore, the steady attrition among the *experten* was not being made good, new arrivals in Africa being almost universally 'green' pilots fresh out of fighter school. On 23 October, the landmark battle of El Alamein opened. The Luftwaffe was on its way out of Africa.

In the hands of a competent pilot, and against primarily fighter opposition, the Bf 109F's three-gun armament proved entirely adequate. The MG 151 was an excellent weapon for its time, with a higher rate of fire and faster muzzle velocity than the MG FF. The shells' trajectory closely matched that of the bullets from the MG 17s, providing a great concentration of fire. However, there were some disadvantages. In the desert the MG 151 was prone to jamming, leaving the Bf 109F with just its two MG 17s, hardly enough to down an aircraft. This problem was not attended to until the Bf 109G series. Another problem, and one which caused much debate, was that the three-gun armament was not sufficient against bomber-sized targets, and it also required a good pilot to employ it with effect.

Increased weight of fire

Accordingly, the first Rüstzustand (equipment condition) was developed for the Bf 109F, allowing for the addition of a pair of 20-mm MG 151/20s in gondolas under the wing, each provided with 120 rounds. This greatly increased the overall firepower, and enhanced the chances of a hit as the shells were more widely spread, but also adversely affected the handling. Not only did the extra weight and drag hamper performance, but the guns caused the Bf 109F to swing like a pendulum, requiring careful use of rudder to counteract the movement. This inevitably caused the Bf 109F-4/R1 to lose much of its effectiveness when used against

The Berlin bear badge identifies this Bf 109F as belonging to II./JG 27. It is seen sharing Martuba airfield with a Ju 88 of LG 1. Virtually all Bf 109s sent to North Africa wore a standard Sandbraun scheme, although the demarcation line along the fuselage varied considerably in position.

Far left: A Bf 109F-3 cavorts for the camera. Most Luftwaffe pilots agreed that the 'Friedrich' was the pinnacle of Bf 109 design from a handling point of view. The aircraft retained the fine handling of the Bf 109E, but rolled faster thanks to the new wingtips and was considerably better performing. The 'Gustav' was faster still, especially at altitude, but the extra weight eroded the handling considerably.

Tactical reconnaissance

Tactical photo-reconnaissance missions were assigned to Bf 109F-4s finished at the factory with various Rüstzustände modifications which permitted them to carry cameras. This aircraft flew with 1.(Fern) Staffel/Aufklärungsgruppe 122 in Sicily.

Sunshades protect the pilots of these reconnaissance-configured Bf 109F-4s from the sun's rays as they prepare for a mission. The reconnaissance aircraft usually had small pipes which ducted excess oil back behind the camera window to avoid the latter being fouled.

Right: Last-minute preparations are undertaken prior to this Bf 109F leaving on a reconnaissance mission. In addition to the factory-installed modification which provided for camera installations, the reconnaissance Bf 109s occasionally had armament removed in the field to make them lighter and faster.

A group of 7./JG 54 Bf 109Fs taxis out for a mission across a snow-covered airfield on the Leningrad front in 1942. Once compacted, snow presented little problem to the Bf 109, but in the summer the mud caused severe wheel-clogging. Note the victory bars on the tail of the aircraft in the foreground.

fighters. Although not seen as such at the time, the Bf 109F-4/R1 was really the point where the rot set in as far as the fighter's ascendancy was concerned. Aircraft so-equipped were nicknamed 'Kanonenboote' ('gunboat'), a nickname which was also used throughout the G series.

A number of Rüstsätze were developed for the Bf 109F, but few reached the front line as the Bf 109G had already largely replaced the F by the time they were ready. One which did see some action was Rüstsatz-6, which added an ETC 250 bomb rack beneath the centreline, this being able to lift a single 250-kg (551-lb) SC 250 bomb, four SC 50 bombs (50-kg/110-lb) on an ER 4 adaptor, or a single 300-litre (66-Imp gal) drop tank. At this juncture it is worth pointing out that the term Rüstsatz covered a field modification kit only, and this in itself was not sufficient to alter an aircraft's designation. The 'R' suffixes in sub-variant designations apply to the Rüstzustand only, being applied at the factory and describing the configuration in which the aircraft left its makers. The 'U' suffix (Umbausatz) covered a factory conversion kit.

Fs with cameras

Additional versions were the F-4/Z with GM 1 boosting and several sub-variants of reconnaissance aircraft built in four Rüstzustände. Previously thought to be the Bf 109F-5 and F-6, the reconnaissance variants are now known to

have been designated Bf 109F-4/R2, R3, R4 and R8. The first three Rüstzustände designations covered aircraft with single vertically-mounted cameras (Rb 20/30, Rb 50/30 and Rb 75/30, respectively) immediately behind the cockpit, and no radios, while the single Bf 109F-4/R8 had either an Rb 50/30 or Rb 75/30 and radio. Available production figures for reconnaissance aircraft are very low, suggesting that they are either wrong, or that many aircraft were converted to the role after leaving the factory. Many had at least the cannon armament removed, and had a slight excrescence under the fuselage on which to mount the optically-flat glass through which the camera peered. As for the F-5 (an undescribed fighter variant), only one aircraft is believed to have been built, while the planned large batches of F-6s and F-8s were not fulfilled.

Foreign Fs

Luftwaffe service for the 'Friedrich' was relatively brief, as it was rapidly superseded by the Bf 109G on both the production lines and in the front line. By the end of 1942 it had largely disappeared from the day fighter forces, although a number were still being used as Jabos. Ex-Luftwaffe aircraft were supplied to other Axis or friendly nations, beginning in mid-1942 with Spain, which received 15 Bf 109F-4s. They were flown by 25 Grupo at Alcalá de Henares to prepare Spanish pilots for the volunteer unit flying on the Eastern Front. Known as the Escuadrón Azul, or more formally as 15.(span.)/JG 51, this Staffel converted from Bf 109Es to Bf 109F-4s in October 1942, and flew the 'Friedrich' until July 1943.

Second foreign recipient of the F was the Magyar Királyi Légierö (Royal Hungarian Air Force), which received Bf 109F-4s to replace the Reggiane Re.2000s of the 1./1 Vadasz Század (fighter squadron) which was serving on the Russian front, known simply as the ungarische Jagdstaffel

(Hungarian fighter squadron). In early 1943 the transfer of Bf 109F-4/R1s and F-4/Bs allowed the transition of two Italian units to the 'Friedrich', these being 3° and 150° Gruppo Caccia Terrestre.

As a test vehicle, the Bf 109F performed useful work, notably for the 'Gustav' which supplanted it on the production lines. One aircraft (V30) was employed to test the G-1's pressurised cabin. Surplus Bf 109Fs were involved in a number of other trials programme, including five assigned to different aspects of the Me 309 fighter project. Two were the third and fourth Bf 109F prototypes, modified with a fixed tricycle undercarriage and a ventral radiator bath, respectively. Other Fs tested the Me 309's inward-retracting undercarriage, air conditioning and cabin pressurisation systems.

Bf 109Fs were flown with both the BMW 801 radial engine and the Jumo 213 with its annular radiator (à la Fw

Above and top: The Hungarian air force received Bf 109Fs in 1942, and its aircraft were soon in action against the Russians in the East. The aircraft at top has the green/white/red Hungarian fin markings, but retains German national insignia. The aircraft above is in full Hungarian markings.

Italy-based 'Friedrich'

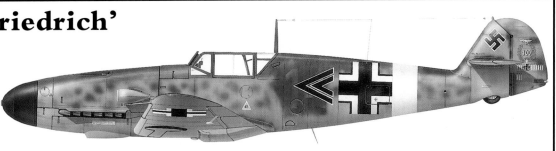

This F-4, the personal aircraft of Leutnant Heinz-Edgar Bär, Kommandeur of I./JG 77, is shown as it appeared while based in southern Italy in July 1942, prior to the move to North Africa. 'Pritzl' Bär had opened his account on 25 September 1939, and scored his last of 220 kills on 28 April 1945, flying an Me 262 jet with JV 44.

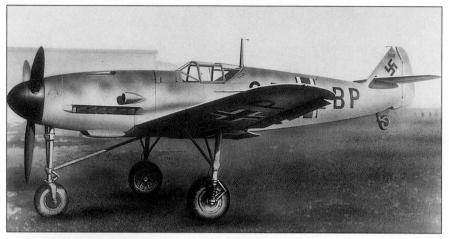

Bf 109Fs for research

When it came to research purposes, the Bf 109F was the major source of airframes, due mainly to their ready availability and general similarity to the 'Gustav'. In addition to powerplant and armament trials, F airframes were used to test aspects of the Me 309 programme, as the upper component of the Mistel combination, and as high-altitude fighter testbeds.

Above: Heavily retouched, this photograph shows the V23 after installation of the tricycle undercarriage intended for the Me 309.

Above right: Another Me 309 testbed was this aircraft, fitted with the wide-track undercarriage and retractable ventral radiator.

Left: This close-up shows the Bf 109F fitted with a BMW 801 radial (which powered the Fw 190A). Another F was fitted with a Jumo engine with an annular radiator.

Right: A Bf 109F-2 was tested at Tarnewitz with the RZ 65 rocket, housed singly in tubes faired into the leading edge. The weapon was tested for anti-bomber duties with both a contact and time-delay fuse, and with just a contact fuse for ground attack work.

190D), while one was tested with a butterfly tail. The latter aircraft first flew with its new empennage on 21 January 1943, with Karl Baur at the controls. The V-tail offered little advantage and plenty of problems, including decreased longitudinal stability and increased swing on landing. It was not adopted. Another F was assigned to Junkers for Mistel trials, acting as the upper component of the prototype.

Zwilling

Although it never flew, another project which initially involved the Bf 109F is worthy of mention – the Bf 109Z 'Zwilling' (twin). Originally proposed for (and carried out on) the Heinkel He 111, the 'Zwilling' concept married two standard fuselages of an existing type by a new centre-section and tailplane. In the Bf 109's case it was proposed as a means of producing a new Zerstörer-type heavy fighter

without the need for much development or for massive disruption to existing production lines.

Two Bf 109F-4s were assigned to the programme, which was initiated in earnest in late 1942. The two component aircraft retained their fuselages and one wing virtually unchanged, but a new straight-chord tailplane and centre-section joined the two halves. All four original radiators were retained, and all four main undercarriage units, although the latter were arranged in pairs under the centre of each fuselage, set much closer together than on the Bf 109F but still retracting outwards, away from the fuselage. A lower fuselage keel member was introduced to support them. There was still enough room between the legs for an ETC 250 bomb rack under each fuselage. The pilot flew the contraption from the left-hand fuselage, the cockpit of the right-hand fuselage being faired over. The prototype Bf

Below and below right: Werknummer 14001, bearing Stammkenn-zeichen (factory code) VJ+WA, was the first of three Bf 109G-0s. The aircraft displays the heavy cockpit framing and lack of quarterlight glazing of the production Gs, but does not have the two small airscoops aft of the spinner.

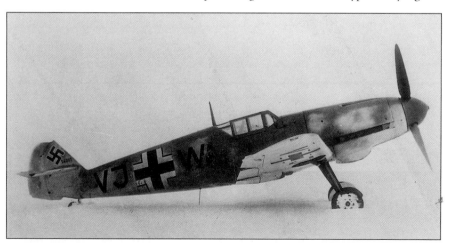

The first 'Gustavs'

Following tests with a Bf 109F fitted with a pressurised cockpit, Messerschmitt produced a batch of three pre-production Bf 109G-0s. Cockpit pressurisation was fitted, but the intended DB 605 engines were not ready in time. Accordingly, the Bf 109G-0s flew with the F's DB 601E powerplant.

Bf 109 replacements

Throughout the life of the Bf 109, Messerschmitt made three serious attempts to provide a follow-on fighter to replace its original masterpiece, these projects running alongside the ongoing work of steadily improving the existing design. All were doomed to failure.

Messerschmitt Me 209

In 1937/38 Messerschmitt had designed a special craft to capture the world speed record, designated Me 209. The second prototype eventually took the record at a speed of 469.22 mph on 26 April 1939, pipping the mark set by the Heinkel He 100 V8. The propaganda machine went into full swing, calling the aircraft an 'Me 109R' and inferring that it was a version of the service fighter. In fact, the Me 209 was much smaller, and bore no resemblance to the Bf 109 apart from having a DB 601 engine.

Spurred on by its success, Messerschmitt studied turning the record-breaking design into a service fighter. The result was the Me 209 V4 (D-IRND), which first flew on 12 May 1939. Initially outwardly similar to the racing aircraft, the V4 had provision for armament (two MG 17s and an engine-mounted MG FF/M), increased vertical fin area, shortened undercarriage and a new, larger wing. The surface evaporation cooling system of the racer was retained, but was soon found to be insufficient, and was replaced by two conventional underwing radiators after just eight flights. These, too, were inadequate, and were eventually replaced by a large single radiator under the centreline. Handling was distinctly unpleasant, leading to two successive increases in wing span.

By mid-1940 the V4's DB 601A had been replaced by a DB 601N, but this did not provide enough extra power to overcome the aircraft's increased weight and wing area, and certainly precluded plans to fit operational Me 209s with the MK 108 cannon in the engine, plus two further weapons underwing. Despite its racing origins, the Me 209 V4 was marginally slower than the Bf 109E then in widespread service, and its ground

The Me 209 V4 was finished with (just visible) provision for armament. It is seen here in its interim configuration with two shallow underwing radiators. The snake motif was purely for propaganda purposes.

and flight handling properties remained atrocious. The new Bf 109F then in development would have left the Me 209 standing, and development was abandoned.

Messerschmitt Me 309

In late 1940, while Bf 109F development was continuing, Messerschmitt began work on an all-new fighter which, it was hoped, would be the natural successor to the Bf 109. Designated Me 309, the new fighter employed many novel features, several of which were tested on Bf 109Fs. Among the most radical were a tricycle undercarriage with wide-track inward-retracting mainwheels, a variable, retractable central radiator bath, and reversible-pitch propeller.

When first proposed, RLM interest in the type was not great: at the time, no-one foresaw the need to develop a successor to the Bf 109. Development continued at a leisurely pace and the first prototype was not completed until June 1942. It first flew, with Karl Baur at the controls, on 18 July. Initially, problems with the cooling system were encountered, and the aircraft showed a lack of directional stability both on the ground and in the air. During the first test of the reverse-pitch in September, the aircraft braked so violently that it damaged the flaps and nosed over, breaking the nosewheel leg.

By November the Me 309 V1 was flying again with enlarged tail surfaces, in time to undergo mock combat trials with a Bf 109G. Although the Me 309 was faster than the 'Gustav', the Bf 109 could easily turn well inside the prototype fighter. On 29 November the V2 joined the test fleet, but not for long – its nosewheel collapsed on landing, the fuselage breaking in two in the ensuing crash. The V2 had the intended DB 605 engine installed, the first aircraft having hitherto flown with a DB 603A. In March 1943 the DB 605-powered V3

Messerschmitt engineers work on the Me 309 V1. The wide-track tricycle undercarriage made the Me 309 a tricky aircraft to taxi, and caused swerving on the runway.

flew, but by then the RLM had lost interest in the design, which it was felt would have been too difficult for the average pilot to operate, and which offered only a marginal speed increase as compensation for poor manoeuvrability when compared with the Bf 109.

Nevertheless, the V4 prototype did make it into the air in July 1943, equipped as the prototype for the Me 309A-2 heavy fighter. It was armed with a powerful battery of weapons for the anti-bomber role, consisting of four MG

The Me 309 V2 is seen in a sorry state at Lechfeld at the end of its one and only flight.

131s, two MG 151/20s and two MK 108s, the latter in the overwing fairings developed for the Me 209 II. The V4 was destroyed in a bombing raid, while the V1 and V3 were used sporadically to test elements of the Me 262 programme and for undercarriage/reverse-pitch research. Proposed variants included the Me 309B dive-bomber and the Me 609 Zwilling, with two fuselages joined by a common centre-section.

Messerschmitt Me 209 II

Although it carried the same designation as its racing predecessor, and the Versuchs (prototype) numbers continued sequentially from the earlier series, the aircraft referred to as the Me 209 II had nothing in common with the earlier machine. The original concept was to provide a fighter with some 65 per cent parts commonality with the Bf 109G but with considerably improved performance. Major changes compared to the Bf 109 consisted of an inward-retracting undercarriage (tested on a Bf 109F), taller fin and a DB 603 engine with annular radiator. Studies soon showed that the Bf 109G wing was impractical, so a new wing was designed. This could not accommodate the planned MK 108 wing guns, leading to a series of redesigns, most of which increased weight and consequently required a more sturdy structure. As a result, the Me 209 V5 emerged with little commonality with the Bf 109G, rendering its chances of being built, at a time when fighter production was being ramped up in the face of an ever more desperate war situation, less likely.

Flugkapitän Fritz Wendel flew the Me 209 V5 for the first time on 3 November 1943. Initially flying with a DB 603A, the aircraft soon acquired a DB 603G, which necessitated an increase in fin size. The V5 was intended to serve as the prototype for the Me 209A-1 series, which had an armament of one engine-mounted MK 108 and two MG 131s in the wingroot. Various Umbausatz conversions added extra cannon in the wings, for which a streamlined fairing was developed (and tested on a Bf 109F) to house the feed system. The fairings extended back over the trailing edge, and were found to provide some hitherto-unexpected aerodynamic benefits – as 'Küchemann carrots', the fairings were later adopted in the jet age by several designs.

Following the V5 was a further prototype powered by a Jumo 213E, intended to serve as the development aircraft for the Me 209A-2. It was armed with the engine-mounted MK 108, but had MG 151/20s in the wingroots. A more radical derivative was the Me 209H, proposed as a specialised high-altitude fighter. It was to be produced by inserting an untapered centre-section to increase wing span and by using either the special DB 628 engine or a turbo-supercharged DB 603E. In the event, the aircraft was completed with a standard DB 603G, pending the availability of the final choice of engine, the DB 627 (a DB 603 with two-stage supercharging). Proposed armament consisted of one MK 108 in the engine, two MG 131s in the forward fuselage and four MG 151/20s in the wings.

In the late spring of 1944 all Me 209 work was abandoned as it had become blatantly obvious that a new fighter type could not be introduced to the existing production lines; all the while, every last Bf 109G was urgently needed on the front line. Despite this, and damage caused during an air raid, the Me 209H V1 was completed in June 1944. No flight records have survived.

This is the DB 603G-powered Me 209 V5 (first prototype for the Me 209 II), seen with the tall vertical fin which accompanied the installation of this powerplant. The Me 209 V6 had a Jumo 213 engine, characterised by smoother lines under the cowling.

Messerschmitt Bf 109

Bf 109G-1

The first production variant of the 'Gustav' was the pressurised G-1, built in small numbers for the specialist high-altitude units based on the Channel Front. When USAAF bombers arrived in North Africa, the variant was dispatched to the region to oppose their operations.

Above: This is an early production Bf 109G-1. An additional airscoop was added behind and slightly below the gun muzzle trough.

Top right: G-1s gave the Luftwaffe a useful capability against high-flying bombers. Most G-1s and G-2s were fitted with retractable tailwheels, although they often flew with them extended.

109Z was believed to be complete when it was destroyed in an air raid.

Production Bf 109Zs would have been based on the Bf 109G airframe (as the Bf 109F had by then long been out of production), and would have been armed with one 30-mm MK 108 cannon firing through each propeller hub, plus a similar weapon in a gondola beneath each outer wing. The centre-section would have housed a 30-mm MK 103 cannon, and carried an ETC 500 bomb rack in addition to the two ETC 250s. As such, this five-cannon heavy fighter would have been formidable, and promised much better performance than other Zerstörer types. However, interest waned considerably after the loss of the

prototype, and the 'Zwilling' project was cancelled in early 1944. Soon Germany would have far more pressing matters with which to contend.

Enter the 'Gustav'

In mid-1941, as the Bf 109F was leading the German charge into Russia, development work was under way for a new version of the Bf 109, the G or 'Gustav', which would become the most numerous of the variants. Not that the Bf 109G was that good, but the circumstances of the mismanagement which had prevailed earlier required it to be built in huge numbers simply because there was nothing else. What should have been built was an entirely new successor, but such an aircraft (the Me 209) was far from ready. That the Bf 109G was in production from early 1942 until the end of the war is ample testament to the ineptitude of the Luftwaffe's overlords.

From the earliest days of Barbarossa it was becoming obvious that the Luftwaffe was suffering much higher attrition than had been envisaged. The German aviation industry had not been geared up sufficiently to cater for such attrition and, as the pressures on the Axis mounted daily from an increasing number of directions, never truly caught up with the demands of war, despite some desperate measures being taken. Similarly, the provision of new types was woeful – even the new Fw 190 was not available in sufficient numbers, and suffered its own share of development problems which delayed its mass appearance at the front lines.

Charged with limiting the damage, Messerschmitt's work on the Bf 109G was by necessity of great haste, with the result that the aircraft was a minimum-change version of the 'Friedrich' with improved basic performance. By 1941 the greatest emphasis was being placed on speed, with handling and manoeuvrability considered to be of lesser importance. Also, the air battle, especially in the west, had moved continuously upwards, and the ability to fight at higher altitudes carried increasing weight. Therefore, the Bf 109G was designed with a more powerful engine – the DB 605 – for greater speed, and cabin pressurisation.

Unfortunately, there was no time to develop the aerodynamic and structural modifications alongside the new equipment. The Bf 109E and F had represented harmony between installed power, aircraft weight and handling. The G, however, lost much of the fine handling at the expense of speed and greater weight. On the other side of the Channel, development of the Spitfire was following a similar line: the Mk IX was hastily being cobbled together by the marriage of the two-stage Merlin 60 series and the

Above: The clean cowling and small tailwheel identify this aircraft as Bf 109G-2. Although unpressurised, the G-2 was fitted with the heavily-framed canopy of the G-1.

This mixed bag of 'Gustavs' consists of a Bf 109G-3 (nearest the camera) fitted with the large, fixed tailwheel, a G-6 (centre) and an early machine (background) with retractable tailwheel, probably a G-2.

'Gustav' in the Med

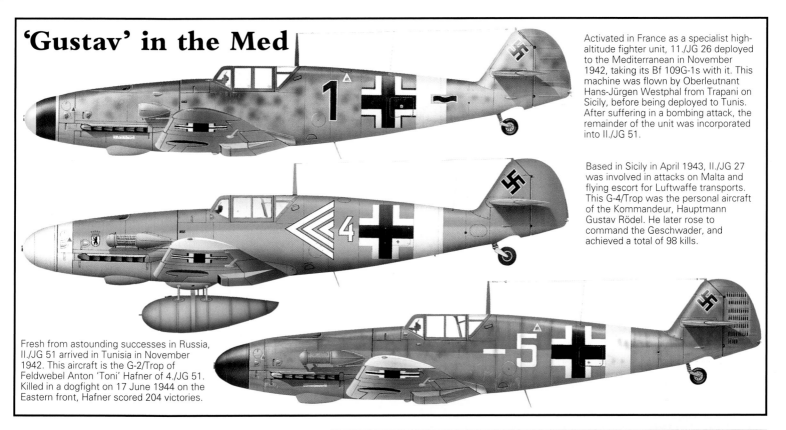

Activated in France as a specialist high-altitude fighter unit, 11./JG 26 deployed to the Mediterranean in November 1942, taking its Bf 109G-1s with it. This machine was flown by Oberleutnant Hans-Jürgen Westphal from Trapani on Sicily, before being deployed to Tunis. After suffering in a bombing attack, the remainder of the unit was incorporated into II./JG 51.

Based in Sicily in April 1943, II./JG 27 was involved in attacks on Malta and flying escort for Luftwaffe transports. This G-4/Trop was the personal aircraft of the Kommandeur, Hauptmann Gustav Rödel. He later rose to command the Geschwader, and achieved a total of 98 kills.

Fresh from astounding successes in Russia, II./JG 51 arrived in Tunisia in November 1942. This aircraft is the G-2/Trop of Feldwebel Anton 'Toni' Hafner of 4./JG 51. Killed in a dogfight on 17 June 1944 on the Eastern front, Hafner scored 204 victories.

existing Mk V airframe, to provide an expeditious means of countering the Fw 190A, which had demonstrated a striking superiority over the Mk V. To illustrate the fickleness of fate, the unmodified Spitfire airframe proved easily capable of absorbing the additional power and weight, and the Mk IX established itself as one of the outstanding fighters of the war. It, too, was also the most produced version (if one includes the nearly-identical Mk XVI with a US-built Merlin).

DB 605 power

Daimler-Benz's new DB 605A for the Bf 109G was closely based on the DB 601E, but introduced greater bore, higher permissible rpm and increased compression ratio. The result was an engine which produced 1,475 hp (1100 kW) for take-off. Although of similar overall dimensions, the engine was heavier, demanding a strengthening of the engine bearers and other parts of the fuselage structure. In turn, the extra weight required a beefing up of the main undercarriage. The engine installation required additional cooling, and the G featured an enlarged oil cooler and four small additional airscoops just aft of the spinner.

Above: Factory-fresh Bf 109G-2s await delivery to a front-line unit. The aircraft have undergone flight-testing, as evidenced by the oil streaks over the wingroot which characterised all Bf 109s.

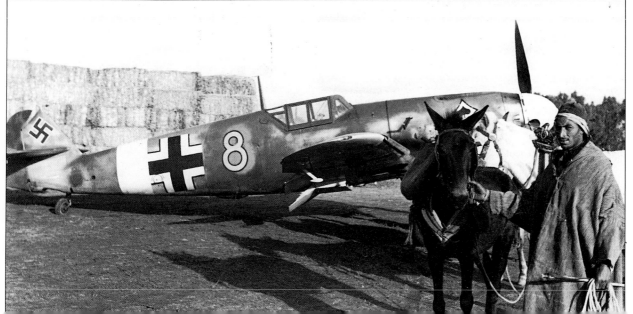

Left: In November 1942 Bf 109G-1s were deployed from France to North Africa to provide high-altitude defence. This aircraft is seen serving with 3./JG 53 in Tunisia in early 1943, having been transferred from 11./JG 2. Note the silica pellets slotted into the sandwich of the canopy glazing.

Expert pair

One of JG 53's stars, Oberleutnant Wolfgang Tonne was Kapitän of 3. Staffel when he arrived in Tunisia, with 101 kills on the Russian front already to his credit. Flying this Bf 109G-4, Tonne shot down another 21 aircraft in the desert before succumbing on 20 April 1943, killed trying to land his badly damaged aircraft.

The other half of a unique pair, Leutnant Wilhelm Crinius was Tonne's wingman and he, too, was a 'centurion' from Russia. After 14 more kills in Tunisia in this Bf 109G-2/Trop 'Kanonenboote' (with Rüstsatz-1 MG 151/20 installation), he himself was killed on 14 January 1943, shot down by a Spitfire while flying as a passenger in a transport aircraft.

A Bf 109G-2 of II./JG 54 is seen at rest on an airfield in northern Russia. Luftwaffe pilots on the Russian front led a somewhat nomadic existence, living in and operating from tents for much of the time, moving forward (and then retreating) through a series of grass airfields with no facilities. A large ground transport effort was required to move the accommodation, equipment, spares and supplies necessary to keep the aircraft flying.

Cabin pressurisation was provided by the expedient means of sealing the original Bf 109 cockpit enclosure without major redesign. The fore and aft bulkheads, walls and floor were all sealed, while the canopy and windshield incorporated rubber seals. The lower quarterlights which had characterised the earlier models were dispensed with, while the canopy had strengthened framing. The glazing was made of a sandwich, which incorporated a silica pellet to dry the air between the layers. The result was a pressure cabin able to withstand 4.4 lb/sq ft of overpressure. To further aid high-altitude operations, Bf 109Gs were built with provision for the GM-1 boost system from the outset,

Two views show the development aircraft for the Bf 109G-2/R1. This aircraft appears to be a G-1 airframe: it has the cockpit scoop and silica pellets in the cockpit glazing.

although this added yet more weight. The GM-1 system did provide welcome extra power at altitude, and the capacity of 115 litres (25.3 Imp gal) allowed its continued use for about 50 minutes.

Construction of the first pre-production batch of three Bf 109G-0s was undertaken at Regensurg in October 1941, but the DB 605A was not yet available. Accordingly, the G-0s were powered by the DB 601E, albeit with the G's revised cowling (minus the four small airscoops). The first production Bf 109G-1s introduced the DB 605A, and they began to leave the factories in the late spring of 1942, in parallel with the Bf 109G-2, which differed only by having the pressurisation equipment and GM-1 provision deleted. To confuse students of the Bf 109, many G-2s were built with some, or all, of the external airscoops which were associated with the G-1's pressurisation system. Identification between Fs and the early Gs is readily possible thanks to the heavier cockpit framing, deletion of quarterlights, the adoption of a deeper oil cooler bath and the addition of two small airscoops on either side the cowling just aft of the propeller.

'Gustav' enters service

Owing to its simpler construction, it was the Bf 109G-2 which entered service first, initial examples reaching the front line in June 1942. The G-1 was not far behind, being dispatched initially to JG 2, and then to JG 26, the two units which remained in the west facing the RAF across the Channel. Both Geschwaders established an 11. Staffel as a dedicated high-altitude unit. 11./JG 2 and 11./JG 26 both

Four-legged Messerschmitt

Under the designation FiSk 199, the Fieseler works modified a Bf 109G to an experimental long-range fighter-bomber configuration (Jabo-Rei). Quite apart from the problem of providing sufficient clearance for the underfuselage bomb, the FiSk 199, with two 300-litre tanks under the wings, was also extremely heavy. It is thought that 10 Bf 109G-2/R1s were built.

Left: After take-off, the extra undercarriage leg's usefulness had ended, and it was jettisoned. A chute was deployed to slow its return to earth, allowing it to be used again.

numbered a few Bf 109G-1/R2s in their complement, this Rüstzustand covering aircraft specially lightened for high-altitude work. The factory-undertaken modifications included deletion of unnecessary equipment and some armour, and fitment of GM-1. The two high-altitude Staffeln were transferred to the Mediterranean in November 1942, resulting in G-1s being subsequently reassigned to JGs 51 and 53 (and probably fitted with tropical filters), while JGs 1 and 5 also received the type. Rüstsätze noted on Bf 109G-1s were R3 (300-litre/65-Imp gal centreline tank) and R6 (gondola-mounted MG 151/20s).

Unpressurised fighter

The unpressurised Bf 109G-2 was built in much larger numbers, and was soon in evidence in all theatres, notably on the Russian front where the first examples arrived in June 1942. Two Rüstzustände were applied to this variant: the R1 and R2. One of the more unusual test programmes concerning the Bf 109 was that undertaken by Fieseler to provide a Jabo-Rei (Jagdbomber mit vergrösserter Reichweit – extended-range fighter-bomber) version of the Bf 109G-2. Quite apart from supporting the overload weight of 4080 kg (8,995 lb), the main problem was providing sufficient ground clearance for the carriage of the intended weapon: a single SC 500 500-kg (1,102-lb) bomb. The solution was an auxiliary undercarriage leg mounted halfway along the rear fuselage. Attached behind the fuel tank, the auxiliary leg was attached with explosive bolts, and after take-off was jettisoned by the pilot. The leg fell to earth

under a parachute for reuse. A single G-2 was modified by Skoda to the new design, being designated the Bf 109G-2/R1 or FiSk 199 (the latter being the Fieseler/Skoda designation). In addition to the extra leg, the FiSk 199 had strongpoints incorporated in the inner wings for the carriage of two 300-litre (66-Imp gal) drop tanks. Trials were successful, but the idea was not taken any further.

The second Rüstzustand was far more conservative, concerning the provision of aircraft for tactical reconnaissance. The Bf 109G-2/R2 had a similar camera installation to that in the F-4, but could change between camera fits. GM-1 was fitted as a matter of course.

Against the Spitfire Mk V, the Bf 109G-2 maintained some of the F's ascendancy in diving and climbing. Initially, the G retained the Bf 109's traditional advantage of being able to bunt away from a pursuing Spitfire, which still did

In summer the frozen ground rapidly turned to mud, proving as much of a hindrance to operations as the snow, with wheel-clogging becoming a real problem. In the summer of 1942 the Germans continued their push east, led by Bf 109s such as this G-2 of II./JG 54.

Above: These Bf 109G-2s are from the II. Gruppe (left) and Geschwaderstab (adjutant's aircraft, right) of Jagdgeschwader 54 'Grünherz'.

Left: The Bf 109G-4 differed only in minor detail from the G-2, the principal improvement being the adoption of FuG 16Z radio, externally distinguished by having the vertical wire on the radio antenna moved aft. Seen in Russia, these aircraft are from III./JG 3 'Udet', the aircraft in the foreground being assigned to the Gruppenkommandeur.

Eastern colours

This Bf 109G-6 was on the strength of IV./JG 5, based at Petsamo in the winter of 1943/44. The fourth Gruppe employed a spot as its badge behind the Balkankreuz. The aircraft sported an unusual winter dapple finish, applied over dark green, this proving very effective over the forested northern sector of the Russian front.

Sporting a garish summer camouflage, this is a Bf 109G-2 of II./JG 54 'Grünherz' at Siverskaya in 1942. JG 54 was heavily involved in the fighting in Russia, serving under Luftflotte I on the northern sector. Tans and greens were found to be highly effective camouflage, but the effect was somewhat ruined by the yellow theatre bands, cowling underside and wingtips.

A Bf 109G-2, probably of I./JG 77, rests on a Tunisian airfield in the spring of 1943, next to the remains of another G-2 and a Ju 52. In the background three Ju 52s can be seen arriving from Sicily. At this time, with the Allies closing in on the Germans in Tunisia, the perilous air bridge from Sicily was the only means of keeping the German forces supplied. In addition to fighting the massed Allied air forces supporting the land push, Bf 109s were heavily involved in attempting to escort the vulnerable transports.

Right: This Bf 109G-2/Trop was operated by 2.(H)/14, a reconnaissance unit. It was shot down in Tunisia on 7 April 1943.

Below: Pilots of 4./JG 53 are seen during a March 1943 'Alarmstart' in Tunisia. 'White 4' was the aircraft of Oberleutnant Fritz Dinger, who scored 67 kills.

not have a negative-*g* carburettor. The ability to employ the GM-1 boost in difficult circumstances saved the neck of many a Jagdflieger.

With the DB 605A, the Bf 109G-2 was slightly faster than the F-4 at high altitude, reaching 640 km/h (398 mph) at 6300 m (20,670 ft), compared with 624 km/h (388 mph) for the 'Friedrich'. At low altitude the F-4 was actually marginally quicker, the G gaining the ascendancy at about 1500 m (4,920 ft). Climb rate was also improved. However, normal loaded weight was raised from 2900 kg (6,393 lb) to 3100 kg (6,834 lb), and would grow even more as the G series developed.

Early 'Gustavs' were subjects of several test programmes, including the fitment of Messerschmitt-designed P6 variable-pitch propellers (Bf 109G-2/U1). A G-2/R2 photo-reconnaissance aircraft was flown with a Waffen-tropfen (WT) 17 pod underneath, containing two aft-firing MG 17 7.92-mm machine-guns. The WT 17 added too much weight and drag for service adoption.

Refined 'Gustav'

Chronologically, the next 'Gustav' variant was the G-4, which began to roll from the lines in October 1942. Like the G-2, it was an unpressurised multi-role fighter built in large numbers and equipping many units. Differences between it and its predecessor were small, the main one being the installation of a FuG 16Z radio in place of the FuG VIIa, with a resultant subtle change in antenna configuration. Early in the G-4 production run, larger main-wheels were introduced (as a result of the increasing weight of the 'Gustav'), which in turn led to the addition of bulges on the top of the wings. These bulges are believed to be the inspiration for the nickname 'Beule' ('bump') which stuck with the Bf 109G throughout its life, although it has

A Bf 109G comes in to land at a Tunisian airfield. It carries two Rüstätze modifications, the R3 centreline tank and the R6 MG 151/20 cannon pods. The latter were handed, and not interchangeable between wings. Visible are the case ejector chutes, which always faced towards the fuselage.

also been attributed to the gun fairings of the G-6. Not all G-4s had the wheel bulges, while several later and rewinged G-2s did. Like its immediate predecessor, the G-4 was regularly seen with Rüstsatz 3 fuel tanks and R6 wing gondolas, although some had the R1 and R2 bomb racks fitted.

Many G-4s were issued to reconnaissance units, some as Bf 109G-4/U3s with MW-50 water-methanol boosting. A specialist reconnaissance variant was the Bf 109G-4/R3, which was a long-range sub-variant with racks for two 300-litre tanks under the wings and a single Rb 50/30 or Rb 75/30 camera in the rear fuselage. The MG 17 machine-guns were removed and the muzzle troughs faired over. At least one G-4 was given a trials installation of three MG 151/20 cannon gondolas, with one mounted on the centreline.

Early Gs were sent to the Eastern Front, where they maintained the ascendancy established by the 'Friedrichs' a year before. However, on the ground the Wehrmacht was suffering and the advance into Russia stumbled to a halt at Stalingrad. Despite the best efforts of the Jagdflieger, the inevitable came on 2 February when the encircled 6th Army surrendered to the Soviets. The last fighter aircraft (Bf 109G-2s of JG 3) had left the Stalingrad pocket a few days earlier. Just as the Red army was finding success on the ground, so the VVS was clawing back the initiative in the air. By late 1942 the Yak-7 and Yak-9 fighters were beginning to make their presence felt, especially against the less experienced of the Luftwaffe pilots. Losses began to mount, but still the leading *experten* added to their scores. Among the new pilots finding their feet was the young Erich Hartmann of JG 52, who scored his first kill in November.

Bf 109G-6

The G-6 quickly followed the early variants on the production line, and remained in production until the end of 1944. More than 12,000 aircraft were built, although the last aircraft differed considerably from the first. All, however, featured 13-mm MG 131 machine-guns in place of the 7.92-mm MG 17s of earlier Bf 109s. These guns could not be fitted into the confines of the existing cowling, requiring bulged fairings just forward of the cockpit to house the spent belt chutes.

Sizeable numbers of both G-2s and G-4s were built as Trops, with dust filter and umbrella stand. The latter was vital to give the pilots some protection from the sun when sitting at cockpit alert, and consisted of two small metal attachments below the port cockpit rail. G-2/Trops appeared in North Africa at the end of June 1942, and G-4/Trops soon after. They were widespread by the time the momentous battle of El Alamein began on 23 October, although many aircraft were lost during the retreat which followed.

Some time after the G-4 had appeared, the Bf 109G-3 entered service, in March 1943. This was a high-altitude pressurised fighter like the G-1, but featured the improvements of the G-4. Only 50 were built, serving at first with the specialist high-altitude units 11./JG 2 and 11./JG 26, although later noted in use with JG 1 and 11./JG 54. The only sub-variant noted was the Bf 109G-3/U2, which had a GM-1 system that could be used for 20 minutes.

G-6 – the definitive variant

By mid-1942 the Bf 109G was being asked to perform an ever-increasing number of differing missions – no longer was it a pure fighter. To cater for this diversity of role without major disruption to the production lines, Messerschmitt

Bottom left: This Bf 109G-6 'Kanonenboote' is from the Gruppenstab of I./JG 27, wearing the chevron/triangle marking of the Gruppenkommendeur himself. Aircraft assigned to schwarm (a four-ship) leaders usually had white rudders. As well as R6 cannons, it appears to have Rüstsatz-1 for the carriage of a centreline bomb.

Left: A close-up of the cowling shows the bulged cowling fairings that characterised the Bf 109G-6. Also visible are the 'Beule' fairings on top of the wings, introduced in 1942 by late G-2s and early G-4s.

Below: A group of Bf 109G-6s undergo final checks outside the factory before delivery to the front. Most, if not all, have the Rüstsatz-6 underwing cannon installation.

Bf 109 colours

Luftwaffe

As Bf 109F production was gearing up in 1941, Messerschmitt produced an official painting guide to incorporate camouflage experience gained in the war's early campaigns. This plan served as the basis for painting the G series from March 1942. By mid-1944, the more defensive nature of the air war and the need to optimise use of manpower and materials led to a new range of grey, green and violet shades and much less consistency in colour and markings application.

The white nose, fuselage band and wingtips were a Mediterranean theatre marking first introduced by I./JG 27 on its arrival in Libya in 1941. The normal marking for a Gruppenkommandeur was a double chevron, but the holder of that office in II./JG 27 during late 1941 sported a triple device on his Bf 109F-4, with the addition of a small tactical number. Such obvious displays of a pilot's rank were outlawed later in the war as they made it easier for the enemy to identify and eliminate the most experienced pilots in a formation.

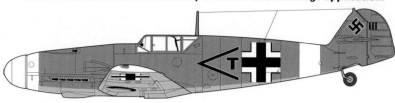

Unlike Bf 109Es in the North African theatre, Bf 109Fs and Gs were not given a topside heavy green mottle on delivery to the front. For the most part, they operated in factory-standard sand-yellow (Sandgelb) 79 over light blue (Hellblau) 78, although later deliveries were often in European theatre colours. On this Bf 109F-4/Z the 'T' within the chevron – indicating the Gruppe technical officer – was a non-regulation marking of a type common to JG 27. Normally this would be '< (chevron) IO' to the left of the fuselage cross.

Another unit in the Mediterranean to use non-standard patterns was II./JG 53 on Sicily in early 1942. This aircraft belonging to 5. Staffel had the basic 79/78 colours oversprayed with a pattern of dark green (Dunkelgrün) 71. Other aircraft of this unit had variations of this, some with a hard-edged application of 71 and others with a mottle blurring the demarcation between upper and lower surface colours.

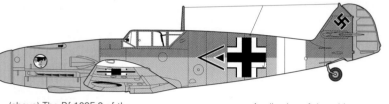

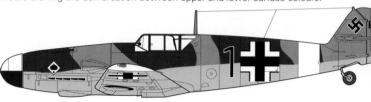

(above) The Bf 109F-2 of the I./JG 27 Gruppenkommandeur during late 1941 featured the higher fuselage colour demarcation common to later batches of 109F Trops. The yellow nose and rudder markings were a hangover from the Balkan campaign seen on desert-camouflaged Bf 109s only during 1941.

Application of the white wingtip markings varied greatly. It could be found above and below both wingtips, on the undersides only or not at all. Otherwise, upper surface colours varied little in North Africa. An exception is the 'scribble' pattern seen below which extended over the wings.

The Bf 109G-4 Trop of the Gruppenadjutant of I./JG 77 in southern Tunisia in early 1943 had 79 topsides with a mottle of olive green (Olivgrün) 80. The yellow panels under the nose remained on many Bf 109s in the theatre long after the full yellow nose marking was discarded.

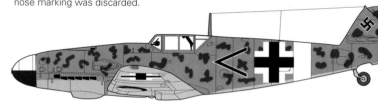

While the basic desert colour schemes on I./JG 27 Bf 109s generally conformed with regulation, local conditions in other parts of the Mediterranean led to variations such as this 'scribble' overspray of dark green (Dunkelgrün) 71 seen on this Bf 109G-2/Trop of 2./JG 77 in Tunisia 1943. The pattern was similar to those seen on Regia Aeronautica fighters and it is believed that the Italians supplied the paints for the first Luftwaffe fighters in the theatre. The sand yellow (Sandgelb) 79 on later fighters was a notably darker shade than that seen initially.

The standard grey camouflage pattern for the Bf 109F (and carried over to the G) was promulgated in August 1941. The colours were Graugrün (grey-green) 74, Grauviolett (grey-violet) 75 and Hellblau (light blue) 76. Although the colour separations appear hard, an overspray of 19 mm (0.75 in) was specified.

At the beginning of 1944, the RLM specified the use of a simplified form of national insignia consisting of an outline only – black against light-coloured aircraft undersides and white against dark backgrounds. Where a white cross was to be placed over a light area, the interior was to be filled with the darker camouflage. In practice, these rules were often not followed to the letter as seen on this example.

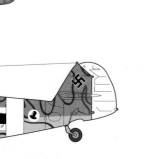

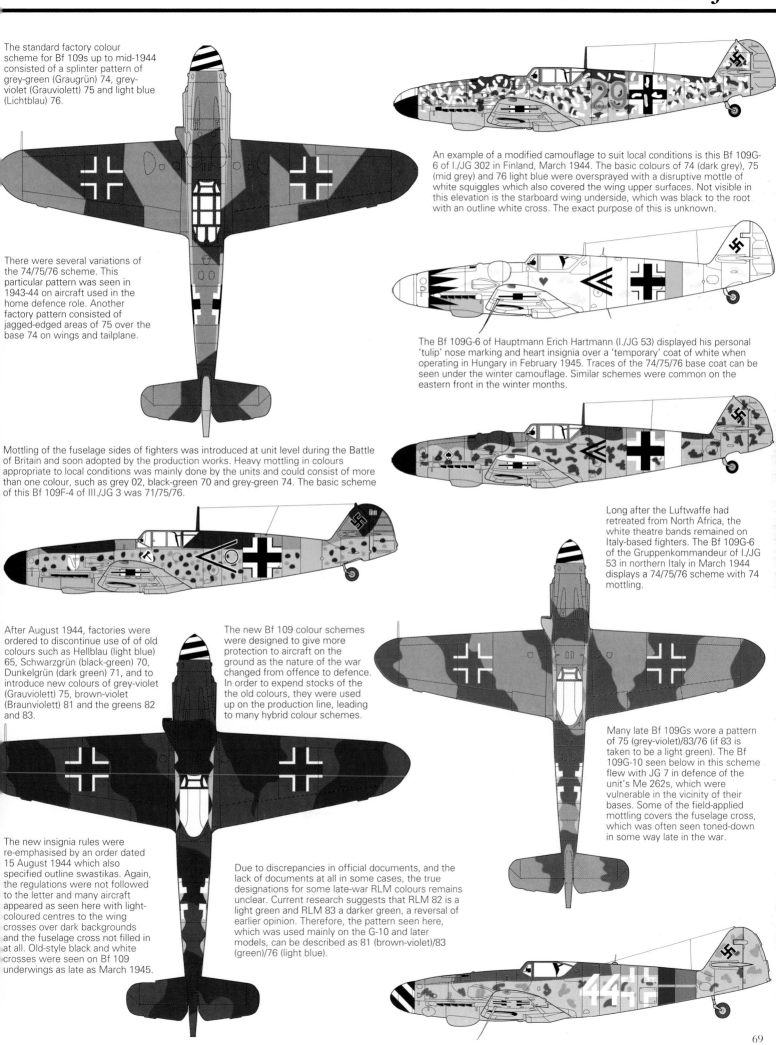

The standard factory colour scheme for Bf 109s up to mid-1944 consisted of a splinter pattern of grey-green (Graugrün) 74, grey-violet (Grauviolett) 75 and light blue (Lichtblau) 76.

An example of a modified camouflage to suit local conditions is this Bf 109G-6 of I./JG 302 in Finland, March 1944. The basic colours of 74 (dark grey), 75 (mid grey) and 76 light blue were oversprayed with a disruptive mottle of white squiggles which also covered the wing upper surfaces. Not visible in this elevation is the starboard wing underside, which was black to the root with an outline white cross. The exact purpose of this is unknown.

There were several variations of the 74/75/76 scheme. This particular pattern was seen in 1943-44 on aircraft used in the home defence role. Another factory pattern consisted of jagged-edged areas of 75 over the base 74 on wings and tailplane.

The Bf 109G-6 of Hauptmann Erich Hartmann (I./JG 53) displayed his personal 'tulip' nose marking and heart insignia over a 'temporary' coat of white when operating in Hungary in February 1945. Traces of the 74/75/76 base coat can be seen under the winter camouflage. Similar schemes were common on the eastern front in the winter months.

Mottling of the fuselage sides of fighters was introduced at unit level during the Battle of Britain and soon adopted by the production works. Heavy mottling in colours appropriate to local conditions was mainly done by the units and could consist of more than one colour, such as grey 02, black-green 70 and grey-green 74. The basic scheme of this Bf 109F-4 of III./JG 3 was 71/75/76.

Long after the Luftwaffe had retreated from North Africa, the white theatre bands remained on Italy-based fighters. The Bf 109G-6 of the Gruppenkommandeur of I./JG 53 in northern Italy in March 1944 displays a 74/75/76 scheme with 74 mottling.

After August 1944, factories were ordered to discontinue use of of old colours such as Hellblau (light blue) 65, Schwarzgrün (black-green) 70, Dunkelgrün (dark green) 71, and to introduce new colours of grey-violet (Grauviolett) 75, brown-violet (Braunviolett) 81 and the greens 82 and 83.

The new Bf 109 colour schemes were designed to give more protection to aircraft on the ground as the nature of the war changed from offence to defence. In order to expend stocks of the old colours, they were used up on the production line, leading to many hybrid colour schemes.

Many late Bf 109Gs wore a pattern of 75 (grey-violet)/83/76 (if 83 is taken to be a light green). The Bf 109G-10 seen below in this scheme flew with JG 7 in defence of the unit's Me 262s, which were vulnerable in the vicinity of their bases. Some of the field-applied mottling covers the fuselage cross, which was often seen toned-down in some way late in the war.

The new insignia rules were re-emphasised by an order dated 15 August 1944 which also specified outline swastikas. Again, the regulations were not followed to the letter and many aircraft appeared as seen here with light-coloured centres to the wing crosses over dark backgrounds and the fuselage cross not filled in at all. Old-style black and white crosses were seen on Bf 109 underwings as late as March 1945.

Due to discrepancies in official documents, and the lack of documents at all in some cases, the true designations for some late-war RLM colours remains unclear. Current research suggests that RLM 82 is a light green and RLM 83 a darker green, a reversal of earlier opinion. Therefore, the pattern seen here, which was used mainly on the G-10 and later models, can be described as 81 (brown-violet)/83 (green)/76 (light blue).

Origins of the 'Kurfürst'

Established by the Reichskriegsministerium on 1 March 1944, the Jägerstab (Fighter Staff) Otto Saur aimed to boost fighter output in the wake of Allied bombing attacks in the late au 1943, which had set back Bf 109 final assembly at a critical time. The aim was to facilitate t release of materials, components and sub-assemblies that had accumulated in the wake of raids, removing 'obstacles' in the production system by improving the movement of compo between the dispersed plants. Saur had the full backing of the Minister of Armaments and v answerable to the Führer, and though the Jägerstab's methods were unsavoury – plant mar were threatened with arrest and worse – it did manage to increase production rates (though control, parts interchangeability and the supply of spare parts all suffered).

A by-product of the Jägerstab's efforts was a new basic model, the Bf 109K (nicknamed 'Kurfürst'), introduced with the aim of standardising, and thereby streamlining, production. T Bf 109K embodied many of the changes introduced in successive variants of the Bf 109G, t examples appearing in service during October 1944. These were Bf 109K-4 aircraft, pressur aircraft based on the planned, but unbuilt, K-2 fighter. In the event, the entire K-4 production amounted to, at the most, 1,700 aircraft, though some sources suggest as few as 754 were

Identifying features

Several features of the Bf 109K-4's airframe had been carried over from late-production 'Gustavs'. These included rectangular upper wing surface bulges to accommodate wider, low-pressure main gear tyres (fitted to improve ground handling), a bulged DB 605D series sump cover (below the leading exhaust nozzle) and the FuG 16ZY radio aerial under the port wing. The rudder usually had a Flettner tab and two fixed trim tabs (to obviate the need for rudder applications when diving and climbing), although some aircraft did not have the fixed tabs.

Unique to the K-4 were a relocated DF loop, a refined lower engine cowling design, a relocated access fuselage hatch, a taller, retractable rear wheel and additional main gear wheel well doors (often removed in the field). Fixed aileron trim tabs were also a feature of the K-4; a few aircraft were also equipped with hinged Flettner aileron tabs.

Engine and propeller

Bf 109K-0 pre-production aircraft and the first K-4s were powered by the DB 605DB variant of Daimler-Benz's inverted-Vee, 12-cylinder, liquid-cooled DB 605. (The DB 605D series was derived from the 605A, featuring a larger supercharger derived from that designed for the DB 603 engine.) Later machines utilised the DB 605DC (referred to in some sources as the 605DM or 605DCM), differing from the 605DB in having a higher maximum supercharger boost pressure and being strengthened accordingly. It was this that resulted in the different designation, something that some sources have incorrectly attributed to the octane of fuel used. The higher boost pressure allowed maximum power output to be attained while using lower-octane fuel, a valuable feature as shortages of first-rate fuel worsened as the war continued.

Like its predecessors, the Bf 109K-4 also used MW-50 (methanol-water) injection to boost power, but only when the engine was running on lower-octane fuel. The DB 605 powered a wide-bladed VDM9-12159A propeller with a 3-m diameter and used fuel that was held in a 400-litre tank located behind the pilot. A Rüstsätze kit (R3) was applied to some aircraft to improve range, with a 300-litre drop tank suspended under the fuselage.

The projected K-14 variant would have been powered by a DB 605L, which boasted a two-stage supercharger and a 40 per cent power increase. It had been assumed that this engine was built in only limited numbers after production of the K-14 was cancelled in November 1944. However, there have been suggestions by some researchers that the 605L may have found its way into Bf 109K-4s during the last month of production, March 1945.

Bf 109K deployment

As well as the various Jagdgeschwader to which the K-4 was issued, a number of other units flew the type. Several Kampfgeschwader were redesignated KG (Jagd) units in the autumn of 1944, and their pilots retrained for fighter operations. A few K-4s were assigned to these units from 1 January 1945 and saw some action against Allied fighters in the closing months of the war.

One Nachtjagdgeschwader (NJG) night-fighter unit, I./NJG 11, supplemented its Bf 109Gs with a few K-4s, while some aircraft also appeared with training units, including JG 110. By the time Germany capitulated, the Luftwaffe had about 800 Bf 109s still on strength, split almost 50/50 between Bf 109Gs and K models. Perhaps the last unit to receive the K-4 was Sonderkommando Elbe, the bomber ramming unit established in February 1945. Its only recorded operation took place on 7 April, in which Bf 109Ks are known to have participated.

In addition, a very small number of K-4s were made available to the Italian Aviazione Nazionale Repubblicana and were employed from airfields in northern Italy from the beginning of April 1945.

Messerschmitt Bf 109K-4
III. Gruppe/Jagdgeschwader 27
Defence of the Reich
Prague-Ruzyne, 1945

Reconnaissance variants

Among the Rüstsätze (retrofit) kits planned for the K-4 were three which gave the type a reconnaissance capability, the R2, R5 and R6. The R2 was to carry an Rb 50/30 or Rb 70/30 vertical camera behind the cockpit, the R5 an Rb 32/7x9 or Rb 12/7x9 and the R6 a BSK 16 gun camera in the port wing leading edge for bomber and fighter-bomber units.

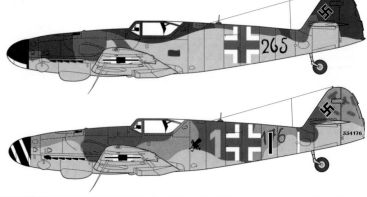

After a directive issued in August 1944 that forbade the use of four-letter factory codes, the last three digits of the Werk Nummer were frequently sprayed on the rear fuselage of Bf 109s as a 'book-keeping' measure. This Bf 109K-4 captured at Amberg, Germany has a non-standard pattern of 81/82 on the fuselage and a quartered (rather than spiral) spinner.

A variation on the 75/83/76 scheme more commonly seen on Bf 109G-14s is that shown here, the main difference being the distribution of colour on the fuselage spine. The actual hue of the late-war colours such as light green (83) and Braunviolett (81) varied greatly. Dispersed production and absence of explicit colour descriptions from the RLM led to much variation in these colours, which also suffered from staining, fading and wear in service, which especially effected 83 light green.

Below right: This Bf 109K-4 of 11./JG 53 in April 1945 wears 82/75/76. This was not a standard combination, but mixing of the older colours such as 75 with the new late-war greens was not unusual.

Foreign users

The allies of Germany that received late-model Bf 109s during the war took delivery of the aircraft in the camouflage specified for Luftwaffe aircraft of the time of manufacture. The majority of Bf 109s remained that way, with the addition of new national insignia, although some aircraft were later repainted in locally-devised schemes. Those aircraft fighting against Russian forces adopted the yellow theatre-identification markings worn by Luftwaffe aircraft. Post-war Messerschmitt operators tended to use whatever paints came to hand as the basis for their schemes.

Czechoslovakia
The S-99s (Czech-built Bf 109G-14) of the National Air Guard were predominantly light blue 76 (or possibly even an older colour such as 65), with red undersurfaces and nose.

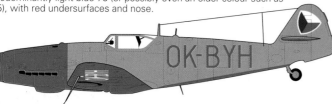

In Czech air force service, the Mezec was usually painted in overall dark green (probably an RLM colour). Note the circular (rather than lozenge-shaped) insignia used by the regular air force.

Finland
Most Finnish Bf 109s appeared in standard Luftwaffe schemes such as this 74/75/76 pattern. Some aircraft wore a locally-devised green/black/light blue scheme. The background to the *hakaristi* (swastika) was white or light grey.

From 1945, the Finns adopted the blue/white roundel and removed the Axis yellow theatre markings used in the Continuation War. Both spiral and quartered spinners were seen on Ilmavoimat Bf 109s.

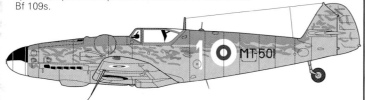

Hungary
The first batch of 80 Hungarian Bf 109Gs was numbered from V-310. Swastikas were uncommon on HAF aircraft, and this G-6 of 5/2 Fighter Squadron in 1943 has had the marking partly removed.

Israel
IAF Avias wore the same blue as used on Czech aircraft. The red/white rudder was the 101 Squadron marking and the black/white band was a recognition for all Israeli fighters in the 1948 war.
The code translates from Hebrew as 'D120'.

Italy Aviazione Nazionale Repubblicana
The ANR adopted a yellow-bordered Italian flag as its insignia, although the German Balkankreuze was often worn under the wings as an additional recognition marking, as seen on this Bf 109G-10.

Spain
Spanish HA-1112-M1Ls wore an overall coat of blue (similar to FS 35050) in the early part of their service. The area affected by exhaust staining was painted black.

Switzerland
The red and white neutrality markings adopted in mid-September 1944 were applied over the base camouflage, which varied considerably between aircraft. Some Gs wore the markings as late as the end of 1945.

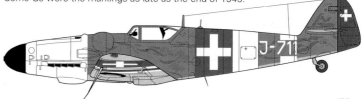

Bf 109 details

The aileron had a horn balance mounted underneath. Bf 109Ks introduced an aileron tab but this was usually locked in the neutral position.

Right: The direction-finding loop of the G-6 and later variants served the Peilrufanlage navigation aid. Some aircraft dispensed with the radio mast, the antenna passing through the loop.

The WGr 21 air-launched mortar installation consisted of a simple launch tube braced to the wing.

This is the late-standard tall wooden fin, as seen on Hans Dittes's Bf 109G/Buchón.

Bf 109G-14 cutaway

1 Starboard navigation light
2 Starboard wingtip
3 Fixed trim tab
4 Starboard Frise-type aileron
5 Flush-rivetted stressed wing skinning
6 Handley Page automatic leading-edge slot
7 Slot control linkage
8 Slot equaliser rod
9 Aileron control linkage
10 Fabric-covered flap section
11 Wheel fairing
12 Port fuselage machine-gun ammunition feed fairing
13 Port 13-mm Rheinmetall-Borsig MG 131 machine-gun
14 Engine accessories
15 Starboard machine-gun trough
16 Daimler-Benz DB 605AM 12-cylinder inverted-Vee liquid-cooled engine
17 Detachable cowling panel
18 Oil filter access
19 Oil tank
20 Propeller pitch-change mechanism
21 VDM electrically-operated constant-speed propeller
22 Spinner
23 Engine-mounted cannon muzzle
24 Blast tube
25 Propeller hub
26 Spinner back plate
27 Auxiliary cooling intakes
28 Coolant header tank
29 Anti-vibration rubber engine mounting pads
30 Elektron forged engine bearer
31 Engine bearer support strut attachment
32 Plug leads
33 Exhaust manifold fairing strip
34 Ejector exhausts
35 Cowling fasteners
36 Oil cooler
37 Oil cooler intake
38 Starboard mainwheel
39 Oil cooler outlet flap
40 Wingroot fillet
41 Wing/fuselage fairing
42 Firewall/bulkhead
43 Supercharger air intake
44 Supercharger assembly
45 20-mm cannon magazine drum
46 13-mm machine-gun ammunition feed
47 Engine bearer upper attachment
48 Ammunition feed fairing
49 13-mm Rheinmetall-Borsig MG 131 machine-gun breeches
50 Instrument panel
51 20-mm Mauser MG 151/20 cannon breech
52 Heelrests
53 Rudder pedals
54 Undercarriage emergency retraction cables
55 Fuselage frame
56 Wing/fuselage fairing
57 Undercarriage emergency retraction handwheel (outboard)
58 Tail trim handwheel (inboard)
59 Seat harness
60 Throttle lever
61 Control column
62 Cockpit ventilation inlet
63 Revi 16B reflector gunsight (folding)
64 Armoured windshield frame
65 Anti-glare gunsight screen
66 90-mm armourglass windscreen
67 Erla-Haube clear-vision hinged canopy
68 Galland-Panzer framed armourglass head/back panel
69 Canopy contoured frame
70 Canopy hinges (starboard)
71 Canopy release catch
72 Pilot's bucket-type seat (8-mm back armour)
73 Underfloor contoured fuel tank (400 litres/88 Imp gal of 87 octane B4)
74 Fuselage frame
75 Circular access panel
76 Tail trimming cable conduit
77 Wireless leads
78 MW-50 (methanol/water) tank (114-litre/25-Imp gal capacity)
79 Handhold
80 Fuselage decking
81 Aerial mast
82 D/F loop
83 Oxygen cylinders (three)

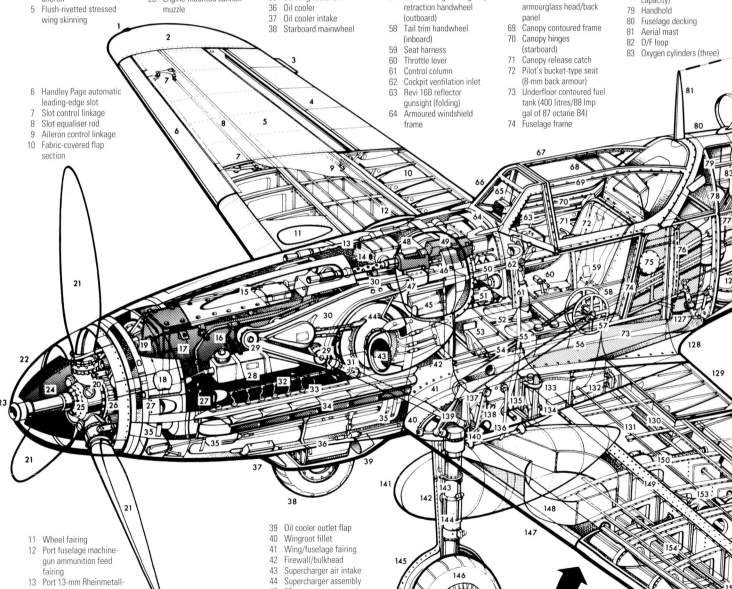

© Aerospace Publishing Ltd

Iain Wyllie

off the
vember,
ing,
ven

and by

that no

luding
ype.

O were minimal,
ariant is hard to
Allies until after
in exactly which
t a distinction
more
the war had
d alongside the

made up an
ts cockpit was
ly applied
gain due to
ottle was

h MW-50
Allied types. Its
craft of superior
y controls' (and
matched for
t that was
Spitfire Mk XIV,
ed by the MW-

bility advantage,
nost cases, a

Colour scheme and markings

This Bf 109K-4 was finished in the RLM 81/82/76 colours
common on Bf 109G-10s. The actual hue of these colours
varied considerably depending on which factory supplied
the paint and which applied it to the aircraft. This was
especially true of the wooden rudders and other tail
components which were manufactured and painted as
sub-assemblies in furniture factories. Age and weathering
also affected the shade.

In particular, the RLM 82 mittelgrün (medium green)
could range from a flat mid-green to a bright almost apple
green, and the RLM 81 braunviolett from brownish-green
to a colour closer to violet, as the German name implies.
A mottled overspray was applied in the field to reduce the
contrast between the wing and upper fuselage and the
pale blue-grey (RLM 76) fuselage sides. The higher
contrast on the fin and rudder is the result of application
by brush or by sponge (rather than sprayed), as well as
the different paint sources mentioned above.

A directive at the beginning of 1944 officially
eliminated black from the fuselage and upper wing
balkenkreuz, substituting the darker of the two
camouflage colours. On the lower surfaces, the
balkenkreuz was to consist of just the white right-angled
portions. The tail swastika was to be displayed in black,
without the white outline, or a white outline only.
However, in reality there were many variations; for
example, most K-4s had a standard black-and-white
swastika, as seen on this aircraft.

Defence of the Reich identification bands
(*Reichsverteidgungsband*) had appeared on day fighters
at the end of 1944. Their use was confirmed by a general
order dated 20 February 1945. The specified width was
900 mm (2 ft 11.5 in) although this varied greatly in
practice. JG 27 used RLM 25 (bright green), over which a
Gruppe marking was often applied, in this case the black
'vertical line' of III. Gruppe.

Proposed K model variants

Though Bf 109K production appears to have been
confined to the K-4, a number of other variants were
planned, as follows:

K-1	initial production variant, based on Bf 109G to latest mod. standard, with DB 605D engine, pressurised cabin, MK 108 engine-mounted cannon; cancelled after MK 108 production delays
K-2	to replace K-1, plans to build K-2/R3 with MG 151/20 cannon and DB 605A engine were drawn up; a small number may have been built; only one 'true' K-2 known to have been completed
K-3	DB 605AS-powered, pressurised variant with MK 108 cannon; cancelled after decision taken to concentrate on K-4
K-6	'bomber destroyer' variant of K-4 with an additional MK 108 in each wing; one prototype trialled
K-8	reconnaissance variant to replace Bf 109G-8; intended to have DB 605L engine, Rb 50/30 vertical camera behind cockpit; armament probably engine-mounted MK 103 or MG 151/20, with MK 108s in wings; believed cancelled after problems with MK 103 installation
K-10	K-4 with engine-mounted MK 103 in place of MK 108; cancelled
K-14	high-altitude fighter with DB 605L engine and four-bladed propeller, three MK 108 cannon and two MG 131 machine-guns; failed to proceed past prototype stage (though 605L believed to have been fitted to a few production K-4s)

Gruppe III./Jagdgeschwader 27

III./JG 77 and III./JG 27 were the first units to re-equip with the Bf 109K-4s, the first of which came
production line in August 1944. The first recorded combat engagement involving K-4s came on 2 N
when JG 27 engaged Allied fighters escorting a large bomber force near Leipzig. In the ensuing fig
JG 27 suffered its worst one-day losses of the war so far – 27 pilots were killed and 11 wounded.
Allied 'kills' were claimed by the unit – all Mustangs.

Later in the month other units received K-4s, including III./JG 3, III./JG 4, III./JG 26 and I./JG 27
1 January 1945, the day of the Luftwaffe's ill-fated Operation Bodenplatte against Allied airfields, th
following Gruppen had also received the variant: II./JG 2, I./JG 4, IV./JG 4 and II./JG 11. It is believe
unit was exclusively equipped with the Bf 109K; a mix of Gs and Ks was the norm.

During January 1945, a number of units equipped with K-4s transferred to the Eastern Front, in
III./JG 27, and during late January and February a number of eastern Gruppen were issued with the

Armament

Bf 109K-4s carried the standard Bf 109G-6 armament of a single,
engine-mounted, Rheinmetall-Borsig 30-mm MK 108 cannon (with
60 rounds) and a pair of Rheinmetall-Borsig MG 131 13-mm
machine-guns above the engine, each with 300 rounds. The
MK 108 was a highly effective weapon, but was prone to jamming
during hard manoeuvring, leaving the aircraft with just two
machine-guns.

As an alternative to the MK 108 (which had suffered reliability
problems during development), the earlier Mauser MG 151/20
20-mm cannon, as fitted to early Bf 109Gs, could be installed, but
this seems not to have been deemed necessary in production K-4s.

The wing of the Bf 109K was built to accommodate not only
Mauser MG 151/20 cannon but, alternatively, two MK 108s using
an internal mount. An anti-bomber variant, the K-6, was to be
equipped to the same standard as a late K-4, but with the addition
of an MK 108 cannon in each wing. The weight penalty was
considerable and handling suffered accordingly. Though prototype
service trials, probably with III./JG 3, were carried out from
February 1945, the K-6 is though not to have entered production.

Various Rüstsätze (retrofit) kits of the type developed for the
Bf 109G could be applied to the K-4. Two of these were related to
the aircraft's armament: R1 was a fighter-bomber modification
allowing the carriage of a 250-kg or 500-kg bomb under the
fuselage, while the R4 allowed the installation of an additional
MG 151/20 under each wing.

'Kurfürst' handling and performance

Differences in performance between the K-4 and the Bf 109G-
though a detailed evaluation of the flying characteristics of the
put together, given that an example was not test flown by the
the war and Luftwaffe pilots appear to have taken little interest
variant they were flying. Log books from the period suggest tha
was made, at least by some pilots, but the latter were probabl
concerned with 'the job in hand' given the desperate stage tha
reached. This was compounded by the fact that Bf 109Ks serv
similar late-build Bf 109Gs.

The K-4 was not an aircraft for the inexperienced pilots tha
increasing proportion of the Luftwaffe's aircrew. Visibility from
poor on the ground and the engine's torque was such that rapi
opposite rudder was vital on take-off. Landing was also tricky,
airscrew torque and the habit of the aircraft to rear up as full th
applied for a 'go round'.

In the air, however, the aircraft was better behaved and, w
injection, gave a reasonable account of itself in combat against
most common adversary was probably the P-51 Mustang, an a
performance in most respects, but one that was prone to 'hea
therefore degraded manoeuvrability) at high speed and could b
speed and climb rate by a K-4 with MW-50 selected. The aircra
perhaps the most feared by K-4 pilots was the Griffon-engined
which could maintain high speeds without the time limits impo
50 system.

On the eastern front, Russian types often had a manoeuvr
but the K-4 was able to counter this with higher speed and, in r
better climb rate.

Above: The Erla-Haube clear-view canopy considerably improved visibility from the cockpit, as did the Galland-Panzer armoured glass backrest and head protection.

Right: The inboard flap section was split in two and acted as a variable ejector for the radiator. The degree to which the two petals opened was controlled by thermostat.

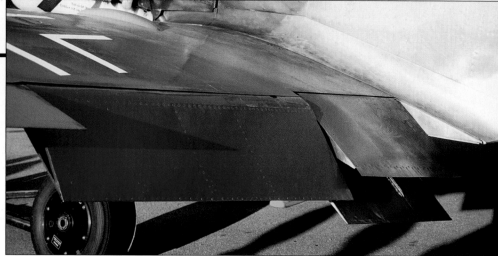

84 Filler pipe
85 Wireless equipment packs (FuG 16ZY communications and FuG 25 IFF)
86 Main fuel filler cap
87 Aerial
88 Fuselage top keel (connector stringer)

95 Starboard fixed tailplane
96 Elevator balance
97 Starboard elevator
98 Geared elevator tab

89 Aerial lead-in
90 Fuselage skin plating sections
91 'U' stringers
92 Fuselage frames (monocoque construction)
93 Tail trimming cables
94 Tailfin root fairing

99 All-wooden tailfin construction
100 Aerial attachment
101 Rudder upper hinge bracket
102 Rudder post
103 Fabric-covered wooden rudder structure
104 Geared rudder tab
105 Rear navigation light
106 Port elevator
107 Elevator geared tab
108 Tailplane structure
109 Rudder actuating linkage
110 Elevator control horn
111 Elevator connecting rod
112 Elevator control quadrant
113 Tailwheel leg cuff
114 Castoring non-retractable tailwheel
115 Lengthened tailwheel leg
116 Access panel
117 Tailwheel shock strut
118 Lifting point
119 Rudder cable
120 Elevator cables
121 First aid pack
122 Air bottles

123 Fuselage access panel
124 Bottom keel (connector stringer)
125 Ventral IFF aerial
126 Master compass
127 Elevator control linkage
128 Wingroot fillet
129 Camber changing flap
130 Ducted coolant radiator
131 Wing stringers
132 Wing rear pick-up point
133 Spar/fuselage upper pin joint (horizontal)
134 Spar/fuselage lower pin joint (vertical)
135 Flap equaliser rod
136 Rüstsatz-3 auxiliary fuel tank ventral rack
137 Undercarriage electrical interlock
138 Wing horizontal pin forward pick-up
139 Undercarriage retraction jack mechanism
140 Undercarriage pivot bevel
141 Auxiliary fuel tank (Rüstsatz-3) of 300-litre (66-Imp gal) capacity
142 Mainwheel leg fairing
143 Mainwheel oleo leg
144 Brake lines
145 Mainwheel fairing
146 Port mainwheel
147 Leading-edge skin
148 Port mainwheel well
149 Wing spar
150 Flap actuating linkage
151 Fabric-covered control surfaces
152 Slotted flap structure
153 Leading-edge slot-actuating mechanism
154 Slot equaliser rod
155 Handley Page automatic leading-edge slot
156 Wing stringers
157 Spar flange decrease

158 Wing ribs
159 Flush-rivetted stressed wing skinning
160 Metal framed Frise-type aileron
161 Fixed trim tab
162 Wingtip construction
163 Port navigation light
164 Angled pitot head
165 Rüstsatz-6 optional underwing cannon gondola
166 14-point plug connection
167 Electrical junction box
168 Cannon rear mounting bracket
169 20-mm Mauser MG 151/20 cannon
170 Cannon front mounting bracket
171 Ammunition feed chute
172 Ammunition magazine drum
173 Underwing panel
174 Gondola fairing
175 Cannon barrel

This is the tall (non-retractable) tailwheel introduced late in the G-6 production run, and subsequently fitted to G-10s and G-14s.

The single-strut mainwheel assembly (right), retracted into a well forward of the wing spar (below). The lower portion of the wheel was left uncovered when retracted. Note the shallow underwing radiator.

DB 605 installations seen on **Black 6** (*left*) and **D-FMBB** (*above*) highlight the sturdy A-frame bearers from which the engine was suspended. Noticeable on the port side of the engine is the circular intake for the supercharger. The upper cowling leaves have apertures through which the fuselage machine-guns fired.

Bf 109 cockpit

Shown above is the cockpit of a Finnish Bf 109G-2, dominated by the Revi 16B sight and by the breech for the engine-mounted cannon, which projected back into the cockpit. Below is the cockpit of a Czech Avia S 199, showing some detail differences compared to the standard Bf 109G, notably the lack of cannon.

Bf 109G-6 cockpit

1 Undercarriage emergency lowering handwheel
2 Tailplane trim wheel
3 Seat height adjustment handle
4 Tailplane incidence indicator panel
5 Fuel injection primer pump
6 Fuel cock lever
7 Throttle
8 Throttle-mounted propeller pitch control thumbswitch
9 Dust filter handgrip
10 Canopy lever
11 Undercarriage switches
12 Undercarriage position indicators
13 Start plug cleansing switch
14 Starter switch
15 Panel light
16 Main line switch
17 Ignition switch
18 Frame struts
19 Armoured glass windscreen
20 Revi 16B reflector gunsight
21 Armament switch
22 Ammunition counters
23 Clock
24 Repeater compass
25 Artificial horizon/turn-and-bank indicator
26 Fine and coarse altimeter
27 Airspeed indicator
28 Gunsight padding
29 Manifold pressure gauge
30 Tachometer
31 AFN 2 homing indicator (FuG 16ZY)
32 Mechanical propeller pitch position indicator
33 Tumbler switch
34 Combined coolant exit and oil intake temperature indicator
35 Fuel warning lamp
36 30-mm MK 108 cannon breech
37 Rudder pedals
38 Firing trigger
39 Gun charging knob
40 Control column
41 Pilot's seat
42 Undercarriage emergency release
43 Electric fuel contents gauge
44 Dual oil and fuel pressure gauge
45 Auxiliary fuel contents indicator
46 Panel light
47 Coolant radiator control
48 Oxygen supply indicator
49 Oxygen pressure gauge
50 Radio switch panel
51 Oxygen supply
52 Radio tuner panel

Above: Bf 109G-6s occasionally flew close support missions, fitted with Rüstsatz-1 which added an ETC 500 IXb bombrack on the centreline. Shown preparing for a bombing mission is a G-6 of JG 3, the Geschwader badge being a stylised 'U' in memory of Ernst Udet.

Above: Between April 1942 and March 1944 Hauptmann Horst Carganico was Gruppenkommandeur of II./JG 5, operating against the Russians in the north. The giant Mickey Mouse replaced the usual chevron markings. Carganico's pet Scottie inspired the badge of his previous command, 6./JG 5.

Above right: Rüstsatz-3 was commonly seen on Bf 109G-6s, consisting of a 300-litre (66-Imp gal) drop tank. Here the carrier is a Stab/JG 54 aircraft.

introduced the Bf 109G-6, which was in many ways the definitive sub-variant of the 'Gustav'. It was also by far the most numerous, accounting for over 12,000 airframes. The principle behind the G-6 was to produce a basic fighter airframe which could accept any one of a number of conversion sets to equip it for its chosen mission. The aircraft could also accept a number of versions of the DB 605.

The cannon malfunction problems encountered by the Bf 109Fs in the desert mentioned earlier had given some cause for concern. While the MG 151/20 remained the cannon armament of the G-6, the MG 17 machine-guns were replaced with the 13-mm Rheinmetall-Borsig MG 131 machine-gun, with 300 instead of 500 rounds per gun. The new weapon provided the Bf 109G with a reasonable weight of fire even if the primary cannon jammed. The muzzle troughs were moved further back, but the most obvious difference was the addition of large fairings over the spent case return feeds of this much larger gun.

G-6s began to issue from the lines in late 1942 and were rapidly fielded in all theatres, although their arrival did not unduly upset the balance of power. Much later, the RAF got the chance to fully evaluate a G-6 when an R6-equipped 'Kanonenboote' landed by mistake at Manston, allowing the Air Fighter Development Squadron at Wittering to mount a series of comparisons with Allied fighters. Against the Spitfire Mks IX and XIV the Bf 109G's only real advantage was in the dive, for the Spitfire was able to outclimb and out-turn the Messerschmitt with ease, also being slightly faster (a marked advantage with the Griffon-powered Mk XIV) and possessing a much quicker roll rate. Against the P-51C (Mustang Mk III) the Bf 109G was

found to be much slower, but could generally outclimb the Mustang. In the dive the P-51 had the edge, and it could easily out-turn the German fighter. Roll rates were identical. Before tests could be performed with a Tempest Mk V, the Bf 109 was lost in a take-off accident.

Interspersed with the G-6 on the production lines were small numbers of Bf 109G-5s. They were essentially pressurised versions of the G-6 with one important external difference. Fitting the larger MG 131 machine-guns caused the pressurisation compressor to be moved to the starboard side of the engine, with the result that a small fairing had to be added to cover it. This adjoined the main bulge covering the MG 131s. The compressor intake scoop was mounted immediately beside it. Just to add further to the enormous confusion surrounding 'Gustav' models, many unpressurised aircraft (G-6s and G-14s) were built, inexplicably, with the extra fairing. G-5s entered service in September 1943, some time after the G-6, and virtually all were assigned to units in the West or on home defence duties.

Conversion kits

As befitted its initial design concept, the G-6 (and G-5) was subject to a bewildering array of conversions and modifications. Many aircraft were fitted with either the GM-1 (U2) or MW-50 (U3) boost systems. Initially, the engine cannon remained the Mauser MG 151/20 with 150 rounds, but increasingly became the Rheinmetall-Borsig MK 108 30-mm cannon with 60 rounds as production of the weapon ramped up from mid-1943 onwards. The heavier cannon was a lethal weapon, with one hit sufficient to bring down any fighter. Fitment of the MK 108 (most numerous among WNF-built aircraft) was covered by the Umbausatz-4 designation. Other U designations also concerned armament: the U5 was an MG 151/20-armed aircraft fitted with MK 108s in wing gondolas, while the U6 was an aircraft with three MK 108s. These latter two schemes remained in the test phase only, and were never deployed.

Rüstzustände designations for the G-6 included the R2 and R3 tactical reconnaissance platforms, with camera installations similar to those of the G-4, while the standard range of Rüstsätze was available, including R1 (centreline ETC 500 bomb rack), R3 (centreline drop tank) and R6 (underwing MG 151/20s). The suffix 'Y' was applied to aircraft fitted with FuG 16ZY radio (with a whip antenna

Captured 'Gustavs'

DB 605D-powered Bf 109G-10 in use with No. 318 'Gdanskski' Sqn (Spitfire Mk IXs) in Italy

Bf 109G-2/Trop, wearing No. 3 Sqn RAAF squadron codes after capture. Flown again in UK, 1991-97, after lengthy rebuild as 'Black 6'

Bf 109G-6/Trop under test by USAAF

Bf 109G-2, RAF serial HK849, used as hack in Italy

Bf 109G-6 (ex-JG 1), RAF serial TP814. Used for comparative trials with Spitfire and P-51

Bf 109G-14, one of two such aircraft tested by the RAF. Note Fw 190 in background

VVS Bf 109G-2 (ex-JG 3)

VVS Bf 109G-2 with Rüstsatz 6, near Leningrad

VVS Bf 109G-2 with Rüstsatz 6, NII trials

under the fuselage), this equipment allowing ground commands to control aircraft in the air. It was consequently usually fitted to the aircraft of unit leaders.

Mediterranean retreat

Following the victory at El Alamein, the Allied forces in the desert slowly steamrollered the Wehrmacht back into Tunisia. The following month, in November 1942, Operation Torch saw Allied forces landed on the Atlantic coast, and at once the German forces were split. Now equipped with Bf 109G-2s, -4s and -6s, the Jagdflieger were also divided as they attempted to prevent the jaws of the Allied

pincers closing. Torch brought with it the first large-scale US involvement, and initially the experienced German pilots found the inexperienced and over-confident Americans easy game. However, the general improvement of Allied aircraft – large numbers of Spitfires and P-38s were now in theatre – together with the sheer weight of numbers combined to create an unstoppable force. By May 1943 the Axis was pushed out of Africa for good.

Post-Torch operations had seen the introduction of large numbers of medium and heavy bombers, and this set the pattern for the remainder of the war in the Mediterranean theatre which had, more than any other, hitherto been a

By necessity the evacuation from Sicily was conducted hastily, the fight being continued from Italian bases. Here British officers inspect a pair of apparently serviceable II./JG 53 Bf 109G-2/Trops left behind at Comiso airfield. The aircraft on the left is a Gruppenstab aircraft, while that on the right is a 'Kanonenboote'.

Sicilian defenders

As soon as Axis forces were ousted from North Africa on 13 May 1943, the Allies immediately turned their attentions to Sicily. For the next two months USAAF bombers pounded the island as a prelude to the invasion which began on 10 July. Bf 109s put up a stout resistance, but were ultimately overwhelmed by the sheer number of fighters which the Allies could muster. In addition to the fighting over the battlefront in the south of the island, the Jagdflieger were tasked with keeping open the escape route to Italy in the east.

Left: This group of Bf 109G-6s is seen at Sciacca airfield on Sicily in June 1943. They belong to 2./JG 77, which fought through to the end of the whole Italian campaign in June 1944. The aircraft exhibit a variety of camouflage patterns, and carry the small individual aircraft numerals common at the time among certain units.

Bf 109G in Italy

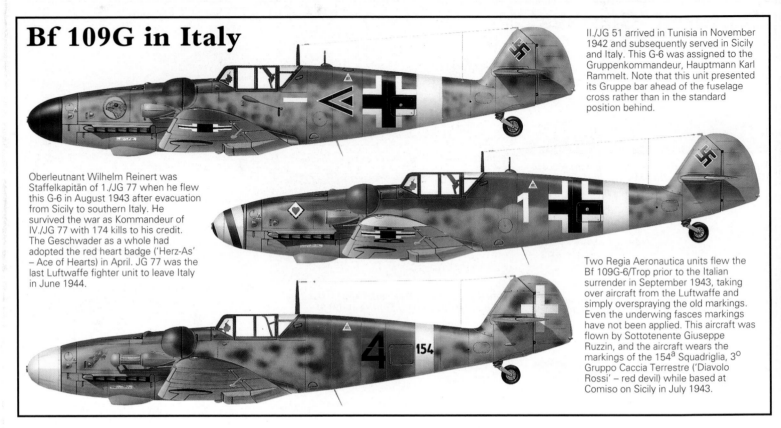

II./JG 51 arrived in Tunisia in November 1942 and subsequently served in Sicily and Italy. This G-6 was assigned to the Gruppenkommandeur, Hauptmann Karl Rammelt. Note that this unit presented its Gruppe bar ahead of the fuselage cross rather than in the standard position behind.

Oberleutnant Wilhelm Reinert was Staffelkapitän of 1./JG 77 when he flew this G-6 in August 1943 after evacuation from Sicily to southern Italy. He survived the war as Kommandeur of IV./JG 77 with 174 kills to his credit. The Geschwader as a whole had adopted the red heart badge ('Herz-As' – Ace of Hearts) in April. JG 77 was the last Luftwaffe fighter unit to leave Italy in June 1944.

Two Regia Aeronautica units flew the Bf 109G-6/Trop prior to the Italian surrender in September 1943, taking over aircraft from the Luftwaffe and simply overspraying the old markings. Even the underwing fasces markings have not been applied. This aircraft was flown by Sottotenente Giuseppe Ruzzin, and the aircraft wears the markings of the 154ª Squadriglia, 3º Gruppo Caccia Terrestre ('Diavolo Rossi' – red devil) while based at Comiso on Sicily in July 1943.

Below right: Having fought in North Africa, II./JG 51 was dispatched to Sardinia on 20 April 1943, where this aircraft is seen. Most of the Gruppe was destroyed on the ground, with the result that when it evacuated to Italy only four G-6/Trops could be mustered for the flight.

Bottom right: A small number of Regia Aeronautica units converted to the Bf 109G-6 in 1943. This aircraft belonged to the 363ª Squadriglia, 150º Gruppo, 53º Stormo.

Below: Partnering the 363ª in the 150º Gruppo was the 364ª Squadriglia. This aircraft wears the 'Gigi Trei Osei' badge of the Gruppo, worn in honour of Teniente Luigi 'Gigi' Caneppele.

fighter vs fighter contest. It did not take the greatest military strategist to work out the Allies' next move, for Sicily lay in all its temptation across the Sicilian Channel. Massed Allied air attacks meant that the Axis defence of the island was doomed to failure, and when Operation Husky, the invasion, was launched on 10 July, the defending Bf 109Gs of Stab and II./JG 27, II./JG 51 and II./JG 77 had just days left before evacuating to the Foggia airfield complex in southern Italy. The evacuation was completed before the end of the month.

September 1943 was a crucial month in the Italian campaign. Allied forces went ashore, to be followed almost immediately by the Italian surrender. This effectively cut the Regia Aeronautica in half; many units reformed and fought for the Allied cause as the Co-Belligerent Air Force, while those staying loyal to the Fascists formed the Aviazione Nazionale Repubblicana. By the end of September the Luftwaffe Bf 109 units had flown to safety to airfields around Rome, and several then continued north back to Germany or to the Eastern Front. The only new arrival was I./JG 4.

German withdrawal from Italy

At the start of 1944 the remaining Bf 109 units were faced with fighter-bombers, medium bombers and heavies in ever increasing numbers, always attended by swarms of escort fighters. Back in Berlin, the German High Command had largely lost interest in Italy, and it was felt that the fighters could be better employed defending Germany itself. Units were slowly withdrawn until only I./JG 4 and JG 77 were left. The fall of Rome on 5 June 1944, and the Allied landings in Normandy the following day, precipitated the final withdrawal, and the last Bf 109s left by the end of the month.

Not that the Germans left Italy entirely to its own fate, for it had nurtured the newly-formed ANR forces (flying Macchi MC.205s and Fiat G.55s) and subsequently

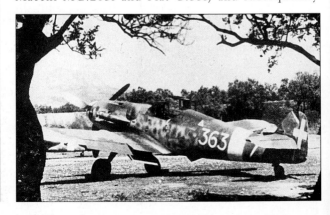

Left: I° Gruppo Caccia was an ANR unit which flew the Bf 109G-10 from January to April 1945, disbanding at Gallarate.

Below: This Bf 109G-6 served with the ANR's 4ª Squadriglia, II° Gruppo.

equipped two Gruppi with Bf 109Gs. The Regia Aeronautica had briefly operated the Bf 109G before the armistice, and this provided a nucleus of pilots who were dispatched to Germany to collect new aircraft. II° Gruppo Caccia was the first to return with Messerschmitts, flying its first operation with the Bf 109G-6 in June 1944. I° Gruppo came back to the front line in January 1945, bringing Bf 109G-10s with it. Both units operated strictly on defensive missions, attempting to hit unescorted bombers operating over northern Italy. Despite their small number and the ultimate futility of their efforts, the ANR Bf 109G units proved to be a constant thorn in the Allied side, and the Italian pilots revealed themselves as skilled and brave opponents.

In the east, the G-6 was continually embroiled in huge battles with massed formations of Soviet aircraft. There was certainly no shortage of trade for the Jagdflieger, although the quality of the opposition had changed out of all recognition compared with that which it had faced in 1941. Still, individual tallies began to mount, notably within Jagdgeschwader 52. In addition to standard G-6s, several

Trop models fought on the Russian front, especially in the south where the summer dust caused engine problems. Despite the fact that the G-6 entered service at a time when the Luftwaffe was in retreat from Africa, large numbers were built with provision for taking the tropical modifications. It was not uncommon to see aircraft in the harsh Soviet winter fitted with sunshade stands.

Anti-bomber operations

By the end of 1942, Germany was facing what was arguably its sternest test: the concerted bombing campaign launched from English soil, and later from southern Italy. Relentlessly, the day bombers of the US 8th Air Force and night bombers of RAF Bomber Command chipped away at Germany's industrial and military complex, while wearing the morale of its populace to the bone. Despite increasing losses in the east and in the Mediterranean, fighter forces had to be diverted to meet the growing threat, and large numbers of 'Gustavs' (mainly G-6s) were employed on home defence duties. Ideally, Bf 109s would put their good

Above: These G-6s equipped the II° Gruppo of the ANR, which was also known as the Aviazione della Repubblica Sociale Italiano. The decision to equip the ANR with the Bf 109G was taken to reduce the identification problem between Macchis and Bf 109s, which had hitherto caused some fratricidal kills.

Top left: Along with I./JG 4, JG 77 was the last Luftwaffe fighter unit in Italy. Here a 4. Staffel aircraft flies in formation with a I° Gruppo MC.205 prior to the Luftwaffe's withdrawal from Italy.

Aviazione Nazionale Repubblicana

After the Italian armistice, many Italian pilots continued flying with the Axis forces as part of the ANR. Two units were Bf 109G-equipped, and these flew missions defending northern Italy. This G-6 was the mount of Capitano Ugo Drago of I° Gruppo Caccia, the ANR's top scorer with 11 kills.

1° Gruppo Caccia was the second ANR unit to convert to the Bf 109, arriving back in Italy in January 1945 with Bf 109G-10/AS fighters. This is the aircraft of the unit's commander, Maggiore Adriano Visconti, who scored seven kills with the ANR to add to the 19 achieved with the Regia Aeronautica. The badge is that of the RA's 153° Gruppo.

Above: 7./JG 27 Bf 109G-6s are seen escorting the He 111 bomber carrying Generals Fiebig and Holle during their inspection of forces on Crete on 1 December 1943. 'White 9' was the aircraft of Staffelkapitän Emil Clade, who survived the war with 26 kills to his credit. Within weeks of this picture being taken, III./JG 27 moved north to Vienna to join the Reich defence effort.

Above right: This unfortunate Bf 109G-6/Trop 'Kanonenboote' was also a 7./JG 27 aircraft, seen at Malemes on Crete after a crash-landing. The aircraft wears the III./JG 27 Gruppe badge on the engine cowling, and the 7. Staffel badge of a pierced apple below the cockpit.

high-altitude performance to use in tackling the escort fighters, while the more heavily-armed Fw 190s took on the bombers. In practice, this was rarely achievable. In recognition of this, the relatively light armament of the Bf 109 was usually augmented by the Rüstsatz-6 cannon installation so that it could attack the bombers.

Other more innovative methods of attacking bombers were introduced. In early 1943 5./JG 11 G-1s experimented with air-burst bombs, using a time-delay fuse to theoretically explode the bomb in the midst of a bomber formation. The USAAF 'heavies' relied on tight formation-keeping to maintain a withering wall of defensive fire against attack from any quarter. If the bombers could be split up, they would become much easier targets for follow-up cannon attacks. The idea persisted throughout the remainder of the war, but never proved worthwhile.

More successful was the use of air-to-air rockets. G-6s (and a few older variants) were modified to carry two launch tubes under the wings for the Werfergranate 210-mm rocket. This was little more than a mortar, but did

have a large 40-kg (88-lb) warhead. Known as *Pulk-Zerstörer* (formation-destroyer), the WGr 21-equipped Bf 109Gs served in specialist Staffeln within the Gruppen assigned to home defence duties, including those in northern Italy, and again the aim was principally to break up the formation. Their first major use came during the 14 October 1943 raid by 8th AF 'heavies' on Schweinfurt, resulting in catastrophic losses to the American formations.

Wilde Sau night-fighters

Bf 109Gs also played their part in the night defence of the Reich, especially between June 1943 and March 1944, when G-6s (and Fw 190s) equipped the specially created night-fighter units of 30. Jagddivision. The large-scale adoption of single-seat fighters for this role had come about following trials of a new tactic known as *wilde Sau* (wild boar), in which fighters roamed above the bombers, stalking them visually over their targets when they were silhouetted against target flares, searchlights and fires on the ground. *Wilde Sau* was the brainchild of Major Hajo Herrmann. To test his ideas, JG 300 had formed on Bf 109G-6s, and initial results were highly promising.

The nascent *wilde Sau* force suddenly gained great importance in July through the RAF's introduction of chaff, known to the RAF as 'Window' and to the Germans as 'Düppel'. It proved to be an effective blinding agent against German radars, rendering the traditional night-fighter force largely superfluous, tied as it was to the Himmelbett radar control system. Two further *wilde Sau* Geschwaders were hastily formed (JG 301 and 302) to form 30. Jagddivision under the control of promoted Oberstleutnant Herrmann. Each Geschwader had three Gruppen, but only one in each Geschwader had its own aircraft assigned. The other two Gruppen borrowed aircraft from co-located day-fighter units.

Greek 'Gustavs'

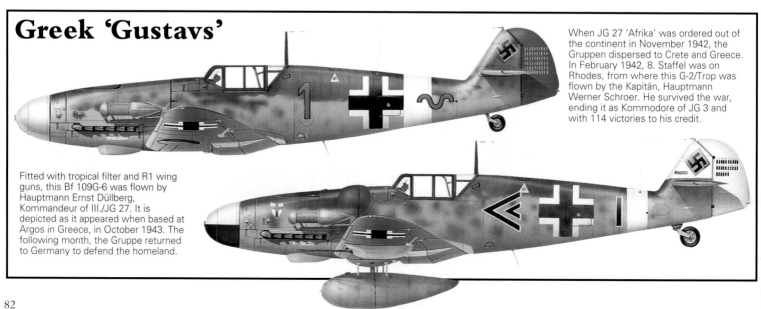

When JG 27 'Afrika' was ordered out of the continent in November 1942, the Gruppen dispersed to Crete and Greece. In February 1942, 8. Staffel was on Rhodes, from where this G-2/Trop was flown by the Kapitän, Hauptmann Werner Schroer. He survived the war, ending it as Kommodore of JG 3 and with 114 victories to his credit.

Fitted with tropical filter and R1 wing guns, this Bf 109G-6 was flown by Hauptmann Ernst Düllberg, Kommandeur of III./JG 27. It is depicted as it appeared when based at Argos in Greece, in October 1943. The following month, the Gruppe returned to Germany to defend the homeland.

Messerschmitt Bf 109G-6/R6
11. Staffel Jagdgeschwader 27 Kalamaki, Greece September 1943

'Red 13' was flown by Heinrich Bartels (then an Oberfeldwebel) during IV./JG 27's sojourn in the eastern Mediterranean from autumn 1943 to spring 1944. Bartels's rudder recorded 56 kills and the award of the Knight's Cross at this time. Bartels's final official tally was 99 victories, 47 of them scored against Russian pilots while flying with JG 5 in Norway. He disappeared during the furious air battles near Bonn on 23 December 1944 after downing a P-47. His victor was possibly Dave Schilling, CO of the 56th FG, who was credited with three Bf 109s destroyed in this area on that day. Bartels's body remained undiscovered until 1967.

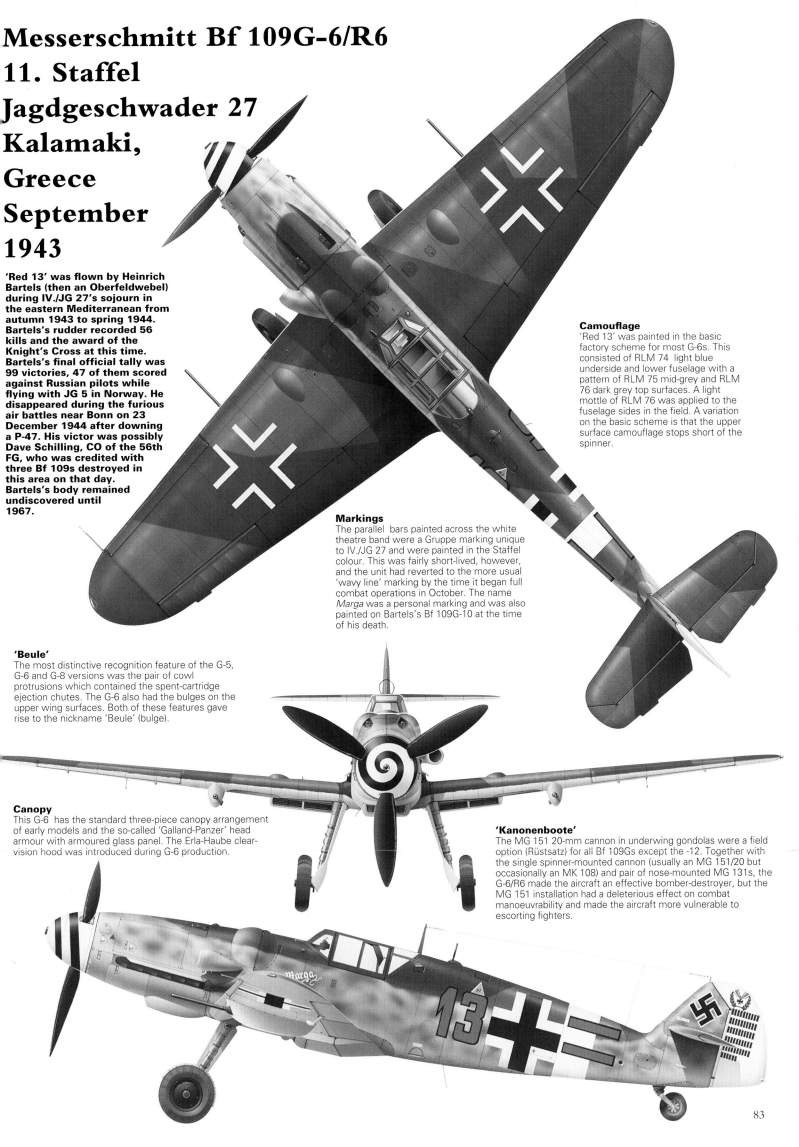

Camouflage
'Red 13' was painted in the basic factory scheme for most G-6s. This consisted of RLM 74 light blue underside and lower fuselage with a pattern of RLM 75 mid-grey and RLM 76 dark grey top surfaces. A light mottle of RLM 76 was applied to the fuselage sides in the field. A variation on the basic scheme is that the upper surface camouflage stops short of the spinner.

Markings
The parallel bars painted across the white theatre band were a Gruppe marking unique to IV./JG 27 and were painted in the Staffel colour. This was fairly short-lived, however, and the unit had reverted to the more usual 'wavy line' marking by the time it began full combat operations in October. The name *Marga* was a personal marking and was also painted on Bartels's Bf 109G-10 at the time of his death.

'Beule'
The most distinctive recognition feature of the G-5, G-6 and G-8 versions was the pair of cowl protrusions which contained the spent-cartridge ejection chutes. The G-6 also had the bulges on the upper wing surfaces. Both of these features gave rise to the nickname 'Beule' (bulge).

Canopy
This G-6 has the standard three-piece canopy arrangement of early models and the so-called 'Galland-Panzer' head armour with armoured glass panel. The Erla-Haube clear-vision hood was introduced during G-6 production.

'Kanonenboote'
The MG 151 20-mm cannon in underwing gondolas were a field option (Rüstsatz) for all Bf 109Gs except the -12. Together with the single spinner-mounted cannon (usually an MG 151/20 but occasionally an MK 108) and pair of nose-mounted MG 131s, the G-6/R6 made the aircraft an effective bomber-destroyer, but the MG 151 installation had a deleterious effect on combat manoeuvrability and made the aircraft more vulnerable to escorting fighters.

Pulk-Zerstörer

Several units involved in anti-bomber operations employed Bf 109G-6s equipped with the WGr-21 rocket for breaking up bomber formations. Most were defending the homeland, but a few units were dispatched to northern Italy. Among them was the newly-formed IV./JG 3 which served in Italy from July to September 1943. This G-6/Trop was the aircraft of the Kommandeur, Major Franz Beyer.

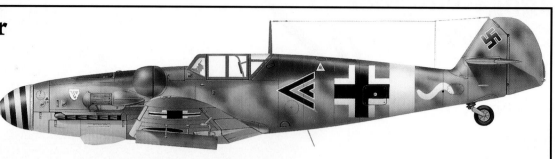

Two photographs show 'Pulk-Zerstörer' Bf 109G-6s armed with the Werfergranate 210-mm rocket. The tubes were more like mortars than rockets, lobbing a heavy warhead. The tubes were angled upwards to achieve adequate range. The projectiles were detonated by time delay, calculated to explode in the middle of a bomber formation. Even if the projectile did not hit a bomber, its effect would cause the tightly held formation to split up, reducing the effect of the mutual defensive fire.

The glazed dome on the spine identifies this aircraft as a Bf 109G-6/N, one of a small batch built with Naxos Z equipment to home on to the bombing radars used by RAF heavy bombers.

30. Jagddivision achieved a great deal of success in the late summer of 1943, by which time the Germans had begun to field airborne radars that could see through 'Window'. A dedicated night-fighter version of the Bf 109G-6 appeared from the factory in early 1944, designated Bf 109G-6/N. This version had Rüstsatz-6 armament, flame-damped exhausts, FuG 16ZY radio for tactical communications and direction-finding, FuG 25a beacon-homing equipment and FuG 350 Naxos Z. The latter was widely used night-fighter equipment, consisting of a receiver which picked up on the emissions from the H2S bombing radar carried by the RAF bombers. On the G-6/N, it was carried in a glass dome mounted on the spine behind the canopy.

Only a handful of G-6/Ns was built, and they were only used by a special cadre of experienced *wilde Sau* pilots within NJG 11. The reason for their non-adoption was the dissolution of 30. Jagddivision in March 1944 after a winter of appalling attrition. Whereas the single-seat fighters had been effective during good weather, many had been lost when the winter weather arrived. Without suitable radio aids (as carried by the traditional night-fighters), many were getting lost or finding landing at night in bad weather impossible. It was far from uncommon for pilots to bale out rather than risk a landing. JGs 300, 301 and 302 all retrained for the day-fighter role, still in defence of the homeland.

'Gustav' in foreign service

From mid-1942, the Bf 109G began appearing in the insignia of several air arms allied to the German cause (in addition to Italy, described above), beginning with Croatia. The fighter component of the Croatian legion fighting in Russia was 15.(kroat)/JG 52, and this unit had converted to the Bf 109G-2 as early as July 1942. By November it was flying the Bf 109G-6, although aircraft availability was very low. Two more Croatian squadrons were planned, the personnel having trained on Bf 109Gs, but in the event they were fielded flying Fiat G.50s and Macchi MC.202s. In the meantime, 15.(kroat)/JG 52, also referred to as simply the kroat. Jagdstaffel, had fought for much of the war in the Crimea, and had retreated with other Luftwaffe units. It converted to the Bf 109G-10 towards the end of the war.

In the Continuation War in the north, Finland found itself facing growing numbers of Lavochkin La-5 fighters, against which the Brewster Buffalo offered no real opposition. Accordingly, in January 1943, Germany delivered a batch of 16 Bf 109G-2s (dubbed 'Mersu' in Finnish air force parlance) with which HLeLv 34 was formed, followed by another similar-sized batch in May. The Finnish pilots immediately took to their new mounts, and began to rack up impressive scores. Highest-scoring was Eino Juutilainen, who achieved 94 kills, mostly in the Bf 109, to become the highest-scoring non-German ace of all time. Amazingly, his aircraft was never scratched by a single bullet from his opponents, a remarkable feat unmatched by any of the major German *experten* (Erich Hartmann, for example, survived 14 force-landings during his 352-kill career).

When the Soviets stepped up their campaign against Finland in 1944, further batches totalling 132 aircraft were supplied to Finland, including G-6s, G-8s, G-10s and G-14s, although the Finns referred to them all as Bf 109G-6s. Two additional units, HLeLv 24 and HLeLv 28, were formed, although their effectiveness was crippled by poor spares supply from Germany. On 4 September 1944 Finland accepted the terms of surrender offered by the Soviet Union, although the Bf 109s did not take part in the ensuing Finnish operation against German forces in Lappland. In December 1944 HLeLv 24 and 34 were redesignated as HLeLv 31 and 33, and with these two units the Finnish Bf 109s continued in service until 1954.

Hungary also acquired Bf 109G-2s in early 1943, these aircraft supplanting the F-4s delivered in October 1942. Two units were formed, 5/1 and 5/2 Vadasz Szàzad, which

The Croatian Legion pilots were organised into 15.(kroat)/JG 52 and fought as part of the Luftwaffe on the Russian front. Aircraft usually wore standard Luftwaffe markings with the Croatian shield displayed prominently.

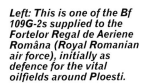

Left: This is one of the Bf 109G-2s supplied to the Fortelor Regal de Aeriene Româna (Royal Romanian air force), initially as defence for the vital oilfields around Ploesti.

Above: These Bf 109G-6s are of the 102 Vadasz Osztaly (fighter group), administered by the Fliegerführer 102 Ungarn. This unit had two constituent squadrons.

Below: Bulgaria received 149 Bf 109Gs, this being a G-6. The aircraft is unusual in being fitted with the G-5 cowling, with additional fairing below the main bulge over the gun.

This poor photograph, taken at Tri Duby, shows one of the two Bf 109Gs used by the Combined Squadron of the Slovakian Insurgent air force during the Slovakian uprising against the Germans in September 1944.

Allies in the East

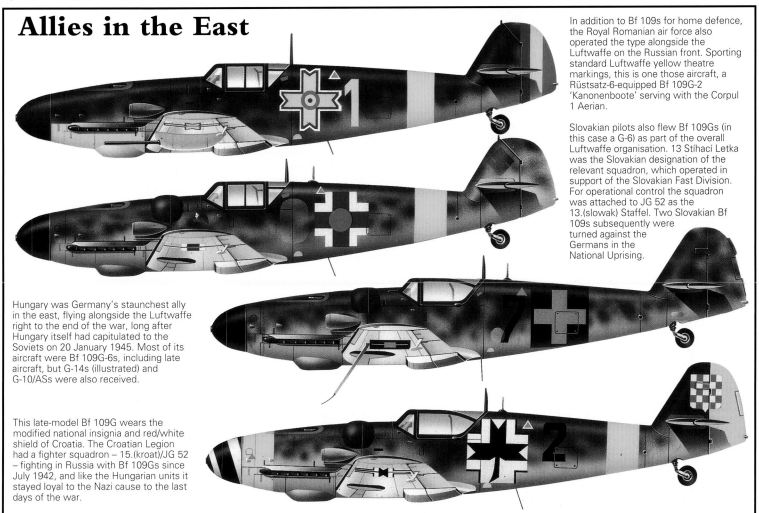

In addition to Bf 109s for home defence, the Royal Romanian air force also operated the type alongside the Luftwaffe on the Russian front. Sporting standard Luftwaffe yellow theatre markings, this is one those aircraft, a Rüstsatz-6-equipped Bf 109G-2 'Kanonenboote' serving with the Corpul 1 Aerian.

Slovakian pilots also flew Bf 109Gs (in this case a G-6) as part of the overall Luftwaffe organisation. 13 Stíhací Letka was the Slovakian designation of the relevant squadron, which operated in support of the Slovakian Fast Division. For operational control the squadron was attached to JG 52 as the 13.(slowak) Staffel. Two Slovakian Bf 109s subsequently were turned against the Germans in the National Uprising.

Hungary was Germany's staunchest ally in the east, flying alongside the Luftwaffe right to the end of the war, long after Hungary itself had capitulated to the Soviets on 20 January 1945. Most of its aircraft were Bf 109G-6s, including late aircraft, but G-14s (illustrated) and G-10/ASs were also received.

This late-model Bf 109G wears the modified national insignia and red/white shield of Croatia. The Croatian Legion had a fighter squadron – 15.(kroat)/JG 52 – fighting in Russia with Bf 109Gs since July 1942, and like the Hungarian units it stayed loyal to the Nazi cause to the last days of the war.

Above: 9./JG 3 was at Bad Wörishofen in September 1943, engaged on Reich defence duties. The Staffel marked its Bf 109G-6s with an eye on the gun fairing: 7. Staffel had a large comet marking in the same position.

Above: II./JG 26 operated this cannon-equipped Bf 109G-6 from France in early 1943. The two Channel-based Geschwaders became increasingly active in trying to take a toll of 8th AF bomber formations on their way to and from Germany.

Right: With the North African campaign behind it, most of JG 27 was pulled back for Defence of the Reich duties. These G-6s are of III. Gruppe, seen at Wiesbaden in 1944.

Bf 109G-6s taxi out for a mission from an airfield in Germany. The G-6 proved better able to tackle the fighters at high altitude than the Fw 190, although it was at a distinct disadvantage from the beginning of 1944 when the Merlin-powered Mustang arrived in service. At altitude the P-51 was much faster and more manoeuvrable than the Messerschmitt.

were engaged on mostly escort duties on the Russian front. In November 1943 they were withdrawn to Hungary and redesignated 102/1 and 102/2. In April 1944 US bombing operations over Hungary were greatly increased, leading to the supply of six squadrons of Bf 109G-6s for service with the 101 Vadasz Ezred (fighter regiment), which formed the main air defence of Hungary. 102/1 and 102/2 continued to support Luftwaffe operations at the front until pulled back to join their compatriots at home. Despite the Soviets overrunning their homeland and forcing an armistice on 20 January 1945, the 101 Vadasz Ezred fought on, ending the war near Linz in Austria.

Romania also began to receive Bf 109G-2s in early 1943, mainly to help the indigenous IAR 80 fighters defend the vital oilfields around Ploesti. On the Russian front the Corpul 1 Aerian (1st Air Corps) took delivery of Bf 109G-6s and G-8s for its operations within I Fliegerkorps, while further G-6s were delivered for use by home units. After the Soviet-forced coup on 23 August 1944, Romanian Bf 109Gs were turned on their erstwhile masters and used in support of Soviet offensives.

Slovakia, too, joined the Bf 109 club in early 1943, receiving 15 Bf 109G-6s to equip the 13.Stíhací Letka (fighter squadron), also known by its Luftwaffe titles of 13.(slowak)/JG 52 or slowak Jagdstaffel. Slovakian 'Gustavs' fought in the Crimea, while at home the 11. Stíhací Letka was also formed. Most of this unit was wiped out in one action with USAAF P-38s. At least two Bf 109G-6s changed sides and were used in the Slovakian uprising in July 1944. The Royal Bulgarian air force received its first 'Gustavs' in early 1944, a mixed bag of G-2s and G-6s for service with the 6 Polk. Principally acquired to defend the capital, Sofia, Bulgarian Bf 109s also fought in Romania, defending the Ploesti oilfields. Deliveries totalled 149, and most of the survivors were destroyed in late 1944 by a heavy RAF attack on the base at Karlovo.

Neutral customers

The final two Bf 109G customers were both neutral countries. The story of the supply of Bf 109G-2 airframes to Spain as a prelude to licence-production, and their subsequent emergence as HA-1109s, is recounted later. Switzerland, on the other hand, acquired its Bf 109G-6s in the most extraordinary manner. On the night of 28/29 April 1944, a lone Messerschmitt Bf 110G night-fighter, pursuing a Lancaster in Swiss airspace, encountered engine trouble and was forced to land at Dübendorf airfield, near Zürich. German officials were highly anxious that the FuG 220 radar and *schräge Musik* cannon installation of the night-fighter should not be examined by Allied agents, and struck a deal with the Swiss whereby the Bf 110 would be burned in return for the release to the Swiss of 12 Bf 109G-6s, which were required to make good attrition suffered by the Flugwaffe's 'Emil' force.

On 20 and 22 May 1944, the dozen 'Gustavs' arrived from Germany, joining a single example which had been interned earlier (and later joined by a further internee). Assigned to Fliegerkompagnie 7, the G-6s represented a considerable increase in the Flugwaffe's ability to defend

Operation Beethoven: the Mistels

By far the most unorthodox trials involving the Bf 109F actually led to an operational weapon: the Mistel. Known as Operation Beethoven, the Mistel (mistletoe) programme employed the use of a piloted fighter mounted on the back of an explosives-laden surplus bomber airframe in a combination nicknamed 'Vater und Sohn' (father and son). The pilot took off, flew the combination to its target, aimed the bomber airframe and then released the shackles holding his fighter to its carrier. He then returned to base. Strictly speaking, the term Mistel applied only to the lower component, but rapidly became the name by which these odd 'combos' were known.

Beethoven was originally inspired by a suggestion concerning the use of piggyback fighters to deliver explosives, but the first airborne tests, conducted in 1942 and termed 'Huckepack', were intended to provide a means of delivering a transport glider. The 'Huckepack' combination employed a Bf 109E mounted on a DFS 230. The idea of a weapon combination was pursued with renewed vigour in 1943, with Junkers providing the engineering and test team. A flying prototype was created using a Bf 109F-4 upper component, attached to a Ju 88A-4 lower component, which had two tripod supports for the fighter, running between the centre-sections of each aircraft. A single spring-loaded strut supported the tail of the fighter, this falling away when the fighter released its carrier.

Junkers received instructions to produce 15 Ju 88A-4 lower components in July 1943, and initial prototype trials (using the Bf 109F-4) proved the feasibility of the project. The initial combinations were called Mistel 1, and employed the Bf 109G-2 upper component. The first few Mistel lower components were completed with a standard Ju 88 bomber nose but with spartan equipment. Designated Mistel S1, these aircraft could be piloted and served as trainers. Standard Mistel 1s were also built with a bomber nose, but this was a quick release section which could rapidly be swapped for a 3800-kg (8,377-lb) hollow-charge warhead, which fired a steel core that could penetrate the heaviest ship armour or nearly 20 m (65 ft) of concrete.

This Mistel 1 (with Bf 109G-2 upper component) is seen shortly after delivery to the Einsatz-staffel of IV./KG 101. The bomber's nose was used for ferrying, and was attached by bolts. It could be rapidly replaced by the hollow-charge warhead.

Above: Operational Mistel 1s of II./KG 200 are seen at a Danish airfield in the winter of 1944/45, where they were gathered in preparation for a raid on the British Home Fleet. The only operational Mistel sorties involving the Bf 109 were the handful of attacks in late June 1944 against ships forming part of the invasion fleet.

Below: The prototype Mistel combination utilised a Bf 109F-4 mounted on a Ju 88A-4. The support struts were considerably strengthened in the operational Mistels, but the prototype suffered no serious problems during trials. Note the rear fuselage support strut, which fell under spring-load into a cradle.

In the spring of 1944 crews began assembling with the Einsatz-staffel of IV./KG 101 at Nordhausen to begin training on the Bf 109G and the Mistel 1. In May the unit moved to St Dizier with five Mistel 1s in preparation for attacks on the Allied invasion fleet. The first operational mission was conducted by one Mistel on the night of 24 June 1944, but was cut short when a Mosquito night-fighter appeared, forcing the pilot to detach from the Ju 88 prematurely. Soon after, the remaining four Mistel 1s were released successfully against Allied ships off the coast of France. All four hit, but none of the ships was sunk.

In October 1944 the Einsatz-staffel of IV./KG 101 became the Einsatz-gruppe III./KG 66, and soon after was redesignated again as II./KG 200. Mistel production had been building up for a major strike, the chosen target being the British Home Fleet anchored in Scapa Flow. Some 60 Mistel 1s were gathered at airfields in Denmark, but the operation could not be launched because of bad weather. When it cleared, bright moonlight kept the combinations on the ground, as they would have been very vulnerable to the fighters which defended the Orkneys and surrounding seas.

By January 1945 the operation had still not taken place, and further bad weather continued to keep the Mistels on the ground. At this juncture a new plan to launch an all-out strike was hatched, this time against Soviet armament production (Operation Eisenhammer). In early 1945, the Bf 109G was removed from the Mistel combination, its place as upper component being taken by the Fw 190A (as the Mistel 2 and 3). In the event, the mass raid never did take place.

Above: The Mistel 1 featured a long proboscis mounting the contact fuse. This was necessary to ensure the penetrating warhead worked correctly. Taxiing the combination required considerable skill from the Bf 109G pilot, a task made all the more difficult by the massive weights at which the Mistel took off.

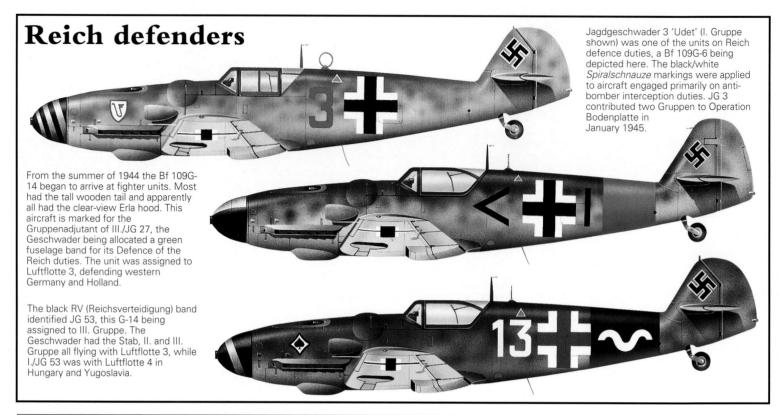

Reich defenders

Jagdgeschwader 3 'Udet' (I. Gruppe shown) was one of the units on Reich defence duties, a Bf 109G-6 being depicted here. The black/white *Spiralschnauze* markings were applied to aircraft engaged primarily on anti-bomber interception duties. JG 3 contributed two Gruppen to Operation Bodenplatte in January 1945.

From the summer of 1944 the Bf 109G-14 began to arrive at fighter units. Most had the tall wooden tail and apparently all had the clear-view Erla hood. This aircraft is marked for the Gruppenadjutant of III./JG 27, the Geschwader being allocated a green fuselage band for its Defence of the Reich duties. The unit was assigned to Luftflotte 3, defending western Germany and Holland.

The black RV (Reichsverteidigung) band identified JG 53, this G-14 being assigned to III. Gruppe. The Geschwader had the Stab, II. and III. Gruppe all flying with Luftflotte 3, while I./JG 53 was with Luftflotte 4 in Hungary and Yugoslavia.

Virtually all Bf 109 'Kanonenboote' flew with the MG 151/20 cannon underwing, but a handful are believed to have received the harder-hitting 30-mm MK 108. This is a test aircraft, showing the much shorter barrel of the larger-calibre weapon.

A Bf 109G-14 of 1./JG 53 'Pik As' sits among Fw 190s at Bad Aibling at the end of the war. The Erla-Haube canopy was fitted to Bf 109s from late 1943, significantly improving visibility from the cockpit.

Swiss airspace, but the aircraft suffered from serious manufacturing defects, symptoms of the poor workmanship and production difficulties that were then facing the German production lines. The Fliegertruppe complained to Germany, and eventually recovered half of the purchase cost, while working hard to remedy the problems. They were never

fully solved, and the flying hours of the 'Gustavs' were limited. In 1947 the type was retired altogether, leaving the original Bf 109Es flying for another two years.

Production line changes

Throughout its production run the Bf 109G-6 was subject to several major modifications, with no resulting change in designation. The first was introduced in about August 1943, when aircraft began to appear with a direction-finding loop antenna on the spine and a corresponding reduction in height of the main radio mast. As with virtually all Bf 109G aircraft configurations, there were many variations, and many aircraft were built with the D/F loop, but had it removed at the front. Some even dispensed with the radio mast altogether, yet retained the D/F, the radio wire antenna passing through the loop.

A common complaint concerned the lack of visibility from the cockpit, and two modifications were incorporated into the G-6 to address this. The first, appearing in the summer of 1943, was the Galland-Panzer, the replacement of the all-metal head armour with armoured glass. More radical was the adoption of the Erla-Haube, a new lightly-framed canopy which replaced both the hinging and rear fixed portions of the old canopy. This appeared at the start of 1944, as did a new, taller vertical fin assembly, characterised by a straight rudder joint and a controllable Flettner tab. The rudder was covered with plywood, which was cheaper to produce, eased the strain on the supply of strategic materials, and utilised the skills of carpenters rather than

metalworkers. Right towards the end of G-6 production, aircraft appeared with a much longer, non-retractable tail-wheel leg which raised the tailplane into the propeller slipstream, improving take-off characteristics.

Experience with the Bf 109G had shown that the GM-1 and MW-50 systems, while useful, were less effective than the provision of extra supercharging, leading to the installation of the DB 605AS engine. This powerplant featured the supercharger which had been developed for the larger DB 603 and gave a maximum output of 1,200 hp (895 kW) at 8000 m (26,250 ft). The DB 605AS had a somewhat larger supercharger, requiring a complete redesign of the engine cowling. The result was a much cleaner cowling which dispensed with the characteristic bulges in favour of larger but more streamlined fairings. First appearing in the spring of 1944, G-6/AS aircraft were produced as both new-build machines and by conversion of older airframes. Most were assigned to home defence duties, where their increased altitude performance was welcome in the ongoing battle with the bombers. A few served with night-fighter units. A small number of Bf 109G-5s also received DB 605AS engines, although it is thought that at least some, if not all, lost their pressurisation capability in the process.

Bf 109G production had included many aircraft destined to serve in the reconnaissance role, but a dedicated variant was produced from August 1943 – the Bf 109G-8. Based on the G-6, the G-8 entered service in November, and swiftly became the standard equipment of the Nahauf-klärungsgruppen. The cameras were mounted further back in the fuselage than on previous reconnaissance Bf 109s, and usually comprised two Rb 12.5/7x9s or a single Rb 32/7x9. Some had a camera installation in the leading edge of the port wing, but this was removed when found to be unsuitable. The standard range of 'Us' and 'Rs' was applicable, but rarely employed. Indeed, many G-8s had the engine-mounted cannon removed to save precious weight. Among the G-8's achievements was taking the first photographs of the Allied invasion fleet on the morning of 6 June 1944, captured by two aircraft from 3./NAGr 13.

Foreign production and trainers

Limited production of the Bf 109G was undertaken in Romania and Hungary. IAR at Brasov assembled 30 Bf 109G-6s from Messerschmitt-supplied kits and constructed another 16 itself before US bombing raids brought a halt to production. In Hungary the production effort was more successful, being centred, initially, on the Györ factory. This built one G-2 (designated Ga-2) and three G/Ga-4s before production got under way with the G-6, engines being provided by Manfred Weiss. Over 600 G-6s and G-14s were delivered from Hungary, production being shifted to the Köbánya brewery in the summer of 1944 after Györ had been bombed.

From the very start of the Bf 109's service career in 1937, it had always been felt unnecessary to have a training version, but by late 1943 the calibre of the young pilots being sent for training had reached the point where they would be lucky to survive their conversion course, let alone

the rigours of combat. Accordingly, the RLM directed that around 500 surplus G airframes should be converted into two-seaters and issued to the Jagdschulen (JGs 101 to 110) to aid conversion to fighter types. G-2s, G-3s, G-4s and early G-6s were involved in the programme.

Designated Bf 109G-12, the two-seater entered service in early 1944. The original cockpit remained in its position, a second cockpit being added behind, cutting fuel capacity from 400 litres (88 Imp gal) to 240 litres (53 Imp gal). Rüstsatz-3 (300-litre/66-Imp gal tank) was regularly installed to boost the endurance of a training mission. The canopy of the front cockpit was essentially similar to that of the single-seater, except that it hinged from the top of the fixed (starboard) panel rather than at the bottom. A fixed glazed section separated it from the rear canopy, which was

Above: A late-model Bf 109, either a G-6 or a G-14, taxis out for a mission in 1944. By the end of the year the Bf 109 production system was in a confusing state, with aircraft being completed with either long or short tailwheels, tall or short fins, DB 605AM or AS engines and with large or small mainwheels.

Left: A Bf 109G-6 lands at a base in the west. The aircraft has the tall fin introduced in early 1944, which dispensed with the characteristic aerodynamic horn balance at the top of the rudder in favour of an inset balance.

Two photographs depict Bf 109G-12s, the aircraft at the bottom being hastily and rather ineffectively camouflaged with foliage.

Bf 109G-12 – two-seat trainer

Trainer versions appeared right towards the end of the war, and reflected the calibre of hopeful pilots rather than any aircraft problems. Based on a variety of G versions, the G-12s retained many of the individual features of the aircraft from which they had been converted.

Above: This Bf 109G-6 or G-14 taxis out at Merzhausen past a construction crew attempting to repair damage caused by Allied bombing. Aircraft of both production series were completed with the DB 605AS engine, distinguished by a larger but more streamlined fairing over the engine gun breeches.

Right: This late-production Bf 109G-6 carries both R3 fuel tank and R6 underwing cannon gondolas. From late 1943 units assigned to the defence of Germany (Reichsverteidigung – RV) applied coloured bands around the rear fuselage of their fighters. This plain band could denote JG 1 (red) or JG 54 (blue).

bulged slightly to give the instructor a measure of forward vision. A hood was fitted in the rear seat for instrument flying, requiring the student and instructor to swap seats for such missions. Although armament was scheduled to have been removed during the G-12 conversion, many retained at least one or both machine-guns, and were used as gunnery trainers. In the last desperate weeks of the Reich, several were used in combat.

High-altitude fighter

By the beginning of 1943, the requirement for a specialist high-altitude fighter had assumed ever-larger proportions, and throughout the year Messerschmitt was working on two Höhenjäger programmes which ran side-by-side. Of these, the most important was the Me 209H, which was intended to be the definitive high-altitude fighter, based on the Me 209 II fighter which was proposed as a replacement for the Bf 109. As it was obvious that no version of the Me 209 could be in production much before the end of 1944, Messerschmitt also worked in parallel on a high-altitude Bf 109 which could be fielded much earlier.

As initially envisaged, the resulting Bf 109H was a Bf 109F-4 with an uprated DB 601 engine and an additional taperless wing centre-section which raised span to 11.92 m (39 ft 1 in). The undercarriage was moved to the outer edges of the new section, which increased its track considerably. As detailed design was being undertaken, the ceiling

requirements were raised, and the F-based fighter could not achieve the new figures. The answer lay in adapting certain features of the parallel Me 209H programme to the Bf 109G.

Among the new aircraft's features was installation of the DB 628A engine, which had a two-stage supercharger. A mock-up of the new engine was tested in a Bf 109G-5, followed soon by a real engine, fitted into a Bf 109G-3 and flown for the first time on 18 May 1943. This aircraft, the V50, featured a ducted spinner and a paddle-blade propeller. The lengthening of the forward fuselage caused by the DB 628A installation upset the centre of gravity, so balance weights were installed in the rear fuselage as compensation. So equipped, the V50 underwent high-altitude trials which achieved 15500 m (50,850 ft), the engine delivering some 1,130 hp (843 kW) at 12000 m (39,370 ft).

Meanwhile, Messerschmitt had been converting a Bf 109G-5 airframe to the Bf 109H configuration, with DB 628A engine, extra centre-section and larger tail surfaces. As the V54, this aircraft first flew in June 1943. Messerschmitt was also producing a batch of Bf 109H-0 aircraft, based on the Bf 109F-4/Z (with DB 601E engines, GM-1 boosting and full armament). This batch was used only for evaluating the problems associated with operating high-altitude fighters.

Service test

The first Bf 109H-1 fighters followed, based on the Bf 109G-5 airframe and powered by a GM-1-boosted DB 605A. In addition to the standard three-gun armament, they had provision for the installation of reconnaissance cameras in the rear fuselage. In early 1944 several were sent to Guyancourt, near Paris, for a service evaluation. Generally found to be satisfactory, the Bf 109H-1 did show some wing flutter, which occasioned Messerschmitt to undertake a series of diving tests. In the course of one of them, a port wing parted company with the aircraft flown by Fritz Wendel.

This Bf 109G-6 was fitted with an experimental auxiliary fuel tank, known as the Irmer-Behälter. The tank had a small fin on the centreline to restore directional stability.

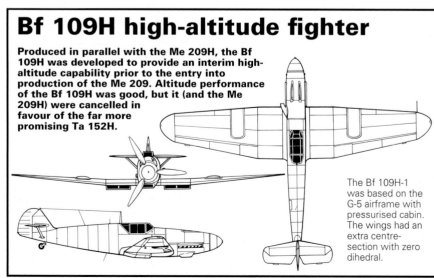

Bf 109H high-altitude fighter

Produced in parallel with the Me 209H, the Bf 109H was developed to provide an interim high-altitude capability prior to the entry into production of the Me 209. Altitude performance of the Bf 109H was good, but it (and the Me 209H) were cancelled in favour of the far more promising Ta 152H.

The Bf 109H-1 was based on the G-5 airframe with pressurised cabin. The wings had an extra centre-section with zero dihedral.

Found at Salzburg by US soldiers in 1945, this is a Bf 109G-10. It has the bulged cowling designed to house the DB 605D engine, although some G-10s with this cowling were fitted with the older DB 605AS.

One other airframe took part in the Bf 109H test programme, the V55. Initially laid down as the Me 209 V6, it was transferred to the Bf 109H programme when the Me 209 was cancelled, and was completed with extra centre-section, lengthened forward fuselage, extended wingtips (total span 13.26 m/43 ft 6 in) and redesigned tail surfaces. First flying on 22 December 1943, the V55 was initially powered by a DB 605B, which was essentially a standard DB 605 fitted with the larger supercharger of the DB 603. When the DB 603G engine, for which the V55 had been designed, failed to materialise, the aircraft subsequently had a Jumo 213E installed. On 25 February 1944 the Bf 109H V55 was destroyed in an air attack, a similar fate befalling the V54 in August. By that time, however, the Bf 109H programme had long been cancelled in favour of development of the Focke-Wulf Ta 152H.

The final 'Gustavs'

Production of the Bf 109 had run at a surprisingly low level for the early part of the war, but in 1943 it began to pick up considerably, peaking in mid-1944. The constant attention of the Allied bombing efforts were met with a dispersal of production, although assembly remained the province of the three main factories: Messerschmitt at Regensburg, Erla at Leipzig and WNF at Wiener Neustadt. Some attempts were made to move engine production into disused mines, but the humidity caused corrosion of the tooling. The big push to increase production was administered by the newly created Jägerstab, which used the threat of imprisonment, or worse, to coerce the factories into producing more and more fighters. The result, inevitably, was bad workmanship, resulting in many aircraft being delivered with serious defects.

However, at the front line the numbers of serviceable Bf 109s did not rise appreciably, for two reasons. Firstly, Allied aircraft were shooting down Messerschmitts almost as fast as they were being built and, secondly, aircraft with relatively minor damage were not being repaired owing to a lack of

Above: This pair of late 'Gustavs' consists of a G-14 nearest the camera and a G-10 behind. The latter has the DB 605D engine fitted, with its characteristic small bulges low down on the sides just behind the propeller. It also has the FuG 16ZY radio antenna under the port wing.

Left: This Croatian Bf 109G-10 was surrendered at Falconara in April 1945. It cannot be seen whether it has the DB 605D engine, or whether it was fitted with the DB 605AS. Until surrender, the Croatian volunteer unit operated under Jagdfliegerführer Ostpreussen.

spare parts. The increased production drive concentrated almost exclusively on building new aircraft, with little thought to the provision of additional components for the field repair of aircraft. Large numbers of aircraft were left lying around airfields while awaiting new parts, a problem exacerbated by the differing configurations of the aircraft themselves.

In July 1944 the first of a new variant – the Bf 109G-14 – entered production, and it was soon active in the skies of western Europe, especially facing the US/Commonwealth forces which had landed in France the previous month. The concept behind the G-14 was to rationalise the production standard of the fighter and to incorporate all of

Left: Seen in May 1945 at Prague-Kbely, this DB 605AS-powered Bf 109G-10 wears the green/white/green RV bands of I./JG 51. The AS and D engines both replaced the engine gun fairings with a neater unit, seen here partially removed.

Below: This Bf 109G-10 was captured and tested by the USAAF. It is seen here in July 1946 at Patterson Field, where it was painted in an approximation of a mottled Luftwaffe scheme. Note that the aircraft has the two additional fixed rudder tabs seen on some aircraft.

Bf 109G-10

To maximise its assets, the Luftwaffe introduced the G-10 variant as a means of bringing older G airframes (G-6s and G-14s) up to the standard of the new-build K-4. However, not all of the K's improvements could be incorporated into all of the remanufactured G-10s, with the result that they were completed in many configurations. The G-10 became the most important variant (alongside the K-4) of the last months of the war, with about 2,600 upgrades completed.

Right: A Bf 109K-4 displays the salient features of the variant: additional main undercarriage doors (rarely fitted in service), retractable long tailwheel, deep oil cooler bath and the relocation aft of the direction-finding loop antenna.

This close-up reveals the installation of the DB 605D in the Bf 109K-4, and how the main undercarriage leg was attached to the fuselage structure rather than the wing spar.

This is another view of the same aircraft. Large numbers of late-model 'Gustavs' and K-4s were found by the Allies in semi-derelict state.

the modifications which had been developed for the G-6 during its long production. From the outset this aim failed abysmally, and G-14s appeared in almost as many combinations as their predecessors. As far as is known all had the Erla canopy, but they appeared with various antenna configurations, long or short tailwheels and tall or regular fins. Engine cannon armament was either the MG 151/20 or MK 108. The first aircraft were powered by the DB 605AM with MW-50 boosting, but were also followed by G-14/AS aircraft with the DB 605AS. One small difference between the G-6 and G-14 was the relocation of the FuG 16ZY antenna (when fitted) from the centreline to under the port wing.

As production continued, some minor improvements were incorporated to some aircraft. In addition to the Flettner rudder tabs, some G-14s were fitted with two fixed tabs above and below the moveable surface, projecting beyond the rudder line. A new rudder of subtly altered shape was introduced, this being fabric- instead of plywood-covered, and tapering to a more pronounced point at its aft-most corner. G-14/AS aircraft appeared with a new, larger oil cooler (although the old unit was inevitably fitted to some aircraft) with a correspondingly deeper chin intake and fairing. At the end of 1944, larger mainwheels were adopted, in turn requiring a wing redesign which dispensed with the characteristic rounded wing bulges in favour of larger, rectangular fairings. To maintain the confusion, many G-6s were refitted with these wings.

As a final twist in the convoluted tale of the 'Gustav', repairable G-6s and G-14s were reworked at the factories to become Bf 109G-10s, this version being roughly equivalent to the Bf 109K-4. The definitive engine for the K-4 was to be the DB 605DM, but apparently few such engines reached the G-10, most being completed as Bf 109G-10/AS aircraft with the DB 605AS. Production got under way in October 1944, and amounted to about 2,500 aircraft. As with the G-14, any attempt at standardisation failed, and the G-10s emerged in a bewildering array of configurations, although most had the tall tailwheel and tall, wooden tail.

One feature which was new to at least some G-10s was a revised cowling, introduced for the DB 605DM engine. The slightly larger size of the new engine required the addition of a small bulge on either side of the cowling just below the forward exhaust stub. The presence of these bulges did not necessarily mean the aircraft was powered by the new engine, for several were completed with the new cowling but retained the DB 605AS. G-10s remanufactured by WNF were known as Bf 109G-10/U4s, the Umbaustaz designation covering the installation of the MK 108 cannon in place of the MG 151/20. Various Rüstsätze were fitted, including R1 (bomb-rack), R3 (auxiliary fuel tank), R5 (gondola-mounted MG 151/20s), R6 (rudder-control autopilot) and R7 (WGr 21 rocket tubes).

Bf 109K

As might be gathered from the descriptions above, the late-model Bf 109Gs represented a minefield of confusion, and positive identification of exact models became virtually impossible without reference to Werknummern. While all this has become a fascinating subject for modern-day researchers, full of conflicting opinions, it represented a serious problem for the Luftwaffe. Of course, the principal problem lay in the massed Allied armies approaching the very Reich itself, preceded by thousands of aircraft flown by well-trained and confident crews. However, the desperate defence against the growing onslaught was not made easier by the wildly differing standards of equipment reaching the front line. The Bf 109K represented a last effort to rationalise the chaotic Bf 109 production programme.

Development of the Bf 109K was spurred by the DB 605DM engine, which offered 2,000 hp (1492 kW) for take-off and 1,800 hp (1343 kW) at 5000 m (16,400 ft). A small batch of Bf 109K-0s was built, featuring the DB 605DB engine, without the MW-50 boosting of the DM.

Messerschmitt Bf 109K-4
III./Jagdgeschwader 53 'Pik As'
Kirrlach
Bavaria
March 1945

Last of the Bf 109s to enter quantity production under the original management, the Bf 109K-4 entered service with home-defence units in October 1944; by the end of November, a total of 534 had been delivered. The K-4 actually preceded the G-10 into service and both types (as well as G-14s) were often mixed within units. III./JG 53 was one of only four Gruppen to be solely equipped with the Bf 109K-4 at some point.

Wings and wheels
One of the improvements made to the basic Bf 109G airframe to make its ground handling more 'friendly' for inexperienced new pilots was the fitting of wider tyres during G-10 production and to all K models. In order to accommodate these wide (660x190 mm) wheels in the thin wing of the 109, large bulges were added to the top surface.

Markings and colours
This JG 53 aircraft wears the 'Pik As' (ace of spades) badge and this Geschwader's black 'defence of the Reich' band on the rear fuselage. On this bar is superimposed the vertical bar marking of the fourth Gruppe, and the yellow colour of the individual number further identifies it as an 11th Staffel machine. The national insignia are of the late-war outline type and the basic scheme is the less common 82 (dark green)/83 (bright mid-green)/76 (light blue) pattern.

Armament
Armament on the K-4 was all concentrated in the fuselage. The R6 gunpacks were a proposed field modification that was never fitted. The main weapon was the devastating MK 108 cannon mounted in the spinner, supplemented by two MG 131 13-mm machine-guns mounted above the engine.

and rudder
tall wooden tail first appeared on some G-5s and was uced into G-6 production in early 1944, although by no ns was it seen on all late examples of this variant. It was dard on the G-10. The unit, which featured a vertical er hinge line, was introduced to give a higher degree of rol during take-off. Being made of wood, it placed less n on the supply of strategic materials. The horizontal liser was also wooden and had a metal sheath on the ng edge.

Last days of JG 53
Despite its nominal Reich defence (bomber interception) role, JG 53 flew mainly tactical support missions after its withdrawal to Bavaria in the last weeks of the war. The Geschwader's last kills (a B-26 and an Auster) were scored on 24 April and its last operation was flown on 2 May. That same day, the surviving aircraft were drained of valuable fuel and burnt at Prien, south-east of Munich, and the personnel dispersed.

Tailwheel
Most K-4s had the long retractable type of tailwheel shown on this aircraft. The longer strut produced a shallower ground angle and improved the pilot's vision over the nose, as well as increasing the clearance for drop tanks and other stores. Many G-10s also had the long strut, but this was a fixed unit.

Reichsverteidigung Bf 109Ks

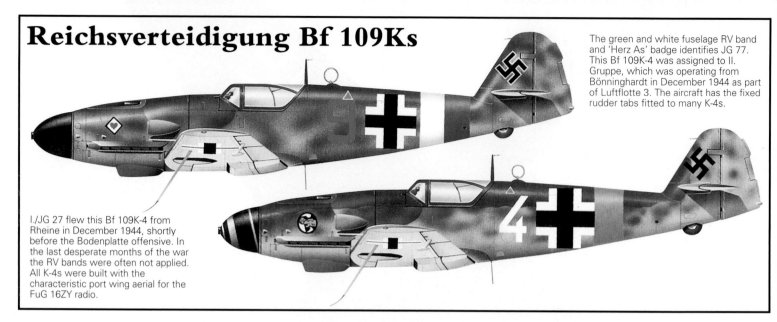

The green and white fuselage RV band and 'Herz As' badge identifies JG 77. This Bf 109K-4 was assigned to II. Gruppe, which was operating from Bönninghardt in December 1944 as part of Luftflotte 3. The aircraft has the fixed rudder tabs fitted to many K-4s.

I./JG 27 flew this Bf 109K-4 from Rheine in December 1944, shortly before the Bodenplatte offensive. In the last desperate months of the war the RV bands were often not applied. All K-4s were built with the characteristic port wing aerial for the FuG 16ZY radio.

Although some test aircraft were built, production of three early variants (the pressurised K-1, standard fighter K-2 and standard/reconnaissance fighter K-3) was cancelled at an early stage to make way for the K-4, which was to be the only mass-produced K variant, incorporating all of the 'standardisation' features of the similar G-10. Among these were DB 605DM engine with characteristic extra cowling bulges, tall fin, long tailwheel, deep oil cooler, wide-bladed propeller, rectangular wing fairings for the larger main-wheels and FuG 16ZY radio antenna under the port wing. The engine-mounted MK 108 was standard, although there are reports of Ks being fitted with the 30-mm MK 103.

Where the K-4 differed was in the relocation of the ADF loop antenna to further back on the spine, the addition of trim tabs for the ailerons (usually locked shut, as they caused a major discrepancy between the stick forces required to operate the tabbed ailerons and untabbed elevators) and the provision of additional undercarriage doors to cover the lower portion of the wheels which had traditionally been left open to the elements. The latter were usually removed by operational units. There were very small numbers of two Rüstzustände, R2 for reconnaissance and R6 with autopilot, while Rüstsätze applied included R1 (bomb), R3 (drop tanks), R4 (underwing cannon) and R6 (gun camera in the port wing).

Further development of the Bf 109K had largely ended by the beginning of 1945, and only the Bf 109K-6 can be ascertained, this being a heavy fighter with an MK 108 cannon installed in each wing (rather than in a gondola) in addition to the standard armament. A K-6 was certainly tested in late 1944, but it is not known if it was put into production. Various accounts mention Bf 109K-8 reconnaissance aircraft, while the K-10 and K-14 fighters may also have been built in small numbers. The last-mentioned was powered by the DB 605L high-altitude engine, allowing the aircraft to attain 727 km/h (452 mph) at 11500 m (37,730 ft), a very respectable performance for an aircraft originally designed 10 years earlier. The K-12 was a planned two-seat trainer.

Defence of the Reich

In the final year of the war the Reich was being squeezed from all sides, and on all fronts the Jagdflieger were very much on the defensive. Every Allied daylight operation was attended by huge numbers of escort fighters. During the early months of the daylight bombing campaign, the German day fighters had exacted a frighteningly heavy toll from the 8th AF heavy bombers, relatively unhindered. The arrival of the Merlin-engined P-51 Mustang at the start of 1944 changed all that, and anti-bomber missions became increasingly dangerous for Bf 109 pilots. The introduction of Bf 109G-10s and Bf 109K-4s could not in any way redress the balance, for even these advanced Bf 109s were no match for the P-51D or Spitfire Mk XIV.

Right: J-704 suffered a number of incidents during its Swiss carreer. After turning over in January 1945, its fin and rudder were replaced by the tall wooden unit. It was written off after a forced landing in November 1946.

Below: Like J-704, J-701 was one of the 12 Bf 109Gs delivered in May 1944. Two Luftwaffe Fs and two other Gs were interned during the war and put into service.

Right: Although heavily retouched, this photograph of an unfortunate Messerschmitt is noteworthy for depicting one of the Yugoslavian Bf 109G-12s, acquired as part of the large batch of aircraft supplied by Bulgaria as war reparations (in return, Yugoslavia also supplied the Bulgarians with much-needed Il-2 spares). The Yugoslavian aircraft differed from standard G-12s in being fitted with an Erla-Haube over the rear cockpit in place of the heavily-framed hood with bulged sides. This modification was almost certainly undertaken in Bulgaria.

Finnish fighters

The Finnish air force operated five sub-types of 'Gustav': the G-1, G-2, G-6, G-8 and G-10. The first appeared in 1943 and were swiftly thrown into the Continuation War with the Soviet Union. The 'Mersu' performed well in Finnish hands, although the numerically superior forces of the Red Army eventually overwhelmed the Finns.

Left: MT-201 was the first of the batch of Bf 109G-2s supplied to Finland in 1943.

On 1 January 1945 the Luftwaffe launched its last concerted offensive – Operation Bodenplatte. Over 800 fighters, including 17 Gruppen of Bf 109G/Ks from JGs 3, 4, 11, 27, 53 and 77, were launched on strafing attacks of 27 Allied airfields in France, Belgium and the Netherlands. Achieving almost complete surprise, Bodenplatte destroyed over 450 Allied aircraft, gaining a brief measure of respite for the ground forces facing the Allied ground attack onslaught. However, those aircraft were swiftly replaced, while the 150-plus pilots lost by the Luftwaffe during the course of the operation were not. These losses left the Jagdflieger reeling from a blow from which it was never to recover. To make matters worse, in the East, where most of the aerial fighting was conducted at low level, the Luftwaffe was facing large numbers of the excellent Lavochkin La-7 and Yakovlev Yak-3, both types which could leave the Bf 109 standing in terms of both speed and manoeuvrability.

As the Reich's territory shrunk by the day, the Luftwaffe found it easier to rapidly redeploy fighter forces to areas where they were most needed, and to the credit of the Germans they put up a savage defence against overwhelming odds on all fronts. Inevitably, the last weeks of war saw some desperate defence measures introduced, notably Operation Wehrwulf, which entailed stripped-down Bf 109s being deliberately rammed into USAAF bombers. A special unit was created for these attacks, the Sonderkommando Elbe. On 7 April 1945 it undertook its only ramming mission, hitting eight bombers for the loss of over 60 fighters.

The final account

Sizeable numbers of Bf 109s were still flying right up to the end, with around 800 on Luftwaffe charge at the end of the war. Many units had simply run out of fuel, while others were caught up in the rapid Allied advances. In early April 1945, the following units were still equipped with Bf 109Gs and Ks: II. and IV.(Einsatz)/JG 1, II. and III./JG 3, III./JG 4, III./JG 6, 1., 4. and 7./NJG 11, I., II. and III./JG 51, Stab, I., II. and III./JG 52, Stab., I., II., III. and IV./JG 53, Stab, I., II. and III./JG 77.

JGs 27, 52, 53 and 77 had flown the Bf 109 throughout the war, and between them had shot down an estimated 22,000-plus enemy aircraft. By far the most successful (and

the most successful fighter unit of all time) was Jagdgeschwader 52, which boasted a combat record of nearly 11,000 kills. Included in its personnel were 67 holders of the Ritterkreuz (Iron Cross), six of the 15 pilots to shoot down more than 200 aircraft, and the Luftwaffe's three top scorers (Erich Hartmann – 352 kills; Gerhard Barkhorn – 301 kills; Günther Rall – 275 kills). Given the

Seen at Erding in Bavaria in early 1943, this group of Finnish pilots relaxes before undertaking the delivery flight of the Bf 109G-2s in the background back to Finland.

After the war the Finns were restricted to 60 combat aircraft by the Allied powers. Of the 102 Bf 109Gs then in service, 42 were put into storage. The swastika insignia was replaced by the blue/white roundel after 1 April 1945. MT-504 'G' was a G-10 serving with HLeLv 31 in 1947.

Post-war operators

The Swiss Fliegertruppe operated a total of 14 Bf 109G-6s, 12 of which were purchased from Germany in a bizarre deal. The other two aircraft were Luftwaffe machines which landed in Switzerland and were interned. The 'Gustav' served with Fliegerkompagnie 7 from 1944 to 1947.

Finland's long association with the Bf 109G lasted until 1954 and encompassed several variants, this being a late-model G-6 with tall fin. The aircraft served with HLeLv 31 at Utti in 1948, and wears the post-armistice roundel markings which replaced the swastika device of the war years.

Above: This photograph is one of the very few to depict an S 99 (Bf 109G-14) in Czechoslovak AF service. The aircraft is marked with a red lightning flash on the fuselage.

Left: Carrying the civilian registration OK-BYH, this S 99 is one of the aircraft allocated to the Czechoslovak National Air Guard. The S 99 featured the standard armament of two MG 131 machine-guns and an engine-mounted MG 151/20 cannon.

Post-war Czechoslovak production

Faced with equipping its nascent air arm in the immediate post-war years, Czechoslovakia naturally turned to the Bf 109, which had been put into production at the Avia factory at Cakovice in the last months of World War II. No Bf 109s were finished during the war, but enough nearly-complete airframes had been built to assemble 20 Bf 109G-14s and a pair of Bf 109G-12s under the designations S 99 and CS 99, respectively. This paved the way for further production, which by circumstance was forced to turn to the Junkers Jumo engine.

Two airframes were completed as CS 99 two-seaters, these being similar to the Bf 109G-12. Both examples were believed to be unarmed, and provided a useful training capability for the young air arm. Although powered by the DB 605AS, the S/CS 99s were completed with the bulged cowling of the DB 605D.

amount of good fortune that must inevitably accompany fighting and flying skills in compiling a huge victory tally, it is perhaps not surprising that all three survived the war. 'Bubi' Hartmann had shot down his 352nd aircraft on the last day of the war, but was subsequently captured by the Russians and held captive for 10 years. Following his release, he returned to Germany, assuming command of the reborn Luftwaffe's premier fighter unit, JG 71 'Richthofen'. Both Barkhorn and Rall also served in the post-war Luftwaffe, the latter becoming the first German to solo in an F-104 Starfighter.

With the end of World War II came an abrupt end to the careers of many Luftwaffe aircraft types. The greatest exception was, of course, the Bf 109. For a start, four countries used the Bf 109 for some years after the end of

the war as front-line equipment. Switzerland had a single Fliegerkompagnie equipped with Bf 109G-6s until 1948, when P-51s arrived. Romania, too, flew the Bf 109G-6/-10/-14 until 1948. Yugoslavia acquired several ex-Luftwaffe and Croatian aircraft at the end of the war, and was also presented with about 60 Bf 109Gs from Bulgaria, including some G-12 two-seaters. They served for some years. The longest-lived Messerschmitts were those of Finland, which kept its fleet of mixed Gs flying until 1954. However, the basic design was to fly and fight for a good deal longer thanks to two indigenous production efforts – in Czechoslovakia and Spain.

Production in Czechoslovakia

In 1944 Germany had established a Bf 109 manufacturing organisation in the vicinity of Prague, feeding a final assembly line in the Avia works at Cakovice. Bf 109G-12 two-seaters and G-14s were produced in small numbers before the German withdrawal. Almost unbelievably, the capacity for Bf 109 production was left almost intact by both the departing Germans and liberating Soviets. At the end of the war, the Czechoslovak government ordered that the assembly line be reopened, plus a second one at the Letov factory at Letnany, to produce Bf 109s for the National Air Guard. Completed components were rounded up and enough gathered to complete 20 Bf 109G-14s, christened S 99 in local service, and two Bf 109G-12 two-seaters, which were designated CS 99.

Plans were hatched for a major production of Bf 109Gs to equip the regular air force (Ceskoslovenske Letectvo), utilising the many partly- or wholly-completed airframes then available and a large stock of DB 605AM engines being held in a sugar refinery warehouse. Unfortunately, the refinery burned to the ground in September 1945, taking with it all the precious DB 605AMs. Nevertheless, the idea was a sound one, promising a cheap and rapid way of providing an air force, so an alternative powerplant was sought. The only one available was the Junkers Jumo 211F (1000 kW/1,340 hp for take-off) and Jumo 211H (1060 kW/1,420 hp for take-off), intended for

Avia S 99 – the Czechoslovak G

The first equipment of the National Air Guard was the Avia S 99, powered by a DB 605AS. All had the tall tail associated with the Bf 109G-14, and were completed with the large mainwheels and corresponding rectangular wing fairings. The tailwheel, however, remained of the short variety. The Air Guard used a curved, triangular marking, later changed to a circular insignia for the Czechoslovak air force.

Avia S 199 – Jumo power

When the stock of DB 605s was destroyed in a fire, Avia had to look to the Junkers Jumo 211 to power its Bf 109 airframes. The result was an inelegant installation which retained the earlier bulges for the fuselage guns but which did not permit the installation of an engine cannon.

A pair of Czechoslovak air force S 199s is caught in flight. The 'Mezec' was armed with a pair of MG 131 machine-guns in the upper fuselage, and usually carried MG 151/20s under the wings in the standard Bf 109 gondolas.

He 111 bombers and by no means ideal, but available in quantity.

Adapting the Bf 109 airframe to take the Jumo was a relatively easy matter, and the first aircraft, designated S 199, first flew at Cakovice on 25 March 1947, with Petr Siroky at the controls. The S 199 was far from a good aircraft. The Jumo drove a VS 11 paddle-bladed propeller with vicious torque and, as soon as the tailwheel rose on take-off, the tail swung alarmingly, requiring an instant boot of rudder to counteract the swing. Handling the aircraft once airborne was demanding, and the performance was sluggish, the S 199 demonstrating a maximum speed of only 550 km/h (341 mph). In service, the S 199 quickly acquired the derisory nickname 'Mezec' (mule).

Deliveries to the CVL

Considerable numbers were built for the CVL, both Jumo 211F- and 211H-powered versions being on strength. First deliveries were made in 1948. Some of the original S 99s were re-engined and redelivered for service

CS 199

Right: CS 199 two-seater production reached 58 aircraft. Early production aircraft retained the original side-hinging canopy inherited from the CS 99/Bf 109G-12.

Below: Part way through the CS 199 production run a new aft-sliding canopy was introduced, greatly improving vision from both cockpits. The angle of the wheel axles was also changed during the production run.

as S 199s. Standard armament comprised two MG 131s in the upper fuselage and two MG 151/20 cannon in underwing gondolas, à la Rüstsatz-6. Some aircraft had MG 131s or MG 17s mounted in the wings in place of the gondola weapons. The 'Erla' hood with which the first aircraft were completed later gave way to an aft-sliding single-piece hood, which was bulged to give the pilot better visibility. To aid pilot conversion, Avia also produced 58 two-seaters, designated the CS 199 and first flying on 24 January 1949. They had armament removed, and initially flew with the standard Bf 109G-12-type side-hinging canopies. Later, a neater three-section aft-sliding canopy was developed and fitted.

S 199.185 was one of the aircraft rebuilt by Avia from a DB 605-engined S 99. The Vojenské Letectvo received its first S 199 in 1948, and the type served for some time into the 1950s before being replaced by modern Soviet jets (MiG-15 and Yak-23).

Large numbers of S 199s of the Czechoslovak air force are seen receiving maintenance. The original Erla-Haube canopy was soon exchanged for a new, bulged, aft-sliding Avia design.

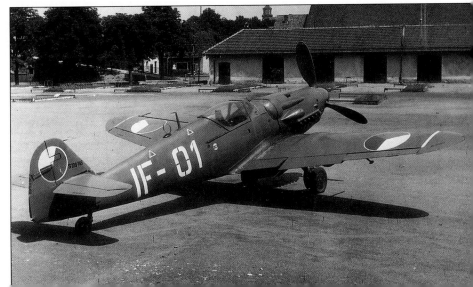

Above: 101 Sqn was the first unit to form in the Chel Ha'Avir, and it flew the S 199 into action within days of the fighters arriving in the newly-proclaimed state of Israel. 101 Sqn marked its aircraft with the now-famous red and white stripes, the rear fuselage bearing identification bands to prevent any confusion with Israeli Spitfires.

Right: 101 Squadron's Chief Technical Officer, Harry Axelrod, poses in front of D-123. Among the unit's pilots was well-known Bell test pilot Chalmers 'Slick' Goodlin.

Far right: A small number of S 199s were completed with MG 131 machine-guns mounted internally in the wings (making a total of four), rather than featuring podded cannon.

Right: This S 199, number 54, is seen at Munich after having been flown in by a defecting Czech political refugee. The national insignia have been hastily taped over.

Although the S 199 served for some years with the CVL and Czechoslovak National Air Guard, it is best remembered for its exploits with the only export customer: Israel. It was not until 14 May 1948 that the Jewish state of Israel had been created came into being, yet the fledgling Israeli air force had been created as early as March. It had money and volunteers in abundance, many of them experienced World War II veterans, but it lacked aircraft. An arms embargo had been placed on exports to the Middle East, preventing the Chel Ha'Avir from obtaining arms from the usual sources. Accordingly, the Israelis turned to Czechoslovakia, which was desperate for hard currency.

On 23 April 1948, a contract was signed covering the supply of 10 S 199s, at a unit price of US$190,000, this also including spares and ammunition. Under Operation Balak, Czechoslovakia was flying arms into Israel using a chartered Douglas DC-4, and it was by this means that the 10 S 199s, plus 15 more signed for in May, arrived, disassembled, in Israel. In the meantime, Israeli pilots had been training at a clandestine school in Rome, before spending two weeks on S 199 conversion in Czechoslovakia.

Within days of the declaration of the state of Israel, attacks came from its Arab neighbours. The rapid procurement and training effort had resulted in No. 101 Squadron at Ekron being made combat-ready on S 199s in time. The first operational sortie, a strafing attack by four aircraft, was mounted on 19 May. During the mission two of the aircraft were lost: one to ground fire and the other in a landing accident. This set the scene for the S 199's less than illustrious career in the Chel Ha'Avir. Disliked by Israeli pilots as much as it was by the Czechoslovaks, the S 199 suffered from an alarming accident rate, while it proved to be nearly useless in combat. Nevertheless, it did achieve a few kills, the first being the shooting-down of two bomb-carrying Egyptian C-47s on 3 June by No. 101 Squadron's commander, Mordechai 'Modi' Alon.

The 'Mule' at war

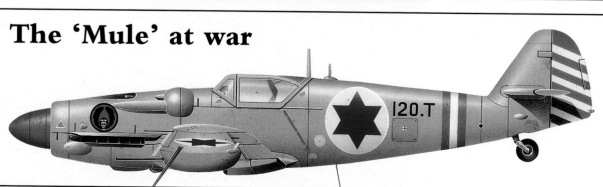

Desperate for fighters, the fledgling Israeli air force (Chel Ha'Avir) was in the market for anything that could get past the United Nations arms embargo. Czechoslovakia was desperate, too, for hard currency, and the Israelis were offering US dollars. A total of 25 early production aircraft was delivered. On 29 May 1948, the S 199 flew its first combat mission in Israeli hands.

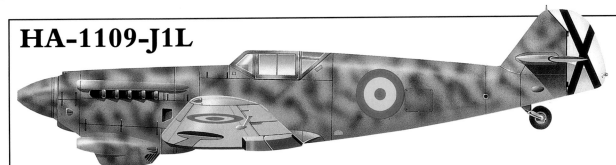

HA-1109-J1L

Twenty-five HA-1109-J1Ls were built up from Bf 109G-2 airframes originally supplied by Germany, with the Hispano-Suiza 12Z 89 engine installed. None was issued for service, although they underwent limited trials. This aircraft is seen as it appeared on trials with the Escuadrón de Experimentación en Vuelo at Cuatro Vientos.

Hispano power

Faced, like Czechoslovakia, with no suitable powerplant for its Bf 109G airframes, Spain turned to the Hispano-Suiza 12Z engine. The physical installation of the engine was painless, but the powerplant was not really suitable for the Bf 109, the resulting aircraft being underpowered and having some less than ideal handling characteristics.

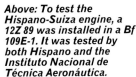

Above: To test the Hispano-Suiza engine, a 12Z 89 was installed in a Bf 109E-1. It was tested by both Hispano and the Instituto Nacional de Técnica Aeronáutica.

Above: 6-119 was the Bf 109E-1 used for the trial engine installation. It had been delivered to the Legion Condor in 1939 and left behind for use by the Ejército del Aire.

Below: Fitting the fuel-injected Hispano-Suiza 12Z 17 engine to produce the HA-1109-K1L certainly improved both the looks and the performance of the Spanish '109, but it was still some way short of being a viable combat aircraft.

Crippling the HA-1109-J1L in terms of drag was the inelegant and bulky carburettor and oil cooler installation under the engine. The fuel-injected 12Z 17 removed the need for a carburettor and cut drag by a large factor.

received Bf 109Fs. Anxious to maintain a modern fighter force, the Spaniards approached Germany in 1942 to acquire a licence to manufacture the Bf 109G-2, resulting in an agreement by which Hispano-Aviación (part of the newly created CASA concern) would undertake the work. Germany would provide 25 broken-down airframes, together with drawings, jigs and tools, followed by armament, propellers and engines for another 200 aircraft.

Delays dogged the establishment of the Hispano production line so that by the time it was ready, the worsening war situation meant that Germany only managed to supply the original 25 airframes (and these lacked tails) and incomplete drawings. Hispano was faced with a considerable struggle to produce a fighter, the major problem being the lack of a suitable engine. By late 1944 it was painfully obvious that the long-promised DB 605s would not appear,

On 18 July two S 199s tackled two Egyptian Spitfires, probably the last time the two old warriors met head-to-head. Alon accounted for one of the Spitfires that day, but it was obvious that the 'Mule' was largely ineffective. It was the S 199 that killed Alon on 16 October 1948 in an accident. Thankfully for the Chel Ha'Avir, Spitfire Mk IXs and P-51Ds soon arrived to redress the balance and allowed the new air force to provide a meaningful defence. By the time the fighting ceased in January 1949, only about five S 199s were still airworthy, flying alongside Spitfires and Mustangs for a short while, but by the end of the year they had disappeared from service. Despite its failure, the S 199 had proved to be an invaluable morale booster at a time when Israel was desperately fighting for its very survival.

Spanish production

Bf 109s, albeit in a rather different guise, were still flying at the other end of the Mediterranean long after the S 199. Spain had made the first combat use of the Bf 109 back in 1937, and it was perhaps fitting that the old warrior should see out its operational days in the Iberian peninsula. The Ejército del Aire was no stranger to the Bf 109, having operated those left behind by the Legion Condor, and later

Armament trials

As it first appeared, the HA-1109-K1L was unarmed, and a series of trials was run to investigate possible armament options for the type. The originally intended weapons were two wing-mounted Breda-SAFAT 12.7-mm (0.50-in) machine-guns under the wings, but a role change from fighter to ground-attack saw the adoption of various rocket, gun and cannon options.

Above: This HA-1109-K1L was fitted with the armament initially specified for the type, namely two Breda-SAFAT 12.7-mm machine-guns in underwing pods. At the time, a fighter role was envisaged for the type.

Above right: The final choice of armament retained the Oerlikon rockets, but added a 20-mm Hispano-Suiza cannon in each wing, necessitating the addition of a prominent wing fence to smooth airflow. With this armament, aircraft were delivered as HA-1112-K1Ls.

Right: In its unarmed HA-1109-K1L form, the Spanish Bf 109 was a sleek aircraft. None was delivered to a service unit, all being used for trials pending delivery of the armed aircraft.

Below: Most of the armed HA-1112-K1Ls were delivered to the Escuela de Caza (fighter school) at Morón for use as advanced ground attack trainers.

Above: The designation HA-1109-K3L covered this aircraft, which flew with no gun armament but with eight launchers for 80-mm Oerlikon rockets under the wings. The HA-1109-K2L was similar but had 12.7-mm machine-guns above the engine.

and so, as in Czechoslovakia, the search was on for a new engine. The answer, initially, came in the form of the Hispano-Suiza 12Z 89, a 12-cylinder engine rated at 970 kW (1,300 hp) for take-off, which had just entered production. One example was tested in a Bf 109E-1 (6-119) by the Air Test and Development Centre at Cuatro Vientos, and although the results were merely satisfactory (the aircraft was at least faster than the Bf 109E), the 12Z 89 was adequate – and, besides, there was nothing else.

Assembly began on the 25 Bf 109 airframes supplied from Germany, followed by production of the 175 remaining airframes from entirely Spanish sources, the Hispano engineers having been able to reverse-engineer some of the parts for which accurate drawings had not been provided. With the designation HA-1109-J1L, the first 12Z 89-powered Messerschmitt flew from Tablada on 2 March 1945, initially fitted with a Hamilton-Standard (VDM) propeller, as the intended production propeller, the Swiss Escher-Wyss V71 L1, had not yet arrived.

Installing the Hispano-Suiza engine required considerable redesign of the cowling, fuel and oil systems and the engine bay, although the original Messerschmitt bearers were easily adapted to the new powerplant. The vertical tail surfaces were also modified to cater for the Hispano's propeller turning to the right, instead of the left as with the DB 605. The self-sealing tanks were replaced by metal units. With the Ejército del Aire designation of C.4J (C=Caza – fighter), the prototype went to the INTA (Instituto Nacional de Técnica Aeronáutica) for testing in January 1946 at Alcalá de Henares. Soon after the Escher-Wyss propeller was fitted. In 1947 the prototype was damaged at Morón.

Initial production variant

That year, the first of the 25 Bf 109Gs flew as a HA-1109-J1L, on 10 July. The remaining 24 aircraft were completed over a period of time, but none was issued to the EdA due to general dissatisfaction with the 12Z 89 engine. A replacement was found in the Hispano-Suiza 12Z 17, which provided a similar power output but was much improved in other areas, including having fuel injection. Both engine types were assembled in Barcelona using major components supplied from the French factory near Paris. The first six of these engines arrived in 1951 and were fitted to three of the original Bf 109Gs and three new-production aircraft, the first flight occurring in the spring. Two of these aircraft were fitted with de Havilland Hydromatic PD-63-335-1 propellers, with no provision for an engine-mounted cannon.

Designated HA-1109-K1L, but retaining the EdA C.4J appellation, the new variant was delivered to the air force from May 1952, initially to 11 Grupo de Experimentación

Below: Among the production of Hispano-engined aircraft was a pair of two-seaters, which remained devoid of armament throughout their lives. Designated HA-1110-K1L, the trainers featured a long, aft-sliding canopy. The first aircraft flew in 1953. Both were later re-engined with Merlins and both are still extant.

Merlin Messerschmitt

Alternative engines for the HA-1112 had been denied to the Spanish due to trade embargoes. In the early 1950s, relationships with the victorious Allied powers began to thaw, and trade sanctions lifted in 1952. This paved the way for an approach to the British for the Merlin in 1953, the Merlin 500-45 driving a four-bladed Rotol propeller being chosen. On 30 December 1954, the first HA-1109-M1L took to the air at San Pablo airport.

(later known as 11 Escuadrón) at Tablada. The first two aircraft were joined by a third in November, by which time the unit had moved to Morón. In 1952 another 19 HA-1109-K1Ls were taken on strength, most serving with the Escuela de Caza at Morón, although four were sent to INTA for tests and a solitary example served with Grupo 23 at Reus.

By the time the HA-1109-K1L entered service, it was obvious that the aircraft could not be used as a fighter, and the originally intended armament of two wing-mounted 12.7-mm (0.5-in) Breda-SAFAT machine-guns was only fitted to one aircraft. Instead, the aircraft was envisaged for ground attack duties, and a series armament trials ensued. One aircraft, designated the HA-1109-K2L, received two Breda-SAFAT guns above the engine and underwing launchers for eight 80-mm Oerlikon rockets. The HA-1109-K3L was a single aircraft with rockets but no guns. Finally, the last of the J1Ls, suitably re-engined with a 12Z 17, had been modified with rocket launchers and a pair of Hispano HS-404 20-mm cannon in the wings. This became the standard configuration, and most of the C.4Js were modified with the new armament, being redesignated as HA-1112-K1Ls in the process. Most were used for operational training.

Meanwhile, in 1951, work had begun on a two-seater version for type conversion, the HA-1110-K1L. Only the two prototypes of this variant were built, flying for the first time in October 1953. The aircraft represented a considerable internal rearrangement, as the normal seat was moved forward to make room for the instructor. The aircraft were unarmed, and the fuel tankage was redesigned and rearranged to bring the quantity (423 litres/93 Imp gal) above that of the 400 litres (88 Imp gal) of the single-seater. The two-seat cockpit was covered by an elegant aft-sliding canopy arrangement which dramatically improved the view compared to the single-seater.

Merlin power

Airframe production had outstripped the provision of powerplants, so that by the end of 1949 80 had left the factory, with more following. Soon after the service introduction of the C.4J it was apparent that the type was not only worthless as a fighter, but it had little combat potential

at all. Again, a new engine was needed to power the large number of completed airframes which were piling up at the factory. The only answer was the Rolls-Royce Merlin. Considering that way back in 1935 it was a Rolls-Royce engine which had taken the first ever Bf 109 aloft, and that the Merlin had powered the Spitfires that had been the Bf 109's main opposition throughout World War II, the choice was supremely ironic.

Earlier, the Merlin had been unavailable due to arms embargoes, but in the early 1950s these were dropped, and an order was placed in the summer of 1953 for the two-speed Merlin 500-45, which developed 1200 kW (1,610 hp) for take-off. A four-bladed Rotol R116/4F5/12 propeller was fitted. The first conversion was aircraft no. 197, and flew for the first time – unarmed – on 30 December 1954 at San Pablo with Fernando de Juan Valiente at the controls. Designated HA-1109-M1L, the aircraft was found to have much improved performance in all areas. It was never as fast as the late-model German aircraft, being capable of 674 km/h (419 mph) at 4000 m (13,125 ft), and in service the armament imposed severe drag penalties, but it was respectable for the task it was asked to perform. Problems in the original design which were never addressed concerned the weak undercarriage and poor brakes, which were to cause a relentless series of accidents throughout the aircraft's career.

Above left: The first and second Merlin-powered Messerschmitts were designated HA-1109-M1L, and were unarmed. Subsequent aircraft were the re-engined armament trials aircraft, resulting in the designations HA-1112-M1L, M2L and M3L. In the event, the original armament of the HA-1112-K1L was retained.

Left: The installation of the Merlin may not have been as elegant as that in the Spitfire, but it dramatically improved the HA-1109's performance. This remained some way short of that achieved by the late-model Bf 109Gs and Ks, but for an aircraft whose task was ground-attack it was nevertheless respectable.

Proudly wearing the badge of Ala 7 de Caza-bombardeo (a diving pelican superimposed on the numeral '7') on its nose, this HA-1112-M1L was assigned to 71 Escuadrón, the first unit to form on the type. When deliveries to the unit exceeded 100 examples, a second Escuadrón (72) was formed, and Ala 7 was created to administer both. A third front-line unit was 364 Escuadrón, part of Ala Mixta 36, whose aircraft wore a white eight-pointed star. Buchóns were initially painted in a dark blue scheme, with a stylish black panel to hide the soot deposits from the exhaust.

Above: The HA-1112-M1L was the only variant of Spanish-built Bf 109 to see widespread service. It also saw limited action, flying close support sorties during the long-running counter-insurgency war in Spanish Sahara (Ifni War). Operations were conducted from the airfield of Gando in the Canary Islands, or from forward bases on the mainland.

Above right: Seen receiving maintenance outside its hangar at Tablada, this 71 Escuadrón Buchón displays the installation of the Merlin. As with the Hispano-Suiza 12 Z engines, the fitment of the Merlin was remarkably easy.

Both two-seaters were also re-engined with Merlins, becoming HA-1112-M4Ls in the process. Whereas Hispano-engined aircraft had been designated C.4J by the Ejército del Aire, all Merlin-powered aircraft were known as C.4Ks.

Armament tests followed soon after, with Merlins being installed in an HA-1112-K1L (to become the HA-1112-M1L), HA-1109-K2L (HA-1112-M2L) and HA-1109-K3L (HA-1112-M3L). In the event, it was the first which was chosen for standardisation, armed with the eight underwing rocket launchers and two HS-404 or HS-808 cannon in the wings. The deep-breasted profile of the Merlin-engined variant led to its being christened the Buchón (pigeon).

HA-1112-M1Ls, with the military designation C.4K, were delivered to the EdA from 1956, and production eventually accounted for 171 HA-1112-M1Ls, including some earlier Hispano-engined aircraft being fitted with the British powerplant. Both two-seaters were also re-engined, becoming HA-1112-M4Ls in the process, and being serialled C.4K-35 and C.4K-112.

Buchón enters service

Initial deliveries went to 71 Escuadrón de Caza-bombardeo at Tablada, which was declared combat-ready in 1957 as part of Grupo 7. In November fighting broke out in the Spanish Sahara when rebels backed by newly-independent Morocco attacked government communications to begin the war of Ifni. 71 Escuadrón was dispatched

to Gando in the Canary Islands, from where the main counter-insurgency effort (using T-6s and CASA 2.111s) was being conducted. To make the long journey, the C.4Ks were fitted with a hastily-produced auxiliary belly tank, and were escorted by CASA 2.111s providing navigation support (it is difficult to imagine that 12 years after the end of World War II Heinkel He 111s and Messerschmitt Bf 109s would be flying off to war again).

Once in theatre, the C.4Ks flew policing patrols from both the Canaries and bases in the desert, strafing and rocketing rebel groups when they were discovered, and occasionally making night attacks with illumination provided by CASA 2.111 flare-ships. Buchóns also provided close air support for motorised penetrations into the Sahara territory, and also for a Spanish Marine amphibious landing near the capital of El Aaiun. While the majority of the C.4Ks returned to Spain in the spring of 1963, a detachment was maintained both at Gando and at several desert strips. Although several were hit by ground fire, no Buchóns were lost to rebel action, although operational accidents accounted for six. The Merlin engines were temperamental in the desert climate, and the armed T-6 and its simple air-cooled engine was found to be a more reliable close support platform. As sufficient numbers became available, the HA-1112-M1L withdrew from the fighting, although they remained on detachment until late 1964.

Deliveries of Buchóns had gathered pace during the campaign, so that a new parent unit, Ala 7, was established to control 71 Escuadrón and the newly-formed 72 Escuadrón, both employing a diving pigeon badge. At this time, the dark blue colour scheme gave way to light grey with blue undersides. The only other operational Buchón unit was 364 Escuadrón, which flew the type only briefly in 1963/64 with Ala Mixta 36, taking over the Gando detachment from Ala 7. One aircraft became the personal mount of the commander of the Academia General del Aire at San Javier.

Back in Spain, at Tablada, Ala 7 was increasingly involved in weapons training, but also kept as reserves for close support operations. In mid-1965 the wing was renumbered as Ala 47, and its inventory, which had once stood at over 100 aircraft, was still a respectable 55, operated by 471 Escuadrón. However, with the wholesale transition to jets (it strains credibility that Spain had F-104Gs and Buchóns in the inventory at the same time), the usefulness of the C.4K, even in the training role, had virtually evaporated. In November 1965, Ala 47 disbanded and its aircraft retired, many heading for the scrapman's torch.

Movie star

Not all of the Buchóns reached the smelting pot, for in 1968 23 were purchased and refurbished for service in the

Hispano HA-1112-M1L Buchón (C.4K) Ala 7 de Caza-bombardeo Ejército del Aire Tablada 1959–65

The first Buchóns entered Ejército del Aire service with Escuadrón 71 at Tablada in 1957. Later in the year the unit moved to El Copero where it remained for a five-year period. This particular Buchón appeared in *Battle of Britain* in 1968, registered as G-AWHM. After filming, the aircraft was one of those purchased by Confederate Air Force 'Colonel' Wilson 'Connie' Edwards, and has been stored at his hangar at Big Spring, Texas to this day.

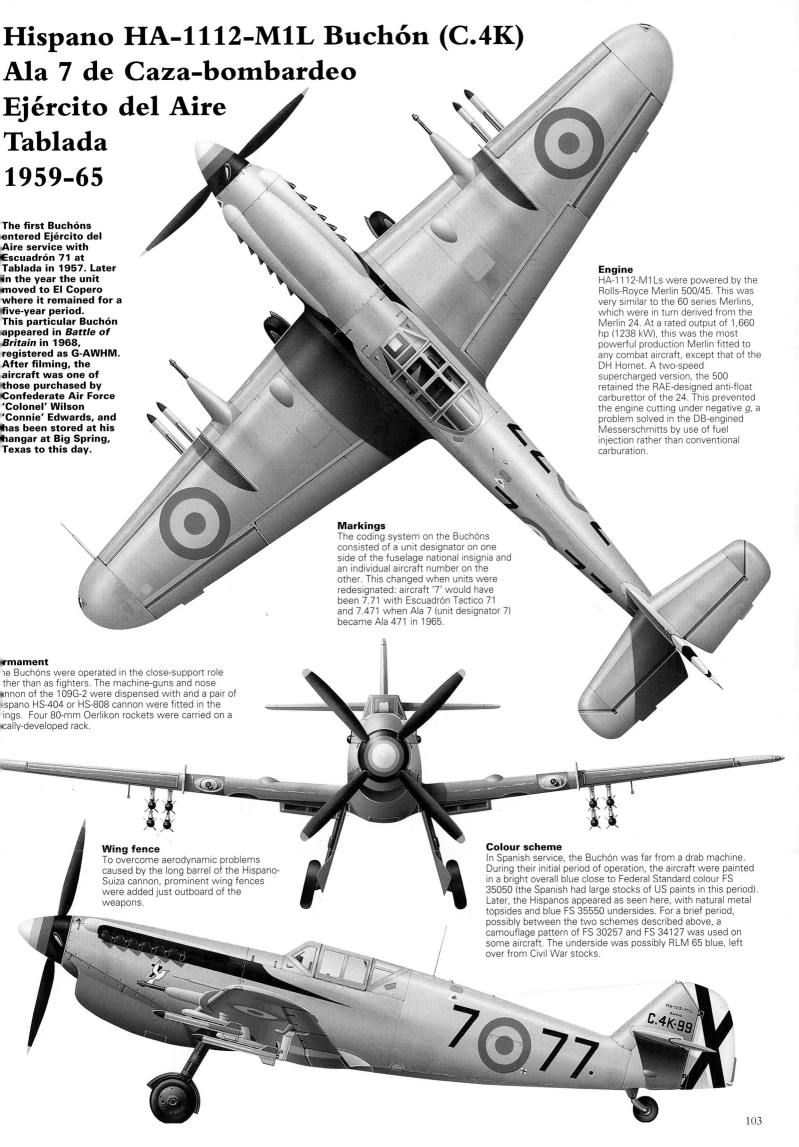

Engine
HA-1112-M1Ls were powered by the Rolls-Royce Merlin 500/45. This was very similar to the 60 series Merlins, which were in turn derived from the Merlin 24. At a rated output of 1,660 hp (1238 kW), this was the most powerful production Merlin fitted to any combat aircraft, except that of the DH Hornet. A two-speed supercharged version, the 500 retained the RAE-designed anti-float carburettor of the 24. This prevented the engine cutting under negative *g*, a problem solved in the DB-engined Messerschmitts by use of fuel injection rather than conventional carburation.

Markings
The coding system on the Buchóns consisted of a unit designator on one side of the fuselage national insignia and an individual aircraft number on the other. This changed when units were redesignated: aircraft '7' would have been 7.71 with Escuadrón Tactico 71 and 7.471 when Ala 7 (unit designator 7) became Ala 471 in 1965.

Armament
The Buchóns were operated in the close-support role rather than as fighters. The machine-guns and nose cannon of the 109G-2 were dispensed with and a pair of Hispano HS-404 or HS-808 cannon were fitted in the wings. Four 80-mm Oerlikon rockets were carried on a locally-developed rack.

Wing fence
To overcome aerodynamic problems caused by the long barrel of the Hispano-Suiza cannon, prominent wing fences were added just outboard of the weapons.

Colour scheme
In Spanish service, the Buchón was far from a drab machine. During their initial period of operation, the aircraft were painted in a bright overall blue close to Federal Standard colour FS 35050 (the Spanish had large stocks of US paints in this period). Later, the Hispanos appeared as seen here, with natural metal topsides and blue FS 35550 undersides. For a brief period, possibly between the two schemes described above, a camouflage pattern of FS 30257 and FS 34127 was used on some aircraft. The underside was possibly RLM 65 blue, left over from Civil War stocks.

In the summer of 1968 the skies over southern England were again filled with the evocative sight of Bf 109s dogfighting with Spitfires during filming of Battle of Britain. *The large setpieces were filmed from a specially modified B-25 Mitchell.*

movie *Battle of Britain*, which was completed the following year. This was not the first time the Buchón had played before the cameras, as several had been used during the filming of *The Star of Africa*, a film about the life of Hans-Joachim Marseille. Of the 23 purchased for the British film, 15 were resurrected as fliers, including one of the HA-1112-M4L two-seaters, all painted in Luftwaffe colours to play the part of Bf 109s. The remaining eight were employed in static roles. Although the Merlin installation had irrevocably altered the distinctive lines of the original Bf 109, the sight of the Luftwaffe-marked Buchóns lined up next to CASA 2.111s, Spitfires and Hurricanes on the airfield at Duxford (first operational home of the Spitfire) was one which would have been thought impossible when the RAF and Luftwaffe had slugged it out in the skies of southern England nearly 30 years earlier. With filming concluded, the aircraft became available for preservation by collectors and museums, joined by others from EdA stocks.

Shooting for *Battle of Britain* was the swansong for the Messerschmitt Bf 109 as a useful tool, although, thankfully, a number of airframes continue to delight air show crowds

in the hands of warbird enthusiasts, with more set to join them. From 1937 to 1965, the Bf 109 was in full military service – an amazing feat given the pace of aircraft development during that period. The Bf 109 was also one of the most numerous aircraft ever, with around 33,000 built. A large percentage of this figure covered the later variants, notably the G-6, which accounted for over a third of this figure.

Although the later variants lost much of the fine handling and fighting ability of the thoroughbred Bf 109E, the huge numbers built ensured that the aircraft remained the backbone of the Luftwaffe throughout World War II, flying in every theatre and doggedly defending the Reich against ever more unfavourable odds, right to the end. Its combat record is unmatched by any other warplane, and it was, by a wide margin, the aircraft type with the most kills. In the event, the Allied industrial machine could always produce more aircraft than the Bf 109 could shoot down, one of the many factors which doomed Germany to its fate. For the reasons above, however, the Bf 109 remains a true classic in the history of air combat. **David Donald**

Below: On the ground, the Buchóns, with their four-bladed propellers, looked a little less like Bf 109Es. All the aircraft seen here had wing cannon, unlike the aircraft above.

Filming *Battle of Britain*

Below: A single two-seat HA-1112-M4L was used in the making of Battle of Britain. *Registered G-AWHC, the aircraft has been stored by 'Connie' Edwards at Big Spring, Texas for nearly 30 years.*

Despite its deep-breasted appearance, the HA-1112-M1L made an acceptable Bf 109E for film purposes, and it was fortuitous that the Spanish air force was retiring the type when the producers of *Battle of Britain* were amassing the armada of vintage warplanes needed for the film. In all, 23 Buchóns were employed during filming, of which 15 were flown. Filming took place in Spain (for the 'France' scenes) and at Duxford, from where Buchóns, CASA 2.111s and RAF fighters operated for the aerial scenes.

Above: A Battle of Britain Hispano 'Messerschmitt' is seen at Duxford together with a CASA 2.111-D (Heinkel He 111H-16). These were used as transports in the Spanish air force and were also Merlin 500-powered.

Messerschmitt survivors

At least 58 post-Bf 109E Messerschmitts are known to exist in some form or other, with the likelihood of more appearing from the former Soviet Union, which has already yielded a number of airframes in recent years. Of the total, more than half are Spanish-built aircraft, including a unique HA-1109-K1L in the Spanish air force museum, which also has a Buchón. Of the 30 HA-1112-M1Ls Buchóns still extant, five remain in storage (along with the sole remaining M4L two-seater) at Big Springs in Texas, and other non-modified, non-flying examples are on display or under restoration to static condition in Canada, France, Germany (three), Spain and the USA (five). Another HA-1112-M1L is on display in the USAF Museum, masquerading as a Bf 109G with a DB 605 fitted. Three Buchóns are flying in the USA with the Confederate Air Force, Planes of Fame Museum and Erickson, while in Europe single airworthy Buchóns reside in Belgium and the UK (Old Flying Machine Company). The OFMC has an additional example being restored to fly, and another aircraft should fly in the USA.

More adventurous have been the projects which have married Buchóns to DB 605 engines for flying purposes. The first was undertaken by Messerschmitt-Bölkow-Blohm (now Daimler-Benz Aerospace) using much of the fuselage of a Bf 109G, DB 605 engine and Buchón parts to create an aircraft which flew again in 1983. The aircraft crashed, and was rebuilt using another airframe. The German Hans Dittes also produced a 'Bf 109G' by using a Buchón and DB 605, with some genuine 'Gustav' parts. This aircraft flies from the Imperial War Museum's airfield at Duxford in England, where it shared hangar space with the IWM's own Bf 109G. Three more Buchóns are being rebuilt to fly again with DB 605s, two in France and one in the USA.

Only three Avia-built aircraft are extant, an S 199 under restoration and a CS 199 on display with the Czech air force museum at Kbely, while the third aircraft, a CS 199, is on display at the Israeli air force museum at Hatzerim.

As far as genuine Messerschmitts are concerned, there are five 'Friedrichs' extant, including two being restored in the UK, one in France and another in Finland. At the time of writing the only example on public display is the immaculate Bf 109F-2/Trop in the South African Military Museum. 'Gustavs' are far more numerous, with at least 16 known to survive. Static examples are on display, in storage or under restoration in Australia, Canada, Finland (two), Italy, Norway, Russia, the USA (NASM and Planes of Fame) and Yugoslavia.

In recent years only one genuine Messerschmitt has been flying, that being the famous 'Black 6' of the IWM in the UK. Captured by the RAAF's No. 3 Sqn in Libya in November 1942, the Bf 109G-2/Trop was used for a series of trials in Egypt and the UK for the remainder of the war, and was subsequently used for static historical displays. In 1972 the painstaking restoration back to flying condition was started, culminating in a 'first' flight on 17 March 1991 at RAF Benson. Painted in its original JG 27 colours, the aircraft was due to fly for three years (subsequently extended to six) before being gracefully retired to static display. However, on 12 August 1997, at the end of what was to be its last ever flight, 'Black Six' was severely damaged in a landing accident at Duxford. Thankfully, the pilot, Air Chief Marshal Sir John Allison, CinC RAF Strike Command, escaped with minor injuries. The aircraft will be repaired back to at least ground display condition, but at the time of writing the world is without a genuine flying Bf 109. That may not be the case for long, for, in addition to a number of Bf 109E projects, two 'Gustavs' (a G-6 and a G-14) are being restored to airworthiness in Colorado.

Above: The Bf 109G-6 at the Finnish Air Force Museum was displayed outdoors at Utti Air Base for many years.

Above: This Bf 109G-6 is now displayed in the Yugoslavian Aviation Museum. A sister aircraft is being restored to fly in the USA.

Above: This CS 199 is now on display at the Czech air force museum at Kbely, near Prague. An incomplete single-seat S-99 is also in the museum.

Below: The Israeli Air Force Museum at Hatzerim displays an Avia S 199 marked as an aircraft of No. 101 Squadron. The aircraft was converted from a two-seat CS 199.

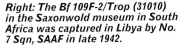

Right: The Bf 109F-2/Trop (31010) in the Saxonwold museum in South Africa was captured in Libya by No. 7 Sqn, SAAF in late 1942.

Above: This Buchón appeared in Battle of Britain, A Piece of Cake and Memphis Belle as a Luftwaffe Bf 109. It is now with the Cavanaugh Flight Museum in Texas.

Below: The only genuine Bf 109 to fly since the 1950s was G-2 'Black 6' (G-USTV), restored 1972-91 and flown 1991-97.

Above: Messerschmitt-Bölkow-Blohm converted a Buchón to DB engine power in the late 1970s. Despite two major accidents, it is currently airworthy.

Above: Hans Dittes owns this Bf 109G/HA-1112 composite (completed as a G-10), operating it from Duxford, from where it flew alongside the IWM's own 'Black 6'.

Bf 109 late-model operators

Luftwaffe

Production of all Bf 109 variants reached around 33,000 airframes, almost all of which were supplied to the Luftwaffe. Of this number, around 27,500 were late-model (Bf 109F, G and K) aircraft, this figure not including the large numbers of 'Gustavs' reworked as G-10s and G-12s. By far the lion's share of production was taken by the G-6, with over 12,000 produced. Throughout the early years of the war Bf 109 production was barely adequate to meet the demands of attrition, with the result that front-line units were spread extremely thinly as the war widened and more theatres of operations were introduced. Continuing to offset this trend were the ongoing successes of the Jagdflieger themselves, although time was swiftly running out.

The first dramatic rise in production occurred at the start of 1943, and it is no coincidence that this occurred soon after the two pivotal reversals at El Alamein (October 1942) and Stalingrad (November 1942). Only when attack turned to defence did the question of fighter production achieve a position of priority. As the war situation worsened, production climbed rapidly, reaching a peak in July to September 1944. From July 1944 production of aircraft other than fighters was phased out to concentrate the efforts of the whole German aviation industry. After September 1944 the figure steadily declined as the effects of the Allied bombing campaign began to bite ever deeper.

Production figures for individual variants vary depending on source, and for some variants records are incomplete. The following figures, taken largely from the excellent reference work *Messerschmitt Bf 109F, G & K Series: An Illustrated Study* (Jochen Prien and Peter Rodeike, Schiffer Military History, ISBN: 0-88740-424-3), are considered to be the most accurate, and provide the best guide as to the numbers of late-model Bf 109s – **F-0:** 14, **F-1:** 208, **F-2:** c.1,830, **F-3:** c. 15, **F-4:** 1,841, **G-0:** 13, **G-1:** 167, **G-2:** 1,587, **G-3:** 50, **G-4:** 1,242, **G-5:** 475, **G-6:** 12,000 plus, **G-8:** 900 plus, **G-10:** c. 2,600 conversions, **G-12:** c. 500 conversions, **G-14:** c. 5,500, **K-4:** c. 1,700.

In October 1940 the Bf 109F-1 entered service with the Geschwaderstab (wing staff flight) of Jagdgeschwader 51 on the Channel coast. It was not until the following spring, however, that the 'Friedrich' got into widespread service. The 'Gustav' followed in June 1942. Deployment of new variants was made rapidly, with the result that the primary Bf 109 units re-equipped with a quick succession of the major variants (F-2, F-4, G-2, G-4, G-6, G-14). From October 1944 G-10s and K-4s began to be delivered, and these became the most important variants of the last months of the war, although only a few units fully converted to the K-4, most retaining various G models on strength alongside the new arrival.

Of the major fighter formations, JGs 3, 5, 27, 51, 52, 53 and 77 stayed largely loyal to the Messerschmitt fighter throughout the war, while others converted to the Fw 190 (JGs 1, 2, 26 and 54). New units were introduced to the Bf 109 during the course of the war (JGs 4, 76, 300, 301 and 302),

A Bf 109G-2 is seen at cockpit alert in the desert, the starting handle already in place.

In 1941 the Bf 109F units were staffed by highly experienced fighter pilots, many of whom would go on to compile huge personal tallies. This group of JG 2 pilots from the Stabsschwarm comprises (from left) Leutnant Egon Mayer (102 kills, first to achieve 100 on the Channel front), Oberleutnant Rudolf Pflanz (52 kills in West), Gescwhaderkommodore Walter Oesau (123 kills) and Oberleutnant Erich Leie (118 kills).

especially as the war situation got worse. In the final months more desperate measures were taken, leading to the hasty conversion of bomber units to a day fighter role with Kampfgeschwader (Jagd) designations. Bf 109s also served with a large number of operational trials, night-fighter, training and tactical reconnaissance units. The following list provides a guide to the units operating the late-model Bf 109s, together with the variants confirmed as having been on strength.

Principal fighter units (Jagdgeschwader)

Stab/JG 1	F-2
I./JG 1	F-1, F-2, F-4, G-1, G-3
II./JG 1	F-4
III./JG 1	F-2, F-4, G-4, G-5, G-6, G-10, G-14, K-4
IV./JG 1	F-1, F-2, F-4
Stab/JG 2	F-2, F-4
I./JG 2	F-2, F-4, G-1, G-4
II./JG 2	F-2, F-4, G-4, G-5, G-6, G-14, K-4
III./JG 2	F-1, F-2, F-4
10./JG 2	F-2, F-4
11./JG 2	G-1, G-3
12./JG 2	G-4
Stab/JG 3	F-1, F-2, F-4, G-2, G-4, G-6, G-14
I./JG 3	F-1, F-2, F-4, G-2, G-4, G-5, G-6, G-10, G-14
II./JG 3	F-2, F-4, G-2, G-4, G-5, G-6, G-14
III./JG 3	F-1, F-2, F-4, G-2, G-4, G-6, G-10, G-14, K-4
IV./JG 3	G-4, G-6
Stab/JG 4	G-6
I./JG 4	G-2, G-4, G-6, G-10, G-14, K-4
III./JG 4	G-6, G-10, G-14, K-4
IV./JG 4	G-6, G-10, G-14
Stab/JG 5	F-1, F-4, G-2, G-6, G-14
I./JG 5	F-2, F-4, G-1, G-2, G-6, G-14
II./JG 5	F-2, F-4, G-2, G-6, G-14
III./JG 5	F-2, F-4, G-2, G-6, G-14
IV./JG 5	F-2, F-4, G-2, G-6, G-14
III./JG 6	G-6, G-10, G-14
II./JG 11	G-3, G-4, G-5, G-6, G-14, K-4
III./JG 11	G-6
Alarmstaffel/JG 11	G-6
Stab/JG 26	F-1, F-2, F-4
I./JG 26	F-2, F-4, G-1
II./JG 26	F-1, F-2, G-4
III./JG 26	F-1, F-2, F-4, G-4, G-5, G-6, G-14, K-4
10./JG 26	F-2, F-4
11./JG 26	G-1, G-3, G-4
12./JG 26	G-4
Stab/JG 27	F-4, G-2, G-6, G-14
I./JG 27	F-4, G-2, G-4, G-6, G-10, G-14
II./JG 27	F-4, G-2, G-4, G-5, G-6, G-10, G-14, K-4
III./JG 27	F-4, G-2, G-4, G-6, G-14, K-4
IV./JG 27	G-2, G-6, G-10, G-14, K-4
10./JG 27	F-4
Stab/JG 51	F-1, F-2, F-3, F-4, G-6, G-14
I./JG 51	F-1, F-2, G-6, G-14
II./JG 51	F-1, F-2, F-4, G-1, G-2, G-4, G-6, G-10, G-14
III./JG 51	F-1, F-2, F-3, F-4, G-6, G-10, G-14, K-4
IV./JG 51	F-1, F-2, F-4
Stab/JG 52	F-2, F-4, G-2, G-4, G-6, G-14
I./JG 52	F-1, F-2, F-4, G-2, G-4, G-6, G-14
II./JG 52	F-2, F-4, G-2, G-4, G-6, G-10, G-14, K-4
III./JG 52	F-2, F-4, G-2, G-4, G-6, G-10, G-14, K-4
Stab/JG 53	F-1, F-2, F-4, G-1, G-2, G-4, G-6, G-14
I./JG 53	F-1, F-2, F-4, G-1, G-2, G-4, G-6, G-10, G-14
II./JG 53	F-1, F-2, F-4, G-2, G-4, G-6, G-14, K-4
III./JG 53	F-1, F-2, F-4, G-4, G-6, G-14, K-4
IV./JG 53	G-14
10./JG 53	F-4
Stab/JG 54	F-1, F-4, G-2
I./JG 54	F-2, F-4, G-2
II./JG 54	F-2, F-4, G-2, G-4
III./JG 54	F-2, F-4, G-2, G-4, G-6
IV./JG 54	G-6
11./JG 54	G-3
I./JG 76	G-6, G-14
III./JG 76	G-6, G-14
Stab/JG 77	F-4, G-2, G-4, G-6, G-14
I./JG 77	F-4, G-2, G-4, G-6, G-10, G-14, K-4
II./JG 77	F-4, G-2, G-4, G-6, G-10, G-14, K-4
III./JG 77	F-4, G-2, G-4, G-6, G-14, K-4
Stab/JG 300	G-6, G-14
I./JG 300	G-5, G-6, G-10, G-14
III./JG 300	G-6, G-10, G-14
IV./JG 300	G-10, G-14
Stab/JG 301	G-6
I./JG 301	G-6
II./JG 301	G-6
III./JG 301	G-6
IV./JG 301	G-6
Stab/JG 302	G-6
I./JG 302	G-6
II./JG 302	G-5, G-6
III./JG 302	G-6

Other fighter units

Jagdgruppe Nord	G-6, G-14
Jagdgruppe Sud	F-2, F-4, G-2, G-4, G-6
Jagdgruppe Ost	F-2, F-4, G-1, G-2, G-4, G-6, G-14
Jagdgruppe West	F-4, G-0, G-1, G-2, G-6, G-14
Jagdgruppe 25	G-6
Jagdgruppe 50	G-6
Jagdgruppe 200	G-6
Jabo-Gruppe Afrika	F-2, F-4
I./EJG 1	G-6, G-14
II./EJG 1	G-5, G-6, G-14
III./EJG 1	G-5, G-6, G-14
IV./EJG 1	G-6, G-14
I./EJG 2	G-5, G-6, G-14
I./NJG 10	G-6

Close up, these wooden dummies did not look much like Bf 109s, but from an attacking aircraft travelling at low level they would have been convincing.

I./NJG 11	G-5, K-4
II./NJG 11	G-5, G-6, G-10, G-14
III./NJG 11	G-14
I./KG(J) 6	G-6, G-10, G-14, K-4
I./KG(J) 27	G-10, G-14, K-4
II./KG(J) 27	G-10, K-4
II./KG(J) 30	G-14
I./KG(J) 55	G-14
II./KG(J) 55	G-6, G-14
Jagdgeschwader 101-112 (fighter schools)	most variants up to and including G-6, G-12
Sonderkommando Elbe	G-6, G-10 (ramming unit)

Reconnaissance units

Aufkl.ObdL	F-4
4.(H)/12	F-4, G-2
2.(H)/14	F-4, G-2, G-4, G-6
(F)/100	F-4
(F)/122	F-4, G-2, G-4
(F)/123	F-4, G-2, G-4, G-5, G-6
(F)/124	G-4, G-6
NAGr 1	G-6, G-8, G-14
NAGr 2	F-4, G-2, G-4, G-5, G-6, G-8, G-10, G-14
NAGr 3	G-6, G-8, G-14
NAGr 4	F-4, G-2, G-4, G-6, G-8, G-10, G-14
NAGr 5	G-6, G-8
NAGr 8	G-6, G-8
NAGr 9	G-4
NAGr 11	G-5, G-6, G-8
NAGr 12	G-4, G-5, G-6, G-8
NAGr 13	G-5, G-6, G-8
NAGr 14	G-6, G-8, G-10, G-14
NAGr 15	G-6, G-8, G-10
NAGr 32	G-8

JG 53 'Pik As' was a stalwart of the Bf 109, flying the type to the end of the war. It served on all fronts, including in the desert where this II. Gruppe G-6 is seen.

Bulgaria

The Vazdushnite na Negovo Velichestvo Voiski (Royal Bulgarian air force) had taken delivery of 19 Bf 109E-4s in 1940, but it was not until 1943 that more Messerschmitts were delivered, in the form of 25 Bf 109G-4s. Further deliveries of G-2s and G-6s brought the VNVV total to 149, allowing the VNVV to largely retire its obsolete fighters such as the Avia B.534. The Messerschmitts served with the two Orliaks (regiments) of the 6th Iztrebitelen Polk (fighter division) for the defence of Sofia, which was under constant attack from USAAF bombers in 1943-44. The two main bases were Bozhouriste and Vrazhdebna. Over 50 kills were claimed by VNVV Bf 109s. Many were destroyed on the ground by Allied bombing attacks.

On 9 September 1944 Bulgaria joined the Allied cause, and VNVV Bf 109s were used against German forces, although there is no record of them having met Luftwaffe Bf 109s in air combat. At the end of the war more than 100 Bf 109G-10/12/14s were handed to Bulgaria after having been found intact in an Austrian factory. Fifty-nine of

Above: Bulgaria received 149 Bf 109Gs, this being a G-2 seen at Bozhouriste. The Bulgarian Bf 109s scored 65 kills, before joining the Allied cause.

Far right: Ground crew turn the propeller of a Croatian Bf 109G-2. The aircraft is marked with the red/white check shield of Croatia, and a coloured spinner.

Bf 109G-6 in France. However, there were not enough Bf 109s available, and so the 2nd and 3rd squadrons converted to the Fiat G.50 and Macchi MC.202. The original unit, now known as the 1st Fighter Squadron, re-equipped in late 1944 with the Bf 109G-10, operating the type from bases in Croatia and Italy until the end of the war.

Croatia

Raised as a volunteer force to fight alongside the German forces on the Russian front, the Croatian Legion included a fighter component established with Bf 109E-7s as the 15.(kroat)/JG 52, or kroat.J.St. This unit converted to Bf 109G-2s as early as July 1942, later converting to G-6s. However, the number of serviceable aircraft dwindled so that, by February 1944, it had only four machines at its base at Karankut in the Crimea.

It had long been planned to form two further Croatian Legion fighter squadrons, and personnel had received training on the

these were sent to Yugoslavia as war reparations. Bulgarian Bf 109s were withdrawn from service in 1946.

Czechoslovakia

At the end of hostilities Czechoslovakia set about creating a new air arm, using the large number of Bf 109G airframes that had

been completed under a late-war licence-construction scheme. A few S 99s and two-seat CS 99s were completed using DB 605 engines, but the bulk were S 199s and CS 199s powered by the Jumo 211 engine.

S/CS 99s served with the National Air Guard while deliveries of the S/CS 199 to the regular air force (Ceskoslovenske Vojenské Letectvo) began in February 1948. Service life was brief, as Soviet-supplied jets

became available in the early 1950s, the S 199 flying on with the National Air Guard until 1954. A few continued in use afterwards as trainers, with armament removed.

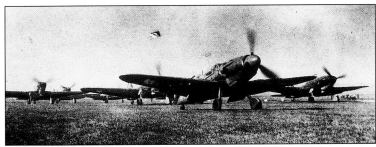

Left: Nineteen S 199s can be discerned in this view of a Czech air base. A handful of aircraft continued in service into the mid-1950s.

Above: An S 199 leads out a section of Il-10s for an attack mission. The S 199 exhibited a vicious swing on take-off.

Finland

The Ilmavoimat established a squadron (HLeLv 34, under Lentorykmentii 3) to operate the Bf 109 on 23 January 1943, but it was not until 13 March that the initial batch of 16 Bf 109G-2s reached Finland. A dozen more were delivered in May to allow HLeLv 34 to reach its operational strength of 28 aircraft. The regiment was divided into three squadrons, 1/HLeLv 34 being based at Malmi for the defence of Helsinki, while 2 and 3/HLeLv 34 operated from Utti. Soon 1 squadron moved to Suulajärvi, 2 squadron and the HLeLv 34 headquarters moved to Kymi, and 3 squadron took over the Malmi base. Finnish Bf 109G-2s found immediate success against the Soviets, shooting down over 100 aircraft (for the loss of six) between May and mid-September.

In April 1944 a batch of 15 Bf 109G-6s arrived for service with HLeLv 34, some of the displaced G-2s going to form a new unit: HLeLv 24. Additional aircraft arrived in May and June, including three G-8s for reconnaissance and G-10s. These deliveries allowed a third unit, HLeLv 28 at Lappeenranta, to partially equip with the 'Gustav'. Spares shortages led to poor serviceability, however. HLeLv 34 moved to Lappeenranta in June, and then to Taipalsaari, while HLeLv 24 deployed to Utti.

A total of 150 'Mersus' were supplied to Finland. By the time of the armistice on 4 September 1944, Finnish Bf 109s had accounted for 270 Soviet aircraft for the loss of 22 aircraft and 11 pilots. Owing to their lack of range, they took no part in the Finnish operations against German forces in Lappland. In December 1944 the two operational units, HLeLv 24 and 34, were

Above: Bf 109G-6s arrived with HLeLv 34 from April 1944, along with some G-8s and G-10s.

Right: MT-216 was from the first batch of Bf 109G-2s supplied to HLeLv 34 in March 1943.

redesignated as HLeLv 31 and 33, respectively, operating from Utti under Lentorykmentit 3 (from 1952 Lennosto 3). Two new units, HLeLv 11 and 13, were established under Lentorykmentit 1 at Luonetjärvi, although by 1952 they had dwindled to a single Hävittäjälentu (fighter flight). HLeLv 31 and 33 continued to operate the Bf 109G from Utti until 1954.

Hungary

As one of Germany's closest allies in the East, the Magyar Királyi Légierö (Royal Hungarian air force) was supplied with Bf 109s from an early stage. Bf 109F-4s were acquired to replace Reggiane Re 2000s in October 1942 for the 1/1 Vadasz Század, which operated as the ungarische Jagdstaffel on the Russian front. In early 1943 1/1 became 5/1 Vadasz Század, and re-equipped with Bf 109G-2s. In May it was joined by 5/2 Vadasz Század. The two units together formed 5/1 Vadasz Osztaly which was operated as part of VIII Fliegerkorps. In November 1943 5/1 Vadasz Század was withdrawn from the Russian front, while 5/2 was redesignated as 102 Önálló Vadasz Század. This was subordinated to Fliegerführer 102 Ungarn, becoming 102/1 when a second Bf 109G squadron, 102/2, was formed in May 1944. 102/2 was formed on the G-6 variant.

By the spring of 1944 two units (101/1 and 101/2) had been formed in Hungary to defend against the growing number of raids mounted by USAAF bombers. In April a third squadron was added, followed by three more by July. The combined six-squadron regiment was known as the 101 Vadasz Ezred. As the Wehrmacht fell back through Hungary, the two squadrons of the 102 Vadasz Osztaly were added to the 101 Vadasz Ezred, which then formed a ninth squadron. Despite the establishment of a Soviet puppet government and Hungary's 'surrender' on 20 January 1945, the 101 Vadasz Ezred continued to fight alongside the Luftwaffe, seeing out the war at Austrian bases. Most aircraft were destroyed prior to surrender in the Linz area.

Hungary operated large numbers of Bf 109s, peaking at nine squadrons. National insignia varied in presentation, but usually featured a white cross on a black square.

Israel

The infant Chel Ha'Avir acquired a total of 25 Avia S 199s with which to equip its first fighter unit, 101 Squadron. While pilots trained in Italy before a brief S 199 conversion course in Czechoslovakia, the aircraft were delivered (air-freighted in a Douglas DC-4) from 20 May 1948. 101 Squadron was based at Ekron, and began combat operations against the Egyptians as soon as it had sufficient aircraft. The S 199 force moved to Herzlea, and flew combat missions until January 1949, when the fighting ceased. By that time only a handful of S 199s were left, the fleet having suffered drastically from accidents and poor serviceability. The type was retired at the end of the conflict, its role having been assumed by the far better Spitfire Mk IX and P-51D Mustang.

This S 199 was seen on display in 1973. Bombs were not carried during the type's brief months of service.

Three of 101 Sqn's pilots pose with an S 199. They are (from left) Chalmers 'Slick' Goodlin, Aaron 'Red' Finkel and Syd Cohen. The squadron badge was a winged skull wearing a flying helmet.

Italy

The Regia Aeronautica received its first Bf 109s in early 1943 when Bf 109F-4s were supplied to form two units. These were the 3° Gruppo Caccia Terrestre (154ª and 155ª Squadriglia) and the 150° Gruppo CT (363ª and 364ª Squadriglia). Bf 109G-6s were subsequently supplied, shortly before the air force was divided into the pro-Allies Co-Belligerent air force and the pro-Axis Aviazione Nazionale Repubblicana. The ANR had two fighter units, of which the II° Gruppo Caccia Terrestre became operational on the Bf 109G-6 in September 1944. I° Gruppo CT became operational on the Bf 109G-10 in January 1945, and both Gruppi flew until surrendering in April 1945 at Udine and Gallarate. A third Gruppo was away in Germany converting to Bf 109s when the war ended.

This is a Bf 109G-10/AS of the ANR's I° Gruppo CT.

Italy's first Bf 109s were F-4s, and they fought in Libya alongside Luftwaffe machines, like this aircraft. It was assigned to the 363ª Squadriglia of the 150° Gruppo Caccia Terrestre. The unit's name was 'Gigi Tre Osei', the badge combining three stylised birds and a palm tree. The badge and name were inherited by the ANR's II° Gruppo.

Romania

Romania's air arm, the Fortelor Regal ale Aeriene Româna (Royal Romanian air force), had acquired 69 Bf 109E-4s from early 1942, and a year later began to receive Bf 109G-2s to equip the Grupul 1 Vinatoare, which was charged with the defence of the vital oilfields around Ploesti (along with earlier Bf 109s and IAR-80s). In mid-1943 Romania's air component on the Russian front, the Corpul 1 Aerian, also received Bf 109s in the form of G-6s and a few G-8s for reconnaissance. The fighter force was based at Zhdanov in the Ukraine, comprising 45, 46, 47 and 48 Escadrile. By the start of 1944 the Romanian contribution to I Fliegerkorps had been reduced to one squadron (rum 49. Jagdstaffel) based at Saki in the Crimea. Further Bf 109G-6 deliveries to units based at home swelled the numbers of the Corpul 1 Aerian, which had been retasked with home defence. 51 Escadrile was based at Tepes-Voda, while 52 Escadrile was at Mamaia. These units fought until the Romanian coup on 23 August 1944, after which they flew in support of the Red army, seeing action against German forces, notably during the battles around Klausenburg.

With the declaration of the People's Republic, the air force was retitled the Fortele Aeriene ale Republicii Populare Româna. In addition to its own aircraft, it took over Bf 109G-10s and G-14s from the Luftwaffe, and operated a mixed bag of 'Gustavs' until 1948.

These 'Gustavs' are two of the original Bf 109G-2s supplied to the home defence unit. The aircraft sport a heavily dappled camouflage.

Slovakia

Slovakia's air arm, the Slovenské Vzdusné Zbrane, had received Bf 109E-7s to equip its 11. Stíhací Letka at Piestany, and also the 13. Stíhací Letka on the Russian front, the latter operating as 13.(slowak)/JG 52 or slowak.J.St. In early 1943 this squadron received Bf 109G-6s, which it used against Russian forces, attached to the Slovak Fast Division. In April 1944 it was transferred back to Piestany to join the 11. Stíhací Letka, which had by then also converted to Bf 109G-6s, to defend Bratislava. By this time, the Slovaks were involved in clandestine discussions with the Allies, and fighting between Slovakian fighters and USAAF bombers was avoided. However, on 26 July 1944 all of 11. Stíhací Letka was wiped out after a fight started, inexplicably, with USAAF P-38s, which were escorting a

Above: This is one of the two Bf 109Gs which flew as part of the Combined Squadron, Slovak Insurgent air force. Note the revised national insignia under the wing.

Left: This Bf 109G Kanonenboote is from the 13. Stíhací Letka, or slowak Jagdstaffel, operating as part of JG 52 on the Russian front. The unit's aircraft wore standard Luftwaffe markings but with a white/blue/red spinner, the colours of the Slovak national flag.

B-24 raid. Two 13.Stíhací Letka Bf 109G aircraft (along with two Bf 109Es) were subsequently used during the Slovakian National Uprising of late August 1944, operating from Tri Duby airfield in 'free' Slovakia.

Spain

Spain's Bf 109 association dates back to the Civil War, when large numbers of 'Emils' were left behind for use by the Ejército del Aire. In early 1942 some Bf 109F-4s were supplied for use by 25 Grupo/23 Regimiento based at Alcalá de Henares. These were principally employed to train pilots for the Spanish volunteer force on the Russian front, which converted from the Bf 109E-7 to the F-4 in October 1942. This unit was known as the Escuadrón Azul, or in Luftwaffe parlance 15.(span)/JG 51.

Spain negotiated in 1942 with Germany to licence-build 200 Bf 109G-2s, of which 25 were supplied in kit form from Germany, together with tooling, jigs, armament and engines for the remaining 175. In the event, the DB 605 engines were not supplied, leading to the development by Hispano-Aviación of the HA-1109/1112 series.

None of the initial batch of HA-1109-K1Ls was delivered to a regular air force unit, being retained for trials purposes. However, the HA-1112-K1L was delivered, although only used as a trainer by the Escuela de Caza at Morón. A single example was operated by Grupo 23 and a number served

The Hispano-engined HA-1112-K1L was the first service type, but it was used almost exclusively for advanced training.

with trials units. It was therefore left to the Merlin-powered HA-1112-M1L Buchón to become the principal service variant. Initial deliveries were made to Escuadrón 71 of Grupo 7 at Tablada, which was soon involved in the war in Spanish Sahara. As deliveries gathered pace, a second squadron was formed, Escuadrón 72, in turn requiring the establishment of Ala 7 to

Only two two-seaters were built, but they had long and productive careers, first with Hispano engines and then with Merlins (illustrated).

parent both Buchón units. For a brief time in 1963/64 Escuadrón 364 operated Buchóns in the Canary Islands as part of Ala Mixta 36. Right at the end of the aircraft's career, Ala 7 was renumbered as Ala 47, by which time the component squadrons numbered just one, this being rechristened 471 Escuadrón. The Buchón was retired in November 1965.

Switzerland

Switzerland's Fliegertruppe had operated the Bf 109D-1 since 1938, subsequently purchasing sizeable numbers of E-3s. During the course of the war it acquired four further Bf 109s (two Bf 109Fs and two Bf 109Gs) through internment of Luftwaffe aircraft, and also by the purchase of 12 Bf 109G-6s in 1944. In the normal course of events Switzerland could not have received the 'Gustavs' at this stage of the war, such was the demand of the Luftwaffe and its allies. However, the Swiss were presented with a powerful bargaining tool in April 1944 when a Bf 110 night-fighter landed at Dübendorf and was interned. Denied its immediate return, Germany was anxious to see it destroyed to prevent Allied agents gaining access to its radar and gun installation, and so it was burned in return for early supply of the required 12 Bf 109s.

Deliveries were made to Dübendorf in two batches of six on 20 and 22 May 1944. The Bf 109Gs (together with the interned aircraft) were allocated to Fliegerkompagnie 7, replacing Bf 109Es. Unfortunately for the Swiss, the workmanship of the Gs was very poor, and their flying was severely curtailed, leading to their eventual retirement in 1946, by which time the Fliegertruppe had been reorganised as the Flugwaffe.

Swiss experience of the Bf 109G-6 was far from happy, as the aircraft showed many manufacturing defects and poor serviceability. Continuing complaints to Germany resulted in a 50 per cent refund of the initial purchase price.

Yugoslavia

Prior to its invasion by German forces in 1941, Yugoslavia had operated Bf 109E-3s, these serving with 32, 51 and 52 Lovácka Grupa. By the end of 1944 Yugoslav pilots were flying alongside liberation forces. Some used Bf 109Gs left behind by the retreating Luftwaffe, while several more 'Gustavs' were acquired when Croatian

pilots defected to the Yugoslav side. These aircraft undertook sporadic strafing and bomber-escort missions against the remnants of the Axis forces, flown by the Independent Headquarters Escadrille. By the end of the war 17 Bf 109Gs were still in service. These were stored until 1947 but were reactivated following the supply from Bulgaria of 59 aircraft. These were war reparations, although Yugoslavia supplied Bulgaria with Il-2 parts in return. The

nascent Jugoslovensko Ratno Vazduhoplovstvo (Yugoslav air force) established two fighter wings with Bf 109s, which were a mixed bag of 'Gustavs' (G-2, G-6, G-10 and G-12). Both the 83rd and 172nd Fighter Wings were based at Cerklje. Training began using three G-12 two-seaters, which were notable for having an Erla-Haube fitted over the rear cockpit. In November 1950 the 172nd Fighter Wing transferred to Zemunik airfield near Zadar.

Both wings were employed on coastal fighter patrols, and both flew sorties during the confrontation with Italy over the free port of Trieste. In JRV service the Bf 109 was operated successfully, the aircraft undergoing several minor modifications such as the installation of Soviet-style radio, gun cameras and new cameras for reconnaissance-configured machines. The aircraft began to fade from service in mid-1952 when new types were received.

109

In 1969 – seven years after the introduction of the MiG-17 and four years after the arrival of the MiG-21 – an intermediate model of the MiG family entered service with the Vietnamese People's Air Force. Such a decision may seem difficult to explain or justify, but the aircraft, the MiG-19 in its Chinese-built J-6 form, found its place in North Vietnam's air defence system in the most crucial months of the air war.

MiG-19 in the Vietnam War

In February 1969, North Vietnam was enjoying a four-month break from American air raids, and in an attempt to strengthen its air force, the Ministry of Defence and the Military Party Committee decided to form a new VPAF fighter unit. In addition to the then-familiar MiG-17F, the 925th Fighter Wing (Trung Doan Khong Quan Tiem Kich 925) was equipped with MiG-19 supersonic fighters. Two bomber battalions equipped with Il-28s were also assigned to the unit temporarily. Nguyen Quang Trung became the wing's commander.

Airmen of the Yen Bai-based wing came from the 910th Air Wing where they had just completed their MiG-17 training, and from Soviet flying schools where they had undergone MiG-21 training. Round-the-clock transition training began after they joined operational squadrons. The syllabus for the 'greenies' emphasised close air combat manoeuvring and demanding air defence sorties flown in formations of four, eight and 12 aircraft. The intense tactical and advanced flying training resulted in nine combat-capable MiG-19 pilots by April 1969.

The bombing operations against North Vietnam had been over for half a year, offering an undisturbed environment for practice, but airmen of the 925th Fighter Wing still faced harsh working and living conditions when compared to their comrades in the 921st and 923rd Fighter Wings. Yen Bai had only one runway, and electricity was provided by generators. Despite every effort, provision even of proper food and accommodation left much room for improvement. Preparation for battle was also hampered by fuel shortages and a high hardware attrition rate caused by the humid climate, poor maintenance and inadequate logistics. Later in the bombing halt, however, the number and skill of personnel in support roles improved, as did the flight servicing, maintenance and repair.

All-weather operations

Control towers were modified to receive new equipment capable of operations in all weather conditions. To simplify air traffic control of the Yen Bai-based 925th, the Kep-based 923rd Fighter Wings and the Gia Lam-based 919th Air Transport Wing, their services were combined.

Regular American reconnaissance flights over North Vietnam meant that fighter units maintained readiness, but no data are available about the launch of MiG-19s against enemy aircraft during the bombing halt. Aerial encounters between reconnaissance aircraft and VPAF fighters involved only the proven MiG-17s and MiG-21s, with limited success. Nevertheless, by the spring of 1972 the MiG-19 force had matured into an effective element of North Vietnam's air defence system, and in forthcoming battles the 925th Fighter Wing challenged the enemy with a certain degree of success.

Into battle

On 30 March 1972 North Vietnamese forces struck across the Demilitarized Zone with massed troop, tank and artillery formations. The heaviest offensive since the Tet of 1968 resulted in the US's Operation Freedom Train, a retaliatory air campaign launched on 6 April 1972. Initially, only targets as far north as the 20th Parallel - like Quang Binh Province, Vinh and Thanh Hoa - suffered from massive air attacks of B-52D Stratofortresses. On 16 April, however, bombs thundered down not only on Vinh and Thanh Hoa but on Hanoi and, following a naval shelling, on quarters of Haiphong. VPAF aircraft received scramble orders and went for the American aircraft sweeping across the northern region. The combined force of 30 Vietnamese fighters of three types, including six MiG-19s of the 925th Fighter Wing, could not engage the B-52s, and finally lost three MiG-21s to USAF Phantoms.

As the focus of the air war shifted back to the north, so all VPAF fighters engaged only above the 20th Parallel. The Yen Bai-based 925th Fighter Wing was ordered to defend the western and northwestern airspace of North Vietnam.

In the spring of 1972 a new stage of aerial warfare began over North Vietnam. VPAF fighter units found themselves facing an enemy who employed refined, improved tactics, the most distinct feature of which was the increased effort to put fairly large fighter forces into the air. Patrols comprised (usually) of 12-ship Phantom formations maintained a fighter screen over the cloud layer, attempting to launch crushing attacks on the emerging MiGs. Soon, the Vietnamese adapted to the new situation and appeared earlier than the enemy could form up over the designated area, so that MiGs were able to succeed on several occasions. Thus, accompanying the 921st and 923rd Fighter Wings, the 925th opened its scoreboard.

On 8 May 1972 President Nixon announced

Photographs of MiG-19s in VPAF service are few, even when the number of aircraft and their activities during the Vietnam war are considered. The first batch arrived in 1969, allowing the 925th Wing three years in which to hone their skills. This photograph appears to show pilots and ground crew with their new aircraft during this period. The former wear leather helmets and plain flight suits, soon discarded in favour of more appropriate gear.

the mining of the most important North Vietnamese ports, under Operation Pocket Money. In addition to the attempt to cut the massive influx of war material, all-out air warfare began under Operation Linebacker against supply lines, military and industrial targets. The VPAF was not caught unprepared; all fighter units had well-defined sorties to fly.

Right: Evidently taken at a later date, this photograph shows pilots on a flight line with their aircraft, probably at Yen Bai, during the period prior to 1972. By this time the MiG pilots appeared to have been issued with anti-g trousers, a vital item of flying kit for the high-speed air combats they were to experience.

First contact

The 925th Fighter Wing was fragged to orbit over Yen Bai airfield and defend, first of all, the Thac Ba hydroelectric power plant. MiG-21s of the 921st Fighter Wing would assist them by distracting the enemy from the MiG-19 force. Flight One with Nguyen Ngoc Tiep, Nguyen Duc Tiem, Pham Hung Son and Nguyen Hong Son was scheduled to circle over the northern confines of the home base, while Nguyen Ngoc Tam, Nguyen Thang Long, Phung Van Quang and Nguyen Manh Tung of Flight Two were assigned to patrol the southern boundaries. To avoid attrition they were briefed to engage the enemy only under favourable conditions and to put them to rout without an own loss only when it was possible. The Vietnamese fighters forming up over Yen Bai would contact the hostile aircraft over Nghia Lo, the selected battle area, and ideally would mix up with the bomber elements.

On the morning of 8 May, Vietnamese radar stations observed a formation of four enemy aircraft approaching Yen Bai at 5000 m (16,400 ft), 35 km (22 miles) south of Moc Chau. At 08.40 a decoy flight of two MiG-21s from the 921st Fighter Wing took off and headed toward Tuyen Quang; seven minutes later four MiG-19s of the 925th Fighter Wing were ordered up. Although summer had already begun, the sky was covered with fairly heavy cloud between 1000 and 1200 m (3,280 and 3,940 ft). Popping up from the cloud layer, Vietnamese fighters veered left and continued climbing, when the controller reported two enemy formations penetrating their airspace at Van Yen. Five minutes later, at 4000 m (13,120 ft), number three, Pham Hung Son, caught sight of an enemy aircraft 6 km (4 miles) away, 40° to port, on the same flight level. It was immediately reported to the MiG-21s.

Phantom four-ship

Pham Hung Son had just identified the enemy fighter as an F-4 when Vietnamese lead Nguyen Ngoc Tiep picked out other Phantoms flying in four-ship formation, and jettisoned the wing tanks right away. His wingman, Nguyen Duc Tiem, did not, and so probably denied himself a victory later in the battle. American fighters must have spotted the MiGs, too, because missiles began whizzing by the Vietnamese. Nguyen Ngoc Tiep ordered a straight flight into the raiders, who were changing their formation from fighting wing to trail. The Phantoms, finally, separated into pairs and

a furious dogfight began.

Vietnamese lead and his wingman went after the left pair while numbers three and four engaged the right one. Covering Nguyen Ngoc Tiep in his pursuit, Nguyen Duc Tiem recognised more Phantoms bearing on them from his six. Evading the two air-to-air missiles launched at him, Nguyen Duc Tiem abruptly broke into the Phantoms and delivered a head-on attack. Vietnamese lead continued to chase an F-4, which dropped its nose, levelled off at 1500 m (4,920 ft) and began a hard break. Nguyen Ngoc Tiep increased his speed, squeezed the trigger – but missed. The Phantom disappeared into a cloud. The Vietnamese pilot turned right, spotted two Phantoms at 2000 m (6,560 ft) and pulled his nose onto them until he was in a firing position. An accurate burst prevented one of his quarries escaping into a cloud; it crashed, and the other disengaged.

In the meantime, Nguyen Duc Tiem reversed again to join his lead. He, however, could not persist in his course, for another Phantom emerging from behind forced him to turn hard back once more. The MiG-19 proved to be a less-than-ideal gun platform at such high g forces with the drop tanks still under the wings, so Nguyen Duc Tiem expended his ammunition ineffectively. Soon he was ordered back to base.

A Phantom with the second Vietnamese pair on his tail dived to 1500 m (4,920 ft). Pham Hung Son was able to follow the evasive manoeuvre and fired his triple cannon, but no hits were observed. The enemy pilot pulled the stick hard back and climbed to 2000 m (6,560 ft) with the MiG stuck on his tail. Despite the Vietnamese pilot's second attempt to shoot it

down with cannon fire, the Phantom escaped unscathed into a cloud.

Number four, seeing that his lead had jettisoned his wing tanks, wanted to do so but in confusion opened his brake chute, which came off instantaneously. Nguyen Ngoc Tiep, keeping an eye on the battle, spotted the chute in the air and thought that another American pilot had bailed out. Finally, Nguyen Hong Son got rid of his drop tanks when he recognised the threat of air-to-air missiles homing on him. He could easily get away with his unburdened MiG by pushing over. An F-4 followed him in his dive but, going much faster, shot past him. The MiG went straight down after the Phantom and started shooting at 1200 m (3,937 ft), with no results. Reaching the top of the cloud layer, the American fighter disappeared.

Fireball

The chase continued through the cloud, and when the MiG emerged from its base the Vietnamese pilot opened fire again. The Phantom's tail section blew up in an enormous fireball. Looking around, Nguyen Hong Son found himself facing a high mountain, so pulled hard around. Low on fuel, he set a course for home and landed at Yen Bai.

The rest of the MiG-19s were ordered back, too. Although having only 1100 litres (240 Imp gal) of fuel left, Nguyen Ngoc Tiep remained airborne until two MiG-19s took off to assume his task. By 09.16 all MiG-19s had returned to Yen Bai.

The 925th Fighter Wing's first battle experience lasted merely eight minutes. The flight of

The VPAF began to equip its MiG-19s with IR-homing air-to-air missiles from the summer of 1972. However, there is no evidence that any were sent into combat so-equipped. This rare, missile-armed aircraft (a Chinese-built Shenyang J-6) is displayed at Da Nang Air Base and does not bear any trace of the customary 'tactical' number on its nose. This machine carries a pair of K-13 AAMs.

The 925th Fighter Wing's famous 'Sons'

Three pilots serving with the 925th Fighter Wing became well known for their similar names – Nguyen Hong Son, Pham Hung Son and Nguyen Hung Son. They soon became known as Son A, Son B and Son C, respectively. All three were successful in downing enemy aircraft and became the best-known MiG-19 pilots of the Vietnam War.

Nguyen Hong Son (Son A) was number four in the flight that fought the first battle involving VPAF MiG-19s on 8 May 1972 and shot down an F-4. Two days later he was in the air again, his MiG receiving serious damage after being hit by an American air-to-air missile. The Vietnamese pilot ejected safely from his doomed fighter, but was fatally injured on landing.

Pham Hung Son (Son B) made his first contact with the enemy on 8 May 1972, attempting unsuccessfully to down an F-4 Phantom with cannon fire. However, two days later his fortunes changed, Son B claiming an F-4 destroyed. On 23 May, he downed another Phantom, claimed by the North Vietnamese to be the 3,600th enemy aircraft shot down over the North.

Nguyen Hung Son (Son C) is seen here in the classic fighter pilot's pose, standing in the cockpit of his MiG-19/J-6. Little detail regarding his exploits has come to light, other than the fact that the destruction of the 3,601st American aircraft over North Vietnam is attributed to him in May 1972. This was the seventh and last of the 925th's J-6 kills.

---

four MiG-19s shot down two F-4 Phantoms without losing any of its own aircraft. The credit of a MiG-19 to an F-4D crew on this day seems to be inaccurate in the light of Vietnamese reports. The second MiG-19 pair apparently did not meet enemy aircraft.

Systematic destruction of military and industrial targets in North Vietnam continued on 9 May. American aircraft flew at least 200 sorties against Vinh, Tho Xuan, Hoa Lac, Yen Bai and Na San in addition to the raids concentrated against vital road and rail lines between Hanoi and Haiphong. The force of these attacks gave an indication of the intensity of the following day's air battle, which became the heaviest in the course of the air war.

Massive strikes

Trying to cope with the massive strikes, the VPAF decided to send all four fighter wings into combat the next day. MiG-21s of the 921st and 927th Fighter Wings, together with the

MiG-17s of the 923rd Fighter Wing, were ordered to defend Hanoi and the key communication lines. MiG-19s of the 925th Fighter Wing were tasked again with the air defence of the northern and northwestern region, enjoying the support of the MiG-21s of the 921st Fighter Wing.

The Vietnamese continuously analysed enemy tactics using data from observations or acquired during interrogations of captured enemy pilots. American fighters avoided turning with the agile MiG-17s and MiG-19s, and stressed vertical fight. Their formations ingressed the combat area with the pairs well spaced, because it required less concentration to maintain the position and the pilots could pay more attention to the MiGs sneaking up on them. When facing a lone MiG, they attacked it by working together. Meeting a pair of Vietnamese fighters, the Americans went after the wingman until they succeeded or the lead could force them to break off. Encountering a larger formation, they separated and engaged the MiGs in pairs.

The greatest battle

The 10 May Haiphong raid – comprising about 70 aircraft – reached its target at 08.30. Two MiG-21s of the 921st Fighter Wing kept on alert at Kep airfield were ordered to intercept the enemy formation. They were only just taking off when patrolling Phantoms caught them and shot the lead down with an air-to-air missile.

At 09.20 a formation of 60-plus aircraft began to attack Hanoi West. By this time the enemy had put up an umbrella of Phantoms to engage the MiGs should they scramble from Noi Bai, Hoa Lac or Kep. Twenty-four minutes later two MiG-21s of the 921st Fighter Wing departed Noi Bai. Heading toward Tuyen Quang, they tried to distract the enemy's attention from the four MiG-19s just about to leave Yen Bai. The deceptive manoeuvre was less than successful, as the MiG-

19s ran into a 20-ship enemy fighter formation patrolling over the cloud top. Overwhelmed by the numbers and the technical and tactical superiority of the Phantoms, the MiGs found themselves in an inferior position. The Vietnamese pilots could rely only on their skill to make the most of the MiG's better manoeuvrability.

The MiGs wound up to altitude and engaged the enemy fighters, beginning with a firing pass from flight lead Nguyen Ngoc Tiep and his wingman Nguyen Duc Tiem, but no hits were observed. Number three, Pham Hung Son, harried a Phantom at 2000 m (6,560 ft) and, after a burst from the triple cannon, the American aircraft caught fire. Closing in to 300 m (985 ft), the Vietnamese pilot squeezed the trigger again, then, with a third barrage of 30-mm shells, finally finished the enemy aircraft which blew up and broke into two.

Pham Hung Son with Nguyen Hong Son on his wing went after another Phantom when they spotted it coming in behind them. The Vietnamese pair reversed, and while the lead fired three bursts ineffectively, an air-to-air missile hit his wingman. Nguyen Hong Son successfully ejected over La Mountain but died from injuries received when he hit the ground.

As the MiGs of the first flight approached the limit of their fuel endurance, a second flight took off from Yen Bai to cover them while landing. The tanks of Nguyen Duc Tiem ran dry on approach and the engines quit at 1600 m (5,250 ft). The Vietnamese pilot glided his fighter back to the base, but because of the excessive landing speed the aircraft was seriously damaged. Nguyen Duc Tiem was unhurt.

Nguyen Ngoc Tiep and Pham Hung Son came under attack on their finals just after extending their landing gear. Pham Hung Son retracted the undercarriage and turned into the attackers to defend his lead, who landed successfully. Then Pham Hung Son returned, too.

The second flight met the enemy immediately after take-off. Number four, Nguyen Manh Tung, managed to get on the tail of a Phantom and sent it crashing into the ground with two bursts of cannon fire. Number three, Phung Van Quang, singled out another enemy fighter and opened fire three times, but was not successful. After being locked in combat for 18 minutes, the MiGs ran low on fuel and were ordered home despite the enemy aircraft

The North Vietnamese paid close attention to recording and publicising the total number of enemy aircraft shot down by any means over their territories. This cartoon commemorated the 3,600th victory claimed by the VPAF.

observed over Yen Bai. Lead, Nguyen Ngoc Tam, landed first. Phung Van Quang overran by 50 m (165 ft) but his aircraft suffered no significant damage. Unfortunately, Nguyen Manh Tung, who ran out of fuel at 1400 m (5,595 ft), had to make an emergency landing at very high speed; his aircraft overran, crashed and exploded. Nguyen Thanh Long had just begun the landing procedure when he was informed of enemy aircraft pursuing him. Turning tail, he saw the Phantoms disengage, then touched down at 10.47.

25 per cent loss rate

With the touch-down of the last MiG-19, the 925th Fighter Wing's participation in this day's air battle was over. Of the eight pilots sent into combat, one was shot down and another was killed in a landing accident. They expended 1,050 cannon shells and destroyed two enemy aircraft. The second part of the fighting which raged in the afternoon of 10 May involved only MiG-17s and MiG-21s. The MiG-19s were sent up again two days later.

From 10 May, the blazing summer sky witnessed fighter combats of unprecedented intensity. The war diary of the 925th Fighter Wing was to be filled with some victories and many losses.

On 12 May a dogfight developed between a flight of four MiG-19s and numerous USAF Phantoms. One of the Vietnamese fell victim to an F-4D of the 555th TFS 'Triple Nickel'. On the morning of 18 May, four MiG-19s shot down an F-4 over Noi Bai. Their victim was probably an F-4D of the 555th TFS flown by

Aircraft '6058' is a J-6 in the custody of the VPAF museum in Hanoi. It carries a different design of AAM launch rail to the aircraft at Da Nang. MiG-19/J-6 aircraft were also fitted with four air-to-ground weapons pylons, each with a capacity of 250 kg. Bombs and rocket pods were typical stores for many MiG-19 operators.

First Lieutenants Ratzel and Bednarek, both of whom are listed as MIA. In the afternoon a pair of MiG-19s attacked a formation of 12 US Navy Phantoms. Both MiGs were downed over Kep by air-to-air missiles launched from two F-4Bs of VF-161 'Chargers'.

Pham Hung Son and Nguyen Hung Son succeeded again in destroying one Phantom each from a 16-ship enemy formation on 23 May. Number two of the four-ship Vietnamese flight, Nguyen Duc Tiem, was hit by a friendly surface-to-air missile and ejected.

A Vietnamese flight departed Gia Lam to intercept the enemy over Kep on 2 June. The battle shifted to the Bac Giang industrial area where a MiG-19 was blown out of the sky again by an overzealous SAM battery. Due to American air superiority, Yen Bai became under the control of the enemy in the second half of 1972, so part of the 925th Fighter Wing had to be deployed to Gia Lam.

On 11 June a MiG-19 flight was jumped when flying along Red River immediately after take-off, losing two aircraft and one pilot. On 27 June the 925th Fighter Wing lost another aircraft: following an uneventful flight, one of

the MiG-19s arriving home developed mechanical failure and exploded upon landing.

As available data suggest, VPAF MiG-19 operations petered out in the summer of 1972. Later in that year attempts were made to equip the aircraft with air-to-air missiles, but Vietnamese pilots recalling the events deny the use of this armament during the Vietnam War. The 925th Fighter Wing received 24 MiG-19s again in 1974. Remaining at Yen Bai, they were responsible for the air defence of the region north and northwest of the capital.

Dr Zoltán Buza and Dr István Toperczer

Known VPAF MiG-19 (J-6) victories

Date	Location	Pilot
8 May 1972	Yen Bai	Nguyen Ngoc Tiep
8 May 1972	Yen Bai	Nguyen Hong Son
10 May 1972	Tuyen Quang	Pham Hung Son
10 May 1972	Tuyen Quang?	Nguyen Manh Tung
18 May 1972	Noi Bai	?
23 May 1972	Yen Bai	Pham Hung Son
23 May 1972	Yen Bai	Nguyen Hung Son

Note: In all cases the downed aircraft were claimed by the 925th FW and identified as F-4 Phantoms.

Shenyang J-6, Vietnamese People's Air Force, 1972

Manoeuvrability
Pitted against missile-armed interceptors, like the F-4 Phantom operated by the USAF and US Navy, the relatively compact J-6 had, like its MiG-17 predecessor, a valuable agility advantage.

Chinese-built MiG-19S
The 54 MiG-19S aircraft delivered to the VPAF's 925th Fighter Wing in 1968/69 are believed to have been examples of the Chinese licence-built Shenyang J-6 (or F-6). The first Chinese J-6s had appeared in 1959 and were based on the radar-equipped MiG-19P.

Interrupted production
Only a handful of MiG-19Ps were built in China, the 'Great Leap Forward' setting the Chinese aviation industry back years. Production resumed in 1961, concentrating on the MiG-19S, though the J-6 designation was retained.

Cannon armament
Like the MiG-19S, the J-6 was armed with three NR-30 cannon; one in which wingroot and a third below and to the right of the engine air intake.

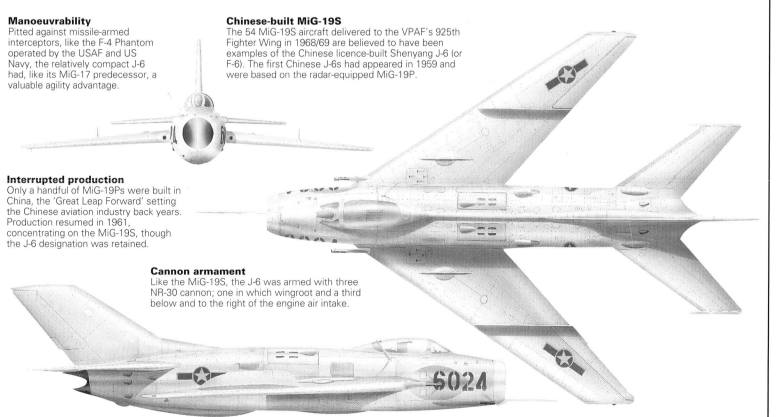

Lockheed P-80 Shooting Star
Variant Briefing

America's first production jet fighter only just missed combat in World War II, but went on to form the backbone of USAF ground-attack forces in the early part of the Korean War. The adaptable Shooting Star was used in many test programmes and later became the basis for the long-lived T-33 trainer and, in turn, the F-94 fighter series.

Within two days of the North Korean invasion, Japan-based F-80 units such as the 49th Fighter-Bomber Group at Yokota, Japan had been rushed to the battle front. With bomb racks now empty and soot around the gun muzzles, a flight of 8th FBS, 49th FBG F-80C-10s returns to its base at Taegu (K-2) from a mission in May 1951. The following month FT-826 was written off as the result of battle damage.

The first operational American jet fighter was created to meet the urgent needs of World War II but instead dominated a revolution in the years afterward, setting one speed record after another and bringing a new form of propulsion to military squadrons. Amid the tension of the Berlin Airlift and the detonation of the first Soviet atomic bomb, the silvery Lockheed F-80 Shooting Star became a stalwart of the newly-independent US Air Force and a symbol of US resolve in its Cold War confrontation with Moscow.

F-80s filled out squadrons of the Air Defense Command (ADC) charged with defending North America against Soviet bombers. The F-80 also became the first operational jet fighter to see prolonged duty in Arctic climes, where red trim on Shooting Stars defending Alaska became a trademark of the times. Beyond the speed records and the strategic readiness, the F-80 is remembered today because it slogged through mud, snow and rain in a ghastly and glamourless air-to-ground war in Korea. It was an ugly kind of triumph for an aircraft that had begun as a beauty — a bright and brilliant concept on the drawing boards of what we know today as the Lockheed Martin Skunk Works.

The saga of the F-80 begins with a young engineer whose schoolmates dubbed him 'Kelly' because he favoured green neckties, despite his Swedish ancestry. On 18 June 1943, Clarence L. ('Kelly') Johnson vaulted up the stairs to the

office of Robert Gross, Lockheed's president, located at the company's headquarters in Burbank, California. In the office, Johnson found Gross and chief engineer Hal Hibbard.

"Wright Field wants us to submit a proposal for building a plane around a British jet engine," 'Kelly' Johnson told the two corporate leaders. "I've worked out some figures. I think we can promise them 180-day delivery. What do you think?"

Johnson — who had pestered Hibbard to allow him to set up an experimental department where designers and artisans could work closely together — knew that the Army had a require-

ment that the new aircraft be completed in 180 days, but committed himself a few days later to a first flight in 150. Gross, Hibbard and Johnson all knew that rosy legends about new aircraft being developed overnight are almost always the stuff of fiction. There were special circumstances when the NA-73X, prototype of the North American P-51 Mustang, went from blueprints to finished airframe in four months. In normal times, even in wartime, it was almost impossible to develop a new aircraft, especially when introducing a new kind of power — the turbojet engine — in any period that could be measured in days, weeks, or months.

In November 1945, after a few false starts, the first American jet fighter group was constituted at March Field, under the designation 412th FG (P-80 Jet). Seen here is a new P-80A-1 (44-84997) being checked by 412th FG personnel. The degree of finish on these early aircraft was high, with all gaps filled, rivets ground flush, and a baked-on final coat of gloss gull grey paint.

While bearing a strong resemblance to later Shooting Stars, the XP-80 was in fact a significantly different aircraft. Many improvements were added to the sound basic design of Lulu Belle, seen here at Muroc during December 1943. These included larger wing and tail surfaces, and a detachable rear fuselage for engine access.

Apparently, at Johnson's behest, Lockheed had established a goal of 180 days to first flight (changed to 150 as measured from 23 June 1943) when the company responded to a 17 May 1943 invitation from the AAF to propose a fighter using the de Havilland-built Halford H-1B engine.

The Bell XP-59A Airacomet was the first American jet aircraft. Test pilot Robert M. Stanley took the XP-59 up for its maiden flight at Muroc Dry Lake, California on 1 October 1942. A mix of American airframe technology and British gas turbine knowledge, the XP-59A was followed by a small production batch of P-59s, tested by US Army and Navy pilots.

Germany's Heinkel He 178, powered by a 750-lb (3.34 kN) thrust HeS 3b engine, became the world's first turbojet aircraft to fly on 27 August 1939, piloted by Flugkapitän Erich Warsitz. Britain's Gloster E.28/39 flew 22 months later on 15 May 1941. Messerschmitt's Me 262 V1 prototype took to the sky under jet power on 25 March 1942. All of them came significantly ahead of the Airacomet, while close on its heels followed the Gloster Meteor (5 March 1943) and de Havilland Vampire (20 September 1943). And the XP-59A, unlike the Meteor or Me-262, was a test aircraft, never viewed as combat capable.

So the United States, in many respects a world leader in science (the word 'technology' did not exist) was slow to develop jet propulsion. Still, America would have been first out of the starting gate, rather than in distant third place, had Washington's military brass listened to Lockheed or to 'Kelly' Johnson.

Lockheed projects

Back in 1939, Johnson's design team – later to be dubbed the Skunk Works – had proposed a jet fighter. In a pre-war environment when the P-39 Airacobra and P-40 Tomahawk were becoming the standard AAF fighters, nothing but bureaucratic indifference greeted Lockheed's model L-133. Engineers drew up plans for several versions on the drawing board, culminating in the model L-133-02-01, a futuristic canard design which would have been powered not by a British import but by two company-designed L-1000 turbojet engines. The AAF simply had no interest, thus forsaking an opportunity for an American 'first'. Nonetheless, their work on the never-to-be L-133 gave Lockheed's engineering team a wealth of experience when opportunity belatedly knocked.

In the latter half of 1943, Johnson and his staff put their new aircraft together ahead of the USAAF's demanding schedule – not in 150 days but in 143.

Brigadier General Franklin O. Carroll, head

44-85004 was one of the first batch of 127 P-80A-1s. The smooth grey finish marginally improved the performance of the Shooting Star but deteriorated quickly when exposed to rain and normal wear and tear. From the P-80A-5 the aircraft were left in natural metal finish.

of the USAAF's engineering division, arranged for 'Kelly' Johnson's design team to receive preliminary design studies undertaken by Bell for the unbuilt XP-59B, as well as the specifications and drawings for the Halford engine. To proceed with engineering work on the L-140, as Lockheed initially named the XP-80, Johnson put together a team which never numbered more than 23 engineers and 105 assembly personnel, including designers W. P. Ralston and Don Palmer. Art Viereck, head of the engineering experimental department, supervised the shop group. Lieutenant Colonel Ralph Swofford was the original USAF project liaison on the XP-80.

Outwardly conventional

Johnson's team concocted an aircraft that superficially appeared quite conventional, as if it might have been flyable with either a jet or a reciprocating engine in the nose. In fact, while the design was sensible and straightforward, it was anything but orthodox. Johnson stressed simplicity. The XP-80 was a clean design with straight wings, tail surfaces, and tricycle gear. To the extent that it incorporated any unorthodox feature, the 'gamble', as Johnson called it, was the wing. Departing from proven airfoil designs, Johnson picked what he called a 'wind tunnel wing' – a low-aspect ratio, laminar-flow surface never tested on a propeller-driven aircraft.

Air intakes positioned on the lower fuselage forward of the wing leading edge fed the de Havilland-built Halford H.1B Goblin centrifugal-flow turbojet, which occupied the rear of the main fuselage section. The aft fuselage, with engine and tail surfaces, was detachable for ready access to the powerplant. The cockpit was well forward and enclosed by a rearward-sliding bubble canopy. The absence of a propeller up front made it easy to install six forward-firing 0.50-in (12.7-mm) machine-guns in the tear-shaped nose. After a full-scale mock-up was evaluated on 20-22 July 1943, only exceedingly minor changes were recommended. Years later, the last F-80 built looked little different from the first XP-80.

The basic design was simple and sensible. To make the powerplant installation accessible and easy to change, Lockheed designed the aft fuselage and tail assembly to be removed as a unit. Three bolts held the tail section in place. Control cables had quick disconnects, as did the engine tailpipe, making it possible for maintenance crews to change engines in as little as 20 minutes.

Engine urgency

The XP-80 prototype was built without the team having an actual Halford engine. They had only blueprints. When Guy Bristow, the de Havilland engine expert, finally arrived with the H.1B powerplant seven days before completion of the airframe, minor changes had to be made which put the XP-80 6 lb (2.7 kg) over the guaranteed contract weight of 8,600 lb (3,900 kg). 'Kelly' Johnson's rule against working on Sunday – the design team's only day off – was broken to install the turbojet.

Lockheed P-80 Variants

Above: Napalm was an effective and widely-used weapon on F-80s in Korea, although the six-tank configuration shown here was only a trial installation – buffet and excess weight meant that it was not adopted operationally. The napalm was ignited by M16 fuses fitted into the tank filler cap and in a new aperture at the rear. When fuses were scarce, only the rear position was used. F-51 pilots found that firing their guns would often ignite napalm leaking from the filler cap while the tanks were still on the wing.

An idea of the low-level environment in which the F-80s operated in Korea can be appreciated in this view of a strike south of Pyongyang taken on 8 May 1952. As it releases its napalm tanks on a supply building and truck park, the F-80 is engaged by a gun position concealed in an embankment. The white blob beneath the aircraft is an AA shell. More than 12,000 US gal (45425 litres) of napalm were dropped in this area during what was then the biggest strike of the war. All the F-80s returned without damage.

The Halford H.1B was to be produced by Allis-Chalmers as the J36. Before the XP-80's first flight, ground run-up tests inflicted damage requiring strengthening of the intake ducts, and the prototype eventually flew with the Halford engine which had to be rushed from the UK where it was awaiting installation in the number two Vampire. The General Electric I-40 (later J33) was well advanced in the design stage in late 1943 and was chosen for subsequent aircraft in the series, designated L-141 or XP-80A.

The spinach-green XP-80 (44-83020), nicknamed *Lulu Belle*, was powered by a de Havilland-built Goblin turbojet delivering a mere 3,000 lb (13.34 kN) thrust. Milo Burcham took the prototype up for its first flight on 8 January 1944. The XP-80 did much of the initial flying and then gave way to I-40-powered developmental aircraft. By war's end, two P-80s were in Italy readying for combat, two more had reached England, and no fewer than 16 were flying. P-80 Shooting Star accidents claimed the lives of Burcham on 20 October 1944 and of America's top air ace,

Major Richard I. Bong, on 6 August 1945, but the development effort forged ahead – even though World War II was one war too early for this jet fighter.

The I-40 (later J33) engine built initially by General Electric in Syracuse, New York and later by Allison in Indianapolis, Indiana, was patterned after the smaller and less powerful British engine. GE boasted that the I-40 had but one moving part, an impeller and turbine connected by a shaft. "The turbine and impeller spin at more than 10,000 revolutions per minute. Air condensed by the impeller frequently is 50° below zero [F], while that pouring from the combustion chambers is blazing hot, 1,500° Fahrenheit or more." Jet power was new to the world, and this press release language was giddy: "Kerosene injected into the combustion chamber burns fiercely in the compressed air." "Velocity of the air and gases is increased by the heat before they strike the turbine buckets. The air gases turn the turbine at great speed and then pass out through the jet exhaust nozzle directly under the P-80 tail assembly."

Alcohol problems

Lockheed experimented with a water injection system for the powerplant. Little or no work had ever been done on a complete installation for water and water-alcohol injection. The installation was able to increase

Right: Operational conditions including poor runway surfaces contributed to many losses in Korea. This 25th FIS F-80C crashed on take-off at K-14 in summer 1951. The pilot was unhurt.

Below: The F-80C was a durable aircraft, as attested to by this 80th FBS pilot who brought his F-80C back to Suwon after MiG-15 gunfire took off a quarter of his right wing in late 1952. Note the T-33 in the background.

Above: A pair of 15th TRS pilots shows how the reconnaissance mission was achieved at Kimpo in 1952.

Above right: Wee Stud was the FP-80A assigned to the commander of the 4th TRS, Col Bob Baselor. The 4th spent its whole existence (1941-1949) in the Caribbean and the Canal Zone, with FP-80s replacing F-6 Mustangs in 1947.

Right: RF-80s were among the few camouflaged jets used by the USAF in Korea. This RF-80A with olive drab top surfaces was assigned to the 45th TRS at K-14 in 1952. It was one of two RF-80As camouflaged as part of Operation Stovepipe, a weather reconnaissance mission into North Korea.

thrust by about 30 per cent and to reduce take-off distance by the same figure. On early aircraft, because compressor pressure was used to drive the flight instruments, the instruments loaded up with water, water got into the wingtip fuel tanks, and the cabin filled with water vapours to cause windshield fogging. Moreover, when water was carried higher than 15,000 ft (4572 m), it froze solid.

'Kelly' Johnson complained that the logical answer to this problem, combining water and alcohol at 50 per cent each, did not prevent water from getting into the wingtips and instruments. "Now," said Johnson, "the problem increased because the pilot became drunk as well as blind." Further work on the design led to a successful (and sober) water-alcohol arrangement beginning with the P-80B production model.

"Buck Rogers space ship"

The Army felt enough confidence in the P-80 Shooting Star two weeks before the end of the war that it trotted out two pre-production examples for simultaneous unveilings to the press at Mitchel Field, New York and in Burbank on 1 August 1945, the 38th anniversary of the AAF. A press release noted that the Shooting Star's "droppable fuel tanks mounted on inner shackles and faired into the extreme tips of the wings give the plane the out-of-this-world appearance of a Buck Rogers space ship." In fact, the P-80 was far cleaner in appearance than the clunky spacecraft of the pre-war comic strip and movie serial, not least because of the jettisonable 'teardrop' wing tanks

which had evolved after eight configurations were tested in a wind tunnel.

Called a 'superfighter' at the time, the Shooting Star was an impressive contrast to propeller-driven fighters, with only air intakes and canopy interrupting the smooth lines of its all-metal, semi-monocoque fuselage. Centreline of the sharp, laminar-flow low wing was 2 in (5 cm) behind the midpoint of the fuselage and the wing was tapered at both leading and trailing edges, with control surfaces that used only 45 per cent of the area of P-38 Lightning flight surfaces.

The US Army's 412th Fighter Group at Bakersfield Army Air Field, California had the distinction of becoming the first American unit

Not all that it seems, this F-80C Shooting Star in apparent standard fighter-bomber configuration is in fact modified with a single K-14 camera, making it an RF-80C. This 45th TRS aircraft has red-painted tubes replacing the gun barrels, and is seen at Kimpo in 1952. The RF-80C designation covered a number of configurations.

to operate jet fighters. The men of the 412th got their first chance to examine this new kind of flying when Major Julius Jacobson, 31st FS commander, brought them the first XP-80 (44-83020) – the famous, lizard-green *Lulu Belle* – to be used in early check flights. When the XP-80A took over the test flight effort, *Lulu Belle* was assigned to the 412th FG for familiarisation.

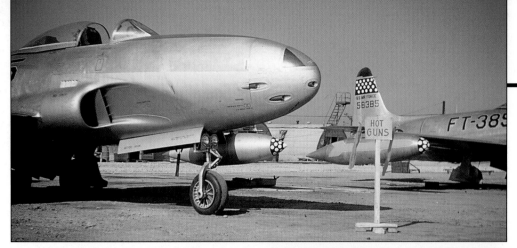

The group relocated to Santa Maria AAF, California on 10 July 1945 and soon afterward Colonel David 'Tex' Hill, a double ace with the wartime 'Flying Tigers', took command. On 29 November 1945, the group made another move, to March Field in Riverside, where a considerable amount of jet pioneering was to be accomplished. On 4 July 1946, the group suffered the first operational loss of a Shooting Star when 71st Fighter Squadron commander Lieutenant Colonel John 'Pappy' Herbst was killed bellying-in a P-80A (44-85083). Herbst was a 12-victory ace from the China Burma India theatre and was flying at an air show at San Diego, California, with Major Robin Olds.

Another well-known flyer, Colonel Bruce Holloway, took over the group on 30 January 1946, and presided over the unit's change in designation to 1st Fighter Group. The 1st FG eventually carried out much of the early operational flying of the P-80 and, later, of the F-86 Sabre.

Racers and record-breakers

The P-80 got a chance to show its stuff when air racing resumed in America in 1946. In the transcontinental Bendix Trophy race covering 2,000 miles (3218 km) from California to Cleveland, Lieutenant Colonel Leon Gray of the 12th PRS/1st FG and Major George Ruddell of the 27th FS/1st FG came in first and second places at the head of a four-ship P-80A cross-country effort. Ruddell later became an ace in Korea.

It was the beginning of a spectacular series of air records and flight performances by the P-80 Shooting Star. In the 1946 Thompson Trophy Race, Major Gustav Lundquist and Major Olds came in first and second places. On 24 June 1946, the 1st FG received its first P-80B models and these became the participants in numerous air racing and record-setting efforts.

The following year, a specially-modified aircraft, the XP-80R, held a world's air speed record – briefly. Colonel Albert Boyd flew the highly-polished XP-80R on 19 June 1947, averaging 623.738 mph (1003.782 km/h). Boyd took the record away from Britain's Gloster Meteor IV. Soon afterward, however, another American jet – the Douglas D-558 Skystreak – snatched the record away.

As for the photo-reconnaissance version of the Shooting Star, which was part of the story virtually from the beginning, the 363rd Reconnaissance Group was activated at Brooks Field, Texas, on 29 July 1946 and took delivery of early FP-80As.

The close of the war brought an end to plans to rush the Shooting Star to the Pacific region, but the P-80A arrived there in March 1946 when the first 24 aircraft, shipped by sea, joined the 67th FS/18th FG at Florida Blanca, Luzon, Philippines. Things began poorly when a P-80A crashed on 9 September 1946, killing squadron commander Major Henry Troolope. There was a pause, but eventually the group's 44th squadron followed as more Shooting Stars arrived. By the time fighting began in Korea four years later, the F-80 Shooting Star was to be the principal US fighter in the Far East.

P-80s to Europe

Apart from four aircraft that reached Europe at VE-Day, the first overseas P-80s were assigned to the 55th Fighter Group under Colonel Horace Hanes, which received 32 Shooting Stars for its 38th FS at Gibelstadt, Germany. This unit evolved into the 31st Fighter Group and at one point was commanded by well-known ace Lieutenant Colonel Donald Blakeslee. By late 1947, these P-80s were returned to the US. When the Soviets blockaded Berlin in March 1948, the only USAF fighter in Europe was the P-47 Thunderbolt.

The famed 56th Fighter Group, the 'Wolfpack', became operational in the P-80 in 1947. Like the 1st FG, it was transferred to Strategic Air Command. Confronted with the

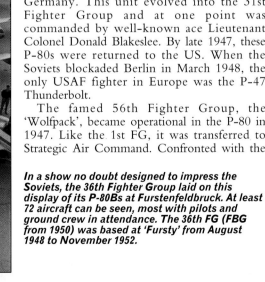

Soviet threat during the Berlin Airlift, the 56th began making the first mass, transoceanic flights by jet fighters. In the summer of 1948 16 P-80As were the first jets to fly the Atlantic from west to east in a flight led by Colonel Dave Schilling. The flight, known as Fox Able (the phonetic abbreviation for 'Fighters Atlantic'), was held up by a month so that the English could fly the Atlantic from east to west with a squadron of Vampires as the first jets across the Atlantic. All 16 made it to Germany and back with no problems other than a hot start on one engine which required a hot start inspection. Soon afterward, the 36th FG became operational with the Shooting Star in Europe – but now the fighter had a new designation.

Designation change

In a change of military designations on 11 June 1948, the US Air Force (which had become an independent service branch in September 1947) dropped the 'P' for pursuit category; the P-80 became the F-80, a 'fighter'. Reconnaissance versions, previously identified as F-14 and FP-80, became RF-80 fighters.

The long career of the Shooting Star in the Air National Guard began in June 1947 when the 196th FS at San Bernardino Field received its first 'B' models. In time, there were to be dozens of ANG squadrons flying the F-80.

Some of the most-photographed Shooting Stars of this era were the brightly-decorated F-80s that flew with the USAF's first jet aerobatics team, the 'Acrojets', at Williams AFB, Arizona beginning in 1948. This was the first of half a dozen aerobatic teams to fly the F-80, eventually including the 'Skyblazers' in Europe and the 'Minutemen' of the Colorado Air National Guard.

This 56th FG F-80B seen in the US wears flags recording its stopovers on the historic Fox Able I tour of Europe in July 1948. For a 45-day period after the 11 June 1948 USAF redesignation order, F-80s (including those on Fox Able I) could be seen with an 'FN' 'buzz number'.

In May 1949, Schilling's replacement, Lieutenant Colonel Irwin Degne of the 56th FG, flew the Fox Able II mission, taking 11 F-80Bs and a T-33 from Selfridge Field, Michigan to Furstenfeldbruck, Germany. It was not until the following year that the first RF-80A reconnaissance ships appeared in Europe with the 32nd TRS/10th TRG at Furstenfeldbruck, Germany.

The 4th Fighter Group at Langley Field, Virginia became the next important F-80 operator. In September 1948, the group's aerial demonstration team performed at the Cleveland National Air Races. Soon afterward, the 81st FG at Kirtland AFB, New Mexico became another F-80 operator. Soon thereafter, other F-80s began to join several Air Defense Command interceptor squadrons.

The first F-80s in Alaska had gone there on TDY (temporary duty) with the 1st FG's 94th FS, the 'Hat in the Ring' squadron, which operated from Ladd AFB. These aircraft remained in Alaska and, beginning in March 1948, equipped the 57th FG at Elmendorf AFB. The F-80 in the brilliant Arctic paint scheme, with red trim on wingtips and tail, was to become another of the much-photographed sights of the era.

Beginning in 1950, many F-80 fighters served as advanced trainers with the USAF's Air

The 'Acrojets' were the first US jet aerial demonstration team, formed in 1948 by the Fighter School at Williams AFB. Its initial purpose was to show the potential of the P-80 to young pilots and those more accustomed to propeller-driven aircraft, but they were soon performing at public air shows. The Korean War forced a transition to T-33s.

Training Command (ATC), filling a role that was later taken over by the derivative T-33.

Korean War

By the time North Korea invaded its southern neighbour on 25 June 1950, the F-80 Shooting Star had replaced the F-51D Mustang as the principal US fighter in the region, and the RF-80 reconnaissance ship was also widely used. In fact, the F-80 was on the scene prematurely. FEAF (Far East Air Force) officers needed a propeller-driven fighter to battle North Korea's Yakovlev and Lavochkin fighters, and arranged to have 145 F-51Ds shipped to the battlezone from stateside. Typically, one F-80 pilot complained that he could not manoeuvre with, or outshoot, the prop-driven North Koreans. The inadequacies of pure-jet fighters in combat with North Korea's propeller-driven warplanes were undoubtedly overworked in Associated Press dispatches of the period, but the impression was left on the general public that the F-80 was the

wrong aircraft for the job. Ironically, the F-51D Mustang was more wrong: the Mustang was far more vulnerable than the Shooting Star to loose metal flying around on low-level air-to-ground sorties.

The 8th, 35th, 49th and 51st Fighter Groups flew F-80s in Korea. At home, the government 'federalised' Air National Guard F-80 squadrons – called them to active duty – to fly air defence missions. As a result of the Korean War, 14 squadrons of the ANG were shifted from fighter to photo-reconnaissance duties, many of them equipped with F-80s that were retroactively converted to RF-80 standard. The converted aircraft differed from purpose-built RF-80s in having a distinctive 'bump' at the curve of the nose, but carried the same camera equipment and performed the same mission.

Although an F-82 Twin Mustang scored the first aerial victory in Korea, the F-80 was part of the air-to-air scuffle from the beginning. On 27 June 1950, Captain Robert Schillereff led a flight of F-80s that shot down three Ilyushin Il-10 *Shturmovik* bombers. On 28 June 1950, 1st Lieutenant Bryce Poe II managed to get aloft from Itazuke in an RF-80A Shooting Star of the 8th Tactical Reconnaissance Squadron for the first photo-snapping sortie of the war. Of F-80s in the Far East, nearly all fighters were 'C' models which proffered the comfort of an ejec-

tion seat. The reconnaissance aircraft, however, were 'A' models. These had less power and, if the pilot had to get out of the aircraft in an emergency, he had no choice but to climb out. On 29 June 1950 – the day North Korean strafers destroyed a C-54 transport on the ground at Kimpo Air Base while ground troops drove on nearby Seoul – F-80 pilots William T. Norris and Roy W. Marsh shot down a Lavochkin La-7 and an Il-10. The next day, F-80s from Itazuke Air Base, Japan tangled with North Korean fighters and Lieutenants Charles A. Wurster and John B. Thomas each shot down a Yakovlev Yak-9. But US Ambassador Muccio ordered a general evacuation as the war continued to go badly and Seoul fell.

Counter-attack at Inchon

In time, North Korea occupied most of the south and General Douglas MacArthur devised an invasion at the port city of Inchon to strike the enemy from behind and turn the war around. F-80s continued to fly daily missions. The 8th Tactical Reconnaissance Squadron, now operating from Taegu, was one of several outfits charged with sizing up Inchon harbour for the planned landings. Lieutenant Poe and another RF-80A pilot went in to reconnoitre enemy-held Inchon and to snap some much-

needed photography. Poe returned safely from the mission; the other pilot did not.

Sergeant John Nossick, a crew chief with the 25th Fighter-Interceptor Squadron, landed at Inchon and helped set up flight operations at Kimpo. "North Korea's last surviving Yak fighter came down and blew up our mail room. It was so cold, our JP-1 fuel wouldn't fire, so had to start F-80s on 140-octane gas and then switch to JP-1 after the engines lit up."

In an unhappy incident on 8 October 1950, two F-80 Shooting Stars strayed across the border between North Korea and the Soviet Union. The fighters strafed a Soviet airfield near Vladivostok. In later years, the pilots portrayed this sorry mishap as a show of resolve which kept Russia out of the war. In fact, it was a stupid mistake and cost the wing commander his job.

Jet combat

On 1 November 1950, F-51 Mustangs were engaged by six swept-wing jet fighters which lashed out at them from across the Yalu River. It was the first appearance of the Soviet MiG-15 – at the time, viewed with awe by American airmen. Days later, Lieutenant Colonel Clure Smith, the F-80C Shooting Star pilot who commanded the 25th FIS/51st FIW, came back from a mission with a gun-camera photo of a MiG-15 limping north across the Yalu trailing smoke.

On 8 November 1950, Lieutenant Russell J. Brown of the 26th FIS was flying an F-80C Shooting Star (49-0717) borrowed from 1st Lieutenant Jack Smith of the 16th FIS/51st FIW on a mission from Kimpo. Brown and his wingmen came upon half a dozen MiG-15s. The American pilots turned aggressively into their attackers and split them up, sending five scurrying back across the Yalu towards Antung. The sixth MiG broke in the wrong direction and appeared below Brown's F-80. "Damn, I'm going to get him," Brown realised.

Brown pushed down his nose and dived behind the plummeting MiG-15. Although all but one of his guns were jammed, Brown unleashed bursts of fire which struck the MiG, set it afire, and sent it spinning in, engulfed in flames. The American pilot had notched up history's first jet-versus-jet aerial victory.

China's entry into the Korean War reversed the situation on the battlefield and put the Allies into retreat. While the Air Force geared up to abandon Kimpo, men in the 51st FIW packed their bags and flew combat at the same time.

The F-80 was used for a variety of experimental programmes, including trials of wingtip ramjets for additional boost in flight. This aircraft was tested at Muroc with Marquardt ramjets of different diameters, including the 20-in (51-cm) diameter units seen here. Another aircraft was tested at Wright Field.

Lockheed P-80 Variants

Captain John Kropenick, operations officer of the wing's 25th Fighter-Interceptor Squadron, played a key role in defending Kimpo. When the Chinese reached the outskirts of Seoul and (at some locations) the north bank of the Han River, Kropenick planned and led a mission in which F-80s took off, fired rockets at the oncoming Chinese, and landed – all in the span of 10 minutes. It was the coldest winter in 177 years, at times -20°F (-29°C), and F-80s had to be started on 40-octane aviation gas, not jet fuel, because jet fuel could not ignite in those frigid conditions. For a time, F-80s were flying sorties as quickly as they could be rearmed and refuelled. By 4 January 1951, the Chinese seized the airfield and F-80 units again had to operate from bases in Japan.

Korea and beyond

In June 1951, the role of the F-80 in Korea began to decline as the 49th FBG re-equipped with the F-84 Thunderjet. Other groups fought on with the F-80, however. 1st Lieutenant Edward Fernandes recalls F-80 operations with the 51st FIW at Suwon:

"Taxiing an F-80 on a rough PSP taxiway, while carrying 1,000-lb (907-kg) bombs or napalm on the mid-wing pylons, was exciting. The armament cleared the taxiway by only a few inches and as you bounced along the bombs would scrape the mat, causing sparks. Compared to the F-84, the F-80 was a sweetheart on take-off. I never had to use JATO (jet-assisted take-off) on an F-80 at K-13. During September 1951, water alcohol was sufficient. The water alcohol would give out just as you reached flap-up speed of 160 mph [257 km/h], which caused the pilot to have his heart beat a little faster, to increase pitch attitude about 10°, and to slowly milk up the flaps.

"During combat missions we usually fired some, if not all, of our ammo on targets of opportunity. The 1,800 rounds of 50-calibre [12.7-mm] ammo was a large load in the nose of the F-80, and made attaining a nose-up attitude for landing difficult."

The 51st FIW converted to the F-86 Sabre in late 1951, while the 8th FBW continued to fly F-80s until early 1953 before making the same conversion.

In post-Korea years, the F-80 became the first fighter to serve with the Air Force Reserve (AFRes) while also operating with Air National Guard units.

Despite its tremendous success as a jet pioneer with US forces, the F-80 Shooting Star never caught on as an export item, even at a time when NATO was expanding rapidly. Foreign users were limited to six Latin American countries: Ecuador with 16 (Fuerza Aérea Ecuatoriana), Chile 30 (Fuerza Aérea de Chile), Brazil 33 (Força Aérea Brasileira), Uruguay 17 (Fuerza Aérea Uruguaya), Colombia 16 (Fuerza Aérea Colombiana) and Peru 16 (Fuerza Aérea del Peru). Peru was a special case, having in 1949 ordered new-build

F-80s which – for reasons no longer clear – were diverted to the USAF. Among Latin air arms, only Peru's used the F-80 on one occasion in earnest: a few low-level passes helped to put down an insurrection by a local garrison in Peru. None of the Latin American users caught much attention with the F-80s, and all examples were retired by 1971.

No F-80 appeared on the warbird circuit, but half a dozen civil F-80s flew with the Federal Aviation Administration on a weather project. In the 1950s, US Navy and Marine Corps TO-1 Shooting Stars were redesignated TV-1.

Successful two-seater

The notion of a two-seat trainer based on the F-80 was raised at an early juncture by Lockheed, which modified an F-80C to accommodate a second seat. As the TF-80C, this ship flew for the first time on 22 March 1948 with company pilot Tony LeVier at the

controls. The renamed T-33 became far more numerous than the fighter from which it was developed: 5,691 were built by Lockheed, 656 by Canadair, and 210 by Kawasaki, for a total of 6,557 – four times the 1,714 F-80s built.

This test ship underwent further modifications to become a flying prototype for the YF-97 interceptor – itself redesignated YF-94 by the time it flew in this configuration on 16 April 1949, again piloted by LeVier. The F-94 was the USAF's first jet-powered, all-weather interceptor and the F-94B model went to war in Korea, where it was credited with history's first air victory achieved solely on instruments, a Lavochkin La-9 shot down on 30 January 1953. The F-94C model (only) was nicknamed 'Starfire' and served with ADC and ANG squadrons. Retaining their resemblance to the F-80 Shooting Star, 854 Lockheed F-94 interceptors were built between 1948 and 1952.

Robert F. Dorr

The first of the F-80 drones was converted from a standard aircraft as early as 1946. Many more were converted under Project Bad Boy from 1951 to 1954. Take-offs and landings (if any) were controlled by a ground operator, while the mission was guided by an operator in a DT-33 – seen here behind the QF-80A. These aircraft belonged to the 3205th Drone Group. Some of these aircraft were used to gather data from atomic weapons tests by flying through fall-out zones; others were used in more 'traditional' ways, such as missile targets. The later JQF-80F shown below reveals its electronic guidance equipment in the bay that once held a sextet of heavy machine-guns.

Lockheed P-80 Variants

XP-80

The XP-80 *Lulu Belle* (44-83020) was revolutionary, from its new method of propulsion to its untried, laminar-flow wing. *Lulu Belle* was the company L-140 and was known early in its development by the military designation MX-409. At the core of the XP-80 design was the de Havilland-built Halford HB.1B Goblin centrifugal-flow turbojet with a thrust rating of 2,460 lb (10.94 kN). Major Frank Halford's engine had been the intended powerplant of the Bell P-59B Airacomet, a contemplated production version of the first American jet aircraft. This aircraft was never built and the earlier Airacomet had never been expected to enter squadron service, leaving the XP-80 to become the prototype for America's first operational jet fighter.

The new fighter owed its origin to a 17 May 1943 meeting of Air Corps officers. Lockheed's H. L. 'Hal' Hibbard and his chief research engineer C. L. 'Kelly' Johnson set up an experimental department to develop and build the new aircraft free of bureaucratic intrusion; this facility later became known as the Skunk Works, based on a setting in Al Capp's 'L'il Abner' syndicated cartoon; in later years, it was the maker of the U-2, SR-71, and other aviation greats.

Lockheed built the prototype Shooting Star without an example of the Halford engine, then made changes when the powerplant increased in girth during final

XP-80 (early configuration)

de Havilland H.1B Goblin engine

Intake lip forward of windscreen

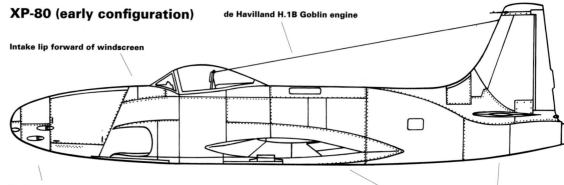

Six Browning M2 0.50-in machine-guns fitted, capacity 200 rpg. Flight-test instrumentation usually fitted in ammunition space

Squared-off wingtips, fin and tailplane (later modified to rounded surfaces)

development. There were monumental delays and difficulties in development of the engine, during which time Lockheed and the Army began to look at the forthcoming General Electric I-40 centrifugal-flow turbojet as an alternative (see XP-80A entry). An unforeseen series of errors occurred with the Halford engine.

The XP-80 was trucked from Burbank to Muroc Army Air Base, California on 8 November 1943 and was ready for flight a week later, 143 days after the signing of the contract. On the night of 15 November 1943, the only Halford engine then available suffered mortal damage during a run-up,

This 1943 impression shows Lockheed's L-140 (MX-409) design in almost final form.

delaying the maiden flight for nearly two months. Britain's de Havilland representative had warned about a gross error (thin intake trunks), without success. The only Halford example available was the one going into the No. 2 Vampire fighter, which the British selflessly sent to Lockheed to replace the destroyed engine.

The XP-80 made its first flight on 8 January 1944 piloted by Milo Burcham. The first flight lasted barely five minutes as Burcham fought in vain to raise the landing gear, but in a second trip aloft that day, Burcham went over the desert and reached the previously-unattained speed of 430 mph (692 km/h). In subsequent flights, the XP-80 proved stable at speeds up to 500 mph (805 km/h), considerably faster than any reciprocating-engine fighter then in service. The XP-80 generally handled well in high-performance flight regimes but was less forgiving closer to earth. At low speeds, it had a nasty tendency to stall and roll sharply to the right with little or no warning. On 17 January 1945 after five flights, *Lulu Belle* was laid up briefly while 'Kelly' Johnson supervised minor modifications. In its original configuration, the 'XP' had been built with blunt-tipped wing and tail surfaces, which Johnson replaced with rounded versions. Wing leading-edge fillets

were added and a number of minor internal changes were made. When Burcham resumed test flights on 7 February 1945, the sudden-stall problem appeared to have been solved.

Lulu Belle had an installed armament of six Browning M2 0.50-in (12.7-mm) machine-guns with 200 rounds per gun. After early ground and aerial firing tests, minor changes had to be made to the gun cartridge ejection doors. Otherwise, the guns performed well at various speeds, attitudes, and levels of g. The M2 gun installation remained essentially unchanged until introduction of the M3 gun in the P-80B model.

The XP-80 had an unpressurised cabin and an aft-sliding bubble canopy. *Lulu Belle* was slightly smaller than every P-80 or F-80 that followed: its wing span of 37 ft (11.27 m) was 2 ft 11 in (0.9 m) less than subsequent aircraft, while fuselage length at 32 ft 10 in (10.0 m) was almost 2 ft (0.6 m) less than later Shooting Star fighters.

Because of its distinctive, spinach-coloured exterior, the XP-80 was dubbed the 'Green Hornet'. It was painted in lustreless F.S. 595A 34092 green on its upper surfaces and F.S. 595A 36440 on its lower portions. This historic prototype was transferred to the National Air Museum in Washington, DC in November 1946, and is on display today at the National Air and Space Museum.

Serial (1): 44-83020

Above: The 'Green Hornet' is seen at Muroc three days before its first flight. It made only five flights in its original configuration with square-cropped fin and wingtips before being laid up for aerodynamic refinements.

Fitting the XF-80 with a taller, rounder fin set the general 'look' of the entire family of aircraft which followed it.

XP-80A

On 2 January 1994, before *Lulu Belle* had flown, Lockheed began engineering work on two L-141 aircraft with the military designation XP-80A. Both were powered by a 4,000-lb (17.79-kN) thrust General Electric I-40 'Whittle' turbojet with air intakes moved somewhat farther aft than on the XP-80. These initial 'A model' Shooting Stars were significantly larger and about 25 per cent heavier than the XP-80 prototype, in order to accommodate the larger powerplant.

The XP-80 also introduced redesigned engine air intake ducts, strengthened landing gear, a detachable fuselage-tail assembly, a quick-change engine

installation, cockpit pressurisation and cooling, and wingtip fuel tanks.

The first of these aircraft (44-83021) was completed in light grey or 'pearl grey' lacquer, leading to the nickname *Gray Ghost*. Built in just 138 days, it was trucked to Muroc like its predecessor and flew on 10 June 1944. Thirty-five minutes into this maiden sortie, pilot Antony 'Tony' LeVier encountered an asymmetrical flight situation, with the right wing flap fully extended and the left flap refusing to budge. The aircraft kept trying to roll

This is the first XP-80A, which differed significantly from the prototype. The main new feature was the General Electric I-40 engine, based on a Whittle design.

violently to port until LeVier made a hot, high-speed landing on Muroc's dry lakebed. In subsequent test flights, the first XP-80A demonstrated that the 'pearl grey' paint scheme did not enhance flying performance

and was a maintenance nightmare.

The XP-80A model introduced the 'teardrop' wingtip tanks that became standard on all Shooting Stars until the Korean War era. Adopted after exhaustive

testing, the tanks reduced drag and improved performance – and could be brought home empty with no penalty in aerodynamic drag. The tanks also improved aileron effectiveness and wing loading.

The second XP-80A (44-83022) was the

Silver Ghost. The name derives from its natural metal surface which permitted comparison between it and the 'pearl grey' finish. This aircraft was optimised as an engine testbed and was heavily instrumented with equipment for recording

The 'Silver Ghost' (second XP-80A) is seen during its time as a testbed for the XF-90's J34 engine, with dorsal spine fillet and revised jetpipe. This aircraft had a second seat installed for an observer.

engine thrust, fuel consumption, intake ram pressure, exhaust temperatures, and other propulsion data. Lockheed installed a second seat behind the pilot's, for the aircraft was considered to be an engine research vehicle and was intended to carry an engineer on some flights. This ship flew for the first time on 1 August 1944.

On some flights, the aircraft carried 'Kelly' Johnson. In due course, the second XP-80A flew against the P-51D Mustang in manoeuvrability trials at Wright Field, Ohio.

Late in its career, the *Silver Ghost* operated as a testbed for the 3,000-lb (13.34-kN) Westinghouse J34-WE-11 turbojet engine used on the Lockheed XF-90 penetration fighter. With this feature, it acquired a dorsal 'spine' like that of the XF-90 and had a much-modified rear fuselage and exhaust area.

After the *Gray Ghost* made a significant contribution to the flight test effort, Lockheed modified it with reduced-size air intake ducts. In this configuration, the *Gray Ghost* suffered engine failure on 20 March 1945. LeVier jettisoned the canopy after the aircraft was ripped by what felt like an explosion. He bailed out successfully and the wreckage of 44-83021 was later found scattered over a wide area.

Serials (2): 44-83021/83022

YP-80A

The YP-80A – which, like all succeeding versions, was called the L-080 in some company documents – was a service-test aircraft intended to pave the way for introduction of the Shooting Star into operational service. It was powered by the 3,850-lb (17.12-kN) thrust General Electric J33-GE-11 or Allison J33-A-9 turbojets also found on the production P-80A that followed – and both redesignations of the I-40 – but for a time the engines were still hand-built and were highly unreliable. Until the proper metals, production techniques, maintenance procedures and fuel controls were developed, engine failure was a frequent cause of accidents.

The Army ordered 13 YP-80As, an unusually large investment at such an early stage, plus an unnumbered static test article. One aircraft was modified on the production line as the sole F-14 reconnaissance ship, leaving a dozen 'YP' models to carry out early development work. The first (44-83023) made a 45-minute maiden flight on 13 September 1944. Produced on an accelerated schedule, all 13 aircraft had been turned over to the Army by 31 December 1944.

Sadly, by then the second ship (44-

83025) had been lost, on 20 October 1944. During take-off at Lockheed's Burbank, California terminal, landing gear and flaps appeared to retract slower than normal, a sign of engine failure. The aircraft achieved a height of about 300 ft (91 m), then plummeted. Unable to clear the rim of a crater off the runway's end, the aircraft came to the ground in a crackling, dry crash that killed the much-admired Milo Burcham. The test pilot, flying the YP-80A model for the first time, apparently had not been briefed on a modification that provided an emergency fuel system back-up in the event of a main fuel pump failure.

Four YP-80As (44-83026/83029) went abroad, two to England and two to Italy, in Project Extraversion – arriving too late to see combat but making a good impression on US allies. On 28 January 1945, a YP-80A (44-83026) crashed at Burtonwood, England, killing pilot Major Frederick Borsodi. Two YP-80As were operated by NACA (National Advisory Committee for Aeronautics).

One of the YP-80As (44-83027) was fitted with a Rolls-Royce B-41 (Nene) engine in England but was damaged beyond repair in a mishap on 14 November 1945.

YP-80A serials: 44-83023 (1); 44-83025/83035 (11)

44-83031 was one of the 12 YP-80As used as service test aircraft. Four of these were sent to war in England and Italy but failed to see action.

P-80A (F-80A)

The first P-80A was accepted by Army Air Forces in February 1945. Production fighters dispensed with the 'pearl grey' external finish. Maintenance demands, high-*g* manoeuvring, rain and sandstorms all contributed to the chipping and scuffing of the paint. The P-80A-5 and all subsequent Shooting Stars emerged from the factory in natural metal.

The first 345 'A models' were powered by a 3,850-lb (17.12-kN) thrust General Electric J33-GE-11 or Allison J33-A-9 turbojet, both developments of the earlier I-40 engine. The P-80A introduced dive brakes and boundary layer bleed ducts and had changes in the design of its armament bay.

The F-80A's wing span of 39 ft 10.5 in (11.85 m) was almost 2 in (5 cm) greater than that of the XP-80, a dimension that remained unchanged in the subsequent F-80B model. Fuselage length of 34 ft 6 in (10.52 m), also shared with the F-80B, was 3 ft 4 in (1.01 m) longer than the XP-80. The F-80A was 1 ft (0.3 m) taller than the XP-80 at a height of 11 ft 3 in (3.43 m), a figure

P-80A

Revised intake design with boundary-layer splitter plates (from P-80A-5). Intake lip moved aft

Landing light

General Electric J33-GE-9/GE-11 or Allison J33-A-9/A-17 engine (with water injection)

Extended rounded tailfin and tailplane

Machine-gun ammunition capacity 300 rpg

Rounded wingtips. Wingtip bomb or fuel tank racks (165 US gal)

Dive brakes under fuselage

Removable rear fuselage

Tailplane incidence raised 1.5°

retained by the F-80B and F-80C models.

The F-80A, B and C all had the same limiting Mach number, maximum dive speed, *g*-load limitation, and fuel tank capacity (when using the same tip tanks).

Although the myth has long been perpetuated that some models had wings of different thickness, the truth is that all production models of the F-80/T-33 had wings of the same thickness. Wing area

was the same for all at 237.60 sq ft (22.07 m²).

The P-80A and all production Shooting Stars had fuselage dive flaps (dive brakes) which opened forward, under the fuselage

Left: Lieutenant Colonel J. Reilly won the 1946 Cleveland National Air Race using this Wright Field Test Division P-80A.

Below: For the bombing role the P-80A could carry a 100-lb (45-kg) bomb under each wingtip, although this severely hampered range.

Left: Seen on the Burbank ramp in 1946, these factory-fresh P-80As proudly wear the legend 'Shooting Star' on the nose. Only the first few aircraft were finished in pearl grey, the majority being left unpainted.

at the wing join. They were adopted after wind tunnel tests showed that other possible installations, such as wing dive flaps, caused high-balancing tail loads. The speed of operation of the dive brakes (two seconds) made them an excellent aid to formation flying. Deploying the dive brakes made it possible to get a nose angle 18° lower at the same relative ground speed, permitting the Shooting Star to make steep dives without exceeding critical Mach.

Armament of the P-80A model consisted of six 0.50-in (12.7-mm) M2 machine-guns with ammunition trays for 300 rounds per gun. The early test aircraft – as well as all aircraft in the P-80A series and the first P-80Bs – were manufactured without the capability to carry underwing ordnance at the mid-wing point. From the 100th 'A model' (44-85091), normal underwing ordnance included provision at mid-wing for two bombs of up to 1,000 lb (454 kg) or eight 5-in high-velocity aircraft rockets.

As production of the 'A model' continued, minor changes were introduced when the P-80A-1-LO gave way to the P-80A-5-LO (from aircraft 44-85337). The 'dash-five' introduced a boundary layer control splitter plate inside the air intakes and relocated the landing gear light from the aircraft's nose to the nosewheel landing gear strut.

After difficulties with equipment ancillary to the latter powerplant, early ships went to the 412th Fighter Group at Muroc for an exhaustive flight test programme. Several P-80A fighters were lost in early flying mishaps. On 1 July 1945 at Long Beach, California, First Lieutenant Joseph Mandl of the 6th Ferrying Group was killed when his P-80A (44-85017) stalled on its take-off run, veered through a fence, and struck a parked A-26 Invader. On 2 August 1945, Major Ira Jones was lost on a flight in a P-80A (44-

83029) from Wright Field, Ohio when the aircraft fell apart in flight over Kentucky. On 6 August 1945, Major Richard I. Bong went down on an acceptance flight in a P-80A (44-85048). Bong escaped from the aircraft but his parachute did not have time to deploy. Bong was the American 'ace of aces', with 40 aerial victories in the Pacific war. As the P-80 came along in its development, numerous other accidents occurred, most blamed on pilots trying to adjust to a new kind of flying.

The first operational P-80As went to the 412th Fighter Group, soon redesignated 1st Fighter Group. This outfit undertook much of the jet pioneering and record flying of the immediate post-war years.

'One-off' examples of the P-80A were plentiful. One aircraft which began on the production line as a P-80A was modified before completion to become the sole XP-80B (44-85200). Another was modified to become the XFP-80A reconnaissance aircraft (44-85201). Yet another (44-85116) was tested with a unique armament installation that included jettisonable racks for 5-in rockets in place of the wingtip tanks and, still later, with a rocket-launcher gun in the nose. A different P-80A, its identity not known today, was tested with four 20-mm cannon.

Two P-80As used as flying testbeds for ramjet power are covered in a separate entry.

Thirty-eight P-80A-5-LOs were completed as FP-80A-5-LO reconnaissance aircraft. A single P-80A became the 'Towed P-80A' (covered by a separate entry) which was pulled through the skies by a B-29 at Wright Field. Another 'A model' (covered in the entry entitled 'Trainable Guns/Prone pilot P-80A' (44-85044)) tested a flexible machine-gun armament. Two P-80As were converted by Bell to become the first

Shooting Star drones.

Lockheed delivered the last P-80A in December 1946. After the Korean War, an unknown number of F-80As were brought up to F-80C standard by Lockheed Air Services and designated F-80C-11 for use in Air National Guard squadrons.

Eighty-three P-80As ordered during the war were cancelled by the Army on 5 September 1945; 123 more were cancelled but then reinstated in the turmoil of the immediate post-war months.

Of 563 airframes that were initially planned as P-80A models, 38 were completed as FP-80A reconnaissance ships (described in a separate entry). The remainder of 525 usually cited for P-80A production includes one aircraft (44-85200) which was completed as the sole XP-80B, later became the XP-80R, and is described separately.

Long after production of 344 P-80A-1-LO and 180 P-80A-5-LO fighters was completed by the manufacturer, Lockheed 'modernised' an unknown number to F-80A-10-LO standard with the installation of AN/ARN-6 radio compass, JATO (Jet-Assisted Take-Off), plenum chamber fire warning units, modified heating, cooling and pressurisation, and other changes.

Additional modifications were made to 26 F-80A-10-LO fighters for operation in extreme cold weather conditions. It is unclear whether these were done by the manufacturer or by the USAF. The changes included replacement of the I-16 emergency fuel pump with the Pseco S-1342A pump,

To celebrate the 30th anniversary of the US Air Mail service, Captain Vermont Garrison flew this 334th FS P-80A from New York-La Guardia to Washington National on 15 May 1948, carrying a sack of mail.

Colonel David Schilling, World War II ace, flew this P-80A when he commanded the 56th FG at Selfridge Field in 1947. The aircraft wears his victory tally, which was ordered removed when the P-80s deployed to Germany in July 1948.

modification to the fuel system to utilise the port leading-edge tank for gasoline starting, installation of an engine-driven fuel pump, and other modifications. These 'winterised' aircraft were 44-85375/85376, 44-85380, 44-85421/85422, 44-85438. 44-85472, 44-85478, 44-85484, 44-85488, 44-8303, 44-8309, 45-8311, 45-8313, 45-8316, 45-8318, 45-8320/8321, 45-8326, 45-8328/8329, 45-8336, 45-8339, 45-8342/8343, 45-8355.

One hundred and twenty-nine F-80A fighters (consisting of 75 F-80A-1-LOs and 54 F-80A-5-LOs) were upgraded to F-80C-11-LO standard by Lockheed Air Services, Inc. Sixty-six aircraft built and put into service as P-80A (F-80A) fighters were later modified to become RF-80A-15-LO reconnaissance aircraft.

P-80A-1-LO serials (344): 44-84992/85199 (208); 44-85201/85336 (136)
P-80A-5-LO serials (180): 44-85337/85382 (46); 45-85384 (1); 44-85386/85398 (13); 44-85400/85424 (25); 44-85426/85432 (7); 44-85434/ 85438 (5); 44-85440/85442 (3); 44-85444 (1); 44-85446 (1); 44-85448 (1); 44-85450 (1); 44-85452 (1); 44-85454 (1); 44-85456 (1); 44-85458 (1); 44-85460 (1); 44-85462 (1); 44-85464 (1); 44-85466 (1); 44-85468 (1); 44-85470 (1); 44-85472 (1); 44-85474 (1); 44-85476 (1); 44-85478 (1); 44-85480 (1); 44-85482 (1); 44-85484 (1); 44-85486 (1); 44-85488 (1); 44-85490 (1); 45-8301 (1); 45-8303 (1); 45-8305 (1); 45-8307 (1); 45-8309 (1); 45-8311 (1); 45-8313 (1); 45-8315/8363 (49)

F-14

F-14 was the generic designation for the prototype photo-reconnaissance version of the Shooting Star. It has been identified in published works as the XF-14, YF-14 or F-14A, although the 'Y' prefix for 'service test' seems unlikely. The Shooting Star was obviously a suitable vehicle to be used as a camera platform, and the initial F-14 design paved the way for distinguished service by later reconnaissance models in the Korean War.

The sole F-14 (44-83024) had initially been ordered as one of 13 YP-80As. The XF-14 carried cameras in place of machine-guns. A window for the camera was built into the hinged-forward lower nose section in front of the nosewheel. This left the sides of the nose unblemished, unlike subsequent photo models which had camera windows on the side ahead of the air intakes.

This F-14 was destroyed in an inflight collision on 6 December 1944. Lockheed pilot Claypool was aloft doing night visual-recognition work with a Lockheed-owned B-25 Mitchell. Claypool's principal purpose was to demonstrate that the Shooting Star did not leave a comet-like exhaust trail at

night, as German jet warplanes reportedly did. He was proven all too right when the F-14 and B-25 collided, with the loss of all on board.

Subsequent reconnaissance ships were designated F-14A and, thereafter, FP-80A. Those with the later FP-80A appellation underwent yet another change when they became RF-80As under the new designation system adopted on 11 June 1948.

F-14 serial (1): 44-83024

F-14

The sole F-14 was the reconnaissance version of the YP-80A. It had only a single downward-pointing camera installation, with optically-flat windows in the lower side of the otherwise standard nose. Gun armament was naturally deleted.

Standard F-80 nose shape without armament | **YP-80A airframe**

Landing light

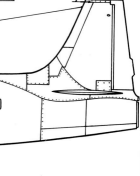

Camera window under nose

F-14A

Shooting Star camera ships beginning with the second aircraft were given the F-14A designation. It is unclear how many airframes were completed under the F-14A nomenclature, or when the AAF decided to change the designation to FP-80A. A P-80A (44-85260) is said to have been the second photo ship, modified as a replacement for the lost F-14 and redesignated F-14A. The exact configuration of this aircraft is unknown, and it is unclear whether cameras were actually installed.

Conflicting evidence suggests that a different P-80A (44-84998) may have become the second reconnaissance aircraft. This was certainly the best-known and most visible of the early photo ships, and wore a data block (the information about designation and serial number stencilled on the fuselage port side beneath the cockpit) identifying it as an F-14A. This aircraft introduced what became the standard mix of viewing ports on all examples to follow – a trapezoid-shaped window on the port side and a much smaller square window on its starboard side, as well as three camera viewing ports on the underfuselage ahead of the nosewheel – all to enable the aircraft to carry a variety of cameras.

Above: 44-84998 was possibly the second photo-reconnaissance P-80, finished under the F-14A designation. Visible through the port-side camera window is a K-14 sensor, set to peer obliquely downwards.

Right: A forward-hinging nose section gave technicians rapid access to the camera bay and film magazines. Flat windows in the lower nose allowed vertical photography.

XFP-80A

The XFP-80A was a modified P-80A (44-85201) with a nose installation of photographic equipment that was more complete than that of the XF-14. As on the earlier aircraft, the nose installation hinged upward to provide access to the camera gear.

XFP-80A serial (1): 44-85201

DF-80A

A small number of F-80s were operated as drone controllers under the designation DF-80A.

Left: This is the nose of the XFP-80A, detailing the camera nose subsequently used on the RF-80A. Note the forward window for the 'dicing' camera.

Above: DF-80A drone controllers were painted yellow, with black stripes on the wings. This example is seen at Wright Field in 1947.

RF-80A (F-14A, FP-80A)

The RF-80A production version of the Shooting Star reconnaissance aircraft (known earlier as F-14A, then FP-80A) covered 38 aircraft that began on the production line as P-80As, plus 114 'new-build' aircraft. In addition, 66 F-80As were later rebuilt to become RF-80As, as noted below.

Initially, the RF-80As were powered by a 3,850-lb (17.12-kN) thrust General Electric J33-GE-11 or Allison J33-A-9 turbojets. Camera installation consisted of one K-17 camera with a 6-in (15.24-cm) lens and two K-22 split-vertical cameras with 24-in (60.9-cm) lens.

FP-80A-1-LO and FP-80A-5-LO were the block number assignments of factory-built aircraft in this series, subsequently redesignated RF-80A-1-LO and RF-80A-5-LO. The latter were built with the J33-A-17 powerplant. The subsequent RF-80A-10-LO block number identifies aircraft modified after entering service. Lockheed 'modernised' an unknown number to RF-80A-10-LO standard with the installation of AN/ARN-6 radio compass, JATO, plenum chamber fire warning units, modified heating, cooling and pressurisation, and other changes. The 'dash 10' block aircraft were powered by J33-A-9A or -9B, and J33-GE-11A or -11B engines.

The RF-80A-15-LO block number assignment went to 66 aircraft initially built as P-80A fighters and converted by Lockheed Aircraft Services, Inc. into photo-reconnaissance ships. They differed from factory-built reconnaissance models in having a less even contour over the nose at the very front of the aircraft. The 'dash 15s'

used J33-A-17, -17A, or -21 engines. The aircraft modified were: 44-85013, 44-85015, 44-85019, 44-85038/85039, 44-85047, 44-85049, 44-85059, 44-85062/85063, 44-85101, 44-85109, 44-85122, 44-85142, 44-85155, 44-85160/85161, 44-85163, 44-85168, 44-85172, 44-85177, 44-85181/85182, 44-85196, 44-85205, 44-85239, 44-85242, 44-85244, 44-85253, 44-85260, 44-85268/85269, 44-85279, 44-85281, 44-85283, 44-85287, 44-85291, 44-85297, 44-85310, 44-85315, 44-85320, 44-85322, 44-85324, 44-85330, 44-85356, 44-85366, 44-85379, 44-85393, 44-85397/85398, 44-85411, 44-85442, 44-85448, 44-85464, 44-85466, 44-85476, 45-8319, 45-8325, 45-8327, 45-8337, 45-8346, 45-8350/8351, 45-8359, 45-8362 and 45-8406.

Above: My Miss Carole B was an RF-80A assigned to the 45th TRS. It has unusual wingtip 'Misawa' tanks of much wider diameter than normal.

Below: Seen alongside F-86s of the 51st FIW, this is an RF-80A of the 15th Tactical Reconnaissance Squadron, assigned to the 67th TRW.

Above: The checkertail fins identified the 363rd Tactical Reconnaissance Wing at Shaw AFB, which operated the RF-80A from 1951 until 1955. The wing also flew the type from 1947 to 1949.

Below: This RF-80A was one of the Block 15 aircraft produced by conversion from standard fighters and identified by the stepped nose contours. It served with the 160th TRS, Alabama ANG.

RF-80A-20-LO and RF-80A-25-LO aircraft – which had no corresponding equivalent in the F-80A 'fighter' series – were conversions of existing -10 and -15 Shooting Stars. They were equipped with J33-A-35 engine, AN/ARC-27 command radio, and AN/APW-11 identification radar.

Six FP-80A reconnaissance aircraft (consisting of four FP-80A-1-LOs and two FP-80A-5-LOs) were modified to RF-80C-11-LO standard.

FP-80A serials: 44-85383 (1); 44-85385 (1); 44-85399 (1); 44-85425 (1); 44-85433 (1); 44-85439 (1); 44-85440/85442 (3); 44-85443 (1); 44-85445 (1); 44-85447 (1); 44-85449 (1); 44-85451 (1); 44-85453 (1); 44-85455 (1); 44-85457 (1); 44-85459 (1); 44-85461 (1); 44-85463 (1); 44-85465 (1); 44-85467 (1); 44-85469 (1); 44-85471 (1); 44-85473 (2); 44-85475 (1); 44-85477 (1); 44-85479 (1); 44-85481 (1); 44-85483 (1); 44-85485 (1); 44-85487 (1); 44-85489 (1); 44-85491 (1); 45-

15th TRS personnel confer at Kimpo in front of Emma Dee, one of the squadron's RF-80As. The raised nose reveals the rack assembly used to mount the cameras.

8302 (1); 45-8304 (1); 45-8306 (1); 45-8308 (1); 45-8310 (1); 45-8312 (1); 45-8314 (1); 45-8364/8477 (114).

ERF-80A

The ERF-80A was a solitary F-80A (44-85042) modified by the Air Materiel Command Photographic Center with a nose of modified contour. It was an airframe that had previously been employed as a ramjet engine testbed.

ERF-80A serial: 44-85042

XP-80B

The first 'B model' Shooting Star (44-85200) introduced an improved J33 engine. Some documents list this powerplant as a 4,000-lb (17.79-kN) thrust Allison J33-A-17, others as a J33-A-21 model with water-alcohol injection. This aircraft was armed with four 0.50-in (12.7-mm) machine-guns, apparently the Browning M2 model found on early variants.

As noted in the entry for the production P-80B, there is no truth to widely published reports that this version introduced a thinner wing design. Wing thickness was identical on all P-80A and P-80B variants.

However, a recognition feature of the 'B model' was the short pitot tube located at the leading edge of the vertical fin (found on the nose on P-80A and P-80C aircraft).

This airframe became better known in a subsequent guise, after it was converted to become the XP-80R for an attempt on the world air speed record.

XP-80B serial: 44-85200

The sole XP-80B was subsequently converted into the XP-80R racer, as seen here in its final configuration. Note the relocated pitot tube mounted on the vertical fin.

P-80B (F-80B)

The post-war P-80B (known in early documents as the P-80Z) was a significantly improved model of the Shooting Star, with virtually all equipment changes occurring beneath the skin. Among other changes, the P-80B was the first operational American warplane to be equipped with an ejection seat, a feature which had been included in Sweden on the Saab J21 and in Germany on the Dornier Do 335. The installation at the time was called a 'jettisonable seat developed along the German lines to provide better escape means at high speed.' The Lockheed-designed ejection seat, together with the capability to use JATO bottles, was also retrofitted on many P-80As.

The 'B model' did not have a thinner wing or thicker skin, as has been reported in articles about the Shooting Star for half a century. The P-80B retained the wing span, length, and height of the P-80A. To create space for water-alcohol tanks, the P-80B sacrificed internal fuel capacity, which dropped to 425 US gal (1609 litres) from 470 US gal (1779 litres). The 'B model' was about 1,000 lb (454 kg) heavier than previous Shooting Stars.

While the 209 P-80B-1 models retained the now-familiar M2 machine-guns, the 31 P-80B-5 fighters were designed to introduce six 0.50-in (12.7-mm) M3 machine-guns, although there were delays in the actual installation. The M3 gun became the standard for US fighters for more than a decade to follow. The P-80B-5 models also had winterised features resulting from cold-

weather tests at Ladd AFB, Alaska.

The first operational P-80Bs went to the 1st Fighter Group at March Field, California on 24 June 1946 and soon began participating in air races and record-setting efforts.

Among noteworthy P-80B airframes was 45-8557, impressed into US Navy service as BuNo. 29060. Others, including 45-8484/8485, 45-8528, 45-8538 and 45-8531, were modified to duplicate the functions and guidance system of the Bell GAM-63 Rascal air-to-surface missile in tests at Holloman AFB, New Mexico in 1953-54.

This F-80B was assigned to the training squadron at Williams AFB, Arizona. It has had the buzz number removed from the nose, and continues to carry the 'Misawa' tanks from its service in Korea.

P/F-80B/TO-1

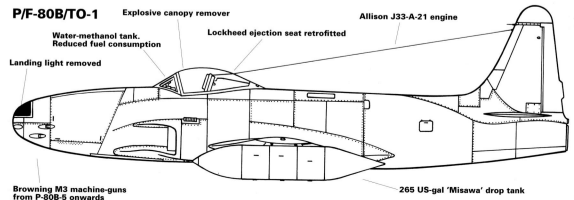

Explosive canopy remover

Allison J33-A-21 engine

Lockheed ejection seat retrofitted

Water-methanol tank. Reduced fuel consumption

Landing light removed

Browning M3 machine-guns from P-80B-5 onwards

265 US-gal 'Misawa' drop tank

Camera nose
The entire nose section of the RF-80A was hinged at a point on the lower fuselage. It could be rapidly hinged forward to allow technicians to remove film magazines or to reconfigure the camera installation.

Camera installation
The reconnaissance nose of the RF-80A allowed for a number of camera installations. Standard equipment consisted of one K-17 camera with a 6-in (15.24-cm) lens and a pair of K-22s with 24-in (60.9-cm) lenses. Some aircraft were seen with one large downward-facing camera, with the side-facing oblique windows empty. Fighters modified in-theatre to RF-80C standard usually had one or two K-14 cameras, facing downwards.

Lockheed RF-80A 15th TRS 67th TRW Kimpo (K-14) Korea 1952

The RF-80A was the USAF's primary tactical reconnaissance platform of the late 1940s and early 1950s, before being replaced by the Republic RF-84. RF-80s often served in mixed units alongside RF-51s and RB-26s. The type was the main tactical reconnaissance tool in Korea, although its vulnerability required it to operate with a fighter escort.

Tip tanks
Eight different configurations of wingtip fuel tank were wind-tunnel tested before Lockheed arrived at the familiar teardrop-shaped 150-US gal (568-litre) design. While this tank had the added benefit of actually reducing drag, it did not give adequate range, and a number of larger tanks were developed.

Refuelled mission
The first air-refuelled combat mission in history was flown by RF-80As of the 67th TRW on 6 July 1951, when a KB-29M topped up the special probe-equipped tanks of three of the wing's aircraft on a mission over North Korea. This installation was not adopted generally.

RF-80 in Korea
The first operator of the RF-80 in Korea was the 8th TRS (Photo), which had been assigned directly to 5th Air Force. It established a detachment at Itazuke for Korean operations, and soon the whole squadron moved, assigned first to the 8th FBW, and then to the 543rd TSG. It moved to Taegu in October 1950. On 24 February 1951 the 543rd was redesignated as the 67th TRW, while the 8th TRS became the 15th TRS. In June 1952 the 45th TRS began operating RF-80s and RF-86s as part of the 67th, having hitherto flown F/RF-51Ds. In addition to RF-80s, the 67th had standard F-80s for armed recce and fighter escort.

Markings
RF-80s served in natural metal finish, with a matt anti-glare panel above the forward fuselage. 'FT' buzz-codes were standard for both fighters and reconnaissance aircraft. The 67th TRW's two RF-80 squadrons employed individual fin-bands: the 15th TRS had a single colour band (yellow or dark green), while the 45th TRS used a dark blue band with white polka dots. A mission tally is carried on this aircraft.

Nose profile
This RF-80A has the smooth nose contours of a factory-produced aircraft. Aircraft produced by conversion had a distinct step in the upper nose profile.

RF-80 in service
The first reconnaissance unit was the 39th Reconnaissance Squadron of the 412th Fighter Group. This became the first squadron of the 363rd Reconnaissance Group which was established in July 1946. Subsequent units to receive the type were the 67th RG, 8th TRS (Photo), 117th TRW, 10th TRW, 66th TRW, 432nd TRG and the 4th TRS. Subsequently, the ANG had five squadrons flying RF-80As.

Above: The ANG received six squadrons of F-80s before the Korean War broke out, but all were taken back for active-duty service. After the end of the war, large-scale equipment of Guard units began. The 188th Fighter Squadron, New Mexico ANG, was one recipient, flying the F-80A, B (illustrated) and C from 1953 to 1958, when the unit upgraded to the F-100A.

Of the 240 manufactured by Lockheed, 31 were P-80B-5-LOs optimised for winter operations with canopy defrosting and special greases and natural rubber for cold-weather duty in Alaska. One hundred and seventeen F-80Bs were partially brought up to F-80C standard by Lockheed Air Services and were redesignated F-80C-12-LO for Air National Guard duty.

P-80B-1-LO serials (209): 45-8478/8480 (3); 45-8482/8565 (84); 45-8596/8717 (122)
P-80B-5-LO serials (31): 45-8481 (1); 45-8566/8595 (30)

Above: The P-80B introduced an ejection seat, among other improvements. These are from Block 1, which retained the M2 machine-guns.

Right: Three F-80Bs from the 36th Fighter Group fly over Germany in 1948, the formation consisting of one aircraft from each of the constituent squadrons (22nd, 23rd and 53rd FS).

F-80C (P-80C)

The definitive model of the first operational US jet fighter, as well as the most numerous, the F-80C was heavier, more powerful, and refined. The F-80C (P-80C until 11 June 1948) was the principal version flown by combat airmen in Korea and established the standard to which early

Having force-landed on a frozen lake, this 65th FIS F-80C was resurrected on skis and, using JATO, flown off the lake and back to its base at Elmendorf.

Shooting Star airframes were partially upgraded.

Early F-80Cs initially were powered by a 4,600-lb (20.46-kN) thrust J33-A-23 turbojet. The final 561 aircraft (from 49-422) were powered by a 5,400-lb (24.02-kN) thrust J33-A-35, which is considered the definitive version of the engine. Included among the more powerful aircraft were four (49-3957/3600) initially intended for Peru but delivered to the USAF.

The F-80C retained the height of the F-80A/B but had a wing span of 39 ft 9 in (12.12 m) and fuselage length of 34 ft 5 in (10.49 m). Armed with the improved M3 machine-guns introduced by the 'B model', the F-80C eventually acquired two additional

wing pylons and provision for 16 5-in HVARs. The existing ordnance stations were strengthened. This made the 'C model' the first Shooting Star to be truly effective in the air-to-ground role.

The F-80C introduced minor changes to the slide-back canopy design, along with the first explosive canopy remover found on a USAF aircraft.

After entering service, F-80C fighters underwent various field modifications, including installation of 265-US gal (1003-litre) underwing 'Misawa' fuel tanks (named for the air base in western Japan) or 230-US gal (871-litre) Fletcher wingtip tanks. When equipped with squared-off wingtips for the latter, wing span of the F-80C was reduced to 38 ft 9 in (11.81 m).

One F-80C (47-171) was constructed almost entirely from magnesium as part of an Air Force structures research programme and was later redesignated NF-80C (which

A common F-80C weapon was napalm, the tanks being made from old F-51 fuel tanks with a hand grenade wired in. This 35th FBS aircraft (seen at K-13 in 1951) also carries a pair of 5-in HVARs.

see). Another (48-356) was modified during production to the two-seat TF-80C operational-trainer version and served as prototype for the T-33 series. Not included in figures for the 'C model' are 49 P-80C-1-LOs and one F-80C-5-LO which went to the US Navy and Marine Corps under the designation TO-1.

In addition to 693 aircraft manufactured as P-80Cs, 129 operational F-80As were modified to F-80C-11-LO standard by Lockheed Air Services, Inc. The conversion consisted of the installation of the J33-A-35 engine, an ejection seat using an M-5

This F-80C was assigned to the 36th Fighter Group at Furstenfeldbruck. Note the open airbrake under the fuselage as the fighter attempts to hold station with the photo-platform.

catapult and M-3 actuator, and provisions for an AN/ARC-27 command radio. The 129 F-80C-11-LO upgrades were airframes 44-84994, 44-85001, 44-85004, 44-85007, 44-85009, 44-85012, 44-85014, 44-85024/85025, 44-85029, 44-85041, 44-85051, 44-85057, 44-85060, 44-85071/85072, 44-85080, 44-85088, 44-85098, 44-85104/85105, 44-85107, 44-85110, 44-85112, 44-85120, 44-85124/85125, 44-85128, 44-85132, 44-85134/85135, 44-85150/85151, 44-85154, 44-85166/85167, 44-85171, 44-85175/85176, 44-85178/85180, 44-85183, 44-85190/85191, 44-85201, 44-85210, 44-85216/85217, 44-85225/85227, 44-85229/85231, 44-85237, 44-85240, 44-85245/85247, 44-85229/85231, 44-85237, 44-85240, 44-85245/85247, 44-85249, 44-85252, 44-85261/85262, 44-85264, 44-85270, 44-85284/85285, 44-85290, 44-85293, 44-85300, 44-85321, 44-85328, 44-85333/85334 (all F-80A-1-LO), and 44-85342, 44-85345, 44-85363/85364, 44-85370/85374, 44-85384, 44-85386, 44-85390, 44-85392, 44-85394/85395, 44-85400/85402, 44-85405/85406, 44-85410, 44-85414, 44-85416, 44-85418, 44-85423/85424, 44-85435, 44-85437, 44-85440/85441, 44-85446, 44-85450, 44-85456, 44-85468, 44-85480, 44-85482, 44-85486, 44-85490, 45-8305, 45-8307, 45-

F-80C/TV-1

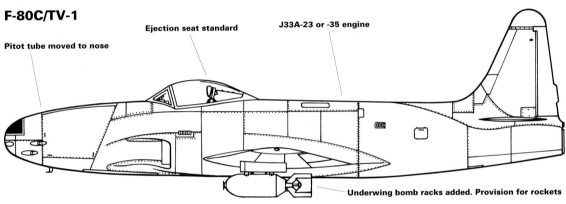

Pitot tube moved to nose

Ejection seat standard

J33A-23 or -35 engine

Underwing bomb racks added. Provision for rockets

Ground crew from the 25th FIS (51st FIG) arm an F-80C during combat operations from K-13 in 1951. The HVAR rocket was widely used on ground attack sorties.

8315, 44-8324, 45-8330/8331, 45-8334/8335, 45-8347/8348, 45-8354, 45-8357/8358, 45-8363 (all F-80A-5-LO).

P-80C-1-LO serials (113): 47-171/217 (47); 47-1395 (1); 48-382/396 (15); 48-863/912 (50)
F-80C-5-LO serials (19): 47-526/600
F-80C-10-LO serials (561): 49-422/878 (457); 49-1800/1899 (100); 49-3597/3600 (4)

NF-80C

The NF-80C designation went to the sole F-80C (47-171) to have virtually all-magnesium construction, in a structures evaluation. It is unclear when the 'N' prefix – which indicates a permanent modification – was applied. The aircraft spent its career in various flight test operations, for example, being used as a chase plane during Muroc flight tests of the Lockheed XF-90 penetration fighter.

Aircraft 47-171 apparently left Muroc in about 1950 and was assigned to the ARDC (Air Research and Development Command) at Wright-Patterson AFB, Ohio. This aircraft was later painted all-white and was tested with a ground transport device known as 'Auto Crawl' with which the aircraft could be towed across rough terrain using tracks. The aircraft was eventually placed on display at the original USAF Museum at Wright-Patterson in the mid-1950s.

The NF-80C rests in the USAFM compound. The aircraft was removed from display after its all-magnesium construction was considered to be a fire risk.

Above: The NF-80C is seen undergoing 'Auto Crawl' tests. It had earlier been used to evaluate magnesium construction.

Above: This close-up shows the 'Auto Crawl' equipment, which consisted of tracked 'boots' which were attached to the wheels. This allowed the aircraft to be towed across rough and muddy terrain.

RF-80C

During the Korean War, an unknown number – possibly as many as 70 – F-80A and F-80C fighters were retroactively modified to RF-80C standard. They were distinguished from most other reconnaissance aircraft by having a smooth fighter-style nose. The guns were replaced by one or two K-14 cameras, with the gun barrels being painted over to give the appearance of retaining weapons.

In addition, six RF-80A reconnaissance aircraft (consisting of four RF-80A-1-LOs and two RF-80A-5-LOs) were modified to RF-80C-11-LO standard by Lockheed Air Services, Inc. The conversion consisted of the installation of the J33-A-35 engine, an ejection seat using an M-5 catapult and M-3 actuator, and provisions for an AN/ARC-27

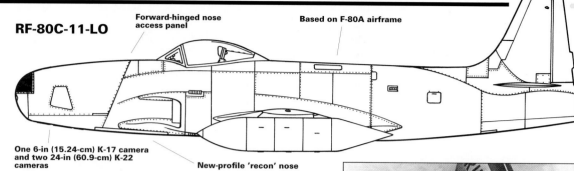

RF-80C-11-LO — Forward-hinged nose access panel — Based on F-80A airframe — One 6-in (15.24-cm) K-17 camera and two 24-in (60.9-cm) K-22 cameras — New-profile 'recon' nose

command radio. The six RF-80C-11-LO upgrades were airframes 45-8372/8375 (all RF-80A-1-LO), and 45-8383 and 45-8421 (both RF-80A-5-LO).

Right: The 'Hybrid-1' added an RF-80A camera nose to a standard F-80C airframe, improving the performance of the basic photo-platform. Several of these conversions were undertaken at Kimpo, by 67th TRW personnel, and at Tachikawa, the main maintenance base for the Korean War F-80 fleet.

Above: An RF-80C from the 45th TRS 'Polka Dots' rests at Misawa in 1952. The aircraft has had its guns removed to make way for a camera.

Right: This RF-80C conversion is also assigned to the 45th TRS. It has 35-mm cameras mounted in leading-edge fairings.

P-80D

The P-80D designation applies to a Lockheed proposal of July 1948, known in company parlance as the Model 680-33-07. The P-80D was to be powered by an Allison J33-A-29 turbojet engine and to have improved instrumentation and cockpit arrangement derived from those of the T-33 trainer. The P-80D was not built.

P-80E

The P-80E (or Lockheed L-181) was a swept-wing version with which Lockheed did not proceed. Aimed at allowing Lockheed to offer a fighter competitor to the F-86 Sabre, the P-80E would have

retained the nose, centre fuselage, unswept vertical tail, and armament of the P-80C. Its aft fuselage was enlarged to house an afterburning Allison J33-A-27 turbojet. The P-80E was to be fitted with a thinner wing and tailplane swept at 35°.

Figures on the P-80E included span 37 ft (11.28 m), length 38 ft 10.25 in (11.84 m), wing area 248 sq ft (23.04 m²), maximum weight 15,200 lb (6895 kg), maximum speed 662 mph (1065 km/h) at sea level, cruising speed 480 mph (772 km/h), initial rate of climb 3,720 ft/min (1134 m/min), service ceiling 37,800 ft (11521 m), and combat range 1,760 miles (2832 km).

At best, the P-80E appears unlikely to have offered serious competition to the F-86. In any event, the USAF did not call upon Lockheed and the P-80E was not built.

P-80N

The P-80N was to be a North American-built P-80A. On 19 January 1945, the USAAF awarded North American Aviation (NAA) a contract to produce 1,000 P-80N fighters, known in company jargon as the NA-137.

In published works, there has long existed a dispute as to whether North American planned to build the P-80A in

Dallas (where it manufactured B-24 Liberators and P-51D/K/M Mustangs and was preparing to build the C-82 Packet) or in Kansas City (where it turned out B-25 Mitchells). In a February 1998 interview, the senior North American official of the era, Lee Attwood, confirmed that Kansas City was the intended P-80N factory, and that, "we had one plane about finished." After VE-Day, the AAF cancelled the contract and no P-80Ns were completed.

XP-80R

The XP-80R, also called *Racey* and converted from the sole XP-80B airframe (44-85200), was a Shooting Star modified at Lockheed's Burbank plant for an attempt on the world air speed record of 615.8 mph (991.0 km/h) set on 7 September 1946 by Group Captain E. M. Donaldson, RAF, in a modified Gloster Meteor F.Mk 4. Changes to the aircraft included experimental NACA flush air intakes and a low-profile canopy. While retaining the Allison J33-A-17, the XP-80R failed in October 1946 to average more than 600 mph (966 km/h) in four passes over a 3-km (1.86-mile) course. Lockheed took the aircraft back to Burbank, where engineers replaced the flush air intakes with conventional ones and installed a 4,600-lb (20.46-kN) thrust Allison Model 400, a highly modified J33 with water injection. This powerplant was essentially the J33-A-23 which later appeared in the F-80C model. Lockheed also clipped the wings and installed sharper leading edges.

Colonel Albert Boyd, chief of flight test at Air Materiel Command, flew the highly-polished XP-80R on a record-breaking flight at Muroc Dry Lake, California on 19 June

1947, averaging 623.738 mph (1003.782 km/h). It was the first time a record had been snared beyond the 1000-km/h figure. Surviving photographs show that the P-80R aircraft was subsequently employed operationally with Air Training Command, which used many F-80s as advanced trainers. The XP-80R eventually was placed on display at the USAF Museum at Wright-Patterson AFB, Ohio.

The XP-80R streaks across the Muroc lakebed during its successful record attempt. In the foreground is one of the timing stations.

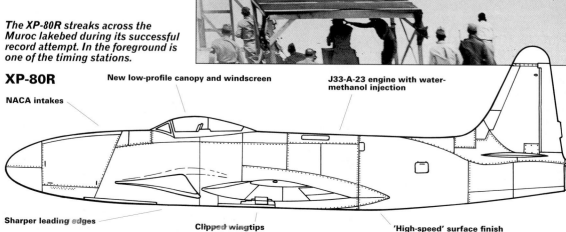

XP-80R — New low-profile canopy and windscreen — J33-A-23 engine with water-methanol injection — NACA intakes — Sharper leading edges — Clipped wingtips — 'High-speed' surface finish

Above: In its initial configuration the XP-80R had NACA-designed flush intakes. The aircraft was not fast enough, causing Lockheed to abandon the intakes in favour of more power and sharper leading edges.

Right: Two views show the XP-80R in its first guise, and then after fitment of standard intakes. Accompanying the latter were sharper-edged, cropped wings and an Allison 400 (J33-A-23) engine.

P-80Z (1st use)

The P-80Z appellation was used for a time in Lockheed documents to refer to swept-wing designs that eventually evolved into the XF-90 fighter. Lockheed's Skunk Works worked on 65 designs including butterfly-tailed, three-engined, and W-winged aircraft. The XF-90 became a wholly different aircraft, a long-range penetration fighter powered by two 3,100-lb (13.79-kN) thrust Westinghouse J34-WE-11 turbojets. It became an unsuccessful competitor to the North American YF-93A and the McDonnell XF-88 Voodoo.

P-80Z (2nd use)

The P-80Z designation was dusted off in March 1947 to appear for a time on company records covering the aircraft that were completed as P-80Bs.

TF-80C

The TF-80C prototype (48-356) introduced the two-seat configuration that was adopted for all T-33 trainers and F-94 fighters. This aircraft made its first flight on 22 March 1948. It was delivered without armament.

QF-80

The first steps to create a drone version of the P-80 began in 1945, although the aircraft did not receive the 'QF' prefix found on later pilotless models. Bell Aircraft took on the job of modifying two Shooting Stars for a radio-control experiment, one aircraft to be a 'mother' ship and the other a drone. Initial plans to use two surviving Project

This pair of drones comprises a QF-80A (background) and a QF-80B. The aircraft were used for the most part as fighter targets.

Extraversion YP-80s in the Bell drone project failed to materialise, and Bell instead modified two P-80As (44-85407/85408). The 'mother' ship and drone reached Muroc in late 1946 and participated in a brief flight test programme with limited goals and accomplishments. It was the beginning of Shooting Star drone programmes that went on for decades.

Sperry Gyroscope began converting eight F-80 fighters to QF-80 drones in 1951 under Project Bad Boy. The first Sperry conversions apparently were P-80A models that became QF-80A drones. A second batch of 14 Sperry QF-80 drone gunnery targets featured enlarged, centre-mounted Fletcher wingtip tanks equipped with

cameras used to record an attacking aircraft's gunnery pattern. The tip-tank cameras were capable of being jettisoned by remote control and lowered by parachutes, located in the rear of the tanks. Although these QF-80 drones were not as fast as the fighters that were employing them as aerial targets, and were difficult to maintain and operate, on several occasions the US Air Force obtained more. As recently as 1962, QF-80 drone aerial targets were being shot down at Eglin AFB, Florida, when the F-105 Thunderchief was being evaluated in the air-to-air role with loads of four and six AIM-9 Sidewinder missiles.

Sperry received contracts for 55 more QF-80 drones (plus 10 DT-33 drone controllers) as Bad Boy continued in November 1954. It appears that most were QF-80C aircraft and that at some later juncture they were redesignated QF-80F – but four decades later, it is no longer

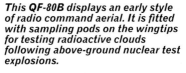

This QF-80B displays an early style of radio command aerial. It is fitted with sampling pods on the wingtips for testing radioactive clouds following above-ground nuclear test explosions.

possible to exactly fix the designations and serial numbers of all of the drone aircraft.

Many QF-80s were employed as pilotless drones to sample radioactive particles by flying through mushroom clouds in the aftermath of atomic bomb tests. The sampling aircraft had large wingtip sampling containers.

Air Force drones were all red but had gloss white or natural metal finish on the top surfaces of both wings. Many, but not all, had arrester hooks and specialised radio receiver equipment.

Above: This QF-80B, complete with Fletcher tanks, was seen on the Nellis ramp in 1958.

Above right: This QF-80C is seen carrying two large ECM pods underwing. In addition to being targets for missile tests, the QF-80s tested the efficiency of countermeasures.

Far right: This drone is a JQF-80F, originally built as a P-80B. In addition to the radio guidance antennas, the aircraft carries a jamming pod.

QF-80A

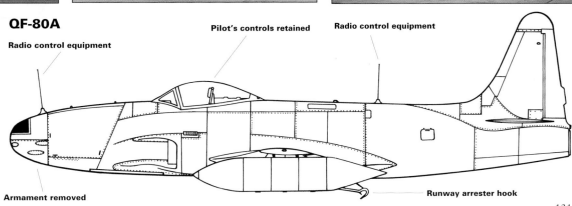

Radio control equipment

Pilot's controls retained

Radio control equipment

Armament removed

Runway arrester hook

Lockheed P-80 Variants

Testbeds

'Catapult P-80A'

The 'Catapult P-80A', or Lockheed Model 180-41-02, is the term that covers a trio of Shooting Stars used to evaluate carrier operations. The US Navy took the transfer of three P-80A fighters (44-85000, 44-85005, and 44-85235) with arrester gear and catapult hook for experimental work. The Navy assigned BuNos 29667, 29668 and 29689 to them. Some published sources which date to 1945 refer to these aircraft using the US Navy designation XFO-1, but no record exists that this designation was ever applied, nor that they were designated TO-1 like other Navy/Marine Corps Shooting Stars that followed.

The first aircraft (BuNo. 29667) was turned over to the Navy on 17 May 1945 and thereafter flew simulated carrier operations at NAS Patuxent River, Maryland, with much of the flying done by Commander Najeeb Halaby. The second ship (BuNo. 29668) reached the Navy on 18 December 1945 and was fitted with catapult bridle and arrester hook. Photos show test pilot Tony LeVier flying the aircraft, tailhook-equipped, on the West Coast. This ship was put through carrier suitability trials aboard the USS *Franklin D. Roosevelt* (CVB-42), flown by Marine Corps Lieutenant Colonel Carl. The air ace celebrated his 31st birthday on 1 November 1946 by making four running take-offs, two catapult launches, and five arrested landings.

The Navy did not see in the Shooting Star any advantages over its McDonnell FD-1 (later FH-1) Phantom fighter then being developed. The P-80A needed a minimum of 900 ft (274 m) for a take-off even with a headwind, and a typical carrier offered only 925 ft (281 m). It did not help that the first two aircraft were lost in mishaps, BuNo. 29667 on 13 February 1947 and 29668 on 4 June 1947.

'Ramjet-powered F-80'

In the 1940s, scientific publications touted the extremely simple and 'pure' athoyd

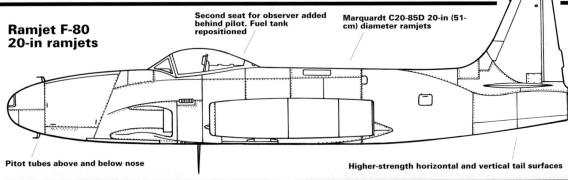

Ramjet F-80 20-in ramjets

Second seat for observer added behind pilot. Fuel tank repositioned

Marquardt C20-85D 20-in (51-cm) diameter ramjets

Pitot tubes above and below nose

Higher-strength horizontal and vertical tail surfaces

44-85214 was the main ramjet-test P-80A, first flying with 20-in engines ignited on 3 December 1947. The aircraft had a second seat added for an observer.

'214 is seen with both of its 30-in Marquardt XRJ-31-MA-1s lit. The larger ramjets were flown first by Herman Salmon on 1 April 1948, and lit on the second flight.

ramjet as the powerplant of the future, overlooking its ravenous fuel consumption. Tests with ramjet-powered P-80As were conducted with two aircraft: one (44-85214) was fitted with a 30-in (76-cm) diameter Marquardt C30-10B unit on each wingtip and flown at Muroc. The other (44-85042) had 20-in (51-cm) diameter Marquardt C20-85Ds and was evaluated at Wright Field. The first flight was made on 12 March 1947.

The tests at Wright Field began with a P-51D Mustang with wingtip ramjets obtained as German war booty, but the P-51D was lost in a mishap. The P-80A used conventional fuel for both the ramjets and its own engine. Pilot Paul Chell, who had parachuted safely from the P-51D, was limited to about 20 minutes in the P-80A. The weight and drag of the wingtip engines limited the Shooting Star to a maximum height of about 20,000 ft (6096 m), which was regarded as somewhat unsatisfactory for these tests.

Engineers at Wright Field determined that it would be unsafe for Chell to test the ramjet-powered 44-85042 in a high-speed, asymmetrical situation. Evaluating a sudden loss of power on one of the two engines, they feared, would cause the P-80A to corkscrew and tear itself apart. They felt the programme had accomplished all it could, when Chell damaged the Shooting Star in a hard landing at Wright Field. 44-85042 was later used to test new camera equipment under the designation ERF-80A-1-LO.

At Muroc, about 100 sorties were made successfully, most by Lockheed pilot Herman R. 'Fish' Salmon. On 17 June 1948, aircraft 44-85214 completed a brief sortie at Muroc using ramjet power only. Another source indicates that Salmon made a longer flight on ramjet power on 21 December 1947, reaching 500 mph (805 km/h) when he ignited both ramjets, shut down the main J33 powerplant, and cruised along creating a great many decibels and burning fuel at a remarkable rate. The ramjet programme was discontinued when it became accepted that fuel consumption would rule out any wider application of the concept.

'Towed F-80A'

A single P-80A (44-84995) carried out tow tests at Wright Field. A Boeing B-29A-10-BN Superfortress (42-93921) towed the P-80A to demonstrate this proposed method of improving a fighter's range. There had been numerous such tests during the war, with a B-17F Flying Fortress and a C-47 Skytrain employed as tow ships, and a P-59 Airacomet, F4F-4 Wildcat and RP-47G Thunderbolt as the towed subjects. If a 'mother' ship could pull a fighter all the way to its target, then turn the fighter loose to wreak havoc with an enemy's air defences, the post-war Strategic Air Command would have a powerful asset.

The Shooting Star went to Wright Field on 1 May 1945. Lieutenant Colonel Pat Fleming flew the fighter and Major Guy Townsend piloted the B-29 tow ship. The tow cable was fitted with an attachment ring, while the P-80 mounted a probe with a hook-link that could be engaged or released by the pilot. The steel cable not only provided the tow but also transferred electrical power to the P-80A from the bomber's APU (auxiliary power unit).

On 23 September 1947, Fleming took off to join with the B-29 at 15,000 ft (4572 m). After trying several times and being beaten around by the turbulence from the B-29, Fleming made the link-up, stopcocked his engine, and was towed for 10 minutes. When it came time to open the hook, it would not release. Fleming struggled unsuccessfully to shake himself free of his

The front end of the prone-pilot P-80 retained the conventional cockpit for a safety pilot. The prone pilot entered via a hatch which also included the rear half of his canopy.

Above and top: A single P-80A was used for towed fighter trials, fitted with an attachment bar at the front. One inflight hook-up was accomplished successfully, although the dismount damaged the tow-bar and led to cancellation of the project.

Prone-pilot P-80A

Prone pilot's entry hatch

Safety pilot in regular cockpit

Cockpit with basic controls for prone pilot fitted in nose section

No armament

BuNo. 29668 was the second of three carrier-capable P-80As tested by the Navy. It was the aircraft which actually tested carrier operations.

Above and below: 44-85116 tested a nose-mounted launcher for 5-in HVAR rockets. The nose incorporated louvres to exhaust gases created by the firing rockets.

bond, then manoeuvred under the B-29 where the bomber's bow wave snapped the attachment point and bent it backward, leaving Fleming with no forward visibility. Fleming landed safely but the programme was halted. Fleming's Shooting Star (44-84995) later served at Eglin, Muroc and with the Air National Guard before being retired.

'Trainable guns/Prone pilot P-80A'

A single P-80A (44-85044) successively was tested with a modified rotating nose, housing four machine-guns which could be elevated up to an angle of 90°, and later with a second cockpit installed in the nose in which a pilot lay prone. The armament test, based on Germany's *schräge Musik* of World War II, was a battery of four upward-firing 0.50-in (12.7-mm) machine-guns mounted on a swivelling platform. The idea was to enable the pilot to approach a target aircraft, a bomber, from below but remain outside its range of defensive fire while locking on and shooting. However, the P-80A bucked and trembled when the guns were fired and the accuracy and merit of the scheme never convinced doubters. This same P-80A apparently was tested with a quartet of forward-firing 20-mm cannon and with a 'rocket gun' firing 4.5-in FFARs (folding fin aircraft rockets); neither

armament package was adopted for operational use.

The prone pilot experiment reflected an interest in the 1950s in finding a new way to assist pilots in sustaining high *g*, or gravity forces. Late P-80 models were stressed for 7.33*g*, while USAF doctrine held that a pilot wearing a *g*-suit could accommodate 5*g*. A pilot in a standard ejection seat was subjected to blood gathering in his mid-section and lower extremities, perhaps causing loss of consciousness. It was understood that when lying flat a pilot's body would be better able to handle the flow of blood. The P-80A (flown after early prone pilot tests in the wingtip of a B-17 and concurrently with British tests employing a Gloster Meteor) was equipped with rudimentary flight controls in the prone nose position with the regular cockpit being occupied by a safety pilot who made take-offs and landings,

The most radically altered P-80 was this B model used as a testbed for the GAM-63 Rascal missile. It was fitted with a missile guidance system in the nose and aerodynamic surfaces on the wings.

navigated, and handled flaps and speed brakes.

In flight, the prone pilot was able to handle 8*g* but had to monitor the safety pilot constantly since the latter was subject to the traditional effect of *g* forces. In the P-80A – although not in an operational prone fighter depicted in paintings in *Popular*

P-80A 44-85354 was used at Wright Field in 1948 as a testbed for a nose installation of four 20-mm cannon.

Mechanics and other magazines – the prone pilot was so far forward that he experienced vertigo during manoeuvres.

Rascal missile testbed

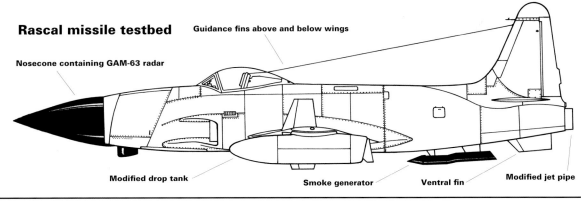

Guidance fins above and below wings

Nosecone containing GAM-63 radar

Modified drop tank

Smoke generator

Ventral fin

Modified jet pipe

TO-1 (TV-1)

TO-1 was the naval designation for the F-80C Shooting Star. The TO-1 flew in

A handful of TV-1s were used as director/observer aircraft for missile programmes, such as the Regulus I.

natural metal with standard Navy markings and had no special modifications or different equipment. Fifty were turned over to the Navy in 1949 to increase its capability to train early jet pilots at the very time when the service was lagging in development of jet fighters like the F2H Banshee and F9F Panther. These fighters served with VF-52, VCN-1, VMF-311 and other units, and were soon relegated to Reserve duty, ending

their service in the mid-1950s.

The designator for Lockheed changed from 'O' to 'V' on 1 April 1952, and all TO-1s were redesignated TV-1. All 50 aircraft had both USAF serials and Navy bureau numbers.

TO-1 BuNos: 33821/33828 (USAF 47-218/224, 47-525) (8); 33829/33847 (USAF 47-601/604, 47-1380/1394) (19);

33848/33870 (USAF 48-382, 47-1396/1411, 48-376/381) (23)

The TO-1 largely served the Navy as a trainer to provide jet experience. This aircraft is Miramar's base hack, and has had two of its nose guns removed and the ports faired over.

The Ye-152A poses with K-9 AAMs during factory tests at Zhukhovskii. The appearance of this aircraft in the 1961 Tushino flypast prompted NATO to assign the reporting name 'Flipper'.

The Big MiGs

Despite a development history hampered by an unpredictable engine and the changing nature of the US bomber threat, the quartet of aircraft that made up the Ye-150/152 programme were the first Soviet aircraft to exceed Mach 2.5 and attain a service ceiling over 22000 m. They paved the way for the Ye-155/MiG-25.

By the late 1950s NATO bombers were becoming a serious threat to the Soviet Union. Not only was the strategic bomber force growing, but the aircraft were getting more capable. The USAF inventory had just been augmented by the Convair B-58 Hustler, a Mach 2 medium bomber with a range of 5000 km (3,105 miles). To counter the bomber threat, the Soviet air defence command (PVO – ProtivoVozdooshnaya Oborona) was in urgent need of new and effective anti-aircraft weapons.

The early anti-aircraft missile systems employed by the PVO had a number of serious

The Ye-152A made at least two public appearances: in 1961 at Tushino and 1967 at Domodedovo. Here it is seen at the latter show, illustrating the wide rear fuselage which easily distinguished the twin-engined variant.

shortcomings, including limited range and a kill altitude not exceeding 20000 m (65,616 ft). Thus, Lockheed U-2 spyplanes were able to overfly Soviet territory with virtual impunity until the mid-1960s because the USSR had no real means of destroying them (the famous Powers shoot-down notwithstanding). Both production MiG-19PM 'Farmer' day interceptors and specially modified MiG-19SV fighters

(V = *vysotnii* – high-altitude) had an insufficient service ceiling, and considerable pilot skill was needed to reach it. None of the experimental Mikoyan I-3U, I-7U and I-75 interceptors (I = *istrebeetel* – fighter) progressed beyond the prototype stage. Still, Artyom I. Mikoyan's design bureau, known as OKB-155 for security reasons, did not give up on the heavy interceptor theme.

The Ye-150 prototype was completed and delivered to the LII (Flight Test Institute) in Ramenskoye (now Zhukhovskii) in December 1958. It was the first of Mikoyan's heavy interceptors to bear Ye series designations, the Ye prefix meant *yedinitsa* – literally 'single unit', i.e., a 'one-off' aircraft. The Ye-150 was to be powered by a single Tumanskii R-15-300 turbojet developing 66.7 kN (14,991 lb st) dry and 99.5 kN (22,376 lb st) in full afterburner. However, the engine was still going through bench testing by the time the airframe was built.

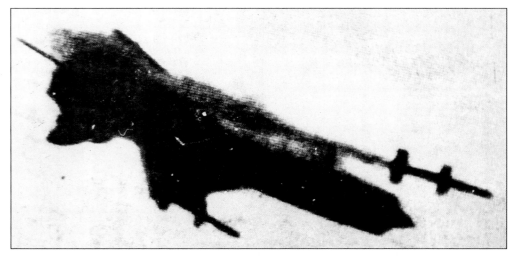

Widely published in the West, this 'action' photograph of a Ye-152A firing a K-9 missile had in fact been doctored by the Soviet authorities and deliberately 'leaked'.

*By the time the **OKB** project had ended on 25 January 1962 (18 months after its first flight), the Ye-150 had flown 42 times with three engines, such was the R-15 turbojet's unreliability.*

The aircraft was very different in appearance from earlier Mikoyan designs. The massive circular-section fuselage looked like a tube with practically no taper at the ends, making the wings and tail appear too small. Four prominent vertical slits were located immediately abead of the nozzle, giving the impression that the Ye-150 was fitted with a thrust reverser like the Saab Viggen; they were really auxiliary air intakes for afterburner cooling.

The low aspect ratio delta wings which had been perfected on the Ye-4 and Ye-5 experimental fighters (precursors of the MiG-21F 'Fishbed-A') had a 60° leading-edge sweep. The small one-piece cast canopy resembled the low-drag canopies of unlimited racing aircraft. It was hinged at the front end, with two prominent lock fairings at the rear, and blended into a shallow fuselage spine running all the way to the base of the fin. The landing gear was very similar to the MiG-21, with a forward-retracting nose unit and inward-retracting main units. During retraction, the mainwheels rotated 90° around the legs to lie vertically in the fuselage.

All-missile armament

The huge circular air intake featured a movable centrebody (shock cone) with a complex curvature in several steps. The dielectric centrebody contained the Uragan-5B (pronounced 'ooragahn', meaning hurricane) fire control radar and terminated in a long pitot boom which promptly earned the aircraft the nickname 'Yedinorog' (unicorn). A ventral fin was fitted to improve directional stability. Fuel was carried in five bladder tanks with a total capacity of 4210 litres (926 Imp gal). The armament consisted of two medium-range air-to-air missiles capable of destroying fast high-altitude targets; no guns were fitted.

Ground system checks took all of five months, ending in June 1959. The aircraft was still without a powerplant at the time due to the engine's protracted test programme. A flight-cleared version of the R-15-300 was finally fitted at the Mikoyan experimental factory

towards the end of the year, and the Ye-150 returned to Ramenskoye on 30 December to commence taxi tests. However, the engine failed during a ground run and had to be replaced, so the aircraft was not ready to fly until mid-1960.

On 8 August, the Ye-150 made its first flight at the hands of Mikoyan test pilot Aleksandr V. Fedotov. The factory trials were completed on 25 January 1962, comprising 42 flights. On its

28th flight, the Ye-150 reached Mach 2.65 (2890 km/h; 1,795 mph) at 19100 m (62,664 ft) – cruising at less than full thrust, however. Take-off weight on that occasion was 10175 kg (22,431 lb). Not all flights went smoothly. The brake parachute failed once and the aircraft overran into soft earth at the end of LII's runway, turning over on its back – luckily, without injuring the pilot or sustaining major damage.

The Ye-150's performance was far superior

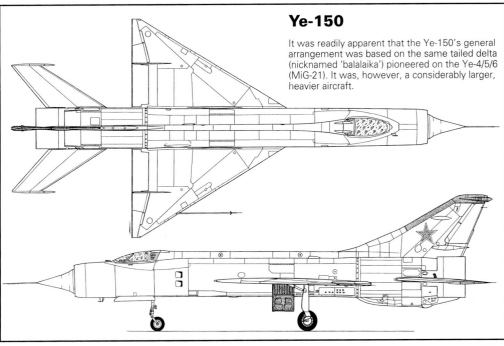

Ye-150

It was readily apparent that the Ye-150's general arrangement was based on the same tailed delta (nicknamed 'balalaika') pioneered on the Ye-4/5/6 (MiG-21). It was, however, a considerably larger, heavier aircraft.

To facilitate engine changes (a repetitive exercise given the R-15-300's problems), Ye-152-1's tail unit was removable as a complete unit.

to contemporary fighters. Ceiling in sustained horizontal flight was 23250 m (76,279 ft); the aircraft climbed to 15000 m (49,212 ft) in two and a half minutes and to 20000 m (65,616 ft) in four and a half minutes. The factory test report contained a table comparing the aircraft to the MiG-21F tactical fighter which was by then in large-scale production, and the Ye-150's climb rate was twice as good. The Mach 2.65 top speed was later repeatedly attained at altitudes up to 22500 m (73,818 ft). In his reports, Fedotov praised the Ye-150's acceleration and climb rate – properties which no doubt are all-important for an interceptor.

Problems with the massive engine persisted, and the aircraft could not enter production with a powerplant which was anything but dependable. Therefore, as soon as the Ye-150 detailed design phase was completed, the Mikoyan bureau started work on two versions of the basic aircraft, designated Ye-152 and Ye-152A, respectively. Outwardly, the two were very similar, differing in aft fuselage structure, wing design and weapons location.

Second engine source

Like its predecessor, the Ye-152 was powered by a single R-15-300. However, the Mikoyan designers were wary of this engine – with good reason, as it turned out. As an insurance policy, the Ye-152A was designed around two production Tumanskii R-11F-300 turbojets rated at 38.05 kN (8,553 lb st) dry and 56.3 kN (12,654 lb st) with reheat. By then, this powerplant had achieved a good reliability record and powered the MiG-21F 'Fishbed-B' and the Yakovlev Yak-28 'Brewer'/'Firebar' light bomber and tactical reconnaissance aircraft. The twin engines placed side by side necessitated an increase in aft fuselage width, resulting in an area-ruled fuselage.

The Ye-152's wings had a cropped-delta planform. Wing area was increased from 34.62 m² (362.2 sq ft) to 40.02 m² (430.3 sq ft), and leading edge sweep was reduced to 53°. The

Ye-152A had pure delta wings but they differed from those of the Ye-150, featuring an area reduced to 32.02 m² (344.3 sq ft). The fin was also recontoured, with a straight leading edge (the Ye-150 had a small fin fillet). The Ye-152A had twin ventral fins canted outboard; by contrast, the single-engined version had a single ventral fin, but the area of the vertical tail was enlarged.

Fuel was carried in six fuselage fuel cells and four integral wing tanks located forward and aft of the main spar; total fuel capacity was 4960 litres (1,091.2 Imp gal). A 1500-litre (330-Imp gal) drop tank could be carried on the fuselage centreline.

The forward fuselage was identical on both aircraft but differed from the original Ye-150. Unusually, the intake centrebody was fixed; air intake area was regulated by moving a ring forming the foremost part of the fuselage. The pitot boom was even longer and was relocated to the underside of the nose, as on the MiG-21F. Unlike the Ye-150, the intake centrebody/radome had a simple conical shape.

Both new versions were armed with two K-9 AAMs; the Ye-152 had missile launch rails at the wingtips, while the Ye-152A featured conventional underwing pylons. There was more to it, however, than just missile location. Like the Ye-150, the Ye-152 was equipped with the same Uragan-5B radar, but the Ye-152A's weapons system was to feature a new radar, designated TsP. (This was not an abbreviation, just a codename.)

Two Ye-152s and a single Ye-152A were built at the Mikoyan experimental plant. Curiously, the latter aircraft was the first to be completed and entered flight test first, beating not only the single-engined version but the original Ye-150 as well. The Ye-152A first flew on 10 July 1959, piloted by Mikoyan chief test pilot Georgi K. Mosolov.

Mosolov and Fedotov took turns flying the aircraft, and the flight test programme was completed on 23 November 1960. At 13700 m

Ye-152A

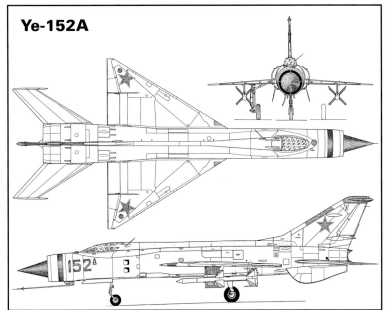

Ye-152-1

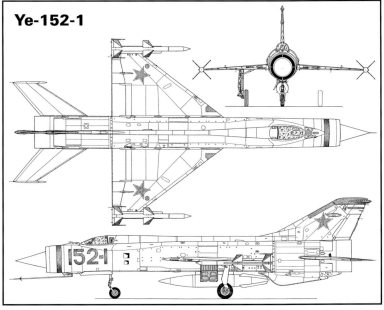

Though it was powered by a pair of the more reliable R-11 turbojets as fitted to the MiG-21F, the Ye-152A remained a 'one-off' and spent its time as a K-9 AAM carry trials aircraft with OKB MiG (below).

The Ye-152A, which predated the single-engined Ye-152-1 and -2 by some months, dispensed with the movable intake shock cone of the Ye-150, replacing it with a moving air intake lip.

(44,947 ft) and 20000 m (65,616 ft), the Ye-152A had a top speed of 2135 km/h (1,326 mph) and 2500 km/h (1,552 mph), respectively. Service ceiling was 19800 m (64,960 ft); 10000 m (32,808 ft) and 20000 m (65,616 ft) could be reached in 1.48 minutes and 7.64 minutes, respectively. MTOW was 13600 kg (29,982 lb) with two K-9 missiles, increasing to 13960 kg (30,776 lb) if a 600-litre (132-Imp gal) drop tank was carried. The curved canopy was soon modified, incorporating an optically flat windshield to reduce distortion – a feature repeated on the later Ye-152.

'Flipper' – the 'MiG-23'

The Ye-152A took part in the 1961 Tushino flypast in Moscow and was promptly allocated the NATO reporting name 'Flipper' – possibly because of the wide rear fuselage. The West could hardly have known that this was a purely experimental aircraft. Some Western observers even went so far as to (mis)identify it as the 'MiG-23' because it surfaced after the MiG-21, only to discover some time later that the MiG-23 was a completely different fighter.

The slimmer 'area-ruled' rear fuselage of the twin-engined Ye-152A is clearly evident in this view.

Subsequently, the Ye-152A was used by the Mikoyan OKB as a weapons systems testbed. It crashed in 1965, killing test pilot A. Kravtsov.

The first single-engined Ye-152 arrived at Ramenskoye on 16 March 1961. It took off for the first time on 21 April with Mosolov at the controls. By 11 September 1962 the Ye-152-1 had made 67 flights, including five with dummy K-9 AAMs. Top speed with missiles at 16200 m (53,149 ft) was 2650 km/h (1,646 mph), with a 14730-kg (32,473-lb) MTOW. The Ye-152-1 climbed to 15000 m (49,212 ft) in 4 minutes 44 seconds in clean condition (i.e., unarmed) and in 5 minutes 55 seconds if toting two missiles; time to 22000 m (72,178 ft) was 6 minutes 40 seconds and 8 minutes 50 seconds, respectively. Ceiling in clean condition was 22680 m (74,409 ft).

On 7 October 1961 the Ye-152-1 set a world speed record, averaging 2401 km/h

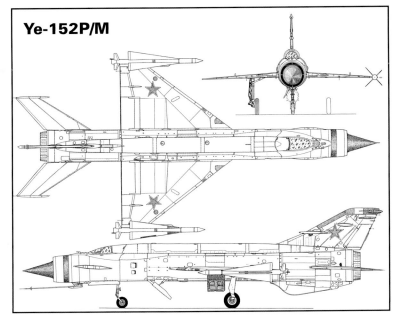

Ye-152P/M

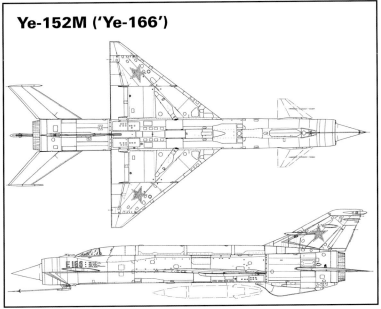

Ye-152M ('Ye-166')

The considerably enlarged dorsal spine of the Ye-152P contained additional fuel tanks. The forward-hinged cockpit was retained, but rearward visibility was reduced even further.

Two K-80 AAMs (as an alternative to K-9s), on wingtip rails rather than pylons, were to arm the Ye-152M. Dummy missiles carried during flight tests were prone to 'flutter'; launch trajectory would have thus been unpredictable.

(1,491.3 mph) over a 100-km (62-mile) closed circuit. On 7 July 1962, the same aircraft flown by G. Mosolov set an absolute world record of 2681 km/h (1,665.2 mph) over a 15/25-km (9.3/15.5-mile) course. These impressive results notwithstanding, the aircraft was still beset by engine problems. Four engine changes were made during the first prototype's test programme but none of five R-15-300 turbojets performed satisfactorily.

Persistent engine problems

The second aircraft, Ye-152-2, was delivered to LII on 8 August 1961 and made its first flight on 21 September. Unlike the first prototype equipped with the Uragan-5B radar, this aircraft was to feature another brand-new radar – the RP-S Smerch (Tornado) later installed on production Tupolev Tu-128 'Fiddler' and MiG-25P 'Foxbat-A' interceptors. This brought about yet another change in radome shape; the new radome with a complex curvature was remarkably similar to that of the original Ye-150.

However, the R-15-300 was proving to be a true can of worms. After making just 16 flights with Mikoyan test pilot Pyotr M. Ostapenko at the controls, the Ye-152-2 was grounded due to persistent engine trouble. The aircraft was converted to take the improved R-15B-300 engine which later was to power the MiG-25, rated at 66.69 kN (14,991 lb st) dry and 100.12

kN (22,508 lb st) in reheat. The re-engined second prototype was originally referred to as the Ye-152P (*perekhvatchik* – interceptor) but, in its ultimate shape, became the Ye-152M (*modifitseerovannyy* – modified).

The Ye-152M had a much deeper fuselage

Fairings either side of the Ye-152PM's nose were evidence of modifications made to the aircraft to accept powered canard foreplanes. Though tested successfully on a modified MiG-21F, they were never fitted to a Ye-152.

Performance comparison of Ye-150/152 family and Sukhoi T-37

	Ye-150	Ye-152-1	Ye-152A	Ye-152M	Sukhoi T-37
Year of manufacture	1958	1961	1959	1961	1960
Powerplant	R-15-300	R-15-300	two R-11F-300	R-15B-300	R-15-300
Thrust, dry	66.71 kN (14,990 lb)	66.71 kN (14,990 lb)	38.06 kN (8550 lb)	66.71 kN (14,990 lb)	66.71 kN (14,990 lb)
Thrust, reheat	99.57 kN (22,375 lb)	100.16 kN (22,510 lb)	56.31 kN (12655 lb)	100.16 kN (22,510 lb)	99.57 kN (22,375 lb)
Radar	Uragan-5B	Uragan-5B	TsP-1	n.a.	TsP
Overall length	18.140 m (59 ft 6 in)	19.656 m (64 ft 5⅞ in)	19.00 m (62 ft 4 in)	19.656 m (64 ft 5⅞ in)	19.413 m (63 ft 8¼ in)
Wing span	8.488 m (27 ft 10⅛ in)	8.793 m (28 ft 10⅛ in)	8.488 m (27 ft 10⅛ in)	8.793 m (28 ft 10⅛ in)	8.560 m (28 ft 1 in)
Wing area	34.615 m² (362.2 sq ft)	40.02 m² (430.3 sq ft)	34.02 m² (344.3 sq ft)	42.89 m² (461.1 sq ft)	34.0 m² (365.6 sq ft)
TOW	12435 kg (27,414 lb)	14350 kg (31,635 lb)	13550 kg (29,872 lb)	11440 kg	10750 kg (23,699 lb)*
Empty weight	8726 kg (19,237 lb)	10900 kg (24,029 lb)	n.a.	18469 kg	7260 kg (16,005 lb)
Maximum speed	2890 km/h (1,795 mph)	3030 km/h (1,882 mph)	2135 km/h (1,326 mph)	2681 km/h (1,665 mph)	3000 km/h (1,864 mph)*
Attained at	19100 m (62,664 ft)	15400 m (50,525 ft)	20000 m (65,617 ft))	n.a.	15000 m (49,210 ft)*
Sustained ceiling	23250 m (76,280 ft)	22680 m (74,410 ft)	19800 m (64,960 ft)	22670 m (74,375 ft)	25-27000 m (82,020-88,585 ft)*
Time to 10000 m (32,810 ft)	n.a.	84 seconds	1.48 minutes	n.a.	–
Time to 15000 m (49,210 ft)	2.5 minutes	n.a.	n.a.	n.a.	–
Time to 20000 m (65,615 ft)	4.5 minutes	5.33 minutes	7.64 minutes	n.a.	–
Range	1500 km (932 miles)	1470 km (913 miles)	n.a.	n.a.	–
Take-off run	935 m (3,067 ft)	1185 m (3,887 ft)**	1295 m (4,250 ft)	n.a.	–
Landing run with chute	1250 m (4,100 ft)	1270 m (4,165 ft)	1600 m (5,250 ft)***	n.a.	–
Armament	two K-7 or K-9 AAMs	two K-9 AAMs	two K-9 AAMs	two K-9 or K-80 AAMs	two K-9 AAMs

* Sukhoi OKB project data   ** with missiles   *** without brake parachute

A group of MiG personnel stand next to the Ye-152M, which is marked with the Ye-152-1's three speed records. In the centre of the group are A. Mikoyan, A. Fedotov, G. Mosolov and P. Ostapenko.

The Ye-152M appeared at the 1967 Domodedovo show, labelled as the 'Ye-166'. For many years it was thought that this aircraft had set the world speed records.

spine housing three additional fuel tanks and a new 'racing-style' canopy without the flat wind-screen. The afterburner cooling problem was apparently not as acute on the R-15B-300 and the characteristic cooling intake slots on the rear fuselage were eliminated. As on the Ye-152, the missiles were to be carried on wingtip launch rails but the K-9 was rejected in favour of the longer-range Bisnovat K-80 AAM developed for the Tu-128.

Canards tested

Originally, the aircraft was to feature canard foreplanes for better manoeuvrability. They were tested successfully on a modified MiG-21F designated Ye-6T-3. Appropriate modifications were made to the Ye-152M, resulting in prominent fairings on the forward fuselage sides, but the idea was abandoned in the middle of the flight test programme and the canards were never installed.

Different missile arrangements were studied at the Ye-152P project stage, including downward-canted wingtips doubling as missile rails, but traditional underwing pylons were finally selected. The choice was influenced by aerodynamics and structural strength considerations.

The Ye-152M suffered the same fate as its predecessors – the still-unreliable engine prevented the aircraft from entering production. However, the 'competition' fared even worse. To meet the same general operational require-

ments, Pavel O. Sukhoi's OKB designed the T-37 heavy interceptor, design work starting in early 1958. It was built around the same R-15-300 turbojet (although the Lyul'ka AL-11 was proposed as an alternative) and looked very similar to the Ye-150/152 series, with a fat tubular fuselage, delta wings with 60° leading-edge sweep, and a small tail unit. As on the Ye-152, the air intake had a fixed centre-body/radome with a complex curvature; engine airflow was controlled by a movable ring forming the foremost part of the fuselage. Four large auxiliary intakes with blow-in doors were located immediately forward of the cockpit.

Unlike the Mikoyan interceptors, the T-37 had an aft-sliding bubble canopy offering the pilot better all-round view, and the nose gear unit retracted aft. Also, unlike the Ye-150/152 series, the aircraft made large-scale use of titanium alloys: the aft fuselage which could be removed for engine maintenance or change was a one-piece welded titanium structure. The afterburner was cooled via eight auxiliary intakes with sprung doors. Armament consisted of two K-9 AAMs on underwing pylons, guided by a TsP radar.

Sukhoi's short-lived alternative

Assembly of the prototype began in February 1960, but then the State Committee for Aviation Equipment (GKAT) ordered the cancellation of the programme and the aircraft was scrapped without ever being flown. It was not until 1965 that the PVO received a long-range interceptor – and it came from neither Mikoyan or Sukhoi. It was the Tu-128, a much larger aircraft powered by proven AL-7F engines.

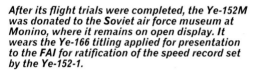

After its flight trials were completed, the Ye-152M was donated to the Soviet air force museum at Monino, where it remains on open display. It wears the Ye-166 titling applied for presentation to the FAI for ratification of the speed record set by the Ye-152-1.

The Ye-152M's air brake arrangement was similar to that of the Ye-150: a single brake below the forward fuselage at the mainplane leading edge.

Upon completion of the flight test programme, the Ye-152M was put on static display at the July 1967 air show in Moscow's Domodedovo airport. It bore the inscription 'E-166' (Ye-166 in Cyrillic) and three 'kill' stars signifying the three world speed records set by the Ye-152-1, accompanied by details of each record. The bogus 'Ye-166' designation was a typical example of Soviet cover-up and misinformation in the Cold War days. It was used to register the aircraft with the International Federation of Aeronautics (FAI) for the speed record attempts. Incidentally, the R-15-300 engine was also entered under a false designation as the R-166. After the show the aircraft was donated to the Russian Air Force Museum in Monino near Moscow, where it is now on display as the sole survivor of the family.

All things considered, it can be said that the Ye-150/152 series was successful in the end. These aircraft were the first Soviet examples to reach Mach 2.5+ and a service ceiling in excess of 22000 m (72,178 ft), proving that fast and high-flying enemy aircraft could indeed be intercepted. New heat-resistant structural materials were employed and new production technologies introduced. Experience gained with the Ye-150/152 series proved invaluable when designing the Ye-155 heavy interceptor and reconnaissance aircraft, which entered production as the MiG-25 and went on to provide sterling service with the Soviet and other air forces.

Yefim Gordon, original translation by Dmitri Komissarov

Sukhoi's rival – the T-37

Powered, like the Ye-150, by the unpredictable R-15-300, the T-37 was similar in configuration to the MiG design, but featured a sliding bubble canopy, affording the pilot a better all-round view. K-9 missile armament would have been pylon-mounted.

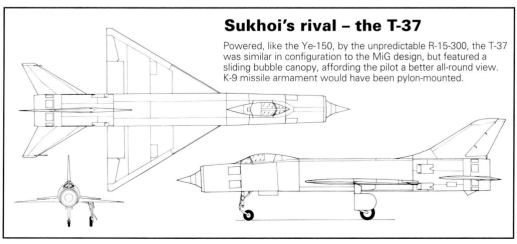

'Second to None'

'Shiny Two', No. II (AC) Squadron, RAF

With battle honours spanning 77 years, from the Western Front to the Persian Gulf, No. II has one of the most distinguished careers of any RAF squadron. Formed just a month after the RFC was established, 'Shiny Two' is one of the very few RAF units to have served almost continuously since, and remains committed to a tactical support role it has performed since World War I.

Mustang Mk Is replaced No. II's Curtiss Tomahawks, reaching operational status in November 1942. Low-level photo-reconnaissance sorties against radar sights on the French coast were among the unit's first missions, before it settled down to general PR duties with flights over land targets (codenamed 'Poplars') and shipping ('Lagoons').

Established on 13 April 1912, the Royal Flying Corps (RFC) absorbed the Air Battalion of the Royal Engineers on 13 May and from this created three flying units – Nos 1, II and 3 Squadrons, RFC. While No. 1 had its origins with No. 1 (Airship) Company, both Nos II and 3 were formed from No. II (Aeroplane) Company at Farnborough, the new No. II Squadron retaining the Company's number plate and becoming established at Farnborough, the former Company's base. (No. 3 Squadron formed at Larkhill.) Thus, No. II can claim to be the oldest fixed-wing squadron in the RAF, and celebrated its 85th anniversary

in 1997. Although Nos 1 and 3 Squadrons challenge this assertion, there is no doubt that No. II was the first squadron to occupy a specifically-designed airfield – Montrose – in 1913.

As far as ascertaining which of Nos II and 3 Squadrons first took a fixed-wing aircraft into the air, an event that took place on 13 May 1912 provides the answer. On that day, the commanding officers of each unit (Majors C. J. Burke and H. R. M. Brooke-Popham, respectively) made a simultaneous take-off from Farnborough. They were the first official flights by each squadron and special care was taken to ensure the aircraft took-off together, so as avoid

any future controversy. That said, a friendly rivalry continued; No. 3 Squadron soon adopted the motto 'Tertius Primus Erit' (Third shall be first).

Major C. J. Burke, a Boer War veteran who had written two papers on the military uses of aircraft and was a firm believer in the future of these new machines, was to be No. II Squadron's commanding officer for the next two and a half years. The squadron was initially equipped with a variety of aircraft types, including the Royal Aircraft Factory 'Blériot Experimental' (B.E.) prototype (number 201), a Bristol Boxkite, at least two Breguet G.3 biplanes and a number of Farman aircraft, including examples of the Longhorn design. A number of other early B.E.2 series machines were taken on charge after successful trials of the prototype.

Scotland base

After nine months at Farnborough, the squadron moved to Montrose on Scotland's west coast, becoming fully established at its new base in late February 1913. Observation and army co-operation, the two main roles envisaged for the new unit, were intensively practised throughout the following summer, and in September a detachment was sent to Limerick, for manoeuvres with the Irish Command. B.E.2s were flown across the Irish Sea safely, no mean feat for these seemingly flimsy aircraft and their crews.

Most prominent among the types assigned to No. II Sqn during the Great War was the Royal Aircraft Factory B.E.2. This B.E.2a was delivered to the RFC on 26 February 1914 and by July was on strength with 'A' Flight of No. II. Some sources suggest that this aircraft was the first British aircraft to land in Europe after the outbreak of war. Flown by Lt H. D. Harvey-Kelly, it is believed to have landed near Amiens at 08.20 on 13 August 1914.

In June No. II deployed to Netheravon for more exercises, this time for a four-week period with other RFC units in an effort to standardise procedures. Tactical exercises, reconnaissance, photography, balloon handling and co-operation were all practised. On 3 August the squadron returned to Scotland.

Long-distance flights

It was later in August 1913 that the first of a number of notable long-distance flights was undertaken by the squadron. On 13 August, Captain Charles Longcroft and Colonel Sykes, then Officer Commanding, RFC, took B.E.2 No. 218 the 540 miles (869 km) from Farnborough to Montrose, with just one stop at Alnmouth, in seven hours and 40 minutes. A special fuel tank was fitted between the pilot and passenger to provide sufficient range. Other flights followed later in the year, including a 650-mile (1046-km) solo effort by Longcroft which earned him the Britannia Challenge Trophy.

However, these accomplishments were to be overshadowed by events further afield. Within a matter of months, No. II was to be mobilised in support of the British Expeditionary Force bound for France and world war.

Britain declared war on Germany on 4 August 1914, and by 12 August No. II had assembled at Dover in preparation for the flight across the Channel. At 08.25 the following day, Lieutenant Harvey-Kelly became the first RFC pilot to land in France, after a two-hour flight in a B.E.2a. He landed near Amiens, and by the end of the day the rest of the unit joined him. By 16 August the squadron had set up a base at Mauberge and was immediately tasked with flying reconnaissance sorties to ascertain the direction and strength of the German advance. The first was flown by Longcroft (by then a major), with Major Bourke as observer, on 20 August.

Two days later, one of the unit's observers became the first member of the RFC to be wounded in battle. On a reconnaissance flight with pilot Lieutenant Noel, during which their aircraft came under rifle and machine-gun fire, Sergeant Major Jillings had the misfortune of being hit in the buttocks.

Within a week the unit was forced to withdraw, but continued to provide details of the enemy's movements. The intelligence collected included photographs of enemy positions which were to prove invaluable, especially once the war had degenerated into trench warfare. The retreat continued into September until the front line stabilised, No. II settling at Vieul Aroy at the end of the month. By then the squadron had moved no fewer than 11 times since arriving in France. On 25 August, Lieutenants Harvey-Kelly and Mansfield became responsible for the RFC's first success in the air against an

enemy aircraft. On that day they forced a single-seat German Taube to land near Merville. The British flyers landed next to the German craft and attempted to chase its escaping pilot on foot. However, he sought refuge in a nearby forested area, where the lieutenants abandoned the chase, returned to their machine and, before departing, set the Taube alight. British troops eventually captured the German flyer.

From September, No. II was engaged in reconnaissance flights in preparation for the first Battle of Ypres, which began with a barrage on 19 October. Flying in support of the First Army Corps from then on, the squadron flew continuously, moving to Merville on 27 November. No. II was to remain here for seven months and joined No. 3 Squadron as part of the First Wing, RFC.

While in France, a mixture of types continued to serve with No. II, including Blériot XIs, Farman Shorthorns and R.E.5s. In February 1915 a number of Vickers F.B.5s, trialled at Farnborough the previous July, appear to have been allocated to the squadron, but for only a matter of weeks.

Photo-reconnaissance

At Merville a number of new techniques were evaluated, including wireless reporting. A flight of wireless telegraphy-equipped machines joined the squadron and began artillery spotting; during the Battle of Neuve Chapelle in early 1915, these techniques were to prove vital, No. II's crews checking the accuracy of artillery fire and radioing aiming corrections to gunners. Neuve Chapelle also saw the first use of cameras

Unit Heritage

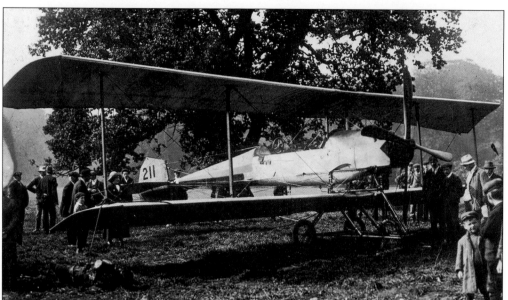

Right: Army aeroplane 206, seen here at Farnborough, was the sixth airframe of 'Bleriot Experimental' (B.E.) type constructed and the third to the B.E.2a pattern. Taken on charge by No. II Sqn on 8 September 1912, the aircraft had transferred to No. 4 in the spring of 1913 and later served with No. 6 Sqn.

Left: Among the various aircraft types taken on charge during the formative years of Army aviation were four Breguet G.3 three-seat biplanes. Aeroplane 211, seen here at Upper Heyford, was the second example and was allocated to No. II Sqn (with 212), between May and December 1912. It later flew with No. 4 Sqn.

to photograph German defences. One of the unit's first photographers was none other than W. Sholto Douglas, later Air Marshal Sir Sholto Douglas and C-in-C RAF Fighter Command from 1940.

Tactical bombing sorties were also undertaken by No. II, railways and road communications being the favoured targets. It was during one such raid, on 26 April, that 2nd Lieutenant W. B. Rhodes-Moorhouse pressed home an attack on a railway junction at Courtrai. His efforts earned him a Victoria Cross, the first such award made to an airman.

During May, No. II was equipped with three B.E.2a, four B.E.2b and five B.E.2c aircraft, but June brought re-equipment with brand new B.E.2cs, two flights of which were detailed with counter-battery sorties (flying reconnaissance missions over the trenches, collecting photo intelligence and artillery spotting), while a third was engaged in trench bombardment. By 1916, crippling losses were being suffered by these outdated machines, often at the hands of Fokker

E.IIIs. Accordingly, No. II had been issued with a fighter flight of Bristol Scouts in June, at the same time moving to Hesdigneul, where the squadron would remain for three years.

A reorganisation of the RFC took place in 1916, No. II losing its Scouts and joining Nos 3, 10 and 16 Squadrons in the First (Corps) Wing, part of the Army Air Brigade. The First Wing was responsible to Corps HQ and carried out tactical tasks. Two other units were attached to the Tenth (Army) Wing, carrying out longer-range sorties for Army HQ.

Unit markings appear

The scope of No. II's operations was revised accordingly, operations continuing and increasing in tempo in preparation for the Battle of the Somme. In May alone, 283 reconnaissance sorties were flown. It was about this time that squadron markings were introduced in an attempt to reduce the incidence of friendly troops firing on RFC aircraft. The triangle motif, which survives to this day in the

squadron's marking, made its first appearance in April; white triangle markings were applied to the sides of camouflaged aircraft, and black to clear-doped machines.

Fighting on the Somme began in July, No. II fielding 10 B.E.2c and eight B.E.2d aircraft and beginning its campaign by bombing Douai railway station alongside B.E.2s from No. 26 Squadron. Soon after, the squadron was split in two, a detachment being sent to Fienviller and overall squadron establishment being increased to 21 aircraft.

Air support sorties over the Somme continued through 1916 and into the following year. After the horrific losses suffered by the RFC during the Arras campaign in 'Bloody April', No. II was at last re-equipped in May, with Armstrong-Whitworth F.K.8s.

'Big Acks'

The 'Big Acks', as they were known to their crews, were a vast improvement over their B.E.2 predecessors, and served No. II for the remainder of the war. These aircraft carried a white zig-zag marking (introduced on the unit's last B.E.2s in April) to help to distinguish them further. In addition to its Army work, the squadron began night bombing, and on the night of 30/31 October dropped 39 20-lb (9-kg) bombs on targets in Henin, Lietard and Billy Montigny.

The award of the squadron's second Victoria Cross came in the final year of the war. On 27 March 1918, Canadian 2nd Lieutenant A. A. 'Babe' McLeod, with his observer Lieutenant A. W. Hammond, took off on a bombing and strafing raid near Bray-sur-Somme. In misty weather, the aircraft became separated and McLeod landed to refuel after flying for two hours, trying to find his target. Airborne once more, he was about to abandon the sortie when he spotted a German balloon and prepared to attack. At this point the F.K.8 was set upon by Fokker Triplanes of Jagdstaffel 10, Jagdgeschwader 1 (an element of Richtofen's 'Flying Circus'). Against overwhelming odds, Hammond shot down three of the German aircraft, McLeod claiming a fourth before the F.K.8 crashed in flames in No Man's Land. Miraculously, both men survived, McLeod receiving a VC for his actions and Hammond a bar to his Military Cross. At just 19 years of age,

B.E.2a 273 is seen here at Castle Kennedy, near Stranraer, in late August 1913, en route to Ireland for army manoeuvres.

Originally delivered to No. 3 Sqn in March 1913, B.E.2a 272 joined 273 in Ireland with No. II Sqn in September 1913.

McLeod was the youngest recipient of a Victoria Cross and the second youngest serviceman of all to receive the gallantry medal.

The Royal Air Force was created on 1 April 1918 by the amalgamation of the RFC and Royal Naval Air Service, and No. II Squadron, RAF moved from Hesdigneul to Floringham in Belgium on 9 April. Two more moves followed in October, the second taking the unit to Genech. From here, No. II Squadron's last operational sorties of the war were flown. By the time of the Armistice, No. II had lost 20 airmen killed, 19 missing, 51 wounded, 12 prisoners of war, three killed in accidents and 14 accidentally injured.

No. II abandoned Genech in February 1919, flying back to England for reduction to cadre status at Bicester. Disbandment came on 20 January 1920 at Weston-on-the-Green.

Between the wars

Just 11 days later, No. II was reformed at Oranmore in Ireland, simply by renumbering No. 105 Squadron, resident at the time. The latter's Bristol F.2b Fighters were the 'new' No. II's first aircraft, still camouflaged from wartime service. No. II, now known as No. II (AC) Squadron in recognition of its army co-operation role, was assigned to No. 11 (Irish) Group, with a flight each at Castlebar and Fermoy.

Drastic defence cuts after the Great War led to a drop in the squadron's efficiency. Its aircraft were obsolete, personnel were changing constantly as a result of demobilisation, and spares were in short supply. Nevertheless, No. II was soon busy again, supporting ground troops against the rioting Irish during the Rebellion. Unarmed non-offensive sorties were flown, including reconnaissance and liaison flights. One aircraft was downed by hostile action during this period: an F.2b flying between Oranmore and Fermoy made a forced landing in the Galtie Mountains after being shot at by rebels. The observer, Flying Officer Mackay, set off to find help, but was captured and not released for some time.

February 1922 saw the unit leave Ireland for Digby, England, but its stay there was short and the unit returned to Ireland four months later, this time to Aldergrove. Little is known of No. II's stay there; in September two flights returned to Farnborough, the remaining one staying until February the following year. By the end of 1922 the entire unit had gathered at Andover.

Based at Shanghai Racecourse

The most distant deployment of the squadron's long career came in 1927, when Chinese Nationalist threats to the British population in China prompted the British government to order No. II (AC) to that country in April as a show of strength. The squadron sailed, with its crated aircraft, on 20 April, arriving on 30 May. Having set up a base at Shanghai

Racecourse, No. II flew its first reconnaissance sortie in China on 17 June.

The squadron remained in China for almost two months, when Fairey IIIDs of No. 441(FR) Flight from HMS *Hermes* arrived on 6 September to relieve the squadron. A number of RAF personnel transferred to the Fleet Air Arm in order to stay in China, although most elected to make the voyage back to Britain, departing on 14 September. By 1 November, No. II was once again fully established, this time at RAF Manston.

For the ensuing 12 years there was little change at No. II. The squadron became part of No. 22 (AC) Group and, though part of the RAF, performed its operational duties for the Army. Typical among its tasks were reconnaissance sorties for the artillery regiments at Larkhill, usually undertaken by a detached flight. The squadron as a whole also took part in annual Army manoeuvres and armament practice camps (APCs). It was at the 1929 APC that the Bristol Fighter had its swansong, a dual-control version of the Armstrong Whitworth

First air Victoria Cross

Second Lieutenant W. B. Rhodes-Moorhouse, of No. II Squadron became the first airman to be awarded a Victoria Cross, on 26 April 1915. During a raid on a road and rail junction near Courtrai, Rhodes-Moorhouse flew his B.E.2c (No. 687) below 300 ft (91 m) through accurate fire to drop his single 100-lb (45-kg) bomb. Sustaining severe injuries and heavy damage to his machine (his fitter later reported counting 95 holes in his aircraft), he managed to return to Merville and deliver a report on the sortie before being treated for his wounds. Tragically, however, he died the following day. His VC was gazetted posthumously, on 22 May 1915. His efforts represented an early use of an aircraft in this tactical support role.

Percival Vega Gull prototype (G-AEYC) which, as a result of the Friday Wood trials, was ordered by the RAF for communications duties, as the Proctor.

In November, rumours that the Audax was to be replaced were confirmed by the arrival of Hawker Hectors, with their unusual Napier Dagger 'H'-form engines and straight upper wing. While the Hector was destined to be the RAF's last army co-operation biplane, its arrival at No. II boosted morale considerably. No. 25 Squadron, a fighter unit also based at Hawkinge, had simultaneously lost its Fury Mk IIs and been forced to operate older Hawker Demons until Gloster Gladiators became available. Thus, No. II had, for a while at least, faster aircraft than the fighter unit!

Hectors enjoyed only a short spell with No. II, for a new purpose-built army co-operation monoplane was on the way. The first Westland Lysander, finished in two-tone camouflage, was delivered in July 1938. Such were the tensions on the continent that a war, for which Britain was ill-prepared, seemed inevitable. Leave was cancelled, and buildings were sandbagged and camouflaged. During the Munich Crisis in September, the Lysanders carried type 'B' roundels and 'KO' squadron code letters were adopted.

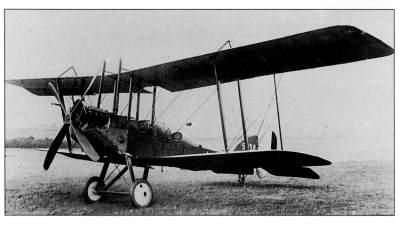

Royal Aircraft Factory B.E.2s served No. II Sqn for around five years before being replaced with more modern types. This Bristol-built B.E.2e, serialled 5858, is seen at Hesdigneul in the spring of 1917. The top corner of the squadron's white triangle fuselage marking is just visible on the rear fuselage.

Atlas arriving in November for conversion duties. The following month the first service examples of the Atlas Mk I were delivered, and at the 1930 APC the squadron's results were much improved, so much so that for the following two years No. II won the APC air gunnery and bombing competitions.

Germany's descent into dictatorship in the 1930s prompted Britain to look towards expanding the RAF. No. II re-equipped with the Hawker Audax in May 1933 and in October 1934 participated in mobilisation exercises. The following year, the squadron moved again, this time to Hawkinge. The squadron establishment at this time was 16 aircraft – three flights of four aircraft each with another four machines in reserve at the unit's workshops. The Audaxes were marked with a large black triangle on the rear fuselage, reviving the wartime motif.

No. II (AC) joins Fighter Command

With the formation of the Air Defence of Great Britain (ADGB), No. II left the Inland Area Command and joined Fighter Command. Army co-operation exercises continued and

often included detachments to advanced landing grounds (ALGs) like Friday Wood, near Colchester. It was during sizeable army manoeuvres in 1937 that an Experimental Communications Squadron was incorporated into No. II. In all, 14 aircraft from various British manufacturers were collected together at Friday Wood for trials. One of these was the

Mobilisation

Affiliation exercises with other RAF units and the usual army co-operation manoeuvres continued into 1939, but on 23 August, Squadron Leader Andrew Geddes, No. II's commanding officer, received the order to mobilise. By the afternoon of 3 September, No.II Squadron was at one hour's readiness

Above: The first Armstrong-Whitworth F.K.8s, or 'Big Acks' as they were often known to crews, arrived in France in 1917; No. II received its first examples in April. A2732 served with Nos II and 8 Sqns on the Western Front, the type remaining in use with the former until February 1919.

Left: No. II Sqn personnel are seen here posing with D5077 (one of a batch of 200 built by Angus Sanderson Ltd of Newcastle-upon-Tyne) at Hesdigneul, France in 1918. Day and night bombing sorties were undertaken by No. II; during the German offensive of March 1918, the latter task was the priority. It was on 27 March that the air battle took place between an F.K.8 flown by 2nd Lt A.A. McLeod and eight enemy aircraft, in which McLeod earned No. II's second Victoria Cross. His observer, Lt A. W. Hammond, shot down three aircraft and McLeod claimed one other before bringing his burning machine down in No Man's Land. Both were wounded six times.

No. II reformed on 1 February 1920 at Oranmore by renumbering No. 105 Sqn, equipped with Bristol F.2b Fighters. It operated them for 10 years, initially in Ireland, where the unit supported the army in actions against Sinn Fein. The crew of this aircraft are seen apparently demonstrating its inherent stability, probably about 1924, after No. II had returned to England. Around this time No. II's F.2bs carried three broad stripes around the rear fuselage. Two red stripes flanked a middle stripe in a colour denoting the flight in which the aircraft belonged – white for 'A' Flt, yellow for 'B' Flt and blue for 'C' Flt.

After No. II moved back to England in 1922, it officially took on an army co-operation role and became No. II (AC) Sqn. Around the mid-1920s, the fuselage stripe markings were replaced with a black triangle on the fin with a white '2', as shown on this 'Brisfit'. The triangle marking dated from 1916, when it was applied to B.E.2s operating over the Somme, according to some sources, as a means of discouraging 'friendly fire'.

with 18 Lysanders. Hawkinge was declared a Recruit Training Pool and No. 25 Squadron took its Blenheims to North Weald, leaving No. II alone on the Kent aerodrome. Within four weeks the unit was being prepared for overseas duty with the Air Component of the British Expeditionary Force (BEF). No. II crossed the Channel on 6 October, en route to Abbeville, where it was to be based with No. 26 (AC) Squadron, another 'Lizzie' unit.

Daily photography sorties began on 13 October, but were hampered by worsening weather, problems with wireless-telegraphy interference and a ban on night flying imposed by the French. The winter of 1939/40 turned out to be particularly harsh; in February numerous sorties were cancelled by snow. By the end of the month the Lysander Mk I fleet had been replaced with new Mk IIs and affiliation exercises with other RAF units and French units continued, although by March Abbeville resembled a quagmire after the spring thaw.

May arrived and the army co-operation squadrons were dispersed, No. II sending a flight each to Labuissière and Senon. On 10 May, German troops invaded the Netherlands and Belgium, and airfields in France, including Senon and Abbeville, were bombed by the Luftwaffe. Although No. II's flights were forced to move yet again, the squadron continued to perform its assigned role, flying reconnaissance sorties for HQ 3rd Army Corps. It was during such a sortie on 19 May that Squadron Leader Geddes claimed an air-to-air 'kill' in his Lysander. While undertaking reconnaissance for the withdrawing 3rd Corps, Geddes and his gunner, LAC Clarke, sighted 20 Ju 87 Stukas preparing to attack the very bridge over which the Corps intended to make their retreat. With the element of surprise, Geddes attacked, and in the ensuing dogfight he succeeded in downing one of the dive-bombers before retreating to land at Wevelghem.

Bombing Lysanders

Later that day, the order for the squadron to withdraw to England finally came; No. II was to regroup at Lympne in Kent, before moving to Bekesbourne on 20 May. However, this did not mean that operations ceased. Tactical reconnaissance flights over France continued as the German army pressed on through France. The Luftwaffe was encountered on more than one occasion; on 22 May, an eventful day for No. II, Flying Officer Doidge and LAC Webborn caught and downed a Stuka and a Henschel Hs 126 reconnaissance machine while over France in the afternoon.

Later in the day, six of No. II's Lysanders undertook a bombing sortie on German targets on roads south of Boulogne. Although the 'Lizzie' was unsuitable for such a role, the general shortage of aircraft necessitated their use

on a raid that was to end disastrously. Each aircraft carried four 20-lb (9-kg) bombs on each stub wing, which, rather than being of the standard HE variety, were of the 'F' type, with a small retarding parachute; they were intended for low-level use.

Unfortunately, the Lysanders' crews had not been informed of this change and during the attack were immediately forced to take evasive action, to avoid hitting bombs dropped by other aircraft. One Lysander failed to return from the raid; its pilot (Pilot Officer Henderson) was killed and gunner (Pilot Officer Kelly) became a POW. Pilot Officer Grant-Govan had the misfortune of having to return to base with his bombs. As he landed, they exploded, killing Grant-Govan's gunner, LAC Jones. Sadly,

Henderson and Jones were No. II's first squadron members killed in action.

On 25 May, as remnants of the BEF and French forces were becoming cut-off at Calais, No. II was detailed, with other RAF and Fleet Air Arm aircraft, to make supply drops to the beleaguered troops. As the Luftwaffe stepped up its attacks and Operation Dynamo, the final evacuation at Dunkirk, began, No. II continued to provide reconnaissance over the Calais area.

No. II Squadron was stood down on 1 June 1940 and rested. On 8 June it received orders to move to Hatfield, an aerodrome north of London owned by de Havilland. At this time the army co-operation squadrons were briefed for a new role – gas spraying. Nos II, 4, 26, 225 and 614 Squadrons were to prepare to carry out

The Armstrong-Whitworth Atlas was the RAF's first army-co-operation aircraft designed for the role from the outset. Powered by an Armstrong-Siddeley Jaguar radial, 446 were built, plus a small fleet of dual-control conversion trainers. This Atlas Mk I, serialled J9552, was used by No. II from RAF Manston in the mid-1930s. Note the retractable message retrieval hook under the fuselage.

Seen at Hawkinge in about 1935, possibly on the occasion of an air display (note the deck chairs in the left background), Audax K3064 had been with No. II Sqn since 15 June 1933. Sources appear to disagree regarding the colour of the fuselage triangle marking; some suggest red, others black.

At this time, Wing Commander Geddes's complaints to his superiors about the obsolescence of the Lysander finally received some attention. Geddes hoped that replacement would come in the shape of Hurricanes, but was informed that Battles and Boulton Paul Defiants would instead be supplied to the unit for trials. Testing dragged on until mid-1941, neither type proving suitable.

In the event, No. II re-equipped with its third batch of Lysanders, this time Mk IIIs. In February 1941 these machines were fitted with new rear armament, twin Browning 0.303-in (7.7-mm) machine-guns, in place of the original single Vickers gun. The new year also brought yet another role to No. II (AC) Squadron – the training of pilots in short take-off and landing at night, pending their eventual posting to Special Duties flights for a secret role, later revealed as the highly risky flights behind enemy lines in support of the Special Operations Executive (SOE).

Mid-year, rumours began to circulate that No. II's Lysanders were about to be replaced. By July, training on the Curtiss Tomahawk was in full swing and in September the unit's pilots had all converted to the type.

Troublesome Tomahawks

Chief among the Tomahawk's teething troubles was a propensity to ground-loop, something that necessitated urgent additional pilot training. Meanwhile, No. 71 Group was disbanded and two wings formed in its place. No. II joined Nos 4 and 268 Squadrons in No. 34 (Recce) Wing. Problems with the Tomahawks continued, however, and led to their temporary withdrawal and replacement with Lysanders towards the end of 1941.

1942 brought further exercises, in which the Tomahawks participated, although the type was destined never to be used operationally by No. II. The type's replacement, in the shape of early examples of the North American Mustang, was soon to arrive. The Mustang offered much improved performance in all respects, particularly speed, climb rate and armament, and was popular with No. II's personnel, especially after their experiences with the Tomahawk. To enhance its abilities in the army co-operation role, an F.24 oblique camera was fitted behind the cockpit.

No. II was ready for operations in the Mustang by April, although training continued apace. In May a No. 26 Squadron Mustang undertook the first of many sorties by Army Co-operation Command aircraft codenamed 'Poplars'. These were photo-reconnaissance sorties over the French coast, made particularly dangerous by German flak and the low-level nature of the mission. Thus, No. II needed to train to fly low, quickly and accurately.

Left: Audaxes of No. II (AC) Sqn are among this large collection of aircraft at an unidentified RAF aerodrome in about 1936. Other home-based army co-operation units equipped with the Hawker Audax were Nos 4, 13, 16 and 26 Sqns. Others served abroad.

this task on beaches along the east coast of the country, in the event of a German invasion. Planning during 1939 had called for 30-lb (13.6-kg) and 250-lb (113-kg) gas bombs and spray tanks to be used, which were also fitted to Bristol Blenheims and Fairey Battles.

Meanwhile, the unit's primary reconnaissance tasks continued, and daily coastal patrols for invasion barges commenced. Officially, No. II was still resting and therefore non-operational, but the importance of these flights was such that No. II was pressed back into service. From 1 August 1940, No. II was based at Marshall's airport at Cambridge, with two flights detached to Sawbridgeworth in support of the 2nd and 11th Army Corps as part of No. 34 (Army Co-operation) Wing, though anti-invasion patrols remained the squadron's most pressing task.

As concerns about a German invasion mounted, plans to mobilise second-line aircraft in the event of an invasion (the 'Banquet Plan') were to effect No. II directly. Training aircraft, like de Havilland Tiger Moths and Miles Magisters, were to be fitted with light bomb racks and commanded by the commanding officer of an army co-operation unit. No. II was allotted 'Banquet-Light' flights provided by No. 22 Elementary Flying Training School (EFTS), also at Cambridge, and No. 6 EFTS. At the height of the Battle of Britain, on 31 August, the squadron was put on alert after ships were reportedly sighted steaming west off the Norfolk coast. Aircraft were bombed-up in preparation for a 'Banquet-Light' sortie, but were stood-down in the early hours of the following morning.

K9738 is a Hawker Hector of No. II (AC) Sqn, again with a black fuselage triangle applied. This aircraft later served with No. 26 Sqn and crashed at Kelmscott on 13 April 1942, while towing two Hotspur gliders with No. 101 Glider Operational Training Unit.

Above: Lysander Mk II L4818, crewed by P/O Shearman and Sgt Spurr, is seen here in May 1940, during the Battle of France. Muddy airfields posed a problem for the Lysanders; note that this aircraft's wheel spats have been partially removed to facilitate cleaning.

On 24 July a press day was organised at Sawbridgeworth, for which 50 correspondents visited the base to see the Mustangs in action. Among the weapons demonstrated was a highly effective, new petroleum jelly substance – napalm.

Exercises continued for No. II through September and October, in preparation for its first operational sortie in the following month; on 14 November, two Mustangs undertook the unit's first mission over occupied territory since 1940. It was a 'Poplar' over Holland intended to photograph a German radar station at Domburg. Photographs were taken from 350 ft (107 m) because of low cloud, instead of the prescribed 1,000 ft (305 m), so the results were unusable, but four days later the sortie was repeated successfully. No. II Squadron was back in business.

Mustang losses

Flak over Flushing brought No. II's first Mustang loss to enemy action on 22 November, when Pilot Officer Ingram's aircraft was hit three times and crashed on landing at Sawbridgeworth. The Mustang was a robust aircraft, often able to survive a crash more or less in one piece, allowing its pilot to fight another day. However, the unit was to lose its first pilot of this new operational phase a week later, when New Zealander Pilot Officer G. M. Cunningham was reported missing on a 'Poplar' sortie. During December bad weather and an often waterlogged aerodrome prompted the detachment of six aircraft to Hunsdon so that operations could continue.

Training carried on, Exercise Spartan taking place in January 1943. This was the biggest Army mobility exercise yet carried out and was intended to test procedures prior to the planned

No. II's first Curtiss Tomahawks were Mk Is, equivalent to the USAAF's P-40, though with four wing-mounted machine-guns. Later Mk IIAs joined the squadron, including AH942 Suzanne, seen at Sawbridgeworth some time in 1941. The Tomahawk Mk IIA, equivalent to a US Army P-40B but with extra armour and self-sealing fuel tanks, was a difficult aircraft for No. II's pilots to master. Ground-looping was a common problem for pilots new to the type, and in the event the Tomahawk was not employed operationally by the squadron.

Above: During the final months of Lysander Mk III use, No. II (AC) Sqn adopted the 'XV' codes more usually associated with the unit's Tomahawks and Mustangs. 'KO' codes, adopted at the time of the Munich Crisis, were the first carried by the unit.

invasion of occupied Europe. No. II was heavily involved, moving to Bottisham on 31 January and posting detachments to four other airfields.

Fowlmere became the unit's base in mid-March and it was while based here that 'Lagoon' (shipping reconnaissance) sorties began off the Dutch coast. During April, 66 'Poplars' and 28 'Lagoons' were flown, 23 pilots flying an

Above: Defiant N1572/'KO-I' was one of two Defiants test flown from Cambridge. Sqn Ldr Geddes, CO of No. II (AC) Sqn at the time of trials aimed at ascertaining whether the Defiant would make a suitable army co-operation aircraft, later admitted that while putting the aircraft through thorough tests he hoped "to find enough reasons to get rid of the crate as quickly and definitely as possible."

impressive 125 hours 44 minutes between them. The unit also returned to Sawbridgeworth during this month.

Risks to the squadron's aircraft and crews were heightened as encounters with Luftwaffe Fw 190As became increasingly commonplace. This was not a problem confined solely to the Allison-engined Mustangs, but affected other fighter types in the RAF, which were no match for this fast, agile Focke-Wulf. A few of the squadron's pilots were able to go to RAE Farnborough, where a captured Fw 190A-3 was flown against, among other types, a Mustang Mk I. Flying as low as possible and carrying out

Odiham were followed by a brief spell at Hutton Cranswick before another stint at Odiham from 6 October. For the move back to Odiham, a Handley Page Harrow provided transport for some of the squadron's kit and those officers who did not have a Mustang to fly to the new location.

Normandy 'Poplars'

Into November, 'Poplars' were being increasingly directed at the beaches of Normandy, though No. II's personnel had no idea that these missions were providing intelligence for the invasion of Europe by the Allies planned for seven months later. 'Rangers', freelance intrusions over enemy territory intended to exhaust the enemy's fighter forces, were also becoming a common tasking. German convoys and trains were typical targets.

Mid-November brought a move to North Weald, but by the end of the month No. II was again at Sawbridgeworth, joining No. 35 (Recce) Wing. These moves had little effect on the squadron's operations. December saw a lot of flying cancelled by bad weather, although the squadron managed a few sorties along the Dutch coast.

The potential threat to Britain posed by the Fieseler Fi 103 'revenge weapon' (V-1), to be launched from sites on the north coast of the continent, was revealed, at least in part, by No. II Squadron. Photographs taken by two of its pilots on 4 January 1944 were the first to show the weapons and their launchers, and prompted further sorties, under Operation Noball.

New aircraft arrived on 12 February, when the squadron swapped its aircraft with No. 186 Squadron's Mustang Mk IAs. They differed from the Mk I in having four 20-mm cannon in place of the machine-guns of the earlier variant.

Gatwick was the destination for yet another move in April, when No. 35 Wing, including Nos 4 and 268 Squadrons, gathered at the Surrey aerodrome. Photo-reconnaissance sorties

steep turns appeared to be the only manoeuvre recommended to Mustang pilots to deal with a Fw 190. This course of action relied on the fact that Mustangs gave their pilots plenty of warning of an impending stall; the Fw 190 apparently did not.

Army Co-operation Command was disbanded on 1 June, No. 34 Wing then coming under the control of No. 12 Group, HQ Tactical Air Force. No. II continued to undertake reconnaissance sorties, moving to Gravesend in July. Meanwhile, 'Distil' operations were introduced to No. II's repertoire, aimed at intercepting mine-laying Junkers Ju 88s. However, the results of these missions were poor.

August brought yet another move, this time to Odiham on 7 August. The unit's role was little changed, although 'Platoons' (convoy escorts) were added to its tasks. Six weeks at

Above: RNZAF P/O Peter Tonkin is seen here running up Mustang Mk I AG550. This aircraft was lost on 26 May 1943 after 'Ranger Asphalt', crashing in Dorset. Its pilot that day, F/O N. J. Miller, was killed.

Below: Machine-gun-armed Mustang Mk Is are seen here during a quiet period between operations at Sawbridgeworth, probably in 1942.

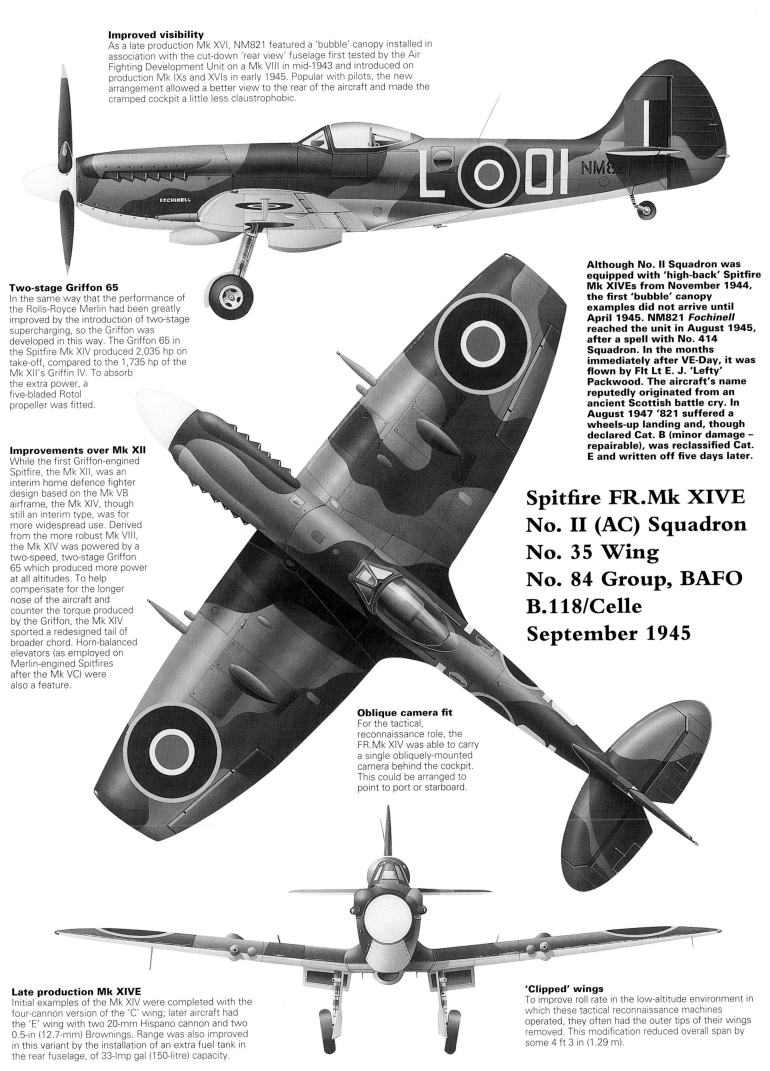

Improved visibility
As a late production Mk XVI, NM821 featured a 'bubble' canopy installed in association with the cut-down 'rear view' fuselage first tested by the Air Fighting Development Unit on a Mk VIII in mid-1943 and introduced on production Mk IXs and XVIs in early 1945. Popular with pilots, the new arrangement allowed a better view to the rear of the aircraft and made the cramped cockpit a little less claustrophobic.

Two-stage Griffon 65
In the same way that the performance of the Rolls-Royce Merlin had been greatly improved by the introduction of two-stage supercharging, so the Griffon was developed in this way. The Griffon 65 in the Spitfire Mk XIV produced 2,035 hp on take-off, compared to the 1,735 hp of the Mk XII's Griffin IV. To absorb the extra power, a five-bladed Rotol propeller was fitted.

Improvements over Mk XII
While the first Griffon-engined Spitfire, the Mk XII, was an interim home defence fighter design based on the Mk VB airframe, the Mk XIV, though still an interim type, was for more widespread use. Derived from the more robust Mk VIII, the Mk XIV was powered by a two-speed, two-stage Griffon 65 which produced more power at all altitudes. To help compensate for the longer nose of the aircraft and counter the torque produced by the Griffon, the Mk XIV sported a redesigned tail of broader chord. Horn-balanced elevators (as employed on Merlin-engined Spitfires after the Mk VC) were also a feature.

Although No. II Squadron was equipped with 'high-back' Spitfire Mk XIVEs from November 1944, the first 'bubble' canopy examples did not arrive until April 1945. NM821 *Fochinell* reached the unit in August 1945, after a spell with No. 414 Squadron. In the months immediately after VE-Day, it was flown by Flt Lt E. J. 'Lefty' Packwood. The aircraft's name reputedly originated from an ancient Scottish battle cry. In August 1947 '821 suffered a wheels-up landing and, though declared Cat. B (minor damage – repairable), was reclassified Cat. E and written off five days later.

**Spitfire FR.Mk XIVE
No. II (AC) Squadron
No. 35 Wing
No. 84 Group, BAFO
B.118/Celle
September 1945**

Oblique camera fit
For the tactical, reconnaissance role, the FR.Mk XIV was able to carry a single obliquely-mounted camera behind the cockpit. This could be arranged to point to port or starboard.

Late production Mk XIVE
Initial examples of the Mk XIV were completed with the four-cannon version of the 'C' wing; later aircraft had the 'E' wing with two 20-mm Hispano cannon and two 0.5-in (12.7-mm) Brownings. Range was also improved in this variant by the installation of an extra fuel tank in the rear fuselage, of 33-Imp gal (150-litre) capacity.

'Clipped' wings
To improve roll rate in the low-altitude environment in which these tactical reconnaissance machines operated, they often had the outer tips of their wings removed. This modification reduced overall span by some 4 ft 3 in (1.29 m).

Personnel of No. II (AC) Sqn pose for an official photograph with eight of their Griffon-engined Spitfires – a mixture of silver, bubble-canopied FR.Mk 14s ('A' Flight) and PRU blue PR.Mk 19s ('B' Flight) at Wahn, West Germany in 1949. The unit's 'OI' codes were adopted in 1944/45 after a period of two years during which No. II's Mustangs were bereft of codes altogether. When No. II converted to Meteors the codes were again dispensed with. The third Mk XIX from the front is believed to be PS915, which was destined to be one of the RAF's last operational Spitfires (retired in 1957) and is today in the care of the Battle of Britain Memorial Flight. The aircraft in the background are Mosquito B.Mk 35s of either No. 14 or 98 Sqn.

Left: With the arrival of Spitfires came the reinstatement of unit codes, the camouflaged machines sporting 'OI' squadron marks. After VE-Day, redundant camouflage was stripped from the FR.Mk XIVEs, but the codes remained. As Meteors were taken on charge, 'B' codes were adopted by the unit, again with a single individual aircraft letter.

continued until the end of May, when all operational flying ceased so that as many aircraft as possible could be made serviceable for the events of early June. Over 400 sorties were flown by No. II Squadron during the month. On D-Day itself, 36 sorties were undertaken by the unit's 20 effective pilots in 10 aircraft, mostly gunnery spotting for the naval bombardment that preceded the invasion. These flights began at dawn, the aircraft landing at Lee-on-Solent after their first sortie to refuel and returning to Gatwick only after a second trip

across the Channel. The last sorties of the day were flown in the evening and were tasked with tactical reconnaissance (Tac/R). In fact, for some time after 6 June, offensive Tac/R of road and rail communications became No. II's main job, at the expense of longer-range photo-reconnaissance.

A No. II Squadron aircraft landed in France (for the third time in the history of the unit) on 20 June, but the squadron, by now equipped with Mustang Mk IIs, did not move across the Channel until 29 July. Its new base was an

advanced landing ground at Plumetot, known simply as B.10. No. II was the only element of No. 35 (Recce) Wing in France until early August, a record month for No. II. No fewer than 624 sorties were carried out, some being 'artillery reconnaissance' (Arty/R) missions of the type carried out by No. II during World War I.

As the Allies advanced, squadron moves were frequent; during September No. II moved four times, finishing up at B.61/St Denis-Westrem in Belgium towards the end of the month. This was a former Luftwaffe airfield and – once buildings had been checked for booby traps – No. II could dispense with its tented accommodation used hitherto. B.70/Duerne-Antwerp played host to the squadron from 10 October. Sortie rates were dropping by this stage, 300 being undertaken during October.

Spitfires and Bodenplatte

New aircraft arrived in November, in the shape of Spitfire FR.Mk XIVEs, the first example, RM805, arriving on 1 November. They were fighter-reconnaissance machines, fitted with two 20-mm cannon, two 0.50-in (12.7-mm) machine-guns and an F.24 oblique camera behind the cockpit. By 18 November, nine examples had been delivered and the first operational sortie with the type (a Tac/R over the Rotterdam area) was flown.

By the end of the month, No. II had moved to B.77 Gilze-Rijen in the Netherlands. Fourteen Spitfires had been delivered and No. II could begin to say farewell to its trusty Mustangs. Ten aircraft left on 29 November, although the remainder saw the year out.

The new year brought the beginning of Operation Bodenplatte, the Luftwaffe's campaign to attack the 2nd Tactical Air Force's airfields, destroying as many aircraft as possible, in an attempt to stem the Allied advance.

Two of No. II's Spitfire FR.Mk XIVEs depart Wunstorf around the time of the unit's move to Wahn in mid-1948. The Hastings transports in the background would soon be busy, flying vital supplies into West Berlin during Operation Plainfare, the RAF's contribution to the Airlift.

Right: Finished in all-over silver dope with black codes when delivered, No. II's armed Meteor FR.Mk 9s were soon camouflaged in a dark green/dark sea grey scheme, with PRU blue undersides. VZ603/'A' was one of the second production batch built by Gloster between 1949 and 1951.

Surprise attacks on New Year's Day almost caught No. II unawares. Early that morning, two of the squadron's Spitfires had taken off on a Tac/R sortie, only to meet a force comprising a few Ju 88s, and a sizeable fighter escort, coming the other way. One of the two Spitfire pilots was able to radio a warning to Gilze-Rijen, also the home of Nos 4 and 268 Squadrons, before it came under attack. Forty minutes later the attack, which had also involved Fw 190s, Bf 109s and Me 262 fighters, was over. Damage to B.77 and its aircraft was remarkably light, and at least three German aircraft were downed by RAF Regiment AA fire, and others damaged. The events of that morning and the apparent lack of success on the part of the Luftwaffe were fairly typical. Bodenplatte cost the Luftwaffe more aircraft than it had cost the 2nd TAF. Worse still, 214 German pilots were killed. It was a gamble that had seemingly back-fired.

Fog hampered operations for the rest of the month. On 17 January the unit flew its last Mustang sortie and the following day the last two examples left. Tac/R and Arty/R operations continued into March, although on 9 January No. II was on the move again, this time to B.89/Mill where crosswinds made Spitfire operations difficult. With the Allies about to cross the Rhine, No. II was detailed to attack river traffic as well as continue its reconnaissance duties. Strafing was to become a unit speciality.

VE-Day

On 1 April, Flight Lieutenant Blundell-Hill's Spitfire was hit by AA fire while on a Tac/R over Apeldoorn. The aircraft crashed, killing the pilot, who was to be the unit's last pilot loss of the war. The first of a batch of new Spitfires arrived on 12 April; they were again FR.Mk

Right: The unloved Swift was never intended as a fighter-reconnaissance aircraft and was adapted for the role after it failed to meet the RAF's expectations as an interceptor. The reworked Swift FR.Mk 5 was the RAF's first jet type equipped with an afterburner, a very necessary addition intended to improve sluggish performance, especially at altitude.

Below: As an RAF Sabre taxis by in the background, 11 of No. II's Swifts are seen at either Geilenkirchen or Jever, in the late 1950s.

XIVEs, but differed from the earlier aircraft in having 'bubble' cockpit canopies, greatly improving the pilot's field of view. Six days later No. 35 Wing moved to B.106/Twenthe, another ex-Luftwaffe aerodrome close to the German border with the Netherlands. Sortie rates increased during the month, but by 4 May Germany had capitulated.

While 8 May brought the celebrations of VE-Day, two No. II Squadron aircraft were sent on a final operation. Reports had been received that German forces, despite their surrender,

were leaving Flensburg by ship bound for Norway. Two Spitfires were dispatched on the long flight to northern Germany, refuelling at Lübeck en route. As it turned out, the report was unsubstantiated, and the sortie was the squadron's last of the war.

From 2nd TAF to BAFO

By the end of May, No. II was at B.118/Celle in Germany. With Celle's runway in a sorry state, most flying was undertaken from nearby B.150/Hustedt, until mid-June

The tails of these Hunter FR.Mk 10s show the traditional white triangle markings (either side of the roundel) adopted again by No. II (AC) Squadron on its camouflaged jet aircraft types. Individual aircraft were identified by a letter in a white triangle on the tail.

sance unit. The PR effort continued throughout the rest of the year, only interrupted by bad weather and a problem with the Spitfire's Griffon 65 and 66 engines. The latter forced the grounding of No. II's aircraft after 100 hours pending modifications by a team from Rolls-Royce, and at one point left the squadron with just five serviceable machines.

From 14 December until 4 January 1947, 'A' Flight was temporarily posted to Gatow-Berlin, a procedure repeated in March and April, and as the weather improved began to undertake sorties over 'targets' as far away as Denmark and the Netherlands. As the 'Iron Curtain' descended, the squadron got busier, with more patrols along the border with the Russian zone of the divided Germany. While official records are short on detail regarding this period of No. II's career, it may be assumed that such patrols occupied the squadron into the early 1950s.

In April 1947, Wunstorf became the unit's base, but only rarely were both flights on the station at the same time; for example, 'A' Flight visited Lübeck in November. The winter of 1947/48 once again wreaked havoc on operations, No. II by then operating 16 aircraft in two flights of eight aircraft each.

Wunstorf to Wahn and back again

Another stint at Gatow for 'A' Flight followed a collision between a Russian fighter and a BEA-operated Vickers Viking airliner, but by the end of June, No. II had moved to Wahn for what was to be a 14-month stay, while Wunstorf was transformed into one of the extremely busy hub airfields during the Berlin Airlift.

Wahn was shared with four de Havilland Mosquito units, two each with B.Mk 35 bombers and FB.Mk 6 fighter-bombers. Here, spare parts and personnel shortages became an increasing problem; most of the Spitfire Mk 19s were grounded by the end of April.

By 1949 the situation had improved, photo-reconnaissance work and various detachments to other bases in Germany continuing, along with

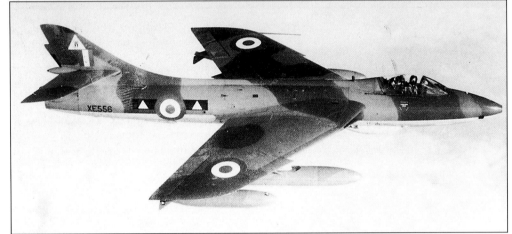

Hunter FR.Mk 10 XE556 poses for the camera above the clouds while flying from No. II's base at Gütersloh during 1969. Four underwing fuel tanks, totalling 660 Imp gal (3000 litres), were often necessary to give the Hunter sufficient range for the reconnaissance mission.

when the squadron returned to England for a two-week armament practice camp at Warmwell. At this time, 2nd TAF was disbanded, its job done, and was replaced in Germany by the British Air Forces of Occupation, or BAFO. No. 84 Group remained as part of this new force, but a start was made in dismantling No. 35 Wing. At the end of August No. 4 Squadron was disbanded, six of its Spitfire PR.Mk XIs becoming 'C' Flight (or the High Level PR Flight) of No. II Squadron.

Operational flying resumed towards the end of the year, despite the fact that the unit's strength was down to 10 pilots and aircraft

serviceability rates left much to be desired. At one point, only three aircraft were available. For these reasons, No. II was reduced to two flights in late 1945/early 1946. 'A' Flight was tasked with Tac/R work, while 'B' Flight re-equipped with Spitfire PR.Mk XIXs, in place of the PR.Mk XIs.

High-altitude flights

In February, 'A' Flight returned to northern Germany for a fortnight's armament camp at Sylt (a trip repeated in August), while 'B' Flight was occupied with various PR tasks, weather permitting. During training, a number of forays to high altitude were made in the Spitfire Mk XIXs, including a couple to 50,000 ft (15240 m). Night flying was also practised, aided by the station's North American Harvard.

No. 35 Wing finally disbanded in June, No. II becoming BAFO's last remaining reconnais-

Amid a cloud of spray, XF457/T lands after another training sortie. The three camera ports are visible in the nose of the aircraft: one in the extreme nose and one either side, in front of the cannon ports. XF457 was later converted to FGA.Mk 70A standard and exported to Lebanon.

Above: Apart from the EMI reconnaissance pod, No. II's suitably modified Phantom FGR.Mk 2s (F-4Ms) were able to carry standard centreline stores associated with the British Phantom, including a General Electric SUU-23 gun pod, seen here aboard XV468 as it 'pops its chute' upon landing at RAF Wildenrath.

gunnery camps in the UK. September brought a return to Wunstorf, Wahn ceasing to be an RAF station on 1 October (though RAF units continued to use the airfield). Serviceability rates had been improved in time for the move, but once the squadron was re-established at Wunstorf, rates dropped again.

June 1950 was an eventful month for the squadron. Eight of No. II's aircraft participated in a flypast as part of the BAFO Air Display and at the end of the month another move took place, this time to Bückeburg. This was to be home for No. II for almost two years, and while here the squadron received its first jet aircraft. In October, a Gloster Meteor T.Mk 7 arrived, with an instructor, for pilot conversion. This process was made tricky by the slippery nature of Bückeburg's runway after rain; more than one pilot went off the end of the runway in the wet conditions.

Into the jet age

On 30 November, the first Meteor FR.Mk 9 arrived and as more were delivered the task of evaluating the type for the Tac/R role began. 'A' Flight's Spitfires departed on 18 January 1951, 'B' Flight's aircraft following in early February, once it had converted to unarmed Meteor PR.Mk 10s. The latter made their first operational sortie in April, but the unit's use of this mark was to be short-lived. Plans to station a full PR squadron, No. 541, in Germany from early June meant that 'B' Flight, No. II Squadron would relinquish its Mk 10s and re-equip with Mk 9s, assuming a fighter-reconnaissance role at the same time.

'A' Flight was, once again, sent on one of the regular gunnery exercises at Sylt in June and on its return experienced the squadron's first ejection. Returning from a training, Sergeant Tickner became disoriented in cloud at 11,000 ft (3353 m) in his Meteor Mk 9 and elected to eject, doing so safely and with little injury.

Right: Phantom FGR.Mk 2 XV430 is seen at RAF Laarbruch on damp day in May 1973. As well as the centreline EMI recce pod, this aircraft is fitted with a photoflash unit in the nose of the port side underwing drop tank. The red in the unit marking was applied in place of the traditional white for a short period from 1973.

Above left and right: XT898, parked among the hardened shelters at Laarbruch in 1976, sports a strike camera (in the port Sparrow recess) as well as a reconnaissance pod. Of British manufacture, the EMI pod contained visual spectrum cameras and an IR linescan unit. Like UK-based No. 41 Sqn, similarly-equipped with F-4Ms tasked with tactical reconnaissance, No. II adorned its pods with sharkmouth markings. Also notable on this aircraft is the fintop ARI.18228 RWR antenna, a feature added to the aircraft from 1975 for the type's impending air defence role. No. II gave up its Phantoms in 1976, replacing them with Jaguars.

Second Allied Tactical Air Force was formed on 1 September 1951, from BAFO, the new name reflecting 2nd ATAF's role within NATO. Spotting for and directing the Army's artillery was still a key tasking for No. II Squadron. That same month the unit's all-weather flying experience netted it the Duncan Trophy for its achievements in this area and in training.

Gütersloh Wing

Second ATAF's reconnaissance wing was finally established at Gütersloh in 1952, when No. II moved to the station in May after its annual armament practice camp at Sylt. There it joined No. 79 Squadron (fighter-reconnais-sance) and No. 541 Squadron (photo-reconnais-sance) and preceded to undertake Tac/R and low-level training prior to the summer and the usual exercises.

New camera equipment was introduced in 1953. The trusty F.24, a relic of the war, was still useful, but not fast enough for use aboard a jet aircraft. Camera manufacturers Vinten had developed the FX.95, a more compact camera with a much larger film magazine than its predecessor. A few aircraft from Nos II and 79 Squadrons were so-equipped; the F.95 was to become the RAF standard later. At the conclusion of these trials, in July, No. II left for Wahn again.

At Wahn, winterisation trials were carried out, four aircraft being parked in the open over

The more accurate navigation and better survivability of the Jaguar helped to compensate for the fact that the aircraft was a single-seater and therefore lacked a second set of 'Mk 1 eyeballs'. Two examples are seen here, with a pair of Phantoms, sometime during the transition period in 1976.

the winter months. Servicing was also undertaken outdoors. Wahn had become, by then, Köln/Bonn Airport and saw a substantial amount of varied air traffic. Nos 68 and 87 Squadrons (Meteor NF.Mk 11s), RAF were also resident, as well as No. 83 Group's Communications Flight (Avro Ansons) and a French ambassadorial Flying Fortress. There were also daily BEA and SABENA flights into the airport.

At Wahn, as part of No. 83 Group, No. II formed part of a Reconnaissance Wing with

Belgian Republic F-84Fs. To this end, four Belgian aircraft arrived to form 'C' Flight. Certain problems arose from integrated operations, namely the Thunderjet's lack of camera equipment and the ease with which the Meteors could out-manoeuvre the larger American-built aircraft. Nevertheless, the flight took part in routine exercises with No. II Squadron, including 1954's Exercise Battle Royal, the main NATO air manoeuvres of the year.

Towards the end of the year, No. II had the honour of being presented with the Royal Standard – a first for a 2nd ATAF unit. Its Battle Honours were 'Western Front 1914-1918', 'Neuve Chapelle', 'Ypres 1915', 'Somme 1916', 'France and Low Countries 1939-1940', 'Dunkirk', 'Normandy 1944' and 'Arnhem'.

From late October 1955 Geilenkirchen became No. II's base, and was home, from the

Left: The Tac/R-tasked Jaguar GR.Mk 1s were able to carry a centreline reconnaissance pod manufactured by British Aerospace. This contained up to five optical cameras and a roll-stabilised ARI.5975 IRLS. Like that fitted to the Phantoms, this was a bulky device, weighing 1,146 lb (520 kg).

following February, of the squadron's new aircraft – Supermarine Swift FR.Mk 5s. First flown in 1951, the Swift had failed in its intended interceptor role, and had been adapted for the fighter-reconnaissance tasks, as a much-needed Meteor FR.Mk 9 replacement. Three F.95 cameras were fitted, along with an after-burning version of the type's Rolls-Royce Avon engine to improve sluggish performance.

Nos II and 79 Squadrons (the latter at Gütersloh) were the only units equipped with the type and, despite their unpopularity with many crews, were employed with some effect. No. II was winner and runner-up in the 1957 NATO reconnaissance competition and was first again in 1959. The Swift's unpopularity stemmed from a number of unsavoury habits, including a tendency to flame-out and poor handling at altitude, without afterburner. Despite being equipped with a large ventral fuel tank, a lack of range was another weakness of the type.

RAF Jever, 200 miles (322 km) north of Geilenkirchen, became the unit's base in October 1957, while on 1 January 1959, 2nd ATAF became RAF Germany, but it was not until October 1960 that the squadron's final Swift was delivered; 31 were allocated to the unit in all, six of which were subsequently written-off in accidents. By April 1961 the entire Swift FR.Mk 5 fleet had been retired, a number being scrapped on site at Jever.

In January 1961 No. II's first Hawker Hunters – five F.Mk 6 fighters – had arrived for familiarisation flying. The first FR.Mk 10 (a variant derived from the Mk 6) arrived the following month, boosting morale considerably. No. II returned to Gütersloh in September.

Libyan excursion

For Exercise Triplex West, four Hunters flew to El Adem, Libya in October 1963. It was the first deployment for the squadron outside Europe since the 1920s, and saw No. II exercising with No. 23 Squadron's Javelins and No. 54's Hunters.

The remainder of the 1960s was taken up with the usual round of NATO exercises and reconnaissance competitions. By the late 1960s, No. II had gained a reputation as one of the RAF's top Hunter units, reinforced by its efforts in the 1970 Big Click competition in which they swept the board, winning every single prize available. However, this was to be the last victory for No. II Squadron in Hunters, for their turn for replacement was nigh. This was to

Mount Etna provides the background for this portrait of a No. II Sqn Jaguar. The aircraft codes carried by No. II's Jaguars were allocated to spell 'SHINYER TWO JAG'.

Above: On the occasion of the 75th anniversary of the squadron, a large squadron badge was applied to the tail of Jaguar XZ104, along with the legend '1912 – 1988' on the RWR fairing.

come in the form of a much larger aircraft, the two-seat Phantom FGR.Mk 2. Laarbruch was to be the unit's base with the new aircraft, but, as it was not ready, Brüggen was chosen to accommodate No. II until May 1971, the first Phantom (XV485) arriving there in December. 'Shiny Two' now had a much more credible secondary ground-attack role, the Phantom having a formidable load-carrying capacity compared to its predecessors on the squadron. The key to its enhanced reconnaissance abilities was an EMI-built reconnaissance pod, carried on the centreline pylon and containing F.95 and F.135 cameras, an infra-red linescan (IRLS) unit and a side-looking airborne radar (SLAR). Although a very capable piece of equipment, it weighed 2,000 lb (907 kg) and imparted considerable drag, which failed to endear it to No. II's Phantom crews.

Photoflash Phantoms

The other major piece of equipment associated with the 'recce Phantoms' was photoflash equipment carried in a compartment in the nose of the Phantom's port drop tank and synchronised for use with the EMI pod's cameras during night time sorties. However, its lack of range necessitated flying as low as 200 ft (61 m) and, while good results were obtained, it did little to reduce the aircraft's vulnerability to AA fire.

The arrival of the Phantoms had not meant the immediate loss of the Hunters. In fact, for about three months there were two No. II Squadrons, a No. II (Hunter) Squadron, still at Gütersloh, which finally disbanded on 31 March 1971, as well as a No. II (Phantom) Squadron. During the 'overlap' period, No. II had its largest complement of aircraft since the late 1930s.

Big Click 1971 was a repeat of the 1970 event, No. II once again taking all the available trophies back to Laarbruch. As well as reconnaissance exercises, No. II was required to practise its air-to-ground capabilities on the Nordhorn range and visited RAF Valley, Wales to fire Sidewinders at aerial targets.

Laarbruch was equipped with hardened

Based at Laarbruch, No. II Sqn supplied six Tornado GR.Mk 1As for Operation Granby, the aircraft forming part of the Dhahran Tornado detachment. All six arrived in Saudi Arabia on 14 January 1991. Three flew the first GR.Mk 1A mission on the first night of the war, 17/18 January, crewed by Nos II and 13 Sqn personnel. Typically, these aircraft flew with four external fuel tanks, giving an 11-tonne fuel capacity.

Above: A flight of No. II's Jaguar GR.Mk 1s in their element, at low level. Each carries a BAe reconnaissance pod and an ARI.18223 RWR in a tailfin-mounted fairing.

Right: 'Shiny Two' Jaguars are seen here on the flight line at Decimomannu, Sardinia during a detachment in 1982. Evident is one of the unit's T.Mk 2 'twin-stick' aircraft used for type conversion and continuation training.

aircraft shelters (HASs) in 1975, in time for the arrival of SEPECAT Jaguars. Again, there was an overlap period during which there were effectively two No. II Squadrons. No. II Squadron (Designate) was formed on 1 June 1976 after the arrival of the first Jaguar GR.Mk 1 (XZ102) in February. Phantom run-down had begun in April, the type finally leaving

No. II in September.

Despite problems with the Jaguar's new British Aerospace centreline reconnaissance pod (containing cameras and an IRLS), No. II was declared operational at the end of November in both the reconnaissance and attack roles. At the height of the Cold War, RAF Germany's Jaguar force was maintained at a high state of readiness,

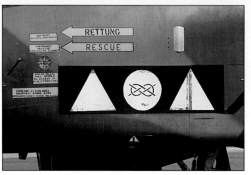

Above: Soluble white distemper provides a measure of winter camouflage for this Tornado GR.Mk 1A bound for exercises in Norway.

Left: No. II's markings, as they appear on the Tornados that equip the squadron in the 1990s, consist of two white triangles, with the central white circle over which the Wake knot has been applied. The latter is the emblem of Hereward, guardian of the Army, and alludes to the strong ties between No. II (AC) Sqn and the Army.

taking part in frequent tactical evaluations (TACEVALs), and was rarely seen outside the HASs, except when flying.

Sixteen single-seat GR.Mk 1s and a couple of two-seat T.Mk 2s were typically assigned to the unit, and were replaced by GR.Mk 1As and T.Mk 2As (the 'A' sub-variant sporting a new FIN.1064 inertial navigation system) in the early 1980s. These aircraft were also re-engined with a more powerful variant of the Rolls-Royce/Turboméca Adour at about this time. In its position as NATO's top tactical reconnaissance unit, No. II attended a number of overseas exercises during the Jaguar era, including Red Flag in the US on three occasions. The squadron's marks at this and a number of other exercises and TACEVALs were excellent. In

1983, the unit deployed to Goose Bay, Canada for low-level training, a task that was difficult to accomplish effectively in Germany. The following year, trials to test the viability of operations from West Germany's autobahn system involved the squadron, while in 1985 No. II was chosen to test night vision goggles (NVG) and their suitability for night sorties. The need for a night reconnaissance capability, especially as RAF Germany re-equipped with all-weather Tornado strike aircraft, became urgent three years later, No. II being tasked with developing tactics for the use of NVGs on a routine basis.

Seventy-five years of service were celebrated by the squadron in 1987; one of the guests of honour at official functions in July was Air Cdre A. J. W. Geddes, No. II's CO during the first two years of World War II.

Detachments to Decimomannu, the NATO Weapons Camp on Sardinia, for weapons exercises, were annual events for No. II, but those

attended in 1988 were to be its last with Jaguars. By then, a dedicated reconnaissance variant of the Panavia Tornado GR.Mk 1 was being readied for service.

No. II Squadron's first Tornado GR.Mk 1A (ZA394) arrived at Laarbruch in September and by mid-December the unit's last Jaguar sortie had been flown. By the end of March 1989, the squadron had just six aircraft as deliveries were held up by delays with the type's reconnaissance equipment. In May No. II had its first trip abroad with the new aircraft, to Goose Bay for low-level flying training.

Combat in the Gulf

The following year was a momentous one for 'Shiny Two', as it was to see the squadron preparing for its first combat in over 45 years. In October 1990 all the squadron's aircraft were sprayed in the 'desert pink' finish, and before Christmas the first crew had left for Tabuk, Saudi Arabia to join No. 16 Squadron personnel. By 14 January 1991, a detachment of six No. II Squadron aircraft (coded 'A', 'C', 'E', 'H', 'O' and 'T' and modified to the latest standard) and a number of crews had joined personnel from the RAF's other Tornado reconnaissance unit, No. 13 Squadron, at Dhahran, Saudi Arabia. There they were to remain for two months.

The heart of the Tornado GR.Mk 1A's capability was a horizon-to-horizon BAe/Vinten Linescan 4000 infra-red linescanner and a BAe sideways-looking infra-red (SLIR), images from which were recorded on a videotape system. The IRLS proved invaluable in the 'Scud' mobile surface-to-surface missile-hunting role with which the aircraft were tasked.

The first of 128 GR.Mk 1A night reconnaissance sorties flown during Operation Granby, totalling 300 flying hours, took place on the night of 17/18 January, when three aircraft (ZA371/C, ZA397/O and ZA400/T) went in search of a 'Scud' launcher reportedly aimed at Israel. The mission was a success, the only damage sustained being a hole in the rudder of ZA400 caused by an AAA round.

By the time the war was over in late February, the unit had earned another Battle Honour ('Gulf 1991') to add to its Royal Standard, having made a major contribution to the coalition campaign. Unlike the RAF Tornado GR.Mk 1 bombers deployed to the Gulf, which switched from low-level to medium-level operations after the first few days, the GR.Mk 1As flew all their operations 'on the deck', relying on their speed and the element of surprise in this high-risk environment. Furthermore, it fulfilled its role without a single loss.

By mid-March, No. II was officially back in Germany, but its stay at Laarbruch was to be short-lived. The Cold War was over and the 'peace dividend' and subsequent defence review by the British government ('Options for Change') saw RAF Germany considerably downsized. No. II Squadron's long association with Germany was brought to an end after over

Before the application of the Medium Sea Grey finish of recent years, the RAF's Tornados wore a standard Dark Green and Dark Sea Grey camouflage, as seen on this aircraft in 1996. This aircraft (ZA395/D) also carries practice bombs, chaff/flare and ECM pods, an AIM-9 AAM acquisition round and two giant 'Hindenburger' 495-Imp gal (2250-litre) drop tanks.

50 years, the unit moving to RAF Marham in December, to form, with Nos 13 and 39 Squadrons, what later became the Marham Reconnaissance Wing of Strike Command.

The legacy of the Gulf War has had a major bearing on No. II's operations in the years since, resulting in further overseas postings for the squadron. The continued presence of British forces in the Gulf (with those of other coalition partners, under Operation Southern Watch) has seen No. II Squadron personnel and Tornado GR.Mk 1A aircraft based in Al Kharj, Saudi Arabia under Operation Jural. Personnel from No. II have also participated in Operation Warden, the detachment of six RAF Tornados to Incirlik, Turkey to assist in Operation Provide Comfort, protecting the Kurdish population of northern Iraq from attack.

85 years of service

In May 1997, the 85th anniversary of No. II's establishment took place, joint celebrations being held with No. 3 Squadron at Farnborough to mark the occasion. The highlight of several days of celebration was the re-enactment of the simultaneous take-off of 13 May 1912, 85 years later to the day. Wing Commander Dick Garwood, OC No. II Squadron in a Tornado GR.Mk 1A, and Wing Commander André Dezonie, OC No. 3 in a Harrier GR.Mk 7, took off together for a 30-minute flight, returning to Farnborough to overfly the familiar hangars known as the 'black sheds', the buildings on the aerodrome that are most likely to have 'witnessed' the event of 85

years ago. The following weekend, celebrations continued at Farnborough. The RAF Museum provided its B.E.2b replica, which was erected in the officer's mess dining room, as a centre-piece for social events in the evening to mark this significant date in the career of the RAF squadron known as 'Shiny Two'.

Postscript

Continuing concerns about Iraq's lack of compliance with the United Nations weapons inspection in the years after the Gulf War peaked in early 1998. Although the UN Secretary General was able to broker a deal with the Iraqi regime in February, the US and UK threatened military action, moving large amounts of equipment and personnel to the Gulf Region. Tornado GR.Mk 1As from No. II Squadron were among eight aircraft despatched to Al Salim Air Base in Kuwait in early February, under Operation Bolton.

John Heathcott

The new millennium is likely to see No. II (AC) Sqn re-equipped with some of the first examples of the upgraded Tornado GR.Mk 4A. As well as improved attack capability, these aircraft are expected to be equipped with a new RAPTOR (Reconnaissance Airborne Pod for Tornado) with medium-level, stand-off, day/night capability.

No. II (AC)'s aircraft over 50 years

Curtiss Tomahawk Mk IIA
No. II Sqn's Tomahawk Mk IIAs were finished at the factory in standard Fighter Command Dark Earth/Dark Green camouflage with Sky undersides. A Sky Fighter Command recognition fuselage band was applied later. Unit codes were in grey, while fuselage roundels were of the early Type 'A1' variety, with a pre-June 1942-type fin flash.

Supermarine Spitfire PR.Mk 19
PR.Mk 19s replaced Spitfire PR.Mk XIs in the photo-reconnaissance role with No. II after World War II. These were finished in standard PRU Blue, with white serial numbers and red 'OI' unit codes, either side of a Type 'C1' roundel.

Supermarine Swift FR.Mk 5
Swifts were finished in the Dark Green/Dark Sea Grey camouflage with Silver undersides as applied to Fighter Command aircraft in the 1950/60s. An individual aircraft letter was applied in white to the tailfin.

Panavia Tornado GR.Mk 1A
No. II (AC) Squadron's current fleet of Tornados is finished in the Medium Sea Grey scheme being applied (with certain variations) to the rest of Strike Command's aircraft. This aircraft has had a temporary 'snow-cam' soluble distemper applied for exercises in Norway.

INDEX

Page numbers in **bold** refer to an illustration

II (AC) Squadron, RAF (see No. II (AC) Squadron, RAF)
IIID (see Fairey)
XI (see Blériot)
2.111 (He 111) (see CASA)
2.111-D (He 111H-16) (see CASA)
198 (see Bristol)
221 (see BAC)
223 (see Bristol)
230 (see DFS)

A

A-26 Invader (see Douglas)
Aérospatiale/BAC Concorde: 38, 41, 42, 44, **45**
Airacobra, P-39 (see Bell)
Airacomet, P-59 (see Bell)
Airacomet, XP-59A/B (see Bell)
Air Combat: 4-27, **4-27**
Albatross, SA-16A (see Grumman)
Anson (see Avro)
Apollo, AW.55 (see Armstrong Whitworth)
Armstrong Whitworth
 Atlas Mk 1: 143, **145**
 AW.55 Apollo: **36**
 F.K.8: 142, **144**
Atlas Mk 1 (see Armstrong Whitworth)
Audax (see Hawker)
Avia
 B.534: 107
 CS 99: 96, 107
 CS 199: 97, **97**, 105, **105**, 107
 S 99: **70**, 96, **96**, 97, 105, 107
 S 199: **77**, 97-99, **97**, **98**, 105, **105**, 107, **107**, 108, **108**
Avro
 Anson: 154
 Lancaster: 86
AW.55 Apollo (see Armstrong Whitworth)

B

B-17/F Flying Fortress (see Boeing)
B-24 Liberator (see Consolidated)
B-25 Mitchell (see North American)
B-29 Superfortress (see Boeing)
B-29A-10-BN Superfortress (see Boeing)
B-52D Stratofortress (see Boeing)
B-58 Hustler (see Convair)
B.534 (see Avia)
Ba 349 Natter (see Bachem)
BAC 221: 32, **33**, 36, 37, **40-45**, 41, 43, 44
Bachem Ba 349 Natter: 32, 33
BAe Harrier GR.Mk 7: 157
Banshee, F2H (see McDonnell)
'Bark' (see Ilyushin Il-2)
'Bat' (see Tupolev Tu-2)
Battle (see Fairey)
B.E.2 (see Royal Aircraft Factory)
B.E.2a *et seq* (see Royal Aircraft Factory)
'Beagle' (see Ilyushin Il-28)
'Beast' (see Ilyushin Il-10)
Beaver, L-20 (see de Havilland Canada)
Belgium
 Air Force (Force Aérienne Belge): 154
Bell
 P-39 Airacobra: 115
 P-59 Airacomet: 32, 115, 132
 X-1: 32
 XP-59A Airacomet: 115
 XP-59B Airacomet: 115, 122
Bf 109 (see Messerschmitt)
Bf 109D *et seq* (see Messerschmitt)
Bf 110/G (see Messerschmitt)
Blackbird, SR-71 (see Lockheed)
Blenheim (see Bristol)
Blériot XI: 141, **143**
'Blériot Experimental' (B.E.) (see Royal Aircraft Factory)
Boeing
 B-17 Flying Fortress: 133, 153
 B-17F Flying Fortress: 132
 B-29 Superfortress: **6**, 7, 10, 16, 124
 B-29A-10-BN Superfortress: 132, 133
 B-52D Stratofortress: 110
 KC-97G: **28**
Boulton Paul Defiant: 146, **147**
Boxkite (see Bristol)
Brazil
 Air Force (Força Aérea Brasileira): 121
Breguet G.3: 140, **142**
'Brewer' (see Yakovlev Yak-28)
Brewster Buffalo: 84
Bristol
 198: 44
 223: 44
 Blenheim: 145, 146
 Boxkite: 140
 F.2b: 143, **145**
 Fighter: 143, **145**
 Scout: 142
Buchón, HA-1112-M1L (C.4K) (see Hispano-Aviación (CASA))
Buffalo (see Brewster)
Bulgaria
 Royal Bulgarian Air Force (Vazdushnite na Negovo Velichestvo Voiski): 86, 94, 107, 109

C

C.4J (HA-1109) (see Hispano-Aviación (CASA))
C.4K (HA-1112-M1 *et seq*) (see Hispano-Aviación (CASA))
C-47 Skytrain (DC-3) (see Douglas)
C-47A (see Douglas)
C-54 (see Douglas)
C-82 Packet (see Fairchild)
C-119/B/C (see Fairchild)
C-121C (L-1049) Constellation (see Lockheed)
C-124A/C Globemaster (see Douglas)
Canadair
 F-86E-6-CAN Sabre (CL-13 Sabre Mk 2): 10, **10**
 T-33: 121
Cape Esperance, USS: 5, 6
CASA
 2.111 (He 111): 102, 104
 2.111-D (He 111H-16): **104**
CASA HA-1109 *et seq* (see Hispano-Aviación)
Catalina, OA-10 (see Consolidated)
Catapult P-80A (see Lockheed)
Chile
 Air Force (Fuerza Aérea de Chile): 121
China
 Air Force: 22
Colombia
 Air Force (Fuerza Aérea Colombiana): 121
Concorde (see Aérospatiale/BAC)
Consolidated
 B-24 Liberator: 109, 130
 OA-10 Catalina: **30**
Constellation, C-121C (L-1049) (see Lockheed)
Convair
 B-58 Hustler: 134
 L-13: 30
 L-13B: **30**
Croatia
 Legion: 84, 85, 91, 107, 109
CS 99 (see Avia)
CS 199 (see Avia)
Curtiss
 Kittyhawk Mk I: 54
 P-40 Kittyhawk: 12, 55, 56
 P-40 Tomahawk: 12, 55, 56, **140**, 115, 146, 147
 P-40B Tomahawk: 147
 Tomahawk Mk I: 147
 Tomahawk Mk IIA: **147**, **157**
Czechoslovakia
 Air Force (Ceskoslovenske Vojenské Letectvo): 70, 96-98, 105, 107
 National Air Guard: 70, 96, 98, 107

D

D-558 Skystreak (see Douglas)
Dassault Mirage I/II/III: 36
DC-3 *et seq* (see Douglas)
Defiant (see Boulton Paul)
de Havilland
 Hornet: 103
 Mosquito: 4, 87
 Mosquito B.Mk 35: **150**, 152
 Mosquito FB.Mk 6: 152
 Tiger Moth: 146
 Vampire: 32, 115, 119, 122
 Venom: 40
de Havilland Canada L-20 Beaver: **18**, **30**
Delta FD.1 (see Fairey)
Delta FD.2 (see Fairey)
Demon (see Hawker)
DF-80A Shooting Star (see Lockheed)
DFS 230: 87
Dornier Do 335: 126
Douglas
 A-26 Invader: 124
 C-47 Skytrain (DC-3): **10**, **29**, 98, 132
 C-47A: **29**
 C-54 (DC-4): **28**, 120
 C-124A Globemaster: **28**, 29
 C-124C Globemaster: **29**
 D-558 Skystreak: 118
 DC-4 (C-54): 98, 108
 RB-26 Invader: 23, 127
Dragonfly H-5/G (see Sikorsky)
Dragonfly H-19A (see Sikorsky)
Dragonfly YR-5A (see Sikorsky)
DT-33 (see Lockheed)

E

E.III (see Fokker)
E.28/39 (see Gloster)
Ecuador
 Air Force (Fuerza Aérea Ecuatoriana): 121
English Electric
 Lightning: 36, 42, 43
 P.1: 36
ERF-80A Shooting Star (see Lockheed)
Exercise
 Battle Royal: 153
 Metrical: 40
 Spartan: 147
 Triplex West: 154

F

F.2b (see Bristol)
F2H Banshee (see McDonnell)
F-4/B/D Phantom II (see McDonnell Douglas)
F4F-4 Wildcat (see Grumman)
F-6 Mustang (see North American)
F9F Panther (see Grumman)
F-14/A (see Lockheed)
F-51/D Mustang (see North American)
F-80 (P-80) Shooting Star (see Lockheed)
F-80A (P-80A) *et seq* Shooting Star (see Lockheed)
F-82 Twin Mustang (see North American)
F-84 Thunderjet (see Republic)
F-86 Sabre (see North American)
F-86A *et seq* Sabre (see North American)
F-86E-6-CAN Sabre (CL-13 Sabre Mk 2) (see Canadair)
F-94/B (see Lockheed)
F-94C Starfire (see Lockheed)
F-100/A/C Super Sabre (see North American)
F-101A (see McDonnell)
F-104 Starfighter (see Lockheed)
F-105 Thunderchief (see Republic)
'Fagot' (see Mikoyan MiG-15)
Fairchild
 C-82 Packet: 130
 C-119: 28, **29**
 C-119B: **29**
 C-119C: **28**, **30**
Fairey
 IIID: 143
 Battle: 146
 Delta FD.1: 32-35, **32**, **34**, **35**
 Delta FD.2: 32, **32**, **33**, 35-41, **36-41**
 Gannet: 34, 38
Fairey Deltas FD.1, FD.2 & BAC 221 - Beyond the Frontiers: 32-45, **32-45**
Farman
 Longhorn: 140
 Shorthorn: 141
'Farmer' (see Mikoyan MiG-19)
'Farmer-C' (see Mikoyan MiG-19S)
'Farmer-D' (see Mikoyan MiG-19PM)
F.B.5 (see Vickers)
FD-1 Phantom (see McDonnell)
Fi 103 (V-1) (see Fieseler)
Fiat
 G.50: 84, 107
 G.55: 80
'Fiddler' (see Tupolev Tu-28)
Fieseler Fi 103 (V-1): 148
Fieseler/Skoda FiSk 199: **64**, 65
Fighter (see Bristol)
Finland
 Air Force (Ilmavoimat): 70, 77, 84, 95, 96, 105, 107
'Firebar' (see Yakovlev Yak-28)
'Fishbed' (see Mikoyan MiG-21)
'Fishbed-A/B' (see Mikoyan MiG-21F)
FiSk 199 (see Fieseler/Skoda)
F.K.8 (see Armstrong Whitworth)
'Flipper' (see Mikoyan-Gurevich Ye-152A)
'Flogger' (see Mikoyan MiG-23)
Flying Fortress, B-17/F (see Boeing)
Focke-Wulf
 Fw 190: 49, 55, 56, 62, **79**, 82, 86, 106, 148, 151
 Fw 190A: 56, 63, 87, 147
 Fw 190A-1: 51
 Fw 190A-2: 56
 Fw 190A-3: 56, 147
 Fw 190D: 49
 Ta 152H: 90, 91
Fokker
 E.III: 142
 Triplane: 142
'Foxbat' (see Mikoyan-Gurevich MiG-25)
'Foxbat-A' (see Mikoyan-Gurevich MiG-25P)
FP-80 Shooting Star (see Lockheed)
FP-80A *et seq* Shooting Star (see Lockheed)
Franklin D.Roosevelt, USS: 132
'Fresco' (see Mikoyan MiG-17)
Fury Mk II (see Hawker)
Fw 190/A/D (see Focke-Wulf)

G

G.3 (see Breguet)
G.50 (see Fiat)
G.55 (see Fiat)
Gannet (see Fairey)
General Aircraft Hotspur: **146**
Germany
 Air Force (Luftwaffe): 48, 49, 51, 53, 54, 57, 62, 67-70, 73, 84-86, 92, 95, 96, 106-109, 145, 147, 150, 151
 Army (Wehrmacht): 53, 67, 79, 108
Gladiator (see Gloster)
Globemaster, C-124A/C (see Douglas)
Gloster
 E.28/39: 115
 Gladiator: 144
 Javelin: 154
 Meteor: 40, 41, 115, 133, 150, 154
 Meteor F.Mk 4: 118, 130
 Meteor FR.Mk 9: **151**, 153, 154
 Meteor NF.Mk 11: 154
 Meteor PR.Mk 10: 153
 Meteor T.Mk 7: 153
Grumman
 F4F-4 Wildcat: 132
 F9F Panther: 20, 133
 SA-16A Albatross: **30**

H

H-5/G Dragonfly (see Sikorsky)
H-19A Dragonfly (see Sikorsky)
HA-1109-J1L (C.4J) (see Hispano-Aviación (CASA))
HA-1109-K1L *et seq* (C.4J) (see Hispano-Aviación (CASA))
HA-1109-M1L (see Hispano-Aviación (CASA))
HA-1110-K1L (see Hispano-Aviación (CASA))
HA-1112-K1L (see Hispano-Aviación (CASA))
HA-1112-M1L Buchón (C.4K) (see Hispano-Aviación (CASA))
HA-1112-M2L *et seq* (C.4K) (see Hispano-Aviación (CASA))
Handley Page
 Harrow: 148
 Hastings: **150**
 HP.115: 44
Harrier GR.Mk 7 (see BAe)
Harrow (see Handley Page)
Harvard (see North American)
Hastings (see Handley Page)
Hawker
 Audax: 144, **146**
 Demon: 144
 Fury Mk II: 144
 Hector: 144, **146**
 Hunter: 33, 38, 41, 44, 154, 155
 Hunter F.Mk 6: 154
 Hunter FGA.Mk 70A: 152
 Hunter FR.Mk 10: **141**, **152**, 154
 Hurricane: 55, 56, 104
 P.1103: 42
 Tempest Mk V: 78
 Typhoon: 48
Hawker Siddeley SST: 43, 44, 45
He 100 V8 *et seq* (see Heinkel)
Hector (see Hawker)
Heinkel
 He 100 V8: 61
 He 111: 54, 60, **82**, 97, 102
 He 178: 115
Henschel Hs 126: 145
Hermes, HMS: 143
Hispano-Aviación (CASA):
 HA-1109-J1L (C.4J): **99**, 100, 101
 HA-1109-K1L (C.4J): **99**, 100, **100**, 101, 105, 109
 HA-1109-K2L (C.4J): 100-102
 HA-1109-K3L (C.4J): **100**, 101, 102
 HA-1109-M1L: 101, **101**
 HA-1110-K1L: **100**, 101
 HA-1112-K1L: **100**, 101, 102, 109, **109**
 HA-1112-M1L Buchón: **70**, **75**, 101-105, **101-105**, 109
 HA-1112-M2L (C.4K): 101, 102
 HA-1112-M3L (C.4K): 101, 102
 HA-1112-M4L (C.4K): 102, **102**, 104, **104**, 105
Hornet (see de Havilland)
Hotspur (see General Aircraft)
HP.115 (see Handley Page)
Hs 126 (see Henschel)
Hungary
 Royal Hungarian Air Force (Magyar Királyi Légiero): 70, 84-86, 108
Hunter (see Hawker)
Hunter F.Mk 6 (see Hawker)
Hunter FGA.Mk 70A (see Hawker)
Hunter FR.Mk 10 (see Hawker)
Hurricane (see Hawker)
Hustler, B-58 (see Convair)

I

I-3U (see Mikoyan)
I-7U (see Mikoyan)
I-16 (see Polikarpov)
I-75 (see Mikoyan)
I-153 (see Polikarpov)
IAR 80: 86, 108
Il-2 *et seq* (see Ilyushin)
Ilyushin
 Il-2 'Bark': 54, 94, 109
 Il-10 'Beast': **107**, 120
 Il-28 'Beagle': 110
Invader, A-26 (see Douglas)
Invader, RB-26 (see Douglas)
Israel
 Air Force (Chel Ha'Avir): 70, 98, 99, 105, 108
Italy
 Air Force (Aviazione Nazionale Repubblicana): 70, 71, 80, 81, 108
 Air Force (Reggia Aeronautica): 68, 80, 81, 108
 Co-Belligerent air force: 108

J

J-6 (see Shenyang)
J21 (see Saab)
Jaguar (see SEPECAT)
Jaguar GR.Mk 1/A (see SEPECAT)
Jaguar T.Mk 2/A (see SEPECAT)
Javelin (see Gloster)
JQF-80F Shooting Star (see Lockheed)
Ju 52 *et seq* (see Junkers)
Junkers
 Ju 52: **66**
 Ju 87 Stuka: 53, 145
 Ju 88: **57**, 148, 151
 Ju 88A-4: 87, **87**
 Mistel: 60, 87
 Mistel 1: 87, **87**
 Mistel 2: 87
 Mistel 3: 87
 Mistel S1: 87

K

Kawasaki T-33: 121
KC-97G (see Boeing)
Kittyhawk Mk 1 (see Curtiss)
Kittyhawk, P-40 (see Curtiss)
Korea
 Royal Korean Air Force: 4

L

L-13/B (see Convair)
L-20 Beaver (see de Havilland Canada)
L-133 (see Lockheed)
L-245 (T2V-1) (see Lockheed)
La-5 *et seq* (see Lavochkin)
Lancaster (see Avro)
Lavochkin
 La-5: 84
 La-7: 95, 120
 La-9: 7, 12, 121
Liberator, B-24 (see Consolidated)
Lightning (see English Electric)
Lightning, P-38 (see Lockheed)
Lockheed
 C-121C (L-1049) Constellation: **28-29**
 Catapult P-80A: 132
 DF-80A Shooting Star: 125, **125**
 DT-33: **121**, 131
 ERF-80A Shooting Star: 126
 ERF-80A-1-LO Shooting Star: 132
 F-14: 119, 123, 124, **124**, 125
 F-14A: 124, 125, **125**, 126
 F-80 (P-80) Shooting Star: 9, 11, 114, 115, **116**, 118-124, **120**, 127, 12[illegible] 130, 131
 F-80A (P-80A) Shooting Star: 128, 12[illegible] 130
 F-80A-1-LO Shooting Star: 124, 125, 129
 F-80A-5-LO Shooting Star: 124, 125, 129
 F-80A-10-LO Shooting Star: 124, 126
 F-80B (P-80B) Shooting Star: 119, **11[illegible]** 123
 F-80C (P-80C) Shooting Star: 4, 7, 15, 26, **116-118**, 120, 121, 123, 124 128-130, **128-130**, 133
 F-80C-5-LO Shooting Star: 128, 129
 F-80C-10 Shooting Star: **114**
 F-80C-10-LO Shooting Star: 129
 F-80C-11 Shooting Star: 124
 F-80C-11-LO Shooting Star: 124, 128, 129
 F-80C-12-LO Shooting Star: 128
 F-80, Ramjet-powered: 132, **132**
 F-94: 114, 121, 131
 F-94B: 121
 F-94C Starfire: 121
 F-104 Starfighter: 96, 102
 FP-80 Shooting Star: 119
 FP-80A Shooting Star: **117**, 118, 124, 125, 126
 FP-80A-1-LO Shooting Star: 126, 130
 FP-80A-5-LO Shooting Star: 124, 126
 JQF-80F Shooting Star: **121**
 L-133: 115
 L-245 (T2V-1): 120
 NF-80C Shooting Star: 128, 129, **129**
 P-38 Lightning: 12, 79, 86, 109, 117
 P-80 (F-80) Shooting Star: 116-119, **119**, **121**, 122-124, **125**, 131
 P-80A (F-80A) Shooting Star: 118, 119 **120**, 123-126, **123**, **124**, 131, 132, **133**
 P-80A-1 Shooting Star: **114**, **115**
 P-80A-1-LO Shooting Star: 124
 P-80A-5 Shooting Star: 115, 123
 P-80A-5-LO Shooting Star: 124
 P-80A, Catapult: 132
 P-80A, Prone pilot Shooting Star: 124, **132**, 133
 P-80A (F-80A), Towed Shooting Star: 124, 132, **132**, 133
 P-80A Trainable Guns Shooting Star: 124, 133
 P-80B (F-80B) Shooting Star: 117, 118 **118**, 119, 122, 124, 126, **126**, 128, **128**, 131, **133**
 P-80B-1 Shooting Star: 126
 P-80B-5 Shooting Star: 126
 P-80B-5-LO Shooting Star: 128
 P-80C (F-80C) Shooting Star: 126
 P-80C-1-LO Shooting Star: 128, 129
 P-80D Shooting Star: 130
 P-80E (L-181) Shooting Star: 130
 P-80N Shooting Star: 130
 P-80R Shooting Star: 130
 P-80Z Shooting Star: 131
 Prone pilot P-80A Shooting Star: 124, **132**, 133
 QF-80 Shooting Star: 131
 QF-80A Shooting Star: **121**, 131, **131**
 QF-80B Shooting Star: **131**
 QF-80C (QF-80F) Shooting Star: 131, **131**
 Ramjet-powered F-80: 132, **132**
 RF-80 Shooting Star: 23, **118**, 119, 120, 127
 RF-80A Shooting Star: 10, **117**, 119, 120, 124-127, **125-127**, 130, **130**
 RF-80A-1-LO Shooting Star: 125
 RF-80A-5-LO Shooting Star: 125, 130
 RF-80A-10-LO Shooting Star: 125
 RF-80A-11-LO Shooting Star: 130
 RF-80A-15-LO Shooting Star: 124, 125 **126**
 RF-80A-20-LO Shooting Star: 126
 RF-80A-25-LO Shooting Star: 126
 RF-80C Shooting Star: **117**, 127, 130, **130**
 RF-80C-11-LO Shooting Star: 126, 130 **130**
 SR-71 Blackbird: 122
 T-33: 114, **116**, 119, 121, 123, 128, 130, 131
 TF-80C (T-33): 120, 121, 128, 131
 TO-1 (TV-1) Shooting Star: 121, **126**, 128, **129**, 133, **133**
 Towed P-80A (F-80A) Shooting Star: 124, 132, **132**, 133

ainable Guns P-80A Shooting Star: 124, 133
-2: 120, 122, 134
F-14: 124, 125
F-90: 120, 129
F-104: 120
FP-80A Shooting Star: 124, 125, **125**
P-80 (L-140) Shooting Star: 115-117, **115**, 122, **122**, 123
P-80A (L-141) Shooting Star: 116, 117, 120, 122, **122**, 123, **123**
P-80B Shooting Star: 124, 126, **126**, 130
P-80R Shooting Star: 118, 124, 126, **126**, 130, **130**, **131**
F-14: 124
F-94 (YF-97): 120, 121
P-80 Shooting Star: 131
P-80A (L-080) Shooting Star: 123, **123**, 124, **124**
ockheed P-80 Variants: 114-133, **114-133**
nghorn (see Farman)
-6 Mosquito (see North American)
sander (see Westland)
sander Mk I/II/III (see Westland)

M

.52 (see Miles)
acchi
MC.202: 84, 107
MC.205: 80
agister (see Miles)
C.202 (see Macchi)
C.205 (see Macchi)
cDonnell
2H Banshee: 133
-101A: 36
F-88 Voodoo: 131
D-1 Phantom: 132
cDonnell Douglas
-4 Phantom II: 110-113, **154**, 155
-4B Phantom II: 115
-4D Phantom II: 111, 113
Phantom FGR.Mk 2 (F-4M): **153**, 155
Me 109R' (see Messerschmitt)
Me 209 *et seq* (see Messerschmitt)
lesserschmitt
Bf 109: 47-50, **48**, 53-55, **53**, 57, 58, 61, 63-68, **69**, 70, **70**, 72, 75-77, **75**, 79-97, **88**, 99-102, 104-108, **104**, **108**, 151
Bf 109D-1: 109
Bf 109E 'Emil': 47, 49-54, 56, 57, 59, 61, 62, 68, 86-88, 100, 104, 105, 109
Bf 109E-1: **99**, 100
Bf 109E-3: 50, 109
Bf 109E-4: 50, 107, 108
Bf 109E-4/B Jagdbomber: 56
Bf 109E-7: 51, 107, 109
Bf 109F 'Friedrich': 47, 49-62, **50-54**, **56-60**, 64, 65, 67, 68, **68**, 78, 87, 99, 106, 109
Bf 109F-0: 50, **50**, 51, 106
Bf 109F-1: 51, **51**, 52, 106
Bf 109F-2: 52, **52**, **53**, 55, **60**, **68**, 106
Bf 109F-2/B Jagdbomber: 55
Bf 109F-2/Trop: 54, **55**, 105, **105**
Bf 109F-2/U1: 55
Bf 109F-2/Z: 55
Bf 109F-3: 55, **55**, **57**, 106
Bf 109F-4: **52**, **53**, 55, **55**, 56, 59, **57-59**, 60, 65, 66, **68**, **69**, 84, 87, **87**, 90, 106, 108, **108**, 109
Bf 109F-4/B Jagdbomber: **52**, 56, **56**, 59
Bf 109F-4/R1: 57, 58, 59
Bf 109F-4/R2 *et seq*: 59
Bf 109F-4/Trop: **52**, 54, 56, **54-56**
Bf 109F-4/Z: **57**, 58, **58**, **68**, 90
Bf 109F-5: 58, 59
Bf 109F-6: 58, 59
Bf 109F-8: 59
Bf 109G 'Gustav': 47-49, **49**, 56-68, **67**, 70-74, **70**, **75**, 77-93, **85**, **87**, **89**, **90**, **94**, 95, 96, 99-101, 105-109, **105**, **109**
Bf 109G-0: **60**, 64, 106
Bf 109G-1: 59, **62**, **63**, 64, 65, 67, 95, 106
Bf 109G-1/R2 *et seq*: 65
Bf 109G-2: **49**, **62-66**, 64-67, **77**, 79, **79**, 84, **85**, 86, 87, **87**, 89, 95, **95**, 99, 103, **105-108**, 106-109
Bf 109G-2/R1: **64**, 65
Bf 109G-2/R2: 65, 66
Bf 109G-2/Trop: **46-47**, 56, 57, **63**, **64**, **66**, 67, **68**, **79**, **82**, 105
Bf 109G-2/U1: 66
Bf 109G-3: **62**, 67, 89, 90, 106
Bf 109G-3/U2: 67
Bf 109G-3 V50/54: 90, 91
Bf 109G-4: **64**, **65**, 66, 67, 78, 79, 89, 106, 107
Bf 109G-4/R3: 67
Bf 109G-4/Trop: **63**, 67, **68**
Bf 109G-4/U3: 67
Bf 109G-5: 78, 83, 89, 90, 93, 106
Bf 109G-6: **48**, **49**, **62**, **66**, 67, **67**, **69**, **70**, 73, **75-82**, 78, 79, 81-84, **84-86**, 86, 88, **88-90**, 89, 91-93, 95, **95**, 96, 104-109, **105-107**, **109**
Bf 109G-6/AS: 89
Bf 109G-6/N: 84, **84**
Bf 109G-6/R1/2/3: 78
Bf 109G-6/R6: 78, **83**
Bf 109G-6/Trop: **48**, **79**, **80**, **82**, **84**
Bf 109G-6/U2 *et seq*: 78
Bf 109G-6/Y: 78
Bf 109G-8: 74, 83, 84, 86, 89, 95, 106-108
Bf 109G-10: **69**, **70**, 73, 74, **76**, **79**, 81, **81**, 83, 84, **90**, **91**, 92-96, **95**, 106-109
Bf 109G-10/AS: **81**, 85, 92, **108**
Bf 109G-10/R1 *et seq*: 92
Bf 109G-10/U4: 92
Bf 109G-12: 89, **89**, 90, **94**, 96, 97, 106, 107, 109
Bf 109G-14: **70**, **75-77**, 78, **79**, 84, **85**, **88**, 89, 91-93, **91**, 96, 105-108
Bf 109G-14/AS: 91
Bf 109H: 90, 91
Bf 109H-0: 90
Bf 109H-1: 90, **90**
Bf 109H V55: 91
Bf 109K 'Kurfürst': 47, 71-74, **75**, 92-95, 101, 106
Bf 109K-0: 70, 92
Bf 109K-1: 74
Bf 109K-2: 72, 74
Bf 109K-3: 74
Bf 109K-4: **70**, 71-74, **71-74**, 91-94, **92-94**, 106
Bf 109K-4/R1 *et seq*: 71, 73, 94
Bf 109K-6: 73, 74, 94
Bf 109K-8: 74, 94
Bf 109K-10: 74, 94
Bf 109K-12: 94
Bf 109K-14: 70, 74, 94
Bf 109Z 'Zwilling': 60, 62
Bf 110: 109
Bf 110G: 86
'Me 109R': 61
Me 209: 61, 62, 90, 91
Me 209 II: 61, 90
Me 209 V1: 61
Me 209 V4/5: 61, **61**
Me 209 V6: 61, 91
Me 209A-1/2: 61
Me 209H: 61, 90
Me 209H V1: 61
Me 262: 32, 33, 59, 61, 69, 151
Me 262 V1: 115
Me 309: 59, 60, **60**, 61
Me 309A-2: 61
Me 309B: 61
Me 309 V1/2: 61, **61**
Me 309 V3/4: 61
Me 609 Zwilling: 61
Messerschmitt Bf 109 Part 2: The later variants: 46-105, **46-105**
Meteor (see Gloster)
MiG-15 *et seq* (see Mikoyan)
MiG-19 in the Vietnam War: 110-113, **110-113**
MiG-25 (see Mikoyan-Gurevich)
'MiG Maulers' - F-86 Sabre in Korea, 1950-53: 4-27, **4-27**
Mikoyan
I-3U: 134
I-7U: 134
I-75: 134
MiG-15 'Fagot': 4-27, **4**, 97, 120
MiG-15bis: 14
MiG-17 'Fresco': 110, 112, 113
MiG-17F: 110
MiG-19 'Farmer': 110-113, **110-112**
MiG-19PM 'Farmer-D': 134
MiG-19S 'Farmer-C': 113
MiG-19SV: 134
MiG-21 'Fishbed': 110, 111, 112, 113, 135, 137
MiG-21F 'Fishbed-A/B': 135, 136, 137, 138
MiG-23 'Flogger': 137
Mikoyan-Gurevich
MiG-25 (Ye-155) 'Foxbat': 134, 138, 139
MiG-25P 'Foxbat-A': 138
Ye-4/5/6 (MiG-21): 135, 137
Ye-6T-3: 139
Ye-150: 134-139, **135**
Ye-152: 134, 136-139
Ye-152-1: **136**, 137-138, 139
Ye-152-2: 137, 138
Ye-152A 'Flipper': **134**, 136, **136**, 137, **138**
Ye-152M ('Ye-166'): **137**, 138-139, **138**, **139**
Ye-152P: **137**, 138, **138**, 139
Ye-155 (MiG-25): 134, 138, 139
Mikoyan-Gurevich Ye-150/152, The Big MiGs - An Industry of Prototypes: 134-139, **134-139**
Miles
M.52: 32
Magister: 146
Mirage I/II/III (see Dassault)
Mistel 1 *et seq* (see Junkers)
Mistel S1 (see Junkers)
Mitchell, B-25 (see North American)
Mosquito (see de Havilland)
Mosquito B.Mk 35 (see de Havilland)
Mosquito FB.Mk 6 (see de Havilland)
Mosquito, LT-6 (see North American)
Mustang (see North American)

N

NA-73X (see North American)
NA-137 (see North American)
NATO (see North Atlantic Treaty Organisation)
Natter, Ba 349 (see Bachem)
NF-80C Shooting Star (see Lockheed)
No. II (AC) Squadron, RAF: 140-159
North American
B-25 Mitchell: 104, 124, 130
F-6 Mustang: 117
F-51 Mustang: 116, 120
F-51D Mustang: 4, 11, 24, 119, 120, 127
F-82 Twin Mustang: 120
F-86 Sabre: 4-27, **4**, **5**, **8**, **9**, **14**, **15**, **19**, **20**, **24**, 32, 38, 118, 121, **125**, 130, **151**
F-86A Sabre: 4-6, **4-5**, **7-9**, **12**, 13, **13**, 21, 23, **23**
F-86A-5 Sabre: **6**, **23**
F-86A-5-NA Sabre: **9**
F-86E Sabre: **4-5**, 7, 9, **10**, **14**, **17**, 22, 25
F-86E-1 Sabre: **10-17**
F-86E-1-NA Sabre: **19**
F-86E-6 Sabre: **11**
F-86E-10 Sabre: **10**, **11**, **14-17**
F-86E-10-NA Sabre: **12**, **15**
F-86F Sabre: 14, 19, **19-22**, **24-27**, 26
F-86F-1 Sabre: **18**, 22
F-86F-1-NA Sabre: **20**
F-86F-2 Sabre: 22
F-86F-10 Sabre: **22**
F-86F-10-NA Sabre: **19**, **20**, **22**
F-86F-30 Sabre: 8, 18, **18**, **21**, **22**, **24-27**, 25, 26
F-86F-30-NA Sabre: **25**
F-86H Sabre: 22
F-100 Super Sabre: 22
F-100A Super Sabre: 128
F-100C Super Sabre: 36, 37, **37**, 40
Harvard: 152
LT-6 Mosquito: 24
Mustang: 146, 147, **148**, **150**, 151
Mustang Mk I: **140**, 148, **148**
Mustang Mk IA: 148
Mustang Mk II: 150
Mustang Mk III (P-51C): 78
NA-73X: 114
NA-137: 130
P-51 Mustang: 48, 73, 96, 114
P-51C Mustang (Mk III): 78
P-51D Mustang: 86, 94, 99, 108, 123, 130, 132
P-51K/M Mustang: 130
RB-45 Tornado: 10, 23
RF-51 Mustang: 23, 127
RF-51D Mustang: 127
RF-86 Sabre: 10, 23, 127
RF-86A Sabre: **23**
T-6 Texan: 4, **10**, 102
YF-93A: 131
North Atlantic Treaty Organisation (NATO): 134, 153, 154, 156
North Korea
Air Force: 4, 7, 10, 13, 14, 22, 120

O

OA-10 Catalina (see Consolidated)
Operation
Balak: 98
Barbarossa: 53
Beethoven: 87
Bestrafung: 53
Bodenplatte: 73, 95, 150, 151
Bolton: 157
Dynamo: 145
Eisenhammer: 87
Freedom Train: 110
Granby: 155, 156
Husky: 80
Jural: 157
Linebacker: 110
Marita: 53
Merkur: 53
Noball: 148
Plainfare: 150
Provide Comfort: 157
Southern Watch: 157
Stovepipe: 117
Torch: 79
Warden: 157
Wehrwulf: 95

P

P.1 (see English Electric)
P-38 Lightning (see Lockheed)
P-39 Airacobra (see Bell)
P-40 Kittyhawk (see Curtiss)
P-40B Tomahawk (see Curtiss)
P-47 Thunderbolt (see Republic)
P-51 Mustang (see North American)
P-51C *et seq* Mustang (see North American)
P-59 Airacomet (see Bell)
P-80 (F-80) Shooting Star (see Lockheed)
P-80A *et seq* Shooting Star (see Lockheed)
P.1103 (see Hawker)
Packet, C-82 (see Fairchild)
Panavia
Tornado: 156, **156**, 157
Tornado GR.Mk 1: 156
Tornado GR.Mk 1A: **141**, 156, **156**, 157, **157**
Tornado GR.Mk 4A: **157**
Panther, F9F (see Grumman)
Percival
Proctor: 144
Vega Gull: 144
Peru
Air Force (Fuerza Aérea del Peru): 121
Phantom, FD-1 (see McDonnell)
Phantom II, F-4/B/D (see McDonnell Douglas)
Phantom FGR.Mk 2 (F-4M) (see McDonnell Douglas)
Polikarpov
I-16: 53, **54**
I-153: 53
Proctor (see Percival)

Q

QF-80 Shooting Star (see Lockheed)
QF-80A *et seq* Shooting Star (see Lockheed)

R

RB-26 Invader (see Douglas)
RB-45 Tornado (see North American)
R.E.1 (see Royal Aircraft Factory)
R.E.5 (see Royal Aircraft Factory)
Reggiane Re.2000: 59, 108
Republic
F-84 Thunderjet: 7, 13, 17, 20, 121, 154
F-105 Thunderchief: 131
P-47 Thunderbolt: 19, 48, 83, 118
RF-84 Thunderjet: 23, 127
RP-47G Thunderbolt: 132
RF-51/D Mustang (see North American)
RF-80 Shooting Star (see Lockheed)
RF-80A *et seq* Shooting Star (see Lockheed)
RF-84 Thunderjet (see Republic)
RF-86/A Sabre (see North American)
Romania
Royal Romanian Air Force (Fortelor Regal ale Aeriene Romåna/Fortele Aeriene ale Republicii Populare Romåna): 85, 86, 96, 108
Royal Aircraft Factory
B.E.2: 140, 141, 142, 145
B.E.2a: **140**, 141, 142, **142**, **143**
B.E.2b: 142, 157
B.E.2c: 142, 144
B.E.2d: 142
B.E.2e: **144**
'Blériot Experimental' (B.E.): 140, **142**
R.E.1: **143**
R.E.5: 141, 143
RP-47G Thunderbolt (see Republic)
Rumpler Taube: 141

S

S 99 (see Avia)
S 199 (see Avia)
SA-16A Albatross (see Grumman)
Saab
J21: 126
Viggen: 135
Sabre, F-86 (see North American)
Sabre, F-86A *et seq* (see North American)
Sabre, F-86E-6-CAN (CL-13 Sabre Mk 2) (see Canadair)
Sabre, RF-86/A (see North American)
Scout (see Bristol)
Seamew (see Short)
'Second to None' 'Shiny Two', No. II (AC) Squadron, RAF: 140-159, **140-159**
SEPECAT
Jaguar: 153, **154**, 155, **155**, 156
Jaguar GR.Mk 1: **154**, 155, **155**, 156
Jaguar GR.Mk 1A: **155**, 156, 157
Jaguar T.Mk 2: **155**, 156
Jaguar T.Mk 2A: 156
Shenyang J-6: 110-113, **111**, **113**
Shooting Star (see Lockheed)
Shorthorn (see Farman)
Short Seamew: **36**
Sikorsky
H-5 Dragonfly: 31
H-5G Dragonfly: **31**
H-19A Dragonfly: **31**
YR-5A Dragonfly: **31**
Skystreak, D-558 (see Douglas)
Skytrain, C-47 (DC-3) (see Douglas)
Slovakia
Air Arm (Slovenské Vzdusné Zbrane): 85, 86, 109
South Africa
Air Force: 24, 25, 54
Soviet Union
Air defence command (PVO - Protivo Vozdooshnaya Oboronа): 134, 139
Air Force (V-VS): 10, 14, 22, 26, 107, 139
3rd Air Division: 7
Fighter Divisions: 14
Army: 67, 95
LII (Flight Test Institute): 134, 135, 138
Spain
Air Force (Ejército del Aire): 70, 86, 99, 102, 105, 109
Spitfire (see Supermarine)
Spitfire FR.Mk XIV/E (see Supermarine)
Spitfire Mk I *et seq* (see Supermarine)
Spitfire PR.Mk XI/XIX (see Supermarine)
SR-71 Blackbird (see Lockheed)
SST (see Hawker Siddeley)
Starfighter, F-104 (see Lockheed)
Starfire, F-94C (see Lockheed)
Stratofortress, B-52D (see Boeing)
Stuka, Ju 87 (see Junkers)
Sukhoi T-37: 138, 139, **139**
Superfortress, B-29 (see Boeing)
Superfortress, B-29A-10-BN (see Boeing)
Supermarine
Spitfire: 48, 79, 98, 99, 104
Spitfire FR.Mk XIV: **149**, **150**
Spitfire FR.Mk XIVE: 149-151, **149**, **150**, 153
Spitfire Mk I: 52
Spitfire Mk II: 52
Spitfire Mk V: 51, 52, 57, 63, 65
Spitfire Mk VB: 149
Spitfire Mk VC: 149
Spitfire Mk VIII: 149
Spitfire Mk IX: 63, 108, 149
Spitfire Mk XII: 149
Spitfire Mk XIV: 73, 78, 94, **149**
Spitfire Mk XIVC: 149
Spitfire Mk XVI: 63, 149, **149**
Spitfire PR.Mk XI: 152, 157
Spitfire PR.Mk 19 (XIX): **150**, 152, **157**
Swift: 33, 38, 41, 154
Swift FR.Mk 5: **151**, 154, **157**
Super Sabre, F-100/A/C (see North American)
Suvla, HMS: 33
Swift (see Supermarine)
Swift FR.Mk 5 (see Supermarine)
Switzerland
Air Force (Fliegertruppe/Flugwaffe): 70, 86, 88, 94, 95, 96, 109

T

T-6 Texan (see North American)
T-33 (see Canadair)
T-33 (see Kawasaki)
T-33 (see Lockheed)
T-37 (see Sukhoi)
Ta 152H (see Focke-Wulf)
Taube (see Rumpler)
Tempest Mk V (see Hawker)
Texan, T-6 (see North American)
TF-80C (T-33) (see Lockheed)
Thunderbolt, P-47 (see Republic)
Thunderbolt, RP-47G (see Republic)
Thunderchief, F-105 (see Republic)
Thunderjet, F-84 (see Republic)
Thunderjet, RF-84 (see Republic)
Tiger Moth (see de Havilland)
TO-1 (TV-1) Shooting Star (see Lockheed)
Tomahawk, P-40B (see Curtiss)
Tomahawk Mk I/IIA (see Curtiss)
Tornado (see Panavia)
Tornado GR.Mk 1A (see Panavia)
Tornado GR.Mk 4A (see Panavia)
Tornado, RB-45 (see North American)
Triplane (see Fokker)
Tu-2 *et seq* (see Tupolev)
Tupolev
Tu-2 'Bat': 7
Tu-28 'Fiddler': 138, 139
Twin Mustang, F-82 (see North American)
Typhoon (see Hawker)

U

U-2 (see Lockheed)
Unit Heritage: 140-159, **140-159**
United Kingdom
British Armed Forces of Occupation (BAFO): 152, 153
British Army: 156
British Expeditionary Force: 145
Long-range Weapons Establishment, Woomera: 34
Royal Aircraft Establishment (RAE)
Aeroplane & Armament Experimental Establishment (A&AEE): 34, 36, 38, 40
Bedford Aero Flight: 39, 41, 44
Farnborough: 34, 39, 41, 43, 52, 147, 157
Royal Air Force: 32, 48, 51, 52, 54, 64, 78, 82, 86, 143-145, 153-156
Air Forces
2nd Allied Tactical: 153, 154
2nd Tactical: 150-152
HQ Tactical: 148
Commands
Army Co-operation: 148
Bomber: 81
Fighter: 144
Strike: 156
Germany: 154, 156, 157
Regiment: 151
Royal Flying Corps: 140-143
Royal Navy
Fleet Air Arm: 143, 145
Special Operations Executive: 46
United Nations
air forces: 4, 11, 22, 24
United States
Air Force: 18, 21, 22, 24-27, 28-31, 110-113, 114, 117-119, 121, 124, 127-132
5th Air Force: 4, 7-12, 15, 16, 20, 21, 26, 127
Air Defense Command: 114, 119, 121
Air Research and Development Command: 129
Air Training Command: 119, 130
Far East Air Force: 4, 10, 16, 119
Military Air Transport Service (MATS)
Atlantic Division: 29
Reserve: 121
Strategic Air Command: 118, 132
Air National Guard: 10, 12, 23, 119, 120, 121, 124, 128, 133
Air Rescue Service: 31
Army: 30
Army Air Force: 79, 82, 95, 107-109, 114, 115, 117, 123-125, 130
8th Air Force: 81, 86, 94
Federal Aviation Administration: 121
Marine Corps: 18, 20, 121, 128
National Advisory Committee for Aeronautics (NACA): 123, 131
Navy: 113, 115, 120, 121, 126, 128, 132, 133
Uruguay
Air Force (Fuerza Aérea Uruguaya): 121

USAF Airlift and Rescue in the 1950s - Supporting the front line: 28-31, **28-31**

INDEX

V

Valiant (see Vickers)
Vampire (see de Havilland)
Vega Gull (see Percival)
Venom (see de Havilland)
Vickers
  F.B.5: 141
  Valiant: 36
  Viking: 152
Vietnam
  People's Air Force: 110-113
Viggen (see Saab)
Viking (see Vickers)
Voodoo, XF-88 (see McDonnell)

W

Westland
  Lysander: 144, 145, 146
  Lysander Mk I: 145
  Lysander Mk II: 145, **147**
  Lysander Mk III: 146, **147**
Wildcat, F4F-4 (see Grumman)

X

X-1 (see Bell)
XF-14 (see Lockheed)
XF-88 Voodoo (see McDonnell)
XF-90 (see Lockheed)
XF-104 (see Lockheed)
XFP-80A Shooting Star (see Lockheed)
XP-59A/B Airacomet (see Bell)
XP-80 (L-140) Shooting Star (see
  Lockheed)
XP-80A (L-141) Shooting Star (see
  Lockheed)
XP-80B Shooting Star (see Lockheed)
XP-80R Shooting Star (see Lockheed)

Y

Yak-3 *et seq* (see Yakovlev)
Yakovlev
  Yak-3: 95
  Yak-7: 67
  Yak-9: 16, 67, 120
  Yak-23: 97
  Yak-28 'Brewer'/'Firebar': 136
Ye-4/5/6 (MiG-21) (see Mikoyan-
  Gurevich)
Ye-150 (see Mikoyan-Gurevich)
Ye-152 (see Mikoyan-Gurevich)
Ye-152A 'Flipper' (see Mikoyan-
  Gurevich)
Ye-152M ('Ye-166') (see Mikoyan-
  Gurevich)
Ye-152P (see Mikoyan-Gurevich)
Ye-155 (MiG-25) (see Mikoyan-Gurevich)
YF-14 (see Lockheed)
YF-93A (see North American)
YF-94 (YF-97) (see Lockheed)
YP-80 Shooting Star (see Lockheed)
YP-80A (L-080) Shooting Star (see
  Lockheed)
YR-5A Dragonfly (see Sikorsky)
Yugoslavia
  Air Force (Jugoslovensko Ratno
    Vazduhoplovstvo): 94, 96, 109

Picture acknowledgments

Front cover: Lockheed. **4:** Warren Thompson, Martin Bambrick via Larry Davis, USAF (five). **5:** USAF. **6:** John Henderson via Larry Davis (two), Irv Clark via Larry Davis. **7:** USAF, Lt. Col. B. Moore via Larry Davis, Irv Clark via Larry Davis. **8:** Warren Thompson (three), Larry Davis, Leo Fournier via Larry Davis, Irv Clark via Larry Davis, W. J. O'Donnell via Larry Davis. **9:** Irv Clark via Larry Davis, Leo Fournier via Larry Davis, Lt. Col. Bruce Hinton via Larry Davis. **10:** Aerospace, Larry Davis, Warren Thompson, Sqn. Ldr. Eric Smith via Larry Davis, Vern Sprague via Larry Davis. **11:** Hank Crescibene via Larry Davis, W. K. Thomas via Larry Davis, Don Prouty via Larry Davis, Sqn. Ldr. Eric Smith via Larry Davis, USAF. **12:** Tuel via Larry Davis, Jeff Dibrell via Warren Thompson. **13:** Warren Thompson, Brig. Gen. Harrison Thyng via Larry Davis, W. K. Thomas via Larry Davis. **14:** Warren Thompson (four), Hank Buttleman via Larry Davis, USAF, USAF via Larry Davis. **15:** USAF (two), USAF via Larry Davis. **16:** Jensen via Larry Davis, USAF via Larry Davis, USAF Museum via Larry Davis, Bob Moler via Larry Davis. **17:** Walt Copeland via Larry Davis, Curtis Eskew via Larry Davis, James Kumpf via Larry Davis, John Nossick via Larry Davis. **18:** Harry Gann, Bob Groszer via Larry Davis, Marty Isham via Larry Davis, D. N. Drew via Larry Davis, Ron Wilson via Larry Davis. **19:** Warren Thompson, Bill Grover via Larry Davis, Keith Johnson via Larry Davis. **20:** Dean Abbott via Larry Davis, Ron Wilson via Larry Davis, Ron Picciani via Larry Davis. **21:** John Atrica via Larry Davis, Larry Hendel via Larry Davis, Cliff Jolley via Larry Davis, Larry Hendel via Larry Davis, via Larry Davis. **22:** Larry Hendel via Larry Davis, Dave Eldredge via Larry Davis, Paul Peterson via Larry Davis, George Amussen via Larry Davis. **23:** Ken Collins via Larry Davis, George McKay via Warren Thompson (three), Warren Thompson (two). **24:** Warren Thompson (four), Richard Kempthorne via Larry Davis, L. J. Vosloo, J. Thompson via Larry Davis, J. Becket via Larry Davis, Gene Risedorph via Larry Davis. **25:** Richard Kempthorne via Larry Davis, Bill Grover via Larry Davis, James Sullivan via Larry Davis, Gelueles via Larry Davis. **26:** Foote via Larry Davis, Larry Davis, Warren Thompson (four), Paul Barrenger via Larry Davis, Ozzie Neidermann via Larry Davis. **27:** Joe Lynch via Larry Davis, C. Martinez via Larry Davis, R. C. Hyatt via Larry Davis, Ozzie Meidermann via Larry Davis. **28:** Lockheed via Robert F. Dorr, via Robert F. Dorr (three), A1C Donald R. Murphey. **29:** via Robert F. Dorr (two), A1C Donald R. Murphey, Ed Burt via Robert F. Dorr, Joe Buebe via Robert F. Dorr (two). **30:** Harry Newell via Robert F. Dorr, Bill Ginn via Robert F. Dorr , Ed Burt via Robert F. Dorr, Pat Tomelden via Robert F. Dorr. Gene Deatrick via Robert F. Dorr. **31:** via Robert F. Dorr (three), USAF via Robert F. Dorr, Charles Hnton via Robert F. Dorr. **32:** Fairey, Aerospace. **33:** Charles E. Brown Collection/RAF Museum, Aerospace. **34:** Fairey (three), MoD, Aerospace. **35:** Charles E. Brown/Aerospace (three). **36:** Charles E. Brown/Aerospace, M.J. Hooks, Aerospace (three). **37:** Fairey via M.J. Hooks, via Michael Stroud, North American, Fairey via M.J. Hooks. **38:** Michael Stroud, Charles E. Brown/Aerospace (two). **39:** Aerospace (three). **40:** via Michael Stroud, via M.J. Hooks (two). **41:** BAC via Michael Stroud, BAC, BAC via M.J. Hooks (two). **42:** BAC, BAC via Michael Stroud, BAC via Jon Lake (three). **43:** BAC (three). **44:** via Jon Lake, Aerospace, BAC via Jon Lake. **45:** David Willis, BAC, Aerospace. **46-47:** Peter R. March. **48:** Bundesarchiv via John Weal, MBB, MacClancy Collection. **49:** Bundesarchiv via John Weal, Bundesarchiv, Imperial War Museum. **50:** Aerospace (five). **51:** Aerospace (three), Bruce Robertson. **52:** MoD, Aerospace (two), USAF, Bruce Robertson, MBB. **53:** Bundesarchiv via John Weal, Bundesarchiv. **54:** Bundesarchiv via Dr Alfred Price, Dr Alfred price, Bundesarchiv, Aerospace. **55:** Aerospace (two). **56:** Aerospace, Bundesarchiv (three), Imperial War Museum via John Weal. **57:** Bundesarchiv via John Weal, Aerospace. **58:** Bundesarchiv (two), Aerospace. **59:** Bundesarchiv, Aerospace. **60:** Aerospace (six). **61:** Aerospace (four). **62:** Aerospace (three). MoD. **63:** Aerospace, Bundesarchiv via John Weal. **64:** Bundesarchiv, Aerospace (three). **65:** Bundesarchiv via Dr Alfred Price, Bundesarchiv (two). **66:** Bundesarchiv via John Weal (two), Imperial War Museum via John Weal. **67:** Bundesarchiv, Aerospace (three). **75:** Tim Senior (three), Aerospace). **76:** Tim Senior (five). **77:** Tim Senior, Aerospace (three). **78:** Bruce Robertson, Bundesarchiv via John Weal (two). **79:** MAP (two), Imperial War Museum, USAF, Aerospace, MoD, Yefim Gordon Archive (three), Imperial War Museum via John Weal, Bundesarchiv via John Weal. **80:** Bundesarchiv, Carmine de Napoli and R. Mancini (two). **81:** Bundesarchiv via John Weal, Carmine de Napoli and R. Mancini (two), Aerospace. **82:** Bundesarchiv via John Weal (two). **83:** Aerospace (three). **85:** Dragisa Brasnovic, Aerospace (two), Bundesarchiv via Patrick Laureau, via Alexander Mladenov. **86:** Bundesarchiv, John Weal, Dr Alfred Price, Bundesarchiv via John Weal. **87:** Aerospace (four). **88:** Aerospace, Imperial War Museum via John Weal. **89:** Bundesarchiv, Bundesarchiv via John Weal, Aerospace (two). **90:** Dr Alfred Price, Aerospace (two), Larry Davis Collection. **91:** Aerospace (four). **92:** Aerospace (three). **94:** Aerospace (three). **95:** Aerospace (two), Dr Alfred Price. **96:** Aerospace (three). **97:** Aerospace (five). **98:** Aerospace (three), Leon Frankel Collection via Shlomo Aloni. **99:** Aerospace (two). **100:** Aerospace (four), Hispano (two). **101:** Hispano, Aerospace, Bruce Robertson. **102:** Aerospace (three). **104:** Aerospace (four). **105:** Carmine de Napoli and R. Mancini (two), Aerospace (two). **106:** Jeremy Flack/API, Simon Watson, MBB, Photo Link, Peter R. March. **106:** Aerospace (three), Bundesarchiv via John Weal. **107:** Alexander Mladenov, Aerospace (five). **108:** Aerospace (two), Israel Ben-Shachar Collection via Shlomo Aloni, Aaron Finkel Collection via Shlomo Aloni, Carmine de Napoli and R. Mancini (two). **109:** Aerospace (five). **110-113:** Dr Zoltán Buza. **114:** Budd Butcher via Larry Davis, via Larry Davis. **115:** Lockheed, Lockheed via Robert F. Dorr. **116:** USAF, Lockheed, Bill Yoakley via Larry Davis, C. Hoggard via Larry Davis. **117:** via Larry Davis, via Harry Gann, Aerospace, Larry Davis (two). **118:** Stanley Newman via Larry Davis, JEM Aviation Slides via Larry Davis, USAF. **119:** Lockheed, Harry Gann. **120:** via Robert F. Dorr, via Harry Gann. **121:** Aerospace (two), Sperry Gyroscope. **122:** Lockheed via Warren M. Bodie, Lockheed via Terry Panopalis, Lockheed (two). **123:** Lockheed via Robert F. Dorr, Lockheed via Terry Panopalis, USAF Museum via Larry Davis, Lockheed Collection (two), Wm. J. Balogh via Larry Davis, Ron Picciani via Baldur Sveinsson. **125:** Lockheed (two), Larry Davis Collection (two), USAF via Larry Davis, Robert F. Dorr. **126:** Ron Picciani via Larry Davis, Stanley Newman via Larry Davis, Aerospace, Lockheed via Terry Panopalis, Dick Gilbert via Larry Davis. **128:** Larry Davis, Aerospace, USAF via Larry Davis, R. Escola via Larry Davis, USAF via Larry Davis. **129:** USAF via Larry Davis, C. Eskew via Larry Davis, David W. Menard via Robert F. Dorr. **130:** Ron Picciani via Larry Davis, USAF Museum via Larry Davis, Stanley Newman via Larry Davis, Aerospace. **131:** Lockheed (three), USAF, via Robert F. Dorr (two), Larry Davis Collection, Swisher/Esposito via Robert F. Dorr. **132:** Lockheed via Terry Panopalis, Lockheed, Aerospace, USAF Museum via Larry Davis, David W. Menard via Robert F. Dorr. **133:** US Navy via Warren M. Bodie, Warren M. Bodie, USAF via Larry Davis, USAF Museum via Larry Davis, René J. Francillon/Aerosphere Research, Vought, Harry Gann. **134-139:** Yefim Gordon Archive. **140:** Charles E. Brown Collection/RAF Museum, Imperial War Museum via Bruce Robertson. **141:** Aerospace, Sgt Rick Brewell/MoD DPR(RAF). **142:** Bruce Robertson (two), MoD via Bruce Robertson. **143:** Bruce Robertson (three), RAF Museum. **144:** Imperial War Museum via Bruce Robertson, Andrew Thomas, Bruce Robertson (two). **145:** Bruce Robertson, Andrew Thomas. **146:** Bruce Robertson (three). **147:** Wilfred Shearman via Andrew Thomas (two), Imperial War Museum via Bruce Robertson, Aerospace. **148:** Imperial War Museum via Bruce Robertson, Aerospace, Bruce Robertson. **150:** RAF Museum (two), MoD. **151:** MoD via Andrew Thomas, Bruce Robertson, MoD. **152:** Aerospace (two), Andrew Thomas. **153:** MoD, MoD via Bruce Robertson, Peter R. March. **154:** Aerospace (two), MoD. **155:** Andrew March, MoD (two), Aerospace. **156:** MoD, Kevin Wills, Dylan Eklund. **157:** Sgt Rick Brewell/MoD DPR(RAF).